PARALLEL
ALGORITHMS

for Digital Image Processing,
Computer Vision and
Neural Networks

⊛ WILEY SERIES IN PARALLEL COMPUTING

SERIES EDITORS:

R.G. Babb II, *Oregon Graduate Institute, USA*
J.W. de Bakker, *Centrum voor Wiskunde en Informatica, The Netherlands*
M. Hennessy, *University of Sussex, UK*
R. Oldehoeft, *Colorado State University, USA*
D. Simpson, *Brighton Polytechnic, UK*

Carey (ed.): Parallel Supercomputing: Methods, Algorithms and Applications

de Bakker (ed.): Languages for Parallel Architectures: Design, Semantics, Implementation Models

Axford: Concurrent Programming: Fundamental Techniques for Real-Time and Parallel Software Design

Gelenbe: Multiprocessor Performance

Treleaven (ed.): Parallel Computers: Object-oriented, Functional, Logic

Williams: Programming Models for Parallel Systems

Raynal and Helary: Synchronization and Control of Distributed Systems and Programs

Eliëns: DLP—A Language for Distributed Logic Programming: Design, Semantics and Implementation

Kacsuk and Wise (eds): Implementations of Distributed Prolog

Pitas (ed.): Parallel Algorithms for Digital Image Processing, Computer Vision and Neural Networks

PARALLEL
ALGORITHMS

for Digital Image Processing,
Computer Vision and
Neural Networks

Edited by

Ioannis Pitas
Aristotle University of Thessaloniki
Greece

JOHN WILEY & SONS
Chichester · New York · Brisbane · Toronto · Singapore

Other Wiley Editorial Offices

John Wiley & Sons, Inc., 605 Third Avenue,
New York, NY 10158-0012, USA

Jacaranda Wiley Ltd, G.P.O. Box 859, Brisbane,
Queensland 4001, Australia

John Wiley & Sons (Canada) Ltd, 22 Worcester Road,
Rexdale, Ontario M9W 1L1, Canada

John Wiley & Sons (SEA) Pte Ltd, 37 Jalan Pemimpin #05-04,
Block B, Union Industrial Building, Singapore 2057

Library of Congress Cataloging-in-Publication Data

Parallel algorithms : for digital image processing, computer vision,
   and neural networks / edited by Ioannis Pitas.
      p.   cm.— (Wiley series in parallel computing)
   Includes bibliographical references and index.
   ISBN 0 471 93566 2
   1. Parallel processing (Electronic computers)   2. Computer
algorithms.   3. Image processing—Digital techniques.   4. Computer
vision.   5. Neural networks (Computer science)   I. Pitas,
I. (Ioannis)   II. Series.
QA76.58.P36   1993
006.3'7—dc20   92–45607
                                                        CIP

British Library Cataloguing in Publication Data

A catalogue record for this book is available from the British Library

ISBN 0 471 93566 2

Produced from camera-ready copy supplied by the authors
Printed and bound in Great Britain by Bookcraft (Bath) Ltd

Contents

3   Parallel FFT-like Transform Algorithms on Transputers ... 53

4   Parallel Edge Detection and Related Algorithms ... 91

Contributors

Ioannis Pitas
Aristotle University of Thessaloniki
Department of Electrical Engineering, Division of Electronics and Computer Science
Thessaloniki 54006, Greece

Leonel Augusto de Sousa, Moisés Simões Piedade
Instituto Superior Técnico, Department of Electrical Engineering
Av. Rovisco Pais, 1, 1096 Lisboa-Codex, Portugal

Reiner Creutzburg, Torsten Minkwitz
University of Karlsruhe
Faculty of Informatics, Institute of Algorithms and Cognitive Systems
P.O. Box 6980, D-7500 Karlsruhe, Germany

Markus Roggenbach, Thomas Umland
University of Karlsruhe
Faculty of Informatics, Department of Informatics for Engineering and Science
P.O. Box 6980, D-7500 Karlsruhe, Germany

Stephen Marshall
University of Strathclyde
Department of Electronic and Electrical Engineering, Signal Processing Division
204 George Street, Glasgow G1 1XW, Scotland

M. Proesmans, A. Oosterlinck
Catholic University of Leuven,
ESAT-MI2 Department of Electronics Systems Automation Technology
Division of Machine Intelligence and Imaging
Kardinaal Mercierlaan 94, 3001 Heverlee/Leuven, Belgium

Robert B. Fisher, Emanuele Trucco
University of Edinburgh
Department of Artificial Intelligence
5 Forrest Hill, Edinburgh EH1 2QL, Scotland

Malcolm D. Brown
Thinking Machines Corp.
University of Edinburgh
Edinburgh Parallel Computing Centre
James Clerk Maxwell Buildings, Kings Buildings,
Mayfield Road, Edinburgh EH9 3JZ, Scotland

Alastair C. Hume
University of Edinburgh
Department of Artificial Intelligence
5 Forrest Hill, Edinburgh EH1 2QL, Scotland

Mark Holden, M.J. Zemerly, J.-P. Muller
University College London
Department of Photogrammetry and Surveying
Gower Street, London WC1E 6BT, England

Stefanos Kollias, Andreas Stafylopatis
National Technical University of Athens
Department of Electrical and Computer Engineering, Computer Science Division
157 73 Zographou, Athens, Greece

Alain Petrowski
Institut National des Télécommunications
Département Informatique
9, rue Charles Fourier, 91011 Evry Cedex, France

Hélène Paugam-Moisy
Ecole Normale Supérieure de Lyon
46, Allée d'Italie, 69364 Lyon Cedex 07, France

Thomas Kilindris
Aristotle University of Thessaloniki
Department of Electrical Engineering, Division of Electronics and Computer Science
Thessaloniki 54006, Greece

Ernest Hirsch
Université Strasbourg-I, Louis Pasteur,
Ecole Nationale Supérieure de Physique de Strasbourg, ENSPS
Laboratoire des Sciences de l'Image et de la Télédétection, LSIT
7, rue de l'Université, F-67084 Strasbourg Cedex, France

Preface

Three years ago, DGXIII of the Commission of the European Community launched the ESPRIT Parallel Computing Action (PCA) aiming at the mobilization of the European universities in the area of parallel computing. Fifty-five universities have been funded to perform research and development. A number of them specializing in the area of digital image/signal processing, computer vision and neural networks have formed the Signal Processing and Neural Networks (SPNN) group. The research activities of this group formed the basic kernel of this book. Its aim is to provide a state-of-the-art coverage in parallel digital image processing, computer vision and neural networks as well as to expose the research advances that have been performed in PCA. Its first aim is particularly important since no tutorial book exists in this topic and the relevant literature is scattered in a large number of journal and conference papers. Therefore almost all book chapters contain a strong tutorial part. Chapter 1 contains a comprehensive, but not exhaustive reference list on parallel digital image processing and computer vision. The book chapters can be split in three parts: Chapters 1–7 cover parallel digital image processing and computer vision. Chapters 8–10 expose parallel implementation of neural networks. Finally chapters 11 and 12 contain descriptions of software and hardware systems for parallel digital image processing. Each chapter is self contained. The editor wishes to acknowledge the support of the SPNN group members in materializing this project, the effort of the chapter authors in providing a very good coverage of the various topics exposed in this book and Mr. Thomas Kilindris, graduate of Department of Electrical Engineering, Aristotle University of Thessaloniki, for secretarial support in preparing the final camera ready book.

Thessaloniki, September 1992
Ioannis Pitas.

1

Introduction to Parallel Digital Image Processing

IOANNIS PITAS

1.1 INTRODUCTION

Digital image processing operations are usually computationally intensive, because of the large amount of data that must be processed and of the complexity of the elementary operations. Typical image sizes range from 256×256 to 1024×1024. Thus, up to 3 MBytes of data must be processed for a single color image. The complexity is at least of the order $O(KN^2)$ for image dimensions $N \times N$ and for relatively simple operations (e.g., point operations, local operations). Computational complexity is much higher for more complex processing (e.g., image transforms). The computational complexity is also very high for complex computer vision tasks (e.g., shape description and recognition, motion estimation, stereo matching) and for certain advanced digital image processing tasks (e.g., image restoration, image compression). In certain cases (e.g., digital video processing, robotic vision) all these calculations must be performed in real-time, i.e., at a rate of 25-30 images per second. Based on the speed requirements, the computational complexity and the data volume, it can be seen that the limits of general purpose computers can be easily reached in digital image processing applications. Parallel processing provides the mainstream solutions to fast digital image processing and computer vision. Its application in this area can be traced back to the work of M.Golay and S.Unger [Gol65, Ung58]. Since then, parallel digital image processing has had an impressive growth. A large number of dedicated machines has been built. Some of them have been just research prototypes, whereas others have had a commercial success. At the same time, a large number of parallel digital image

Parallel Algorithms for Digital Image Processing, Computer Vision and Neural Networks, ed. I. Pitas
© 1993 John Wiley & Sons Ltd

processing algorithms has been developed. Thus, a large amount of literature has been published in this area especially in the form of edited books [Can86, Dew89, Duf81, Duf83, Duf85, Duf86, Kit85, Lev85, Lev86, Pre82, Uhr86, Uhr87]. One of the aims of this book is to review several such algorithms that appeared in the literature and to present new results in this area. The goal of Chapter 1 is to provide an introduction to parallel digital image processing and computer vision as well as a comprehensive, but not exhaustive, list of relevant references.

1.2   FORMS OF PARALLELISM IN DIGITAL IMAGE PROCESSING

Parallel digital image processing and computer vision have exhibited a tremendous growth in the past decades. This process has been driven not only by the need for fast processing but also from the fact that parallelism suits well to the tasks of digital image processing and to the nature of the digital images. The following types of parallelism can be identified in digital image processing [Dan81]:

1. Geometrical parallelism

2. Neighborhood parallelism

3. Pixel-bit parallelism

4. Operator parallelism.

Digital images are usually sampled on a rectangular grid and are stored on a two-dimensional array [Gon87, Jai89]. Therefore, they possess an inherent geometrical parallelism. This parallelism can be exploited by using a large two-dimensional array of processors, possibly one per image pixel. However, this is not possible for image sizes greater than 128×128 approximately, by current technological standards. Thus, the image is segmented in square $M \times M$ ($M < N$) blocks or in strips and each block/strip is assigned to a specific processor. The only problem that is encountered in such a solution is the border effects that are created due to image split in many processors.

Many digital image processing algorithms are essentially local neighborhood operations of the form :

$$y_{ij} = \mathcal{F}(x_{i+r,j+s}) \quad (r, s) \in A \qquad (1.1)$$

where x_{ij}, y_{ij} are the input, output image respectively. $\mathcal{F}$ is an operator (linear or nonlinear) and A is its processing window. The most frequently used window is square of size 3×3. It contains the pixels having city block distance 1,2 from the central pixel. Neighborhood parallelism denotes the parallel execution of local neighborhood operations. In this case a local processor must have access or communication to its neighbor data or processors.

Pixel-bit parallelism exploits the fact that an image can be decomposed in b bit planes, where b is the number of bits in the image pixel (usually $b=1$ or 8). Several image processing operators, notably the linear operators, can be performed on each bit plane independently. The arithmetic that is performed on bit planes is called *distributed arithmetic.* One-bit Processing Elements (PE) have been constructed to exploit bit-plane parallelism [Duf78, Red79, Bat80].

Two types of operator parallelism exist in digital image processing operations: *pipelining* and *parallel decomposition.* Pipelining is the most commonly used and can be expressed by:

$$Y = F(X) = F_n(F_{n-1}(\ldots F_2(F_1(X))\ldots)) \tag{1.2}$$

where X is the input image or image subregion, Y is the output image, F is an operator and F_i, $i = 1, \ldots, n$ is its cascade decomposition. Typical example of pipelining is the cascade realization of linear digital filters [Dud83]. Another example of a digital image processing pipeline is the computation of morphological operations, namely erosion and dilation [Ser83, Pit90]:

$$Y = X \ominus B = (\ldots(X \ominus B_1) \ominus B_2) \ominus \ldots) \ominus B_n \tag{1.3}$$

Low-level digital image processing usually involves homogeneous pipelines, whereas intermediate and high-level digital image processing involves heterogeneous pipelines in most cases. Parallel decomposition involves operators of the form:

$$Y = F(X) = F_1(X)\|F_2(X)\|\ldots\|F_n(X) \tag{1.4}$$

where $\|$ denotes parallel execution. A typical example of this type of parallelism for low-level vision is the parallel realization of two-dimensional digital filters [Dud83]. Another typical example for pattern recognition is statistical decision making of the form:

$$\text{Find } \min_{1 \leq i \leq n} d(\mathbf{x}, \mathbf{x_i}) \tag{1.5}$$

where $\mathbf{x}$ denotes the feature vector, $\mathbf{x}_i$, $i = 1, \ldots, n$ denote the reference vectors and $d(\mathbf{x}, \mathbf{x_i})$ denotes the distance between $\mathbf{x}$, $\mathbf{x_i}$. In this case, the calculation of the various distances (and even the calculation of the minimum) can be performed in parallel.

1.3 PARALLEL ARCHITECTURES AND ALGORITHMS FOR DIGITAL IMAGE PROCESSING

Parallel architectures can be classified in two large classes: Single Instruction Multiple Data (SIMD) and Multiple Instruction Multiple Data (MIMD) machines. SIMD machines are the first ones that appeared in digital image processing and computer vision applications. Most of them exploit extensively bit-plane parallelism and are called *cellular logic arrays* [Duf78, Red79, Bat80]. They consist of large arrays of simple one-bit processing elements. The processing elements are connected to their immediate neighbors and form a processor grid. Local neighborhood operations can be easily performed by using local data transfers. Thus, cellular logic arrays exploit at the same time both geometrical and neighborhood parallelism. Instructions are broadcast to all PEs. The main problem of cellular arrays is their small size (usually 128 × 128) compared to the image size (512 × 512 or 1024 × 1024). Thus, image must be segmented and each segment must be processed independently. This approach causes border effects that become a serious problem when multiple local operations must be applied in pipeline.

It also introduces heavy IO load to the system. Another disadvantage of cellular arrays is their limited use in high-level vision applications. In this case the nature of the tasks is not well suited for such an architecture.

An alternative approach is *pipeline* architectures. They exploit operator parallelism (pipelining). Pipelines of Digital Signal Processors (DSPs) have been extensively used in the implementation of low-level digital signal/image processing algorithms (e.g., digital filters). Pipelines for morphological image processing are also very efficient [Ste83b]. Heterogeneous pipelines can also be constructed by using special purpose boards operating on a high-speed image bus. Such processors can be optimized for certain tasks each (e.g., histogram, linear FIR filtering, nonlinear filtering). Sometimes the starting and the end processor of a pipeline are connected to form a *loop*. Such an architecture is useful when the same operation must be performed on the data repeatedly. The functionality of the pipeline is controlled from a host (usually a Unix workstation) by using board drivers.

Massive MIMD machines for digital image processing applications have had a widespread use in the last decade. They can be divided in two large classes: *distributed memory* and *common memory* machines. In the case of common memory architectures, all processors access the same memory. They suffer from conflicts in memory access. However, they have the advantage that images are stored in the common memory and can be accessed by any processor any time. In the case of distributed memory architectures, each processor has its own local memory and communicates to the other by using communication links or a common bus or both. In both cases, the images must be split in strips or blocks and must be distributed to the processors. Data exchanges are needed during the execution of most digital image processing algorithms. This fact creates a heavy communication load that deteriorates the speedup that could be achieved. Common bus architectures suffer from bus congestion. Communication by parallel or serial links is widely used in machines based on transputers or on certain Digital Signal Processors (e.g., Texas Instruments TMS320C40). The basic problem in this case is the small bandwidth of the serial links for most digital image processing applications. Thus, mixed topologies having both communication links (for message passing) and a high-speed common bus (for image transfer) are preferable for such applications. Typical programming environment on current MIMD machines consists of conventional languages (FORTRAN, C) plus message and data passing mechanisms. The user writes the code which runs on every processor separately. A unique processor identifier is used to determine message destinations. Thus, the program organization is quite complex, despite its user friendly appearance. Despite the MIMD capabilities, SIMD operation is used for several digital image processing operations. In this case, each node (PE) runs the same code with the other PEs but processes its own image segment. Subroutine libraries have been constructed for such operations.

The natural interconnection scheme for PEs in digital image processing applications is the two dimensional *mesh*. PEs having four communication links are required for the implementation of a mesh. Transputers have four serial links and can be easily used to construct a mesh of any size. The top and bottom rows and the leftmost and rightmost columns are also connected to form a torus, as shown in Figure 1.1.

A machine that does not have the "wrap-around" connection can simulate a torus machine with an increase in time by a constant factor [Cyp89]. If the image size is the same as the mesh size, each image pixel can be stored in one PE. If the digital image has size larger than the mesh size, it is split in a rectangular grid of image blocks and each block is stored in the local memory of a PE. The blocks overlap with each other, so that local operations (e.g., convolution by a small mask) can be easily performed on each PE independently without need for communications. After processing, the output image blocks can be collected back to the host. Input image distribution and output image collection can be performed in a row-wise and column-wise manner by exploiting the mesh links. Data distribution and collection causes a heavy communication load that deteriorates the speedup that could be achieved by the mesh computer. Data transfer from one PE to any other PE can be performed in no more than $N-1$ moves in an $N \times N$ mesh. Communication time increases as $O(N)$. This is the biggest problem for mesh topologies, especially when long-distance data transfers are desired (e.g., in digital image transforms). This problem can be partially solved by superimposing a binary tree on a mesh (whose size N is a power of two). The leaves of this tree are the mesh PEs. The intermediate nodes of the tree serve primarily for communication purposes. Thus, PEs lying far apart can communicate by sending messages that go up and down the binary tree by choosing appropriate routes. In this case the communication load is reduced to $O(\log_2 N)$. The tree can also be used efficiently for image data distribution and collection.

Another interconnection scheme that is used in digital image processing is the *pyramid* shown in Figure 1.2. It has one root PE, a base of $N \times N$ PEs and $\log_2 N - 1$ intermediate levels ($\log_2 N + 1$ levels in total). Each level $0 \le i \le \log_2 N$ is a mesh having $(N/2^i) \times (N/2^i)$ PEs. Such a pyramid has $(4N^2 - 1)/3$ processors. Each processor (except for the root) must have 9 links: 4 for its children PEs, 4 for its neighbor PEs and one for its parent PE. Any two nodes can communicate by using at most $2 \log_2 N$ links. Examples of image processing pyramids are the HCL Pyramid [Tan87], the MPP pyramid [Sch85], SPHINX [Mer85], PAPIA [Can85] and Warwick pyramid [Nud89]. Pyramid computers differ from mesh plus tree computers, because they provide local horizontal interconnections at every pyramid level. In most classical digital image processing algorithms their performance is similar to that of mesh plus tree machines [Cyp89]. Therefore, mesh plus tree computers are preferred, because they

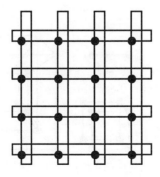

Figure 1.1 Mesh topology. Each node denotes one PE.

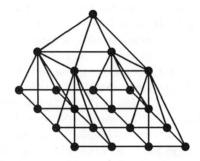

Figure 1.2 Pyramid topology.

need a smaller number of links (5 instead of 9). However, pyramid machines can perform digital image processing at all intermediate pyramid levels. The digital image can be stored locally in a different resolution at each pyramid level. Thus, a multiresolution image representation results. Pyramid topologies are very well suited for multiresolution image processing, due to their structure. Multiresolution techniques in digital image filtering, edge detection, region segmentation and coding have exhibited impressive growth in the past decade [Lev85]. All related algorithms can be efficiently implemented on a pyramid machine.

The basic disadvantage of both mesh and pyramid topologies is that their performance in far data transfers is small. Thus, other connection schemes providing fast communications between long-distance PEs must be explored. Such an interconnection is the *hypercube* [Hay89]. A hypercube of dimension n has $N = 2^n$ PEs. Hypercubes having 2, 4, 8, 16 PEs are shown in Figure 1.3. The interconnections form an n-dimensional hypercube, whose corners are the PEs. A hypercube of order $N = 2^n$ can be constructed from two hypercubes having $2^n - 1$ PEs each, by connecting their corresponding corners. The graph Q_n of a hypercube of dimension n is given by the

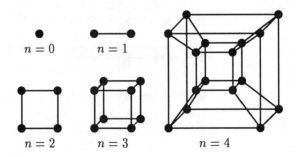

Figure 1.3 Hypercube topology.

following recursive relation [Hay89]:

$$Q_1 = K_2 \tag{1.6}$$
$$Q_n = K_2 \times Q_{n-1} \tag{1.7}$$

where K_2 is a complete graph having two nodes and $\times$ denotes the cartesian product of graphs. Each PE is assigned a number from 0 to $N-1$ in binary notation. Two PEs are connected if and only if the binary representations of their indices differ in one bit only. For example, processor 0000 is connected to the processors 0001, 0010, 0100 and 1000. Each node has n links. This fact poses problems in the construction of large hypercubes, because the number of links per node may become too large to be implemented by current technological standards. The overall number of links is $nN/2$. Any two PEs are at most n links apart. The average internode distance is $(n2^{n-1})/(N-1)$. When n increases, the average internode distance approaches $n/2 = \log_2 N/2$. Thus, far data transfer can be easily performed. No edge or boundary PEs exist that need special treatment. Mesh interconnection can be embedded in hypercube interconnection so that adjacent nodes in the original structure are mapped on adjacent nodes in the hypercube. However, there are problems in simulating mesh computers on hypercubes. A right shift operation on a $N^{1/2} \times N^{1/2}$ mesh computer requires $\log_2 N$ operations on the hypercube of order N and vice-versa [Cyp89]. An image of dimensions $N^{1/2} \times N^{1/2}$ can be stored in several ways on a hypercube of order N. The easiest way is to store pixel (i, j) in the PE having order $iN^{1/2} + j$ (row-wise storage). Alternatively, both row and column numbers can be coded by the Gray code [Cyp89]. This code is a list of integers $0 \leq i \leq N^{1/2} - 1$ arranged so that consecutive integers differ in exactly 1 bit position. Let $C(i)$, $0 \leq i \leq N^{1/2} - 1$ be the Gray code table. The pixel (i, j) is stored on the PE having order $N^{1/2}C(i) + C(j)$. Such an image storage has certain advantages on hypercubes: horizontally or vertically neighboring pixels are stored on PEs that are directly connected, i.e., they are one link apart. This does not hold for row-wise storage. If the size of an image is much larger than $N^{1/2} \times N^{1/2}$, the image can be split in a square grid of blocks. The image blocks can be stored on the hypercube in a row-wise or in a Gray code order. They can be distributed in the hypercube by embedding a pseudo-binary tree on it [Lee87]. Hypercube machines are very efficient in certain cases where far data transfers are essential. This is the case of two-dimensional Fast Fourier Transform algorithms [Ang90]–[Ang92IOS]. There are several hypercube machines, namely Cosmic Cube [Sei85], NCUBE [Hay86] and Connection Machine [Hil85]. NCUBE/ten is an MIMD hypercube having 1024 PEs. Each of them has a 32-bit floating point processor and 128 Kbytes of memory. The Connection Machine has up to 65536 SIMD PEs. Each PE is a bit-serial processor with 4 Kbits memory. Finally, hypercubes of size up to 16 PEs can be easily constructed on transputer machines having reconfigurable topology.

The biggest problem of the hypercube computers is the large number of links per PE for large hypercubes. Thus, several alternative topologies have been proposed in the literature that retain some of the nice topological properties of the hypercubes while they have a relatively small number of links per PE. Such topologies are the shuffle networks [Sto71, Bur92a], the cube-connected networks [Pre81, Sie89] and the de Bruijn networks [Sam89]. A shuffle network is shown in Figure 1.4. Such networks are very good at implementing digital image transform algorithms [Ang92IOS]. They

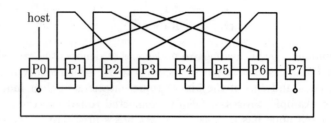

Figure 1.4 Shuffle network computer.

can also implement efficiently hypercube algorithms. However, their performance in mesh algorithms is poor.

Several parallel digital image processing algorithms appeared in the literature in the past two decades. Many of them are reviewed in the subsequent chapters of this book. Two review papers, [Cyp89] and [Cha90], give a very good overview of this area. However, the complete classification and comparative study of these algorithms is very difficult, because each of them is designed to fit a particular parallel digital image processing architecture. Perhaps the best approach to the classification of parallel algorithms is the one presented in [Cyp89]. The algorithms for SIMD machines are split in three classes, according to the topology they use: mesh, pyramid and hypercube algorithms. The following problems can be studied within each class:

1. Pointwise operations

2. Communication operations

3. Geometrical transformations

4. Two-dimensional convolution and local operations

5. Histogram calculation

6. Two-dimensional Fast Fourier Transform

7. Hough transforms and edge following

8. Template matching

9. Region segmentation and relaxation labeling

10. Connected component labeling

11. Computational geometry problems

Each of these classes has its own characteristics and poses different problems to algorithm design. For example, local and pointwise operations can be performed in general without any communications after image distribution. On the contrary, image transforms and connected component labeling require global information, i.e., long-distance communications. Some classes have fixed communication requirements (e.g., convolution, image transforms), whereas other classes have communication loads that depend on the image content (e.g., region segmentation, connected component labeling). Thus, benchmarking of a parallel computer in digital image processing applications must employ a number of algorithms of these classes in order to take into account the above mentioned (sometimes conflicting) aspects.

This chapter contains a relatively comprehensive list of references to the various parallel algorithms and architectures that have been scattered in the literature. This list is far from being complete. It is complemented, of course, by the reference lists in the various chapters of this book. Most of these chapters contain review sections, where the interested reader can find details on the various classes of parallel digital image processing algorithms and architectures.

1.4 CONCLUSIONS

An introduction to parallel digital image processing has been presented in this chapter. It has been observed that the performance of a parallel image computer depends on the task to be performed, on the structure of the processing element and on the interconnection scheme used. SIMD machines dominated in parallel digital image processing in the past. Currently, MIMD computers are progressively taking their place. The main reason for this trend is the wide availability of general purpose MIMD computers and their use by mainstream scientists and engineers. Some of these machines (e.g., transputer and DSP-based) are attractive because they combine low cost and high numerical performance. Such machines can have reconfigurable architecture and they can be easily used to construct meshes, hypercubes and shuffle networks. Mesh computers are ideal for local operations (e.g., look-up tables, convolution). They also operate fast in intermediate image processing applications. Their main disadvantage is their poor performance in long-distance communications. Pyramid computers perform extremely well in multiresolution image processing. They perform well in many low- and intermediate-level image processing tasks. However, horizontal connections seem to be useful only at the bottom level in most applications. Thus, their performance is similar to mesh plus tree computers in most applications. Pyramid computers have poor performance in pointer-based communications. Therefore, they are not the best choice for high level vision tasks. The hypercubes have very good performance in long-distance communications. Their local communication properties vary from moderate (plain hypercube) to very good (hypercube with independent communication). Mesh computers can be easily simulated on hypercubes. Therefore, it seems that hypercubes can be powerful both for low-level and for high-level vision systems. However, they are inferior to the mesh and pyramid computers when performing local neighborhood operations. In general, their performance has to be studied better on practical parallel image processing systems. Their main disadvantage is the number of links required. Shuffle networks can be used instead. These networks can be used to implement hypercube algorithms effectively. However, they cannot simulate mesh computers efficiently. They are less efficient then mesh computers in local neighborhood operations and have many long-distance communications.

REFERENCES

[Agg86] A. Aggarwal. Optimal bounds for finding maximum on array processors with k global buses, *IEEE Trans. Comput.*, C-35:62–64, 1986.

[Agg87] A. Aggarwal and Lena Nekludova. A parallel $O(\log N)$ algorithm for finding connected components in planar images, *Proc. Int. Conf. Parallel Processing*, 1987.

[Agr81] D. P. Agrawał and R. Jain. A multiprocessor system for dynamic scene analysis, *Proc. Workshop Comp. Arch. for Pattern Anal. Mach. Intell.*, 1981.

[Ahu82] N. Ahuja and S. Swamy. Interleaved pyramid architectures for bottom-up analysis, in *Proc. Int. Conf. Pattern Recognition*, Munich 1982, pages 388–390.

[Ahu84] N. Ahuja and S. Swamy. Multiprocessor pyramid architectures for bottom-up analysis, *IEEE Trans. Pattern Anal. Machine Intell.*, PAMI-6:463–475, 1984.

[Aln87] H. Alnuweiri and V.K. Prasanna Kumar. Efficient image computations on VLSI architectures with reduced hardware, in *Proc. IEEE Workshop Comp. Arch. Anal. Machine Intell.*, pages 192–202, Oct. 1987.

[Ang90] G. Angelopoulos and I. Pitas. Parallel implementation of 2-D FFT algorithms on a hypercube, *Proc. Parallel Computing Action*, Workshop ISPRA, Dec. 1990.

[Ang91a] G. Angelopoulos and I. Pitas. Two-dimensional FFT algorithms on hypercube machines, *Proc. Transputer Applications 91*, Glasgow, 1991.

[Ang91b] G. Angelopoulos and I. Pitas. Two-dimensional FFT algorithms on hypercube machines, in *Applications of Transputers 3*, vol.2, T.S. Durrani, W.A. Sandham, J.J. Soraghan and S.M. Forbes, editors, pages 754–759, Aug. 1991.

[Ang92a] G. Angelopoulos and I. Pitas. 2-D FFT algorithms with parallel bit reversion on hypercube computers, *Proc. EUSIPCO92*, Brussels, 1992.

[Ang92b] G. Angelopoulos and I. Pitas. Two-dimensional FFT algorithms on hypercube and mesh machines, *Signal Processing*, in press, 1992.

[Ang92IOS] G. Angelopoulos, P. Ligdas and I. Pitas. Two-dimensional FFT algorithms on parallel machines, in *Transputing for Numerical and Neural Network Applications*, G.L. Reijns, editor, IOS Press, 1992.

[Ant88] A. Antola, R. Negrini and N. Scarabottolo. Arrays for Discrete Fourier Transform, *Proc. EUSIPCO 88*, Grenoble, Sept. 1988.

[Ave90] A. Averbuch, E. Gabber, B. Gordissky and Y. Medan. A parallel FFT on an MIMD machine, *Parallel Computing* 15:61–74, North-Holland, 1990.

[Bat] K.E. Batcher. The STARAN computer, in *Infotech State of the Art Report: Supercomputers*, vol. 2, C.R. Jessope and R.C. Hockney, editors, Infotech, Maidenhead, England.

[Bat68] K.E. Batcher. Sorting networks and their applications, in *AFIPS Conf. Proc. Apr.*, pages 307–314, 1968.

[Bat80] K.E. Batcher. Design of a massively parallel processor, *IEEE Trans. Comput.*, C-29:836–840, 1980.

[Ber84] P. Bertolazzi and M. Pirozzi. A parallel algorithm for the optimal detection of a noisy curve, *Comp. Vision Graphics Image Processing*, 27, 1984.

[Bha88] S.K. Bhaskar, A. Rosenfeld and A.Y. Wu. Parallel processing of regions represented by linear quadtrees, *Comp. Vision Graphics Image Processing*, 42(3), 1988.

[Bla87] R.P. Blanford. Dynamically quantized pyramids for Hough vote collection, *Proc. IEEE Workshop Comp. Arch. Anal. Machine Intell.*, pages 145–152, Oct. 1987.

[Bok81] S.H. Bokhari. MAX: An algorithm for finding maximum in an array processor with a global bus, in *Proc. 1981 Int. Conf. Parallel Processing*, pages 302–303, 1981.

[Bra86] A. Brass and G. S. Pawley. Two and three dimensional FFTs on highly parallel computers, *Parallel Computing* 3:167–184, 1986.

[Bur81] P.J. Burt, T. Hong and A. Rosenfeld. Segmentation and estimation of image region properties through cooperative hierarchical computation, *IEEE Trans. Syst. Man. Cybernetics*, SMC-11:802–809, 1981.

[Bur87] P.J. Burt and G.S. van der Wal. Iconic image analysis with Pyramid Vision Machine (PVM), *Proc. Workshop Comput. Arch. for Pattern Anal. Mach. Intell.*, pages 137–144, 1987.

[Bur92a] H. Burkhardt, B. Lang and M. Noelle. Aspects of parallel image processing algorithms and architectures. In H. Burkhardt, Y. Neuvo and J.C. Simon, editors, *From Pixels to Features II*, pages 65–84, Elsevier, 1992.

[Bur92b] H. Burkhardt, Y. Neuvo J.C. and Simon, editors. *From Pixels to Features II*, Elsevier, 1992.

[Can83] V. Cantoni and S. Levialdi. Matching the task to an image processing architecture, *Computer Vision, Graphics and Image Processing*, 22:301–309, 1983.

[Can85] V. Cantoni, M. Ferretti, S. Levialdi and F. Maloberti. *Integrated Technology for Parallel Image Processing*, A pyramid project using integrated technology, pages 121–131, Academic Press, London, 1985.

[Can86] V. Cantoni and S. Levialdi, editors. *Pyramidal System for Computer Vision*, Springer Verlag, New York, 1986.

[Can88] V. Cantoni, V. di Gesu and S. Levialdi, editors. *Image Analysis and Processing II*, Plenum Press, 1988.

[Can90] S.R. Cannon and S.J. Allan. A parallel processing subsystem for the generation of 3-D cardiac images from CT, *Proc. 3rd Conference North American Transputer Users Group*, pages 75–82, 1990.

[Cha88a] R. M. Chamberlain. Gray codes, fast Fourier transforms and hypercubes, *Parallel Computing*, 6:225–233, North-Holland, 1988.

[Cha88b] J. H. Change, O. H. Ibarra, T. C. Pong and S. M. Sohn. Two-dimensional convolution on a pyramid computer, *IEEE Trans. Pattern Anal. Mach. Intell*, 10(4), July 1988.

[Cha90] V. Chaudhary and J.K. Aggarwal. Parallelism in computer vision: a review, in V. Kumar, P.S. Gopalakrisnan and L.N. Kanal, editors, *Parallel Algorithms for Machine Intelligence and Vision* , pages 271–309, Springer Verlag, 1990.

[Che92] K. Chen and C. Svensson. A 512-processor array chip for video/image processing, in *From Pixels to Features II*, H. Burkhardt, Y. Neuvo and J.C. Simon, editors, pages 187–200, Elsevier, 1992.

[Chi81] Y. P. Chiang and K. S. Fu. Parallel processing for distance computation in syntactic pattern recognition, *Proc. Workshop Comput. Arch. for Pattern Anal. Mach. Intell.*, 1981.

[Chi83] Y. P. Chiang and K. S. Fu. VLSI architectures for syntactic pattern recognition, *Proc. IEEE Conf. Comp. Vision Pattern Recognition*, 1983.

[Chi84] Y. P. Chiang and K. S. Fu. Parallel parsing algorithms and VLSI implementations for syntactic pattern recognition, *IEEE Trans. Pattern Anal. Mach. Intell.*, May 1984.

[Chi85] Y. P. Chiang. Array processing for syntactic pattern recognition, *Proc. Workshop Comput. Arch. for Pattern Anal. Mach. Intell.*, 1985.

[Chi87] R. T. Chin, H. K. Wan, D. L. Stover and R. D. Iverson. A one-pass thinning algorithm and its parallel implementation, *Computer Vision Graphics Image Processing*, 40(1), Oct. 1987.

[Chu85] H. Y. H. Chuang and C. C. Li. A systolic array processor for straight line detection by modified Hough transform, *Proc. Workshop Comput. Arch. for Pattern Anal. Mach. Intell.*, 1985.

[Chu88] C.Y. Chu. Comparison of two-dimensional FFT methods on the hypercube, *Proc. 3rd Hypercube Conference*, ACM, pages 1430–1437, 1988.

[Coh87] F.S. Cohen and D.B. Cooper. Simple parallel hierarchical and relaxation algorithms for segmenting noncasual Markovian random fields, *IEEE Trans. Pattern Anal. Mach. Intell.*, 9(2), Mar. 1987.

[Cor77] L. Cordela, M.J.B. Duff and S. Levialdi. Thresholding: A challenge for parallel processing, *Computer Graphics Image Processing*, 6:207–220, 1977.

[Cor78] L. Cordela, M.J.B. Duff and S. Levialdi. An analysis of computational cost in image processing, *IEEE Trans. Comput.*, C-27:904–910, 1978.

[Cyp87a] R. Cypher, J.L.C. Sanz and L. Snyder. Practical algorithms for image component labeling on SIMD mesh connected computers, *Proc. 1987 Int. Conf. Parallel Processing*, pages 772–779, 1987.

[Cyp87b] R. Cypher, J.L.C. Sanz and L. Snyder. Hypercube and shuffle-exchange algorithms for image component labeling, *Proc. IEEE Workshop Comput. Arch. Pattern Anal. Mach. Intell.*, pages 38–60, 1987.

[Cyp87c] R. Cypher, J. L. C. Sanz and L. Snyder. The Hough transform has $O(N)$ complexity on SIMD $N \times N$ mesh array architectures, *Proc. Workshop Comput. Arch. for Pattern Anal. Mach. Intell.*, pages 115–121, 1987.

[Cyp87d] R. Cypher, J. L. C. Sanz and L. Snyder. EREW PRAM and mesh connected computer algorithms for image component labeling, *Proc. Workshop Comput. Arch. for Pattern Anal. Mach. Intell.*, pages 122–128, 1987.

[Cyp89] R. Cypher and J. L. C. Sanz. SIMD architectures and algorithms for image processing and computer vision, *IEEE Trans. Acoustics, Speech and Signal Processing*, ASSP-37(12):2158–2174, Dec. 1989.

[Dag83] E.L. Dagless, M.D. Edwards and J.T. Proudfoot. Shared memory in CYBA-M multiprocessor, *IEE Proc. part E*, 130, pages 116–123, 1983.

[Dan81] P. Danielson and S. Levialdi. Computer architectures for pictorial information systems, *IEEE Computer*, 53-67, Nov. 1981.

[Dar90] T. Darell and K. Wohn. Depth from focus using a pyramid architecture, *Pattern Recognition Letters*, 11:787-796, 1990.

[Der87] H. Derin and C. H. Won. A parallel image segmentation algorithm using relaxation with varying neighborhoods and its mapping to array processors, *Computer Vision Graphics Image Processing*, 40(1), Oct 1987.

[Dev85] J.E. Devaney. The MPP—a totally different approach to programming, in *Proc. IEEE Workshop Comput. Arch. Pat. Anal. Image Database Man.*, pages 420–427, 1985.

[Dew89] P.M. Dew, R.A. Earnshow and T.R. Heywood, editors. *Parallel Processing for Computer Vision and Display*, Addison-Wesley, 1989.

[Dix87] V. Dixit and D. I. Moldovan. Semantic network array processor and its application to image understanding, *IEEE Trans. Pattern Anal. Mach. Intell.*, 9(1), Jan. 1987.

[Don86] H.S. Don and K.S. Fu. A parallel algorithm for stochastic image segmentation, *IEEE Trans. Pattern Anal. Mach. Intell.*, 8(5), Sept. 1986.

[Dru86] M. Drumheller and T. Poggio. On parallel stereo, *Proc. IEEE Int. Conf. Robotics Automation*, 7(10):1439-1448, Apr. 1986.

[Dud83] D.E. Dudgeon and R.M. Mersereau. *Multidimensional Digital Signal Processing*, Prentice-Hall, 1983.

[Duf76] M.J.B. Duff. CLIP–4: A large scale integrated circuit array parallel processor, in *Proc. IEEE Int. Joint. Conf. Pat. Rec.*, pages 728–733, Nov. 1976.

[Duf78] M.J.B. Duff. Review of CLIP image processing system, *Proc. Nat. Comp. Conf.*, pages 1055–1060, 1978.

[Duf81] M.J.B. Duff and S. Levialdi, editors. *Languages and Architectures for Image Processing*, Academic Press, 1981.

[Duf83] M.J.B. Duff, editor. *Computing Structures for Image Processing*, Academic Press, 1983.

[Duf85] M.J.B. Duff, editor. Real applications on CLIP 4, in *Integrated Technology for Parallel Image Processing*, pages 153–165, Academic Press, 1985.

[Duf86] M.J.B. Duff, editor. *Intermediate-Level Image Processing*, Academic Press, 1986.

[Dye81] C. R. Dyer and A. Rosenfeld. Parallel image processing by memory-augmented cellular automata, *IEEE Trans. Pattern Anal. Mach. Intell.*, PAMI-3:29–41, 1981.

[Dye82] C. R. Dyer. Pyramid algorithms and machines, in *Multicomputers and Image Processing Algorithms and Programs*, pages 409–420, Academic Press, New York, 1982.

[Edw85] M.D. Edwards. A review of MIMD architectures, in *Image Processing Architectures*, J. Kittler and M.J.B. Duff, editors, Research Studies Press, 1985.

[Fai85] J. Fairfield. A cellular automaton for image segmentation using Voronoi diagrams, *Proc. Workshop Comput. Arch. for Pattern Anal. Mach. Intell.*, 1985.

[Fan85] Z. Fang and X. Li. Parallel algorithms on image template matching on hypercube SIMD computer, *Proc. IEEE Workshop Comput. Archit. Pattern Anal. Image Database Management*, pages 33–40, 1985.

[Fan86] Z. Fang, X. Li and L. Ni. Parallel algorithms for 2-D convolution, in *Proc. 1986 Int. Conf. Parallel Processing*, pages 262–269, 1986.

[Fav83] A. Favre and H. Keller. Parallel syntactic thinning by recoding of binary pictures, *Computer Vision Graphics and Image Processing*, 23, 1983.

[Fel85] J.A. Feldman. Connectionist models and parallelism in high level vision, *Computer Vision Graphics Image Processing*, 31, 1985.

[Fis82] J.P. Fishburn and R.A. Finkel. Quotient networks, *IEEE Trans. Comput.*, C-31:288–295, 1982.

[Fis85] A.L. Fisher and P.T. Highnam. Real-time image processing on scan line array processors, in *Proc. IEEE Workshop Comput. Arch. Pat. Anal. Image Database Man.*, pages 484–489, Nov. 1985.

[Fis87] A.L. Fisher and P.T. Highnam. Computing the Hough transform on scan line array processor, in *Proc. IEEE Workshop Comput Arch. Pattern Anal. Mach. Intell.*, pages 83–87, Oct. 1987.

[Fou85] T.J. Fountain. Plans for the CLIP7 chip, in *Integrated Technologies for Parallel Image Processing*, pages 199–214, Academic Press, 1985.

[Fre86] K.A. Frenkel. Evaluating two massively parallel machines, *Commun. ACM*, 29(8):752–758, 1986.

[Gam85] J.P. Gambotto and O. Monga. A parallel and hierarchical algorithm for region growing, *Proc. IEEE Conf. Comp. Vision Pattern Recognition*, 1985.

[Ger83] F.A. Gerritsen. A comparison of the CLIP4, DAP and MPP processor–array implementations, in *Computing Structures for Image Processing*, M.J.B. Duff, editor, pages 15–30, Academic Press, 1983.

[Gil92] W.K. Giloi. Whither image analysis system architecture?, in *From Pixels to Features II*, H. Burkhardt, Y. Neuvo and J.C. Simon, editors, pages 105–120, Elsevier, 1992.

[Gio86] A. Giordano, M. Maresca, G. Sandini, T. Vernazza and D. Ferrari. A systolic convolver for parallel multiresolution edge detection, *Proc. IEEE Conf. Comp. Vision Pattern Recognition*, 1986.

[Gol65] M.J.E. Golay. Apparatus for counting bi-nucleate lymphocytes in blood, US Patent 3,214,574, 1965.

[Gon87] R.C. Gonzales and P. Wintz. *Digital Image Processing*, Addison-Wesley, 1987.

[Got83] A. Gottlieb, R. Grishman, C.P. Kruskal, K.P.McAuliffe, L. Rudolph and M. Snir. The NYU ultracomputer—designing an MIMD shared memory parallel computer, *IEEE Trans. Comput.*, C-32:175–189, 1983.

[Gro86] W.I. Grosky and R. Jain. A pyramid-based approach to segmentation applied to region matching, *IEEE Trans. Pattern Anal. Mach. Intell.*, 8(5), Sept. 1986.

[Gue85] C. Guerra. A VLSI algorithm for the optimal detection of a curve, *Proc. Workshop Comput. Arch. for Pattern Anal. Mach. Intell.*, 1985.

[Gue86] C. Guerra. Systolic algorithms for local operations on images, *IEEE Trans. Comput.*, 35(1), Jan 1986.

[Gue87] C. Guerra. Parallel algorithms for line detection on a mesh, in *Proc. IEEE Workshop Comp. Arch. Pat. Anal. Mach. Intell.*, pages 99–106, 1987.

[Gue89a] C. Guerra and S. Hambrusch. Parallel algorithms for line detection on a mesh. *J. Parallel and Distributed Computing*, 6:1-19, 1989.

[Gue89b] C. Guerra and S. Levialdi. Computer vision: algorithms and architectures, in *Advances in Machine Vision*, Springer Verlag, 1989.

[Gun92] A. Gunzinger, W. Guggenbuehl, E. Hiltebrand, S. Mathis, P. Schaeren, B. Schneuwly, D. Stokar and M. Zeltner, in *From Pixels to Features II*, H. Burkhardt, Y. Neuvo and J.C. Simon, editors, pages 121–136, Elsevier, 1992.

[Har86] J.G. Harris and A.M. Flynn. Object recognition using the Connection Machine's router, *Proc. IEEE Conf. Comp. Vision Pattern Recognition*, 1986.

[Hay86] J.P. Hayes, T. Mudge and Q.F. Stout. A microprocessor based hypercube supercomputer, *IEEE Micro*, pages 6–17, Oct. 1986.

[Hay89] J. P. Hayes and T. Mudge. Hypercube supercomputers, *Special Issue on Supercomputer Technology, Proc. IEEE*, 77(12):1829–1841, Dec. 1989.

[Hil84] W.D. Hillis. The Connection Machine: A computer architecture based on cellular automata, *Physica*, 1984.

[Hil85] D. Hillis. *The Connection Machine*, MIT Press, 1985.

[Hil86] W. D. Hillis and G. L. Steele, Jr. Data parallel algorithms, *Commun. ACM*, 29(12):1170–1183, 1986.

[Hir79] D.S. Hirshberg, A.K. Chandra and D.V. Sarwate. Computing connected components on parallel computers, *Comm. ACM*, 22(8):461–464, Aug. 1979.

[Hir92] E. Hirsch. Heterogeneous parallel processing structures for real time image processing applications: reconfigurable and flexible structures versus modular functional structures, in *From Pixels to Features II*, H. Burkhardt, Y. Neuvo and J.C. Simon, editors, pages 327–346, Elsevier, 1992.

[Hou89] D.H. House. A parallel algorithm for object localization within the binocular visual field, in *Parallel Processing for Computer Vision and Display*, P.M. Dew, R.A. Earnshow and T.R. Heywood, editors, pages 225-238, Addison-Wesley, 1989.

[Hui89] W. Huiskamp, P.M. Eigershuizen, A.G. Langenkamp and P.L.J. van Lieshout. Visualization of 3-D empirical data: the voxel processor, *Proc. 10th OCCAM User Group*, pages 82–94, Enschede, 1989.

[Hui92] W. Huiskamp and P.L.J. van Lieshout. VOXTROT: Voxel data processing on transputer networks, in *From Pixels to Features II*, H. Burkhardt, Y. Neuvo and J.C. Simon, editors, pages 349–358, Elsevier, 1992.

[Hum86] R. Hummel. Connected component labeling in image processing with MIMD architectures, in *Intermediate–Level Image Processing*, M.J.B. Duff, editor, pages 101–127, Academic Press, 1986.

[Hun79] G.M. Hunter and K. Steiglitz. Operations on images using quadtrees, *IEEE Trans. Pattern Anal. Mach. Intell.*, 1:145–153, 1979.

[Hun81] D.J. Hunt. The ICL DAP and its application to image processing, in *Languages and Architectures for Image Processing*, M.J.B.Duff and S.Levialdi, editors, pages 275–282, Academic Press, 1981.

[Hwa84] K. Hwang and F.A. Briggs. *Computer Architecture and Parallel Processing*, McGraw-Hill, New York, 1984.

[Ibr85] H.A.H. Ibrahim, J.R. Kender and D.E. Shaw. The analysis and performance of two middle–level vision tasks on a fine grained SIMD tree machine, in *Proc. IEEE Int. Conf. Comput. Vis. Pattern Recog.*, pages 248–256, June 1985.

[Jai89] A.K. Jain. *Fundamentals of Digital Image Processing*, Prentice-Hall, 1989.

[Jam86] L.H. Jamiesson, P.T. Mueller and H.J. Siegel. FFT algorithms for SIMD parallel processing systems, *J. Parallel and Distributed Computing*, 3:48–71, 1986.

[Jes92] H. Jeschke, H. Volkers and T. Wehberg. A multiprocessor system for real-time image processing based on a MIMD architecture, in *From Pixels to Features II*, H. Burkhardt, Y. Neuvo and J.C. Simon, editors, pages 173–186, Elsevier, 1992.

[Jra87] A.M. Jrad and R.W. Hall. The OFC enhanced mesh architecture: A performance study, in *Proc. Workshop Comput. Arch. Pat. Anal. Mach. Intell.*, pages 184–191, Oct. 1987.

[Kam88] R.A. Kamin and G.B. Adams. Fast Fourier transform algorithm design and tradeoffs on the CM–2, *Proc. Conf. Scientific Applications of the Connection Machine*, pp.134–160, California, 1988.

[Kas88] A. Kashko, H. Buxton, B.F. Buxton and D.A. Castelow. Parallel matching and reconstruction algorithms in computer vision, *Parallel Processing*, 7:3-17, 1988.

[Ken85] E.W. Kent, M.O. Shneier and R. Lumia. PIPE: Pipeline image processing engine, *Int. Conf. Syst. Sci.*, Hawaii, Jan. 1985.

[Kim88] D. Kim and K. Hwang. Mesh-connected array processors with bypass capability for signal image processing, *Int. Conf. Syst. Sci.*, Hawaii, Jan. 1988.

[Kit85] J. Kittler and M.J.B. Duff, editors. *Image Processing System Architectures*, Research Studies Press, 1985.

[Kru82a] B. Kruse, B. Gudmundson and D. Antonsson. In Multicomputers and image processing algorithms and programs, K. Preston and L. Uhr, editors, pages 31–45, Academic Press, 1982.

[Kru82b] T. Krusner, A.Y. Wu and A. Rosenfeld. Image processing on ZMOB, *IEEE Trans. Comput.*, C-31:943–951, 1982.

[Kue85] J.T. Kuehn, J.A. Fessler and H.J. Siegel. Parallel image thinning and vectorization on PASM. *Proc. IEEE Conf. Comput. Vision Pattern Recognition*, 1985.

[Kun81] H.T. Kung and P.L. Picard. Hardware pipelines for multidimensional convolution and resampling, *Proc. Workshop Comput. Arch. for Pattern Anal. Mach. Intell.*, 1981.

[Kun82] H.T. Kung. Why systolic architectures?, *IEEE Computer*, 15, Jan. 1982.

[Kun83] H.T. Kung, L.M. Ruane and D.W. Yen. Two-level pipelined systolic array for multidimensional convolution, *Image Vision Computing*, 1, Feb. 1983.

[Kun85] H.T. Kung and S.W. Song. A systolic 2-D convolution chip, *Proc. Workshop Comput. Arch. for Pattern Anal. Mach. Intell.*, 1985.

[Kus82] T. Kushner, A.Y. Wu and A. Rosenfeld. Image processing on MPP: 1, *Pattern Recognition*, 15(3):121–130, 1982.

[Lee85] S.Y. Lee, S.Yalamanchili and J.K.Aggarwal. Parallel image normalization, *Proc. IEEE Conf. Comput. Vision Pattern Recognition*, 1985.

[Lee86] S.Y. Lee and J.K. Aggarwal. Parallel 2-d convolution on a mesh connected array processor, *Proc IEEE Conf. Comput. Vision Pattern Recognition*, pages 305–310, 1986.

[Lee87] S.Y. Lee and J. K. Aggarwal. Exploitation of image parallelism via the hypercube, *Hypercube Microprocessors*, SIAM, pages 427–437, 1987.

[Lev85] S. Levialdi, editor. *Integrated Technology for Parallel Image Processing*, Academic Press, 1985.

[Lev86] S. Levialdi, editor. *Multicomputer Vision*, Academic Press, 1986.

[Li86] X. Li and Z. Fang. Parallel algorithms for clustering on hypercube SIMD computers, *Proc. IEEE Conf. Comp. Vision Pattern Recognition*, 1986.

[Li87] H. Li and M. Maresca. Polymorphic torus: A new architecture for vision computation, in *Proc. IEEE Conf. Comp. Vision Pattern Recognition*, pages 176–183, Oct. 1987.

[Li92] J.J. Li, S. Miguet, Y. Robert and S. Ubeda. Image processing algorithms on distributed memory machines, in *From Pixels to Features II*, H. Burkhardt, Y. Neuvo and J.C. Simon, editors, pages 13-29, Elsevier, 1992.

[Lim89] W. Lim, A. Agrawal and L. Nekludova. A fast parallel algorithm for labeling connected components in image arrays, in *Parallel Processing for Computer Vision and Display*, P.M. Dew, R.A. Earnshow and T.R. Heywood, editors, pages 169–189, Addison-Wesley, 1989.

[Lin90] W.M. Lin and V.K. Prassana Kumar. Efficient histogramming on SIMD machines. *Computer Vision Graphics and Image Processing*, 49:104-120, 1990.

[Lit87a] J.J. Little, G. Blelloch and T. Cams. How to program the connection machine for computer vision, in *Proc. IEEE Workshop Comput. Pattern Anal. Mach. Intell.*, pages 11–18, Oct. 1987.

[Lit87b] J.J. Little, G. Blelloch and T. Cams. Parallel algorithms of computer vision on the Connection Machine, *Int. Conf. Comput. Vision*, 1987.

[Liu85] H.H. Liu and T.Y. Young. VLSI algorithms and structures for consistent labeling, in *Proc. Workshop Comput. Arch. for Pattern Anal. Mach. Intell.*, 1985.

[Liu88] H.H. Liu, T.Y. Young and A. Das. A multilevel parallel processing approach to scene labeling problems, *IEEE Trans. Pattern Anal. Mach. Intell.*, 10(4), Jul. 1988.

[Llo87] S.A. Lloyd, E.R. Haddow and J.F. Boyce. A parallel binocular stereo algorithm utilizing dynamic programming and relaxation labeling, *Comput. Vision Image Processing*, 39:202–225, Aug. 1987.

[Lu85] H.E. Lu and P.S.P. Wang. An improved fast parallel thinning algorithm for digital patterns, *Proc. IEEE Conf. Comp. Vision Pattern Recognition*, 1985.

[Man89] M. Manohar and H.K. Ramapriyan. Connected component labeling of binary images on a mesh connected massively parallel processor, *Comput. Vision Graphics Image Processing* 45:133-149, Feb. 1989.

[Mar86a] M. Maresca and H. Li. Morphological operations on mesh connected architecture: A generalized convolution algorithm, *Proc. IEEE Conf. Comp. Vision Pattern Recognition*, 1986.

[Mar86b] M. Martin, D.M. Chiarulli and S.S. Iyengar. Parallel processing of quadtrees on a horizontally reconfigurable architecture computing system, *Proc. Int. Conf. Parallel Processing*, pages 895–902, 1986.

[Mcm89] B.M. McMillan and L.M. Ni. A reliable parallel algorithm for relaxation labeling, in *Parallel Processing for Computer Vision and Display*, P.M. Dew, R.A. Earnshow and T.R. Heywood, editors, pages 190–209, Addison-Wesley, 1989.

[Mei86a] G.G. Mei and W. Liu. Quadtree problems on a two dimensional shuffle exchange network, *Proc. IEEE Conf. Comput. Vision Pattern Recognition*, pages 140–147, 1986.

[Mei86b] G.G. Mei and W. Liu. Parallel processing for quadtree problems, *Proc. Int. Conf. Parallel Processing*, pages 402-454, 1986.

[Mer85] A. Merigot, B. Zavidovique and F. Devos. SPHINX, a pyramidal approach to parallel image processing, *Proc. IEEE Workshop Comput. Arch. Pattern Anal. Image Database Manag.*, pages 107–111, 1985.

[Mil85a] R. Miller and Q.F Stout. Varying diameter and problem size in mesh–connected computers, in *Proc. 1985 Int. Conf. Parallel Processing*, pages 697–699, Aug. 1985.

[Mil85b] R. Miller and Q.F Stout. Geometric algorithms for digitized pictures on a mesh-connected computer, *IEEE Trans. Pattern Anal. Mach. Intell.*, March 1985.

[Mil87] R. Miller and Q.F. Stout. Data movement techniques for pyramid computer, *SIAM J. Comput.*, 16(1):38–60, 1987.

[Mil89] S.M. Miller and H.F. Silverman. Optimized implementation of the 2-D DFT on loosely-coupled parallel systems, *Proc. 1989 IEEE Int. Conf. Acoustics, Speech and Signal Processing*, pages 1536–1539, Glasgow, 1989.

[Mil92] R. Miller, V.K. Prassana Kumar, D.I. Reisis and Q.F. Stout. Image processing on reconfigurable meshes, in *From Pixels to Features II*, H. Burkhardt, Y. Neuvo and J.C. Simon, editors, pages 85–101, Elsevier, 1992.

[Miz91] H. Mizusawa and S. Kato. Still picture coding system using transputer and DSP, in *Transputing 91*, P. Welch *et al.*, editors, pages 845-858, 1991.

[Mol85] D.I. Moldovan, C.I. Wu, J.G. Nash, S. Levitan and C. Weems. Parallel processing of iconic to symbolic transformation of images, *Proc. IEEE Conf. Comp. Vision Pattern Recognition*, 1985.

[Mor79] K. Mori, M. Kidode, H. Shinoda and H. Asada. Design of local parallel pattern processor for image processing, *Proc. AFIPS Conf.*, 1979.

[Mor92] P.J. Morrow and D. Crookes. Using a high level language for image processing on transputers, in *From Pixels to Features II*, H. Burkhardt, Y. Neuvo and J.C. Simon, editors, pages 313–326, Elsevier, 1992.

[Mud85] T.N. Mudge. Vision algorithms for hypercube machines, in *Proc. IEEE Workshop Comput. Arch. Pat. Anal. Image Database Manag.*, pages 38–60, Nov. 1985.

[Mur86] D.W. Murary, A. Kashko and H. Buxton. A parallel approach to the picture restoration algorithm of Geman and Geman on an SIMD machine, *Image Vision Computing*, 4(3), Aug. 1986.

[Nas80] D. Nassimi and S. Sahni. Finding connected components and connected ones on a mesh connected parallel computer, *J. SIAM Comput.*, 9(4):744–757, 1980.

[Nas81] D. Nassimi and S. Sahni. Data broadcasting in SIMD computers, *IEEE Trans. Comput.*, C-30:2–7, 1981.

[Nas82] D. Nassimi and S. Sahni. Parallel permutation and sorting algorithms and a new generalized connection network, *J. of ACM*, 29(3):642–667, 1982.

[Ni85] L.M. Ni and A.K. Jain. A VLSI systolic architecture for pattern clustering, *IEEE Trans. Pattern Anal. Mach. Intell.*, 7(1), Jan. 1985.

[Nud89] G.R. Nudd, T.J. Atherton, R.M. Horvarth, S.C. Clippingdale, N.D. Francis, D.J. Kerbyson, R.A. Packwood, G.J. Vandin and D.W. Walton. WPM: a multiple SIMD architecture for image processing, *Proc. 3rd IEEE Conf. Image Processing and its Applications*, 1989.

[Onu92] L. Onural and M.I. Gurelli. Generation and parameter estimation of Markov random field textures by highly parallel networks, in *From Pixels to Features II*, H. Burkhardt, Y. Neuvo and J.C. Simon, editors, pages 31–46, Elsevier, 1992.

[Pet88] N. Petkov. Running order statistics on a bit-level systolic array, in *Lecture Notes in Computer Science 342, Parcella88*, G. Wolf, T. Legendi and U. Schendel, editors, pages 317–325, Springer, 1988.

[Pie81] M. Pietkanien and A. Rosenfeld. Image segmentation by texture using pyramid node linking, *IEEE Trans. Syst. Man. Cybern.*, SMC-11:822–825, 1981.

[Pit86] I. Pitas and M.G. Strintzis. An efficient and systematic way for the parallel implementation of DFT algorithms, in *Signal Processing III: Theories and Applications*, I.T. Young, editor, North-Holland, 1986.

[Pit89a] I. Pitas. Fast algorithms for running ordering and max/min calculation, *IEEE Trans. Circuits and Systems*, CAS-36(6):795–804, 1989.

[Pit89b] I. Pitas and A.N. Venetsanopoulos. A new filter structure for the implementation of certain classes of image operations, *IEEE Trans. Circuits and Systems*, CAS-35:636–647, 1989.

[Pit90] I. Pitas and A.N. Venetsanopoulos. *Nonlinear Digital Filters: Principles and Applications*, Kluwer Academic, 1990.

[Pit91] I. Pitas. Parallel image processing algorithms and architectures, in *Computing with Parallel Architectures: T.Node*, D. Gassilloud and J.C. Grossetie, editors, pages 153–172, Kluwer Academic, 1991.

[Pot83] J. L. Potter. Image processing on the massively parallel processor, *IEEE Computer*, pages 62–67, Jan. 1983.

[Pot85] J. L. Potter. *The Massively Parallel Processor*, MIT Press, 1985.

[Pot89] J. L. Potter and W. C. Meilander. Array processor supercomputers, *Special Issue on Supercomputer Technology, Proc. IEEE*, 77(12):1896–1914, Dec. 1989.

[Pra85a] V.K. Prassana Kumar and C.S.Raghavendra. An enhanced mesh connected VLSI architecture for parallel image processing, *Proc. IEEE Conf. Comp. Vision Pattern Recognition*, 1985.

[Pra85b] V.K. Prassana Kumar and C.S. Raghavendra. Image processing on enhanced mesh connected computers, *Proc. Workshop Comput. Arch. for Pattern Anal. Mach. Intell.*, 1985.

[Pra87] V.K. Prassana Kumar and M.M. Eshaghian. Efficient image template matching on hypercube SIMD arrays, *Proc. 1978 Conf. Parallel Processing*, pages 902–912, 1987.

[Pre81] F.P. Preparata and J. Vuillemin. The cube-connected cycles: a versatile network for parallel computation, *Commun. ACM*, 24(5):300–309, 1981.

[Pre82] K. Preston, Jr. and L. Uhr, editors. *Multicomputers and Image Processing: Algorithms and Programs*, Academic Press, 1982.

[Qu87] X. Qu and X. Li. Parallel image template matching algorithms, *Proc. Int. Conf. Parallel Processing*, pages 223–226, 1987.

[Ram86] D.V. Ramanamurthy, N.J. Dimopoulos, K.F. Li, R.V. Patel and A.J. Al-Khalili. Parallel algorithms for low level vision on the homogeneous multi- processor, *Proc. IEEE Conf. Comp. Vision Pattern Recognition*, 1986.

[Ran87] S. Ranka and S. Sahni. Convolution on SIMD mesh connected multicomputers, *Proc. Int. Conf. Parallel Processing*, pages 211–217, 1987.

[Ran88a] S. Ranka and S. Sahni. Image template matching on SIMD hypercube multicomputers, *Proc. Int. Conf. Parallel Processing*, pages 84–91, 1988.

[Ran88b] S. Ranka and S. Sahni. Image template matching on MIMD hypercube multicomputers, *Proc. Int. Conf. Parallel Processing*, pages 92–99, 1988.

[Red79] S.F. Reddaway. *The DAP Approach*, Infotech Ltd, 1979.

[Red80] D.R. Reddy and R.W. Hon. Computer architecture for vision, in *Computer Vision and Sensor-based Robots*, Plenum Press, New York, 1980.

[Ree80] A.P. Reeves. On efficient global information extraction methods for parallel processors, *Computer Graphics and Image Processing*, 14:159–169, 1980.

[Ree82] A.P. Reeves and A. Rostampour. Computational cost of image registration with a parallel binary array processor, *IEEE Trans. Pattern Anal. Mach. Intell.*, 4:4, July 1982.

[Ree84a] A.P. Reeves. Parallel computer architectures for image processing, *Computer Vision Graphics Image Processing*, 25:68–88, 1984.

[Ree84b] A.P. Reeves. Parallel Pascal: An extended Pascal for parallel computers, *J. Parallel and Distributed Computing* 1:64–80, 1984.

[Ree89] A.P. Reeves. Meshes and hypercubes for computer vision, in *Multicomputer Vision*, S. Levialdi, editor, Academic Press, 1989.

[Rei85] D. Reisis and V.K.P. Kumar. Parallel processing of the labeling problem, in *Proc. IEEE Workshop Comput. Arch. for Pattern Anal. Mach. Intell.*, 1985.

[Rit87] G.X. Ritter and P.D. Gader. Image algebra techniques for parallel image processing, *J. Parallel and Distributed Computing*, 4:7–44, 1987.

[Ros83] A. Rosenfeld. Parallel image processing using cellular arrays, *IEEE Computer*, pages 14-20, 1983.

[Ros86] A. Rosenfeld, J. Ornelas, Jr. and Y. Hung. Hough transform algorithms for mesh-connected SIMD parallel processors, *Comput. Vision Graphics Image Processing*, 41(3):293–305, Mar. 1986.

[Ros90] F.U. Rosenberger, G.C. Johns, D.G. Politte and C.E. Molnar. Transputer implementation of the EM algorithm for PET image reconstruction, *Proc. 3rd Conf. North American Transputer Users Group*, pages 51-62, 1990.

[Sam89] M.R. Samatham and D.K. Pradhan. The De Bruijn multiprocessor network: a versatile parallel processing and sorting network for VLSI, *IEEE Trans. Computers*, C-38:567–581, Apr. 1989.

[San85a] P. A. Sandon. A pyramid implementation using a reconfigurable array of processors, in *Proc. IEEE Workshop Comput. Arch. Pat. Anal. Image Database Manag.*, pages 112–118, 1985.

[San85b] J.L.C. Sanz, E.B. Hinkle and I. Dinstein. Computing geometric features of digital objects in general purpose image processing pipeline architecture, *Proc. IEEE Conf. Comp. Vision Pattern Recognition*, 1985.

[San87] J.L.C. Sanz and I. Dinstein. Projection based geometrical feature extraction for computer vision: Algorithms in pipeline architectures, *IEEE Trans. Pattern Anal. Mach. Intell.*, 9:1, Jan 1987.

[San89a] M.B. Sandler, L. Hayat, L. Costa and A. Naqvi. A comparative evaluation of DSPs, microprocessors and the transputer for image processing, *Proc. IEEE Int. Conf. Acoustics, Speech and Signal Processing*, pages 1532–1535, Glasgow 1989.

[San89b] J.L.C. Sanz, editor. *Advances in Machine Vision*, Springer Verlag, 1989.

[Sch85] D.H. Schaefer, D.H. Wilcox and G.C. Harris. A pyramid of MPP processing elements: experience and plans, *Proc. Hawaii Int. Conf. Syst. Sci.*, pages 178–184, 1985.

[Sch87] P.N. Schwartzrauber. Multiprocessor FFTs, *Parallel Computing*, 5:197–210, 1987.

[Sch89a] I.D. Scherson, S. Sen and Y. Ma. Two nearly optimal sorting algorithms for mesh connected processor arrays using shear sort, *J. Parallel and Distributed Computing*, 6:151–165, 1989.

[Sch89b] H. Schomberg. Image processing on a transputer-based perfect shuffle machine, *Microprocessing and Microprogramming*, 25:277–280, North-Holland, 1989.

[Sei85] C.L. Seitz. The Cosmic Cube, *Commun. ACM*, 28:22–23, Jan 1985.

[Ser83] J. Serra. *Image Analysis and Mathematical Morphology*, Academic Press, 1983.

[Sha84] D.E. Shaw. SIMD and MIMD variants of the NON-VON supercomputer, *Proc. COMPCON*, Feb. 1984.

[Sha85] M. Sharma J.H. Patel and N. Ahuja. NETRA: An architecture for a large scale multiprocessor vision system, in *IEEE Workshop Comput. Arch. Pat. Anal. Image Database Manag.*, pages 311–319, Nov. 1985.

[Sha90] M. Shamash and I. Gertner. A new parallel algorithm for the multidimensional Fourier transform processing, *Proc. 1990 IEEE Int. Conf. Acoustics, Speech and Signal Processing*, pages 1993–1996, Albuquerque, 1990.

[Shi82] Y. Shiloach and U. Vishkin. An $O(\log n)$ parallel connectivity algorithm, *J. Algorithms*, 3:57–67, 1982.

[Sib85] T.M. Siberberg. The Hough transform on the Geometric Arithmetic Parallel Processor, *Proc. Workshop Comput. Arch. for Pattern Anal. Mach. Intell.*, 1985.

[Sie84] H.J. Siegel, T. Schwederski, N.J. Davis and J.T. Kuehn. PASM: a reconfigurable parallel system for image processing, *Computer Architecture News*, 12(4):7–19, 1984.

[Sie89] H.J. Siegel, W.G. Nation, C.P. Kruskal and L.M. Napolitano Jr. Using the multistage cube network topology in parallel supercomputers. *Proc. IEEE*, 77(12):1933–1953, 1989.

[Sny83] W.E. Snyder and Alan Cowart. An iterative approach to region growing using associative memories, *IEEE Trans. Pattern Anal. Mach. Intell.*, 5(3), May 1983.

[Spe89] Special issue on supercomputer technology, *Proc. IEEE*, Dec. 1989.

[Ste83a] M.E. Steenstrup, D.T. Lawton and C. Weems. Determination of the rotational and translational components of a flow field using a content addressable parallel processor, *Proc. IEEE Conf. Comp. Vision Pattern Recognition*, 1983.

[Ste83b] S.R. Sternberg. Biological image processing, *Computer*, 16(1):22–34, 1983.

[Ste89] C.V. Stewart and C.R. Dyer. Simulation of a connectionist stereo algorithm on a shared-memory multiprocessor, in *Parallel Algorithms for Machine Intelligence*, Springer-Verlag, 1989.

[Sto71] H.S. Stone. Parallel processing with the perfect shuffle, *IEEE Trans. Computers*, C-20:153–161, 1971.

[Sto83] Q.F. Stout. Sorting, merging, selecting, and filtering on tree and pyramid machines, in *Proc. 1983 Int. Conf. Parallel Processing*, pages 214–221, 1983.

[Sto86a] Q.F. Stout. Meshes with multiple buses, *Proc. IEEE Symp. Foundations Comp. Sci.*, pages 264–273, 1986.

[Sto86b] Q.F. Stout. An algorithmic comparison of meshes and pyramids, in *Evaluation of multicomputers for image processing*, L. Uhr, S. Levialdi, K. Preston, Jr. and M.J.B. Duff, editors, pages 107–121, Academic Press, 1986.

[Sto86c] Q.F. Stout. Algorithm-guided design considerations for meshes and pyramids, in *Intermediate-Level Image Processing*, M.J.B. Duff, editor, Academic Press, 1986.

[Sto87] Q.F. Stout. Supporting divide-and-conquer algorithms for image processing. *J. Parallel and Distributed Computing*, 4:95–115, 1987.

[Str85] J. P. Strong. The Fourier transform on mesh connected processing arrays such as the massively parallel processor, in *Proc. IEEE Workshop Comp. Arch. Pat. Anal. Image Database Manag.*, pages 190–196, Nov. 1985.

[Sun87] M.H. Sunwoo, B.S. Baroody and J.K. Aggarwal. A parallel algorithm for region labeling, *Proc. Workshop Comput. Arch. for Pattern Anal. Mach. Intell.*, 1987.

[Swa87] P.N. Swarztrauber. Multiprocessor FFTs, *Parallel Computing*, 5:197–210, North-Holland, 1987.

[Tan80] S.L. Tanimoto and A.L. Klinger. *Structured Computer Vision: Machine Perception through Hierarchical Computation Structures*, Academic Press, 1980.

[Tan82] S.L. Tanimoto. Programming techniques for hierarchical parallel image processors, in *Multicomputers and Image Processing Algorithms and Programs*, pages 421–429, Academic Press, 1982.

[Tan83a] S.L. Tanimoto. A pyramidal approach to parallel processing, in *Proc. ACM Int. Symp. Comp. Arch.*, pages 123–141, 1983.

[Tan83b] S.L. Tanimoto. Algorithms for median filtering of images on a pyramid machine, in *Computing Structures for Image Processing*, M.J.B. Duff, editor, Academic Press, 1983.

[Tan84] S.L. Tanimoto. A hierarchical cellular logic for pyramid computers, *J. Parallel Distributed Comp.*, 1:105–132, 1984.

[Tan85] H.T.Tanaka, D.H.Ballard, S.Tsuji and M.Curtiss. Parallel polyhedral shape recognition, *Proc. IEEE Conf. Comp. Vision Pattern Recognition*, 1985.

[Tan87] S.L. Tanimoto, T.J. Ligocki and R. Ling. A prototype pyramid machine for hierarchical cellular logic, in *Parallel Hierarchical Computer Vision*, L. Uhr, editor, Academic Press, 1987.

[Tan91] A.C. Tan and R. Richards. Developing the MGI workstation, in *Transputing 91*, P. Welch *et al.*, editors, IOS, 1991.

[Tan92] S.L. Tanimoto. Steps towards automating the evaluation of image processing architectures, in *From Pixels to Features II*, H. Burkhardt, Y. Neuvo and J.C. Simon, editors, pages 3–12, Elsevier, 1992.

[Tro92] L. Troiano, P.L. Mantovani and M. Carovaglie. Implementation of an adaptive compression algorithm onto a Transputer network, in *Parallel Computing: from Theory to Sound Practice*, W. Joosen and E. Milgram, editors, pages 384–392, IOS Press, 1992.

[Tse85] P.S. Tseng, K. Hwang and V.K. Prassana Kumar. A VLSI-based multiprocessor architecture for implementing parallel algorithms, in *Proc. Int. Conf. Parallel Processing*, pages 657–664, Aug. 1985.

[Tuc92] L.W. Tucker. Data parallelism and image understanding, in *From Pixels to Features II*, H. Burkhardt, Y. Neuvo and J.C. Simon, editors, pages 159–172, Elsevier, 1992.

[Tuo83] D.L. Tuomenoksa, G.B. Adams, H.J. Siegel and O.R. Mitchell. A parallel algorithm for contour extraction: Advantages and architectural implications, *Proc. IEEE Conf. Comp. Vision Pattern Recognition*, 1983.

[Uhr84] L. Uhr. Algorithm-structured computer arrays and networks, in *Architectures and Processes for Images, Percepts, Models, and Information*, Academic Press, 1984.

[Uhr86] L. Uhr, K.Preston, Jr., S. Levialdi and M.J.B. Duff, editors. *Evaluation for Multi-Computers for Image Processing*, Academic Press, 1986.

[Uhr87] L. Uhr, editor. *Parallel Computer Vision*, Academic Press, 1987.

[Ung58] H. Unger. A computer oriented toward special problems, *Proc. IRE*, 46:1744–1750, 1958.

[Vai92] O. Vainio, L. Yin and Y. Neuvo. Parallelism in generalized median operations, in *From Pixels to Features II*, H. Burkhardt, Y. Neuvo and J.C. Simon, editors, pages 359–372, Elsevier, 1992.

[Vii89] J. Viitanen, P. Hanninen, R. Saarela and J. Saarinen. An efficient method for image pattern matching, in *Parallel Processing for Computer Vision and Display*, P.M. Dew, R.A. Earnshow and T.R. Heywood, editors, pages 210–224, Addison-Wesley, 1989.

[Vii92] J. Viitanen, T. Korpiharju, J. Takala and H. Kiminkinen. Data flow principle of programming for image processing on sea-of-gates cellular processors, in *From Pixels to Features II*, H. Burkhardt, Y. Neuvo and J.C. Simon, editors, pages 137–156, Elsevier, 1992.

[Wal87] S.R. Walton. Performance of the one-dimensional fast Fourier transform on the hypercube, *Hypercube Microprocessors*, SIAM:530–535, 1987.

[Wee85] C. Weems, D. Lawton, S. Levitan, E. Riseman, A. Hanson and M. Callahan. Iconic and symbolic processing using a content addressable parallel Processor, *Proc. IEEE Conf. Comp. Vision Pattern Recognition*, 1985.

[Wil85] S.S. Wilson. The PIXIE 5000: A systolic array processor, in *Proc. IEEE Workshop Comput. Arch. Pat. Anal. Image Database Manag.*, pages 477–483, Nov. 1985.

[Wil86] L.R. Williams and P. Anandan. A coarse-to-fine control strategy for stereo and motion on a mesh-connected computer, *Proc. IEEE Conf. Comp. Vision Pattern Recognition*, 1986.

[Wu81] A.Y. Wu, T. Dubitzki and A. Rosenfeld. Parallel computation of contour properties, *IEEE Trans. Pattern Anal. Mach. Intell.*, May 1981.

[Wu88] A.Y. Wu, S.K. Bhaskar and A. Rosenfeld. Parallel computation of geometric properties from the medial axis transform, *Comput. Vision Graphics Image Processing*, 41(3),
March 1988.

[Yal85] S. Yalamanchili, K.V. Palem, L.S. Davis, A.J. Welch and J.K. Aggarwal. Image
processing architectures: A taxonomy and survey, in *Progress in Pattern Recognition 2*,
L.N. Kanal and A. Rosenfeld, editors, Elsevier, 1985.

[Zap90] E. L. Zapata, F. F. Rivera, I. Benavides, J. M. Carazo and R. Peskin, Multidimensional fast Fourier transform into SIMD hypercubes, *IEE Proc.*, Vol. 137, Pt. E, No. 4,
July 1990, pp. 253–260.

2

Low Level Parallel Image Processing

LEONEL SOUSA, MOISÉS PIEDADE

2.1 INTRODUCTION

Computer vision in general, and image processing in particular, requires an enormous amount of computation. For the time being, parallel processing systems seem to be the more economical and flexible solution for achieving the computing power required by image processing applications. The successful development of several parallel systems and algorithms, over the last twenty years, has had an important impact on the practical application of image processing theory and principles.

Image processing can be loosely classified into hierarchical levels. Three different hierarchical levels may be considered [MC85]: *data*, *information* and *knowledge* levels. At the data level, the lowest one, the image is composed of a pixel array without explicit information about structures or objects contained in it. At the information level, features of the image are extracted and manipulated, resulting in a qualitative change and quantitative data reduction of the image representation. At the knowledge level, the highest one, the reduced data obtained in the previous processing levels is submitted to typical operations involving object recognition, scene description or 3-D modeling.

The hierarchical image processing levels require computational machines with different requirements. Several classifications of computer architectures have been proposed [HB84]. The most commonly used is Flynn's classification which is based on the multiplicity of the instruction and data streams. Four different classes are identified: SISD (Single Instruction Single Data stream), SIMD (Single Instruction Multiple Data stream), MISD (Multiple Instruction Single Data stream) and MIMD (Multiple Instruction Multiple Data stream). The SISD architecture corresponds to the classi-

Parallel Algorithms for Digital Image Processing, Computer Vision and Neural Networks, ed. I. Pitas
© 1993 John Wiley & Sons Ltd

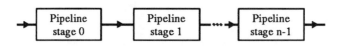

Figure 2.1   Pipeline processing with n stages.

cal sequential systems, and the MISD class has no practical interest. So far, parallel architectures can be loosely classified as SIMD and MIMD architectures. By analyzing today's systems two main subclasses of MIMD architectures can be identified: *shared memory* and *distributed memory* MIMD architectures [Dun90]. In the former, the multiple processors share a main memory (or parts of it). In distributed memory architectures each processor has access only to its local memory, using one or more inter-processor communication channels to exchange information with other processors.

An important concept in present computers is *pipelining*. A pipelined computer overlaps computations in order to exploit *temporal parallelism*. This concept is applied in most digital processors to increase efficiency. The phases needed for executing an instruction are pipelined, and different stages of the pipeline manipulate different instructions at the same time. An N stage pipelined processor can theoretically be N times faster than a non-pipelined processor. Pipeline processing can also be applied at a higher level, by using multiprocessor systems. Information comes from one of the stages, and flows through the other processors of the pipeline, resulting in overlapped processing (Figure 2.1).

In the context of this book, we are concerned with low-level image processing, namely processing at data level, and its implementation on parallel systems. Most low-level image processing algorithms have common features which influence the choice of the more adequate image processing parallel systems. As an example, most of these algorithms are *context-insensitive* and *position-invariant*. The first feature means that the algorithm's parameters are fixed beforehand independently of local image features. The second feature makes the processing independent of the location of the image pixels. Moreover, the image is represented by a regular structure. These characteristics influenced the first generation of specific parallel image processing SIMD and pipeline architectures [Ree84].

Recent technological advances have led to the development of more powerful and flexible processors, some of them adapted to the MIMD architectures [INM89, Tex90], thus spreading the use of these architectures (namely those with distributed memory). Some attention will be given to MIMD architecture systems, which are less covered in the literature.

This chapter begins by presenting the characteristics of low-level image processing algorithms, with emphasis on their computational aspects. Parallel architectures used in the image processing systems are then referred to. Image processing algorithms for the different parallel architectures are discussed in the last two sections. The first of these sections presents a set of local image processing algorithms for parallel systems. The implementation of local image convolution on a parallel MIMD system with a reduced number of processors is described. A review is made of the local algorithms for parallel systems with a large number of processor elements (of the order of the number of pixels in the image array). This review may constitute an introduction for researchers interested in this area, or a tutorial for students of the subject (a large number of references can be found at the end of the chapter). The last section is concerned with parallel global image processing algorithms. Experimental work is included in this section.

Some evaluation of parallel image processing algorithms and systems is presented. Image processing parallel systems are evaluated with respect to the complexity of the algorithms, speed-up obtained and efficiency of the parallel machines.

2.2 LOW LEVEL IMAGE PROCESSING ALGORITHMS

Low level digital image processing techniques and algorithms have been developed during the last twenty years, and play an important role in image processing systems. The main objective of low-level image processing is to enhance the image, or features of the image, to make it more suitable for subsequent processing, or for human analysis and understanding. Higher level algorithms to extract features of the image as well as to classify or model the scene that it represents, have to receive pre-processed information as an input. Processing of the image pixel array can improve the image quality in different ways [WVL83], namely by reducing the noise, by locating pixels that are possible edge points, by reassigning the image quantization levels, by normalizing the pixel values of an image or portions of an image, etc.

Low level digital image processing algorithms have different computational aspects and produce different results, but all of them require an enormous amount of computation. These algorithms, typically, use a large number of simple arithmetic and logic operations to combine the information contained in the pixel array values. A relevant computational aspect of the algorithms, namely for parallel processing, is locality. In parallel systems, operations which use pixels sparsely located through the image array to compute the value of a pixel will not benefit from a neighborhood type connection between processor elements.[1]

Low level image processing operators can be classified loosely as *local*, *point-wise* and *global* operators.

2.2.1 Local Operators

With local operators, the value of a processed pixel depends only on its value and on the values of the pixels placed in its neighborhood. These operators, also referred to in the literature as *window-based* operators, use different neighborhoods (windows), but in general they have a square or rectangular geometry. Because of the large number of elementary operations performed in single-processor systems ($O(M^2 \times N^2)$ for $N \times N$ image size and $M \times M$ window sizes[2]) these operators are important candidates for implementation in parallel systems.

---

[1] The designation *processor element* refers to a processor or processing element.
[2] $F(N) = O(f(N))$ means that there exist constants k and n such that $F(N) \leq k \times f(N)$ for all $N \geq n$.

$$I'(X,Y) = I(X,Y) * T[K,M]$$
$$I'(i,j) = \sum_{k=0}^{M-1} \sum_{m=0}^{M-1} T(k,m) \times I(i+k, j+m) \qquad (2.1)$$

Image convolution [Hor86] with local kernels (masks) (equation 2.1) is a widely used local linear operation for image smoothing and edge enhancement.

In some cases non-linear local operators can be used for image noise smoothing with some advantages (e.g., to reduce the image noise without loss of edge information). This is the case of two-dimensional and separable median filters [Nar81, HYT79]. The intensity of each pixel of the image is replaced by the median value of the pixels contained in a window centered on that pixel.

Image correlation [GW87, Lim90] is another example of a local operation which is commonly used for template matching. Correlation measures the similarity between a pattern and a portion (window) of an image. The image obtained by correlating a template with an image has values between −1 and +1 with values near 0 indicating little similarity between the template and the image.

The implementation of local operations on parallel computing structures is usually made by splitting the images into sub-images which are distributed by the processor elements. Two different approaches are used for the parallelization of local convolution algorithms [SSF82]: the *complete sums approach* and the *partial sums approach*.

The complete sums approach assumes that all the data needed by a processor element to process its local sub-image is transferred to it. With the partial sums approach each processor element makes as much computation as possible using the local data and then transfers the partial results to other processor elements. The first approach requires more memory (in direct proportion to the number of processors and the window size) and the transfer of more data to the parallel system at the image load phase. However, it does not imply any interprocessor communication, as in the second approach. The two approaches can be extended to the parallelization of most of the image processing local algorithms.

When the number of processor elements is less than the number of pixels, a mapping of the image pixel array onto the processor elements [Red88] has to be established. The image pixel array can be divided into sub-images with a size equal to the number of processor elements, processing each sub-image sequentially. The other possibility is to divide the image pixel array into a number of sub-images equal to the number of processor elements and process the sub-images in parallel.

2.2.2 Point-wise Operators

With point-wise operators the value of a processed pixel depends only on the original value of that pixel, or on the value of the same pixel in different images.

Useful point-wise operators are the difference between time-sequenced images (for movement detection or inter-frame coding) and the modification of the image quantization levels.

Parallel point-wise algorithms do not require any communication between processor elements. These algorithms can work on image partitions without the need of synchronization for sharing information. The simplicity of the point-wise algorithms leads to their direct implementation on hardware or firmware in a large number of image processing systems.

2.2.3   Global Operators

A global operation uses the information spread in the image pixel array to compute the value of each pixel of the processed image. Histogram equalization, image coordinate transformations and component labeling are some examples of global operations usually applied in low and intermediate level image processing.

$$H(L_i) = H(L_i) + 1; \qquad L_i \text{ denotes the value of pixel } i \qquad (2.2)$$

The histogram of an image represents the first order probability density function of a given quantization level in the image pixel array given the values of all the image pixels (equation 2.2). The image histogram is computed from the values of all image pixels without explicit reference to their location. Re-assignment of the quantization levels [Pav82] and image binarization [SSWC88] are two frequently used operations which can be performed by using the information conveyed by the histogram.

The labeling of a binary image consists of assigning a label to each 1-pixel (pixels which do not belong to the image background) so that two 1-pixels have the same label if, and only if, they are in the same connected component. Two 1-pixels are in the same connected component if there is a path of connected 1-pixels linking them together. Two contiguous 1-pixels are connected if they are adjacent vertically, horizontally, or diagonally (only vertically and horizontally adjacent pixels can be considered for connectedness) [RK82]. Image labeling is an interesting problem because it has features of both local and global image operators. Labels can be assigned locally with respect to contiguous pixels but the label assigned to one pixel may depend on the label of another image pixel in a distant location within the image. The labeling of components of binary images is an operation often used for image segmentation and analysis.

If the data partition method is used to parallelize global algorithms, the processor elements have to access data distributed all over the parallel computing structure. The implementation of a fully connected architecture, with each processor element connected to the remaining processor elements, becomes impractical for large systems; the cost of the implementation of a fully connected network grows with the square of the number of the processor elements. Global communication among the processors can be made by explicit and general procedures [CS89], or information from the different processors can be combined in different phases of an algorithm according to a particular pattern. This last solution is algorithm dependent but allows the search for better results by using problem oriented solutions. For instance, in the computation of an image histogram, information can be combined in different phases in a recursive way (section 2.5).

Two dimensional image coordinate transformations constitute a class of tools often used in low-level image processing and computer graphics. Image translation, rotation and scaling are typical image coordinate transformations. These transformations may be used for image data normalization as regards size, orientation or position. These transformations exhibit different computational aspects, but they can all be loosely classified as global operators. It is true that image translation can be performed by successive local shifts of the image; however, this principle is more difficult to apply to rotation, where any rotation point and rotation angle can be defined.

Algorithms for the parallel implementation of these operations will be presented in the next sections.

2.3   PARALLEL SYSTEMS FOR IMAGE PROCESSING

Parallel computing systems provide a set of resources (processor elements, memory, etc.) which must be used uniformly. The challenge with parallel systems is to distribute the processing load, programs and data, among the processor elements in a balanced way in order to keep the resources active during as much time as possible. The two paradigms of programming parallel systems are *data parallelism* (which is also called *image parallelism* for image processing) and *task parallelism*.

Image parallelism means that the image is divided by the processor elements all of which execute the same program. With task parallelism an algorithm is split into sub-tasks which are assigned to different processor elements and run concurrently. Task parallelism has the main limitation of being difficult to apply when the number of processors grows, because of the maximum number of sub-tasks found in a single algorithm. Most often, image parallelism seems to be more adequate for implementing low-level image processing algorithms on parallel computing systems [MP88]. The algorithms and operators process large image pixel arrays using a great number of elementary arithmetic and logic operators.

Pipelined processors for real time low-level image processing have been developed [Ree84, BB87]. These processors accept data in raster scan format and pass it along the pipeline of processing stages. Each stage performs a pre-specified function, performing the same operation on every element of the data sequentially. The main advantages of this type of processor are the possibility of processing the image in real time (input data can be taken from the image sensing device), no need for storing the intermediate processing results and simplicity of communication between processing stages. The main drawback of these processing devices is their lower flexibility. Once set up for a particular algorithm, no changes can be made. Pipelined processors for local and point-wise image processing algorithms have been proposed [Ree84].

2.3.1   Parallel Architectures for Image Processing

A classical approach to the subject of parallel architectures for image processing always begins by discussing the dichotomy between SIMD and MIMD architectures. SIMD architectures are used for low-level image processing, and MIMD architectures are reserved for high-level image processing. Intermediate processing [Tan86] is a hybrid inter-level processing stage which uses both architectures or a mixed type of architecture called MSIMD (Multiple SIMD) [SSM+81]. Moreover, pipelined architectures can also be used for different processing levels. At the lower levels, the pipeline specialized processors referred to above are used, while at the other levels pipeline multi-stage architectures can be used to exploit sequential task parallelism for a processing algo-

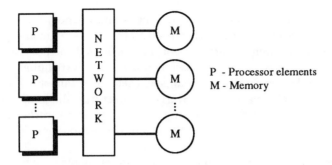

Figure 2.2   Shared memory systems.

rithm or a set of processing algorithms. Although this approach is important, it may be an interesting exercise to adopt some other views of the parallel image processing problem.

An important feature of the parallel systems used for image processing is their granularity. In a loose way, granularity is associated with a comparison of the number of processors, or processing elements, with the size of the image pixel array. Three granularity types are usually considered: *fine grained*, *medium grained* and *coarse grained*. In fine grained systems the cost of interprocessor communication is low, and is comparable to that of a basic arithmetic operation; on the contrary, the communication cost in coarse grained systems is high with respect to that for a basic arithmetic operation.

The simplicity of the SIMD architectures with one single control unit, a program memory unit and several processing elements interconnected by a fixed network, allowed, in the past, the implementation of fine grained systems for low-level image processing [Ree84]. Technological advances have led to the development of flexible MIMD architectures with a large number of processors. Today, medium grained MIMD computing systems can be efficiently used for low-level image processing.

Computing systems with MIMD architectures use two basic different mechanisms for sharing information. *Shared memory* multiprocessor (or *tightly coupled* multiprocessor) architectures provide a common storage device which is shared by the processor's system (Figure 2.2). *Distributed memory* multiprocessor (or *loosely coupled* multiprocessor) architectures provide single or multiple channels for interprocessor communication.

Low-level image processing parallel algorithms for complete shared memory architectures have similarities with the sequential algorithms. Mechanisms of mutual exclusion (e.g *lock* and *unlock*) are necessary to coherently update shared variables or execute critical sections of a program. The main limiting factor for expanding shared memory parallel computing systems is the decrease of performance due to memory access contention—multiple processors trying to access simultaneously the same memory unit. Memory caches are usually introduced in order to reduce processing time. In this case, the systems have to provide cache coherency mechanisms.

Recently, a class of new MIMD *pseudo-shared* memory architectures have been proposed for image processing [HTK89, THK85, SCP91]. These architectures have a set of orthogonal buses which are used to share the memory in an orthogonal way, thus avoiding access conflicts in the memory buses and memory units. Pseudo-shared memory orthogonal architectures with n processors require n^2 memory modules.

Distributed memory architectures do not include shared memory, and use communication channels to pass messages between processors. Distributed memory MIMD systems use multiple communication channels, each one establishing a point-to-point processor communication path. As in SIMD architectures, different networks can be used to allow interprocessor communication. Some of these networks are topologically equivalent [FLN86], but others are not. Some interconnection networks are considered in this section (Figure 2.3).

In a two-dimensional *mesh* network, the processor elements may be viewed as being physically arranged in a two-dimensional array (greater dimensionality can be used). Each processor element of this network is connected to four other processors in the north, south, east and west directions. A slight modification of the architecture can be made by connecting the processor elements on the opposite edge, thus creating a closed toroidal surface—this is the *toroide* network.

A *hypercube* network with N processor elements has a dimensionality of $q = \log_2 N$. Each processor element is directly connected to the processors with indices differing by only one bit, i.e., at a unitary Hamming distance. In a q-dimensional hypercube network each processor is linked to q adjacent processors.

Shuffle-exchange networks require three connections per processor element independently of the dimensionality q. A processor element p with a binary representation $p = p_{q-1}p_{q-2}...p_1p_0$ is connected to the processor elements represented in binary by $p_{q-2}p_{q-3}...p_0p_{q-1}$ (*shuffle*), $p_0p_{q-1}...p_1$ (*unshuffle*) and to $p_{q-1}...\overline{p}_0$ (*exchange*).

The *pyramid* network is a quaternary tree with the processors in the same level of the tree connected to form a mesh. A pyramid network with N^2 processors in the base has a depth of $\log_2 N$ with the processors in level i, $0 \leq i \leq \log_2 N$ (level 0 is the base level), connected as an $N/2^i \times N/2^i$ mesh network. This type of network differs from the *tree* network by introducing direct communication between the processors in the same tree level.

The quite different features of shared memory and distributed memory parallel systems make their comparative performance difficult to assess. Some experimental comparative work has been done on real systems using low-level image processing local operators [PC90]. A shared memory MIMD system and a distributed memory system with a hypercube network have been used. Some normalization of the system elements' characteristics has been made in order to make the comparison as fair as possible. With a small number of processors (typically 20 processors) the shared memory system produced better results than the hypercube based system. By increasing the number of processors, the performance of the shared memory architecture degrades much faster than the performance of the distributed memory system. The two main degrading effects are the increased shared memory references and the requirement of more critical sections for the shared memory programs.

2.3.2   A MIMD Distributed Memory Processing System

Processors with specific characteristics for the implementation of distributed memory MIMD systems have been developed. The *transputer* is the first microprocessor designed for this purpose. Among its specific characteristics [Cok91] the following should

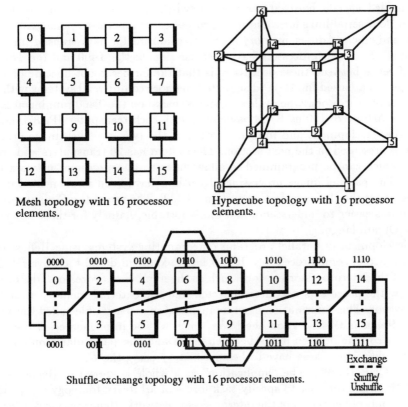

Mesh topology with 16 processor elements.

Hypercube topology with 16 processor elements.

Shuffle-exchange topology with 16 processor elements.

Exchange ---

Shuffle/
Unshuffle

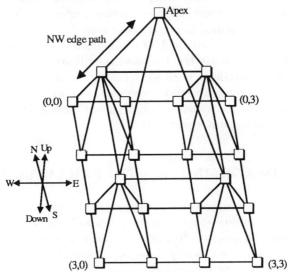

Pyramid topology with base size of 4^2=16 processor elements.

Figure 2.3 Interconnection of processor elements.

be emphasized: specific hardware for context switching between processes on the same processor, four serial links for connecting processors on a point-to-point basis, on-chip memory and efficient direct memory access mechanisms for data transfer, in and out of the links. Two such processors have been developed: the T400 and the T800. The main difference between these processors is that the former is not floating point.

Transputers are used in MIMD distributed memory commercial systems with different number of processors. One of these systems, based on the T800 running at 20 MHz and with 4 MByte of 100 ns RAM associated with each transputer [Pei87], has been used in the development and implementation of the two low-level image processing algorithms presented in the next section. The system has 20 transputers and crossbar switches which can be programmed to allow different interprocessor network configurations. The parallel image processing algorithms have been implemented in the C language under the Helios operating system [Sof89]. The use of the C language makes the programs easier to understand, and more portable, namely for those not familiar with the Occam language [Cok91].

The development of parallel programs on computing systems using Helios requires the observance of some procedures. Helios has to know in detail the physical characteristics of the interprocessor network, such as the number of processors, the processor types, how the processors are interconnected and the external memory available for each processor. This information must be included in a special file called the *resource map* file. Helios must also know the tasks which will be implemented in the system, the various communication paths between them and the particular requirements of the individual tasks. These have to be specified by using the *Component Distributed Language*, CDL [Per90]. The "application" as a whole is known to Helios as a *task force*. CDL allows the user to specify task forces of arbitrary topology independently of the size and configuration of the interprocessor network. Helios provides a *task force manager* which attempts to reconcile the resource requirements specified in the CDL file with the resources specified in the resource map file.

Helios provides different levels of I/O communication between tasks. The implemented programs use the posix I/O level and the library calls **read, write**.

The transputer computing system used has one *root transputer* which interfaces the host and all its peripherals (disks, console, etc.) with the parallel system. The information from and to the outside world is passed through this transputer—images, convolution masks, histogram vectors, etc.

2.4   LOCAL IMAGE PROCESSING PARALLEL ALGORITHMS

This section reviews several low-level local parallel image processing algorithms presented in the specialized literature in recent years and discusses their implementation on various machines. Asymptotic complexity analysis of the algorithms is presented based on communication complexity. Speed-up, efficiency and execution are parameters used to characterize the different machines.

The parallelization of image point-wise algorithms is straightforward due to their characteristics. The processor elements of the parallel systems do not need to share information, working in an independent way. Point-wise *lookup table* operations on grey level images can be performed by broadcasting one lookup table value at a time, and by allowing the processor elements with the correspondent lookup table entry to change the image values.

Low-level parallel image processing local algorithms have been proposed for the different architectures referred to in the previous section. Most of these algorithms divide the image into a number of sub-images equal to the number of processor elements. Each processor element takes charge of the processing of a sub-image.

Parallel algorithms for image local convolution follow the two main approaches already referred to. The partial sums approach is used in systems with different grained types while the complete sums approach can be used with the medium or coarse grained parallel systems. In the partial sums approach, the processor elements multiply the pixels by one or more mask coefficients and store the partial result in a local memory. The image, or the partial results, are then moved and the operation is repeated. The results are accumulated, until the final result is achieved.

2.4.1   Local Algorithm for Coarse and Medium Grained MIMD Architecture

A simple coarse grained algorithm for local image processing in the transputer based system, referred to in the previous section, will now be presented. The algorithm has been implemented in the system using the C language and the Helios operating system; it accepts the image size and mask size as input parameters (images should have 256 quantization levels).[3]

The coarse grained algorithm uses image parallelism to distribute the processing load by the processors. The "task force" (see section 2.3) has two types of processes: a single master and a number of workers (Figure 2.4) (referred to as a farm topology) [Per90]. By using the complete sums approach, referred to in the previous sections, the master process is responsible for the distribution of the sub-images and the mask coefficients by the processors (each processor receives all data needed to convolve its sub-image). All the workers run the same program, making the calculations on each sub-image locally and outputting the maximum and minimum values found on the processed sub-image. Each worker then sends these values to the master. The master computes the maximum and minimum values found on the whole processed image. These values are broadcast to all workers which normalize the processed sub-images, using $I' = ((I - I_{min}) \times 255)/(I_{max} - I_{min})$. The sub-images are sent back to the master process. Each worker will process the same amount of data, so the processing load is balanced.

The **master** program performs the following actions:

- Read the number of workers, which is an input parameter;
- Allocate memory to the image and read it from a file;
- Read the mask from a file (the file contains the size of the mask followed by the value of the mask coefficients);
- Start one thread for each worker. This thread sends initial information to the workers, such as size of the sub-images, the appropriate part of the picture, the mask size, and the coefficients;

---

[3] The experimental work has been partially supported by the EEC under contract ESPRIT–PCA 4121.

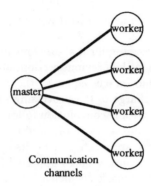

Figure 2.4   Non-balanced farm topology with 4 workers.

- Read the maximum and minimum values of each sub-image sent by the workers;
- Compute the absolute maximum and minimum values and send them to all workers;
- Wait for all workers to finish their task by reading the processed image back.

The **worker** program performs the following actions:

- Read the height and width of the sub-image and the size of the mask;
- Allocate memory to its part of the image;
- Read in the sub-image and the mask coefficients;
- Convolve its part of the image and compute the maximum and minimum values;
- Send the maximum and minimum values found to the master;
- Read the maximum and minimum values found over the whole image;
- Normalize the processed sub-image;
- End the process by sending the processed sub-image back.

The algorithm has been implemented in the parallel computer using 4, 8 and 12 transputers with the network topologies presented in Figure 2.5. The number of workers is equal to the number of transputers in the networks. The master and one of the worker processes run in the same transputer. No degradation of performance occurs since when one of these processors is active the other is blocked (waiting for information). Although Helios can implement the topology in any interprocessor network, the process topology should match the interprocessor network configuration in order to obtain a good system efficiency. The useful diameter of the network, which is the longest of all of the shortest distances between the master and the workers, is 1 for the network with 4 processors and 2 for the other two networks.

The time spent running the algorithm on the different networks is presented in Figure 2.6. The performance of the parallel system is evaluated by using a relative efficiency measure E which compares the time taken for a sequential version of the algorithm T_1, with the time taken for the concurrent version T_n.

$$E = (T_1/(n \times T_n)) \times 100\% \tag{2.3}$$

The results presented in Figure 2.6 were obtained by running the same programs on the system with a different number of transputers. The time T_1 would probably be reduced if an optimized sequential version of the algorithm had been developed. The

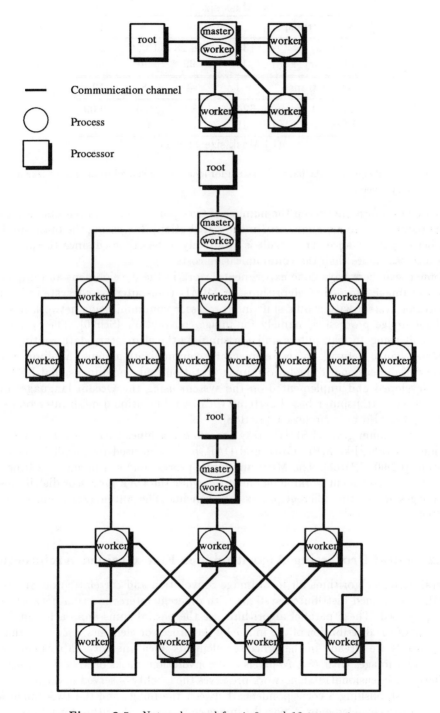

Figure 2.5 Networks used for 4, 8, and 12 transputers.

(a) Mask size 7 × 7

No. of transp.	1	4	8	12
Time(s)	136.92	38.28	18.96	12.93
Efficiency(E%)	100	90	90	88

No. of transp.	1	4	8	12
Time(s)	324.89	88.03	45.52	30.09
Efficiency(E%)	100	93	91	89

(b) Mask size 11 × 11

Figure 2.6   Efficiency of the parallel system for local image convolution (image size 512×512 with 256 grey levels).

decrease of performance when the number of transputers increases reflects an increase in the relative communication cost (image distribution). Increasing the mask size leads to a better performance. This result is intuitively to be expected since the processing load increases more than the communication costs.

Some researchers have done experimental work in the development and implementation of image processing algorithms on MIMD transputer based systems. A multiprocessor system with shuffle-shift interprocessor communication network has been used for image processing, namely for image convolution [Sch90]. The system has been built using 16 transputers and can simulate the elementary data routing of the shuffle-exchange network in two elementary communication steps. Medium grained image two-dimensional convolution, image rotation and one-dimensional FFT have been developed and implemented on the system using the Occam language. Image convolution in transputer based systems with two-dimensional mesh interconnection networks has also been proposed [SRH88].

Several medium grained SIMD array processor machines with mesh type interconnection networks, like MPP, CLIP and DAP, have been used for parallel image convolution [LD90, SRH88]. The MPP and CLIP process one sub-image at a time with each processing element working on one pixel, while the DAP processor distributes the sub-images among the different processing elements. The sub-images are processed in parallel.

2.4.2   Local Processing Algorithms for Fine Grained Architectures

Several parallel algorithms for local image convolution and correlation on SIMD and MIMD fine grained distributed systems with different interconnection networks have been proposed. These parallel algorithms use the partial sums approach and do not take care of the distribution of the image by the processor elements, assuming that the image pixels are already in the processor elements' local memory. In this subsection we consider images with $N \times N$ pixels and convolution masks of $M \times M$ dimension.

The two-dimensional mesh network preserves the locality observed in the image pixel array, by establishing a correspondence between the image and the two-dimensional array of processor elements. A parallel image convolution algorithm for a SIMD mesh architecture with N^2 processing elements and M memory locations per processor has been proposed [FLN86]. The algorithm processes one convolution mask column at a

Processor Element	Image Pixel	Phase 0			Phase 1		
		AB	T	AB'	AB	T	AB'
0	I_0	I_0I_1	T_0	I_0I_1	I_1I_2	T_1	I_1I_0
1	I_1	I_2I_3	T_1	I_2I_1	I_1I_2	T_0	I_1I_2
2	I_2	I_2I_3	T_0	I_2I_3	I_3I_4	T_1	I_3I_2
3	I_3	I_4I_5	T_1	I_4I_3	I_3I_4	T_0	I_3I_4
4	I_4	I_4I_5	T_0	I_4I_5	I_5I_6	T_1	I_5I_4
5	I_5	I_6I_7	T_1	I_6I_5	I_5I_6	T_0	I_5I_6
6	I_6	I_6I_7	T_0	I_6I_7	I_7I_0	T_1	I_7I_6
7	I_7	I_0I_1	T_1	I_0I_7	I_7I_0	T_0	I_7I_0

Figure 2.7 Execution trace of one-dimensional convolution with 8 processors and a mask of 2 coefficients.

time, storing the partial results (equation 2.4). The image is rotated up one row per mask column coefficient, while the partial sum of M products is being computed.

$$I'(i, j + m) = \sum_{k=0}^{M-1} T(k, m) \times I(i + k, j + m) \qquad 0 \le m \le M - 1 \qquad (2.4)$$

By rotating the image left one position at a time, the different columns of the mask are applied, and the results are accumulated. The time complexity of the algorithm is $O(M^2)$.

A parallel image processing convolution algorithm for an N^2 SIMD mesh architecture with $O(1)$ memory locations per processor (*i.e.*, a constant number of memory locations), has been proposed [RS90]. The algorithm uses, as a basic step, the computation of the one-dimensional convolution.

A one-dimensional convolution algorithm for a $1 \times N$ mesh (the mesh has a single row) with $O(1)$ memory locations per processor element is used. An image row is naturally mapped onto the processing elements with the pixel $I[i, j]$ being at processing element $P(j)$. The N processing elements can be partitioned into N/M blocks of M contiguous elements and one copy of the M mask coefficients is broadcast to all blocks. The one-dimensional algorithm begins by pairing pixel values in the processing elements in such a way that the processing element P stores the values of the pixels $(A(P), B(P)) = (I[(q+2k) \bmod N], I[(q+2k+1) \bmod N])$, with $q = \lfloor P/M \rfloor M$ and $k = P \bmod M$ (Figure 2.7). This pairing operation can be achieved in M unit routes. The one-dimensional convolution is performed by rotating the pixel A and the convolution mask clockwise, one position at a time, permuting A with B and computing the partial sums by multiplying $A(P)$ by the mask coefficient of the respective processing element. $B(P)$ stores the next pixel value required by processing element P. Initially, this is true for all processing elements except element P such that $P \bmod M = M - 1$. The problem is solved by substituting the value of B in these processing elements by the value of B' (Figure 2.7). After the j rotation, the value B of a processing element $P \bmod M = M - 1 - j$ has to be replaced by the pixel value initially stored in that processing element. The number of unit routes required to perform the one-dimensional convolution with a mask of M coefficients is at most $3M$.

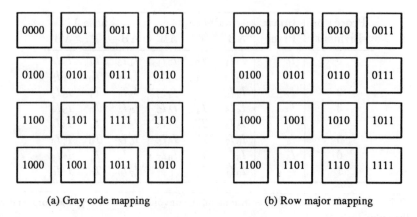

(a) Gray code mapping   (b) Row major mapping

Figure 2.8   Image mappings on two-dimensional hypercubes with 16 processor elements.

The two-dimensional convolution algorithm assumes that N is a multiple of M and that the $N \times N$ image pixel array and the processing elements can be viewed as N^2/M^2 arrays of size $M \times M$ each. It also assumes that the processing element $P(i, j)$ has the value of $T(i \bmod M, j \bmod M)$. The two-dimensional convolution is computed in M phases by calculating N/M lines of the image pixel array per phase—on phase i the lines computed have an index I such that $I \bmod M = i$. On the phase i, the two-dimensional convolution for line I is performed by having the processing elements $P(i + r, j)$ computing the one-dimensional convolution of line $(i + r)$ and column j (with $0 \leq r < M$). The two-dimensional convolution results are obtained by repeatedly shifting the results up M times and by adding the partial sums on processing elements $P(I, j)$. At the end of each phase, the convolution mask is shifted and the process is repeated. The total unit routes of the algorithm is $4M^2 + O(M)$.

Some algorithms have also been proposed for image convolution and correlation on SIMD and MIMD architectures with hypercube interconnection networks. Almost all of these algorithms assume that N and M are powers of 2.

Two different mappings of image pixels onto processor elements have been used in these algorithms. The SIMD hypercube convolution algorithms assume a row major order mapping, while the MIMD algorithms use the Gray code mapping (Figure 2.8).

The Gray code mapping uses the binary reflected Gray code. A binary Gray code with i bits, S_i, is defined recursively as: $S_1 = 0, 1; S_k = 0[S_{k-1}], 1[S_{k-1}]^R$ where $[S_{k-1}]^R$ is the reverse of the $k-1$ bit code S_{k-1} and $b[S]$ is obtained from S by prefixing b to each entry of S. If $N = 2^n$, then S_{2n} is used. This mapping has the property that neighboring pixels are assigned to neighboring hypercube processor elements.

In the row major ordering mapping, neighboring pixels may not be assigned to neighboring processors in the hypercube. For an $N \times N$ array, the index of the processor element at position (i, j) of the array is obtained by multiplying the row index by N and by adding the column index, $i \times N + j$. Therefore, with Gray code mapping a hypercube connected system with the possibility of communicating across different dimensions at a time can simulate a mesh connected system with no loss of efficiency. If the processing elements of the hypercube system can communicate only across one dimension at a time, the simulation of the mesh connected system involves a loss of speed of $\log_2 N$ independently of the code mapping used [CS89].

The parallel algorithms presented for the mesh networks can be applied to the hypercube networks with the number of unit routes of the algorithms multiplied in the worst case by $\log_2 N$.

Fang, Li and Ni [FLN86] have proposed an image convolution parallel algorithm for SIMD fine grained hypercube architecture with M memory locations per processing element and with broadcast capability. Each column of the image is locally divided into N/M segments, where each segment has M consecutive elements. One convolution mask column is sent to the local memory of the processing elements at a time. Then, the elements are permuted in each segment, each pixel is multiplied by a mask coefficient and the results are accumulated. These "permute-multiply-accumulate" steps are repeated, so that every element of the segment appears once in each position of the segment. Since only elements of the same segment are permuted, only half of the products are generated in this phase of the algorithm. After rotating the image up M positions, the "permutation-multiply-accumulate" steps are repeated in order to generate the remaining half of the products required (to recover the original position of the image after this phase the image is rotated down M positions). The image is rotated to the left one position each time a new convolution mask column is input and the process is repeated. The time complexity of the algorithm is $O(M^2 + \log_2 N)$. The algorithm can be extended for systems with L^2 processors, with $M \leq L \leq N$, leading to a time complexity of $O(N^2 M^2 / L^2)$.

Other efficient algorithms to compute two-dimensional convolutions with fine grained SIMD hypercube architectures, with different amounts of memory per processor element, have been proposed. These algorithms use the property that a hypercube of size N^2 can also be viewed as two hypercubes of size $N^2/2 \times N^2/2$ or as N^2/M^2 hypercubes of size M^2 with additional connections. Kumar and Krishnan have proposed an algorithm for template matching on SIMD hypercube architectures with constant local storage size per processing element [KK87]. The hypercube is initially viewed as blocks of size $M \times M$ with all the image values required to compute the convolution within a block sent to it (this operation takes $O(\log_2 N)$ unit routes). The data in each block is circulated recursively so that each data item visits all the processing elements of the block. The algorithm takes $O(M^2 \times \log_2^* M + \log_2 N)$ (where $K = \log_2^* M = \text{Min}\{k \mid \log_2 \log_2 ...k \text{ times}\, (M) \leq 1\}$). The algorithms proposed by Ranka and Sahni [RS88b] for the image convolution with fine grained SIMD hypercube architectures compute the one-dimensional convolution as a basic step of the algorithm. The numbers of unit routes of the algorithms are $2M^2 + O(M + \log_2 M)$ and $12M^2 + O(M \times \log_2 M) + O(\log_2 N)$ for $O(M)$ and $O(1)$ memory elements per processing element, respectively. These last algorithms do not require broadcasting mechanisms to pass the mask coefficients to the processing elements.

Fine grained and medium grained MIMD hypercube algorithms have also been proposed [RS88a]. The number of unit routes of the algorithms is $M^2 + O(M \log_2 M)$ and $2M^2 + O(M \times \log_2 M)$ for $O(M)$ and $O(1)$ memory elements per processor, respectively. Medium grained parallel convolution algorithms have been developed for the $NCUBE/7$ hypercube [PC90] with up to 64 processors. The partial sums approach and the complete sums approach parallel algorithms have been evaluated. It can be seen that the run time for the complete sums algorithm is much lower than for the partial sums algorithm for small size convolution masks. This run time difference is reduced when the size of the convolution masks is increased. Two main reasons have been pointed out for the differences in run time of the two algorithms: the program is more complex for the partial sums approach, thus introducing a greater overhead, and the data transfer rate from the host to the processors is much higher than that between processors.

An algorithm for convolving the image with a two-dimensional mask on a SIMD fine grained shuffle-exchange architecture has been proposed [FLN86]. The basic steps of this algorithm are the same as in the SIMD hypercube algorithm proposed above [FLN86]. The only difference is in data routing. *Exchange*, *shuffle* and *unshuffle* are used to simulate data transmission in the hypercube model. For example, in a hypercube model, processor element p is connected to processor $p^{(b)}$ (only changes the value of bit b on p), with $0 \leq b < (q = \log_2 N^2)$, and the fundamental data transmission is $I(p^{(b)}) \leftarrow I(p)$. The following procedure in the shuffle-exchange architecture models the basic data transmission in the hypercube model (Figure 2.3).

```
procedure hypercube-model(register R, int b)
{
int i;
for (i=1; i<=b; i++)
 R(unshuffle(p)) = R(p); // unshuffle b times where b is the dimension
R(exchange(p)) = R(p);   // exchange
for (i=1; i<=b; i++)
 R(shuffle(p)) = R(p);   // shuffle b times where b is the dimension
}
```

A parallel algorithm for image convolution on MIMD pyramid connected architectures has been proposed [CIPS87]. The operation of the processors is synchronized by a global clock and the data flows through the architecture in a systolic way. The algorithm is divided into three distinct phases (the image is mapped on the base mesh of the pyramid). In the first phase, the size M of the mask is input to the apex processor as a string of $(M-1)$ 1's followed by a special symbol. By transmitting messages serially between the apex and the base processors, these last are partitioned into N^2/M^2 blocks of size $M \times M$ (without loss of generality, it is assumed that N and M are powers of two). In the second phase, the mask is transmitted to the base processors in a row major order. The mask coefficients are sent in serial form, with each row marked with a special symbol and the last entry marked with another special symbol. The mask coefficients are sent by the apex processor to all four children and the procedure is repeated till all coordinators (coordinators are the processors at level $\log_2 M$ which coordinate the processing) receive the mask. The coordinator $CORD(i,j)$ passes the entries to the base processor $P(iM, jM)$ which are the NW (North-west) processor of each block (Figure 2.3). The entries are then rolled into the remaining processors of the block, row by row. The third phase comprises the computation of the two-dimensional convolution. Each subpyramid under $CORD(i,j)$ calculates the convolution values of the pixels $(k,l) = (iM \leq k \leq (iM + M - 1), jM \leq l \leq (jM + M - 1))$. At every time interval the processors at the base contain the image pixel values needed to compute the convolution for one pixel of the block. Each base processor performs a multiplication of a pixel value with a mask coefficient and sends the partial result up the subpyramid. Then, it performs a W (West) shift or an N (North) shift according to the presence or absence of the change row special symbol. Partial results are summed

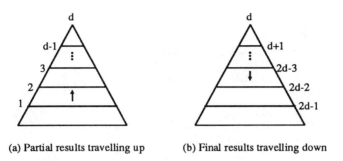

(a) Partial results travelling up   (b) Final results travelling down

Figure 2.9   Flow of information in the pyramid image processing convolution algorithm.

when they go up, level by level, in the subpyramid. The coordinators receive the final
results and broadcast them down the subpyramids (Figure 2.9). The time complexity
of the algorithm is $O(M^2 + \log_2 N)$.

2.5   GLOBAL IMAGE PROCESSING PARALLEL ALGORITHMS

Global image processing parallel algorithms do not have the possibility of directly
using the local interconnection between processor elements in the SIMD and MIMD
distributed memory architectures, since the information needed by the global operators
is spread over all the image. The communication load in the algorithms increases with
the increasing number of processor elements. The use of shared memory architectures
allows the access of each processor element to all the image pixels. Care must be taken
in order to assure mutual exclusion in the access to the shared variables and to reduce
memory access conflicts which degrade the performance of these systems.

2.5.1   Image Histogram Calculation

One of the most typical global operations used in low-level image processing is the image histogram calculation [GW87]. The histogram of an image provides global information about the distribution of image quantization levels. Parallel algorithms developed
for image histogram generation also use the image parallelism paradigm. Conceptually,
the algorithms have two distinct phases. In the first phase histograms of sub-images are
computed, and are then combined in the subsequent phase to generate the histogram
of the whole image.

Parallel algorithms for histogram generation in shared memory systems use the
possibility of having the histogram information in the shared memory accessed by
the processors that update it. These algorithms require mutual exclusion for updating
a value of the histogram since wrong results can otherwise be obtained. Histogram
algorithms for SIMD and MIMD distributed architectures are dependent on the interprocessor network used. For the majority of these algorithms the computation of the
sub-image histograms is performed in parallel, so that each processor element contains
in its local memory the value of an L-bin partial histogram (the grey level of a pixel is
represented by an integer in the range 0 to $L-1$). The local histograms may be combined by using a double recursive procedure [Sie81]. A SIMD algorithm to compute

Processor
Element

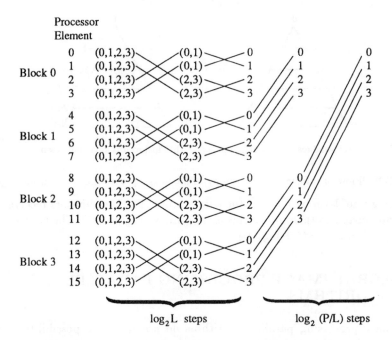

Figure 2.10 Histogram calculation using 16 processing elements (the histogram has 4 bins and $(a,...,b)$ represents the bins from a to b).

the L-bin histogram of $N \times N$ images using $P \geq L$ processing elements has been proposed [SSS82]. The local histogram of each $N/\sqrt{P} \times N/\sqrt{P}$ sub-image is computed in parallel by the different processing elements. By grouping the P processing elements in groups of L processing elements the partial histograms are first combined within each block (in $\log_2 L$ steps) resulting in a new partial histogram with one bin per processing element (Figure 2.10). The next $\log_2 P/L$ steps also use recursive doubling to combine the results of the different blocks and generate the histogram of the image, the result of bin j being stored in processing element j (Figure 2.10). The algorithm takes N^2/P additions to compute the local histograms and $(L - 1 + \log_2 P - \log_2 L)$ "transfer and add" steps.

Another algorithm has been proposed for histogram generation using a form of recursive doubling to combine "local" histograms [CA90]. For an image with L-bins and a system with P processors, processors p_{2l+1}, where $l = 0...(P/2 - 1)$, initially accumulate the sums for the $L/2$ least significant bins stored in its memory and the memory of their right hand side neighboring processor p_{2l+2}. On the other hand, processors p_{2l+2}, where $l = 0...(P/2 - 1)$, accumulate the $L/2$ most significant bins contained in their memory and the memory of the left hand side neighboring processor p_{2l+1}. In the next step, processors p_{4l+1}, where $l = 0...(P/4-1)$, transfer the $L/2$ least significant bins located in their memory to the neighboring processors p_{4l+2}. Similarly, p_{4l+4}, where $l = 0...(P/4-1)$, transfer the more significant bins to p_{4l+3}. At this stage, processors p_{4l+2} and p_{4l+3} ($l = 0...(P/4 - 1)$) contain partial L-bins histograms. The process is repeated until the complete histogram of the image is achieved. The result can be found in processor $p_{P/2}$.

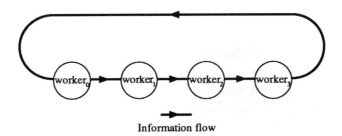

Information flow

Figure 2.11   Ring topology used for communication between 4 workers.

Histogram calculation algorithm for coarse and medium grained MIMD architecture

A histogram generation algorithm has been developed and implemented in the transputer based parallel system referred to in section 2.3. The computation of the histogram of an image can be performed using a task force and interprocessor network configurations (Figure 2.5) similar to those used for the local image convolution described in the previous section. The master process distributes the image among the workers which compute the histograms of each sub-image. These partial histograms are sent to the master which combines them and calculates the histogram of the whole image. This approach seems to be poor, since part of the algorithm, corresponding to the combination of the partial histograms, is performed sequentially. Moreover, all the workers have to transmit information on all bins of the partial histogram to the master, which then sends the histogram of the whole image to the workers, and this involves additional communication time.

A task force is implemented with the two types of processes referred to above, master and work processes, but the workers communicate between them using a ring topology (Figure 2.11). The sub-images are sent to the workers which compute the partial histograms. This information is transmitted through the different workers and the histogram of the whole image is computed using a form of double recursive procedure. Each worker stores two types of histogram vectors that we call *HISTO* and *HISTOEXT* (Figure 2.12). The first vector stores the histogram of a sub-image (*HISTOn* corresponds to the histogram of processor n), while the *HISTOEXT* stores histograms, or sums of the histograms, of different workers. In a first phase, the workers with even index send their *HISTO* to workers with odd index. Then, according to the index parity of the workers, the following actions are taken:

if worker index is even

- Read **HISTOEXT** from the preceding worker
- Add **HISTOEXT** to **HISTO**
- Send **HISTOEXT** to the following worker

if worker index is odd

- Add **HISTOEXT** to **HISTO**
- Send **HISTOEXT** to the following worker
- Read **HISTOEXT** from the preceding worker

The procedure is repeated until the histogram of the whole image is stored in the

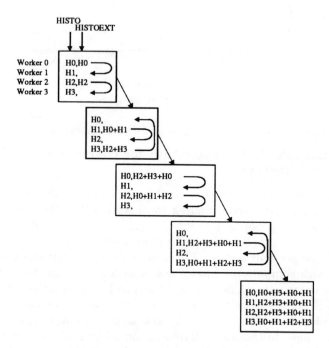

Figure 2.12 Generation of the image histogram using 4 workers (Hi denotes the partial histogram of worker i).

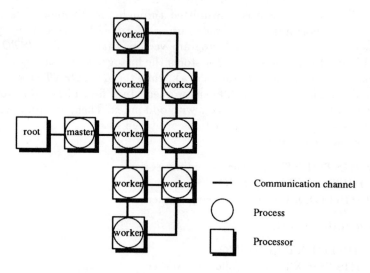

Figure 2.13 Network of 8 transputers.

No. of transp.	1	4	8	12
Time(ms)	1350	500	400	310
Efficiency(E%)	100	68	42	36

Figure 2.14 Efficiency of the parallel system for histogram generation (image size 512x512 with 256 grey levels).

vector *HISTOEXT* of all workers. The image histogram can then be read from the master.

Summarizing, the master process determines the number of workers, allocates memory and reads the image, and starts one thread for each worker. These threads distribute the image among the workers, send the worker identifiers, and one of them waits for the reception of the histogram. Each worker computes its local histogram, determines the parity of its index and performs part of the histogram calculation according to the procedure referred to above. Only one of the workers sends back the histogram of the whole image to the master.

The algorithm has been implemented in the parallel computer using either 4, 8 or 12 transputers [SBCP92]. The 8 transputer network configuration is shown in Figure 2.13. The time spent running the algorithm in the different networks, as well as the performance measurement E (equation 2.3), is presented in Figure 2.14.

Histogram calculation algorithms for fine grained architectures

Algorithms for image histogram calculation in SIMD architectures with mesh and hypercube networks have been developed [CS89]. Beginning with each pixel value stored in a processing element ($N \times N$ processing elements), the algorithms combine partial histograms in a recursive way for the calculation of the final values of the image histogram.

Algorithms for SIMD mesh architectures (with $L \leq N$), in general, calculate the histograms for horizontal or vertical one-dimensional sections of the image (image rows or columns) in parallel, and combine these partial histograms by shifting and adding them along the other direction. Assuming that the edge processing elements are linked (toroidal network) the histogram of the different rows of the image can be calculated by shifting the image horizontally one position at a time and incrementing a counter in each processing element whenever its column number matches the pixel value. The content of the processing element j of a given row has the number of pixels with value j in that row. By successively shifting the histograms of the rows vertically in $\log_2 N - 1$ phases, in phase i a 2^i shift is performed ($0 \leq i < \log_2 N - 1$), and by adding the partial histograms, the final histogram is calculated and stored in one of the edge rows of the network. The algorithm takes $O(N)$ unit routes.

Parallel algorithms for histogram calculation in fine grained hypercube connected SIMD architectures (with $L \leq N^2$) use double recursive procedures. A typical image histogram calculation algorithm, using double recursive procedures, for SIMD hypercube architectures takes $O(L + \log_2 N^2)$ unit routes and requires $O(L)$ memory size per processing element [CS89].

2.5.2   Image Processing Algorithms with Data Dependent Communication

There are global image processing algorithms, at the different processing levels, where communication among processor elements should be done in a *data dependent way*. Communication among processor elements is "random" in the sense that the processor elements define the destination (or source) of the data they intend to send (or receive). *Random Access Read* (RAR) and *Random Access Write* (RAW) are two routines often used with this purpose. These routines allow a processor element to write or read another processor by defining the destination or source address. Several RAW and RAR algorithms have been developed for different types of architectures [CS89]. These algorithms send data through intermediate destinations, trying to sort the data among the processor elements according to the destination or source addresses.

An RAW algorithm for SIMD connected architectures (toroidal) with N^2 processing elements and $O(N)$ memory elements per processor with a complexity of $O(N)$ has been presented [CS89]. Each processing element stores the source data and the destination address in a record which circulates through the system by shifting the records horizontally N times. After a shift, each processing element finds out whether the column of the destination processor in the incoming record matches its own column number. If the items are coincident, the processing element stores the record in a position of its local memory indexed by the row of the destination processing element. In a second phase, each processor element creates a record with its row number and a data destination register initialized with a large number. These records are shifted vertically (cyclically) and the row field is used to index the memory in each processing element. If the memory contains a source record, then the destination data record is filled with the content of the source data register. After N vertical shifts the algorithm is completed. The algorithm can easily be changed to respond to the cases where different processor elements try to send data to the same destination. The same methods used in RAW algorithms can be used to develop a RAR algorithm for mesh connected networks.

Several parallel algorithms for image coordinate transformations use RAR and RAW procedures. Parallel algorithms for image coordinate transformations have been proposed [RS89] for SIMD and MIMD hypercube fine grained architectures. As for image convolution algorithms, the images are mapped on the processors by using Gray code mapping for the MIMD architecture, and row major order for the SIMD architecture. The algorithms assume $O(1)$ memory locations for each processor element. Image translation algorithms are based on hypercube shift algorithms. Successive shifts of the image are made in both orthogonal directions. The time complexity of these algorithms is $O(\log_2 N)$ in both SIMD and MIMD hypercube architectures.

Parallel algorithms for image rotation and scaling use data dependent communication procedures to send data in the image from the original coordinates to the new ones defined by the transformation. The algorithms use particular RAW routines—row and column reordering. In row reordering the destination processor element is always in the same row as the source processor. Column reordering uses the same principle applied to the columns. Image rotation of an arbitrary angle θ, $0 \leq \theta < 360^0$, is cast in one of the forms:

$$\theta = \left\{ \begin{array}{ll} \theta' & \\ \theta' \pm 90^0 & -45^0 \leq \theta' \leq 45^0 \\ \theta' \pm 180^0 & \end{array} \right.$$

Parallel algorithms to rotate the image by $\pm 90^0$, $\pm 180^0$ or $|\theta| \leq 45^0$ have been developed and have a time complexity of $O(\log_2 N)$. To perform an image rotation by $|\theta| > 90^0$, first a $\pm 90^0$, or $\pm 180^0$ rotation is made, and this is followed by a θ' rotation.

Scaling algorithms have also been developed, and have a time complexity of $O(\log_2 N)$, for both types of architectures. Image scaling algorithms, in addition to routing the pixels to their destination, have to reconnect the image boundary and fill in the objects when the scale factor is larger than 1.

Image component labeling is an intermediate level image processing operation which has been applied to image segmentation. This operation is usually applied to binary images with the main objective of getting a new representation of the image in order to extract features and identify or classify objects. Image component labeling is an interesting problem because it can be solved using local or global algorithms.

The local algorithms initially assign labels to the pixels, and then propagate these labels locally across the image in a sequence of phases. A simple local algorithm assigns a label to each 1-pixel (e.g., the address of the pixel in the image array) and then updates the label of each pixel by replacing it with the minimum value of its labels and those of its 1-pixel neighbors. The procedure is repeated until there is no change in any label of the image pixels. This type of algorithms is not efficient if the image contains long objects—assuming an image with a component with two 1-pixels connected through a path with k 1-pixels (which is the shortest path connecting these two pixels) the algorithm takes $O(k)$ local update phases to label this component. Faster local algorithms for image component labeling have been developed. These algorithms use shrinking and expansion operations and have a complexity of $O(N)$ [AK89, Lei92].

Global image component labeling algorithms recursively divide the image in sub-images with a smaller size [Lei92, CS89]. The sub-images are then labeled and the problem of inconsistencies along the borders of the sub-images is solved by merging components that contain adjacent pixels across the boundary of the sub-images. To merge components across the sub-image borders, RAR and RAW routines are used. The 1-pixels in the borders are sent to the appropriate processing elements and an algorithm for computing the connected components of a graph is applied [Lei92]. Recursive algorithms for image component labeling on hypercube and mesh connected architectures have a complexity of $O(N)$.

2.6   CONCLUSIONS

This chapter has reviewed some important computational aspects of low-level image processing operators and their influence on the architecture of the parallel systems for image processing. An overview was given of the concurrent algorithms for low-level image processing for different parallel systems. Time complexity of the different algorithms has been referred to.

Two types of coarse or medium grained parallel image processing algorithms implemented on a parallel distributed memory computer (based on transputers) have been presented. One is a local algorithm, that performs local image convolution, while the other algorithm provides global information on the distribution of grey levels in the image, by computing its histogram. Their different computational aspects lead to the implementation of different interprocessor network configurations. The algorithms have been used to evaluate the performance of the parallel system for image processing applications.

We hope that the material presented will be useful for students and researchers interested in parallel algorithms and systems for image processing.

ACKNOWLEDGEMENTS

We would like to thank Prof. Medeiros Silva for reviewing our manuscript. Special thanks are due to the researchers of the *Signal Processing Systems* group of INESC, namely graduate students António Ramos Costa, Jorge Garrido Bárrios and Teresa Mendes de Almeida.

REFERENCES

[AK89]   Hussein M. Alnueiri and V. K. Kumar. Fast image labeling using local operators on mesh-connected computers. In Fred Ris and Peter M. Kogge, editors, *Proc. International Conference on Parallel Processing*, volume 3, pages 32–39. Penn State University, The Pennsylvania State University Press, August 1989.

[BB87]   Anup Basu and Christofer M. Brown. Algorithms and hardware for efficient image smoothing. *Computer Vision, Graphics and Image Processing*, 40(2):131–146, November 1987.

[CA90]   Vipin Chaudhary and J. K. Aggarwal. *Parallel Algorithms for Machine Intelligence and Vision*, chapter Parallelism in Computer Vision: a Review, pages 269–309. Symbolic Computation–Artificial Intelligence. Springer-Verlag, London, 1990.

[CIPS87] Jik H. Chang, Oscar H. Ibarra, Ting-Chuen Pong, and Stephen M. Sohn. Two-dimensional convolution on a pyramid computer. In Sartaj K. Sahni, editor, *Int. Conference on Parallel Processing*, pages 780–782. Penn State University, The Pennsylvania State University Press, August 1987.

[Cok91] Ronal S. Cok. *Parallel Programs for the Transputer*. Prentice-Hall, London, 1991.

[CS89]   Robert Cypher and Jorge L. S. Sanz. SIMD architectures and algorithms for image processing and computer vision. *IEEE Transactions on Acoustic, Speech, and Signal Processing*, 37(12):2158–2174, December 1989.

[Dun90] Ralph Duncan. A survey of parallel computer architectures. *IEEE Computer*, 23(2):5–16, February 1990.

[FLN86] Zhixi Fang, Xiaobo Li, and Lionel M. Ni. Parallel algorithms for 2-D convolution. In Kay Hwang, Steven M. Jacobs, and Earl E. Swartzlander, editors, *Proc. International Conference on Parallel Processing*, pages 262–269. IEEE Computer Society and Association for Computing Machinery, IEEE Computer Society Press, August 1986.

[GW87]   Rafael C. Gonzalez and Paul Wintz. *Digital Image Processing*. Addison-Wesley, Wokingham, second edition, 1987.

[HB84]   Kay Hwang and Fayé A. Briggs. *Computer Architecture and Parallel Processing*. McGraw-Hill, London, 1984.

[Hor86]   Berthold K. Horn. *Robot Vision*. The MIT Press, London, 1986.

[HTK89]   Kai Hwang, Ping-Sheng Tseng, and Dongseung Kim. An orthogonal multiprocessor for parallel scientific computations. *IEEE Transactions on Computers*, 38(1):47–61, January 1989.

[HYT79]   T. S. Huang, G. Y. Yang, and G. Y. Tang. A fast two-dimensional median filtering algorithm. *IEEE Transactions on Acoustic, Speech, and Signal Processing*, 27(1):13–18, February 1979.

[INM89]   INMOS, Bristol. *The Transputer Databook*, second edition, 1989.

[KK87]   V. P. Kumar and Venkatesh Krishnan. Efficient image template matching on hypercube SIMD arrays. In Sartaj K. Sahni, editor, *Proc. International Conference on Parallel Processing*, pages 765–771. Penn State University, The Pennsylvania State University Press, August 1987.

[LD90]   D. L. Lee and W. A. Davis. On linear speedup of a class of neighborhood functions in an array processor. In *IEEE Symposium on Parallel and Distributed Processing*, pages 441–446. IEEE Computer Society, IEEE Computer Society Press, December 1990.

[Lei92]   F. Thomson Leighton. *Introduction to Parallel Algorithms and Architectures: Arrays, Trees and Hypercubes*, volume 1. Morgan Kaufmann Publishers, California, first edition, 1992.

[Lim90]   Jae S. Lim. *Two-Dimensional Signal and Image Processing*. Prentice-Hall Signal Processing. Prentice-Hall International, London, 1990.

[MC85]   M. M. McCabe and P. V. Collins. *VLSI Image Processing*, chapter Image Processing Algorithms, pages 52–98. McGraw-Hill, London, 1985.

[MP88]   Philip J. Morrow and R. H. Perrott. *Parallel Architectures and Computer Vision*, chapter The Design and Implementation of Low-Level Image Processing Algorithms on a Transputer Network, pages 243–260. Clarendon Press, Oxford, 1988.

[Nar81]   Patrenahalli M. Narendra. A separable median filter for image noise smoothing. *IEEE Transactions on Pattern Analysis and Machine Intelligence*, 3(1):20–29, January 1981.

[Pav82]   Theo Pavlidis. *Algorithms for Graphics and Image Processing*. Computer Science Press, Rockville, 1982.

[PC90]   Silvio Picano and Thomas L. Casavant. An experimental analysis of image correlation on shared vs. non-shared memory MIMD parallel computers. In Pen-Chung Yew, editor, *Proc. International Conference on Parallel Processing*, volume 3, pages 92–96. The Pennsylvania State University, The Pennsylvania State University Press, August 1990.

[Pei87]   Gerhard H. Peise. *Transputer Processor Module*. Parsytec, Germany, July 1987.

[Per90]   Perihelion Software, Bristol. *The CDL Guide–Helios*, first edition, January 1990.

[Red88]   Stewart Reddaway. *Parallel Architectures and Computer Vision*, chapter Mapping Images onto Processor Array Hardware, pages 299–314. Clarendon Press, Oxford, 1988.

[Ree84]   Anthony P. Reeves. Parallel computer architectures for image processing. *Computer Vision, Graphics and Image Processing*, 25(1):68–88, January 1984.

[RK82]   Azriel Rosenfeld and Avinash C. Kak. *Digital Picture Processing*, volume 2 of *Computer Science and Applied Mathematics*. Academic Press, London, second edition, 1982.

[RS88a]   Sanjay Ranka and Sartaj Sahni. Image template matching on MIMD hypercube multicomputers. In David H. Bailey, editor, *Proc. International Conference on Parallel Processing*, volume 3, pages 92–99. Penn State University, Pennsylvania State University, August 1988.

[RS88b]   Sanjay Ranka and Sartaj Sahni. Image template matching on SIMD hypercube multicomputers. In David H. Bailey, editor, *Proc. International Conference on Parallel Processing*, volume 3, pages 84–91. Penn State University, Pennsylvania

State University, August 1988.

[RS89] Sanjay Ranka and Sartaj Sahni. Hypercube algorithms for image transformations. In Fred Ris and Peter M. Kogge, editors, *Proc. International Conference on Parallel Processing*, volume 3, pages 24–31. Penn State University, The Pennsylvania State University Press, August 1989.

[RS90] Sanjay Ranka and Sartaj Sahni. *Parallel Algorithms for Machine Intelligence and Vision*, chapter Parallel Algorithms for Image Template Matching, pages 360–399. Symbolic Computation–Artificial Intelligence. Springer-Verlag, London, 1990.

[SBCP92] Leonel A. Sousa, Jorge Bárrios, António Costa, and Moisés Piedade. Parallel image processing for transputer based systems. In *International Conference on Image Processing and its Applications*, pages 33–36. Electronics Division of the Institution of Electrical Engineers, Institution of Electronic Engineers, April 1992.

[Sch90] Hermann Schomberg. A transputer-based shuffle-shift machine for image processing and reconstruction. In *10th International Conference on Pattern Recognition*, volume 2, pages 445–450. International Association for Pattern Recognition, IEEE Computer Society Press, June 1990.

[SCP91] Leonel Sousa, José Caeiro, and Moisés Piedade. An advanced architecture for image processing and analysis. In *IEEE International Symposium on Circuits and Systems*, volume 1, pages 77–80. IEEE Singapore Section, The Institute of Electrical and Electronics Engineers, May 1991.

[Sie81] L. J. Siegel. *Languages and Architectures for Image Processing*, chapter Image Processing on a Partitionable SIMD machine, pages 293–300. Academic Press, London, 1981.

[Sof89] Perihelion Software. *The Helios Operating System*. Prentice-Hall, London, 1989.

[SRH88] Andrew C. Sleigh, C. J. Radford, and Gordon J. Harp. *Parallel Architectures and Computer Vision*, chapter RSRE Experience Implementing Computer Vision Algorithms on Transputers, DAP and DIPOD Parallel Processors, pages 133–156. Clarendon Press, Oxford, 1988.

[SSF82] Leah J. Siegel, Howard J. Siegel, and Arthur E. Feather. Parallel processing approaches to image correlation. *IEEE Transactions on Computers*, 31(3):208–218, March 1982.

[SSM+81] H. J. Siegel, L. J. Siegel, F.C. Mueller, P. T. Mueller, H. E. Smalley, and S. D. Smith. Pasm: A partitionable SIMD/MIMD system for image processing and pattern recognition. *IEEE Transactions on Computers*, 30(12):934–946, December 1981.

[SSS82] Leah J. Siegel, Howard J. Siegel, and Philip H. Swain. *Multicomputers and Image Processing–Algorithms and Programs*, chapter Parallel Algorithms Performance Measures, pages 241–252. Notes and Reports in Computer Science and Applied Mathematics. Academic Press, London, 1982.

[SSWC88] P. K. Sahoo, S. Soltani, A. K. Wong, and Y. C. Chen. A survey of thresholding techniques. *Computer Vision, Graphics and Image Processing*, 41(2):233–260, February 1988.

[Tan86] S. L. Tanimoto. *Intermediate-Level Image Processing*, chapter Architectural Issues for Intermediate-Level Vision, pages 3–18. Academic Press, London, 1986.

[Tex90] Texas Instruments, Texas. *TMS320C40x User's Guide*, December 1990.

[THK85] P. S. Tseng, K. Hwang, and V. K. Kumar. A VLSI-based multiprocessor architecture for implementing parallel algorithms. In Douglas Degroot, editor, *Proc. International Conference on Parallel Processing*, pages 657–664. IEEE Computer Society and Association for Computing Machinery, IEEE Computer Society Press, August 1985.

[WVL83] David C. Wang, Anthony H. Vagnucci, and C. C. Li. Digital image enhancement: a survey. *Computer Vision, Graphics and Image Processing*, 24(3):363–381, December 1983.

3

Parallel FFT–like Transform Algorithms on Transputers

REINER CREUTZBURG, TORSTEN MINKWITZ,
MARKUS ROGGENBACH, THOMAS UMLAND

3.1 INTRODUCTION

3.1.1 Overview – Motivation

With the growing availability of parallel computing hardware, more signal processing operations become attractive. If an operation can be computed with algorithms, which are highly parallel in nature, a network of Transputers may be used to speed up execution significantly. Ideally, the algorithms should be data parallel, so that the work can be evenly spread out to many Transputers. Therefore, a significant speedup can be achieved. Convolutions and orthogonal transforms form a class of algorithms which allows a great deal of data parallelism [Aga74, Ahm75, Nus81].

The convolution property of certain transforms can be used to compute the cyclic convolution of two signals. Signal filtering or correlations are thereby easily computed which are recurring operations in digital signal processing. One of the mentioned transforms is the discrete Fourier transform (DFT) in the modified version of the fast Fourier transform (FFT), which operates on signals in the field of complex numbers. The FFT of length N requires $(N/2)\log_2(N/2)$ complex multiplications which take most of the computation time. In addition, the FFT implementation introduces round-off errors, thus deteriorating the signal-to-noise ratio.

Number-theoretic transforms (NTT) were introduced as a generalization of the DFT over residue class rings of integers in order to implement fast cyclic convolution and correlation without round-off errors and with better efficiency than the FFT [McC79]. The applications for such a fast method are in fast digital filtering, image processing, fast coding and decoding of error correcting codes and fast computation of the FFT.

A large number of transform methods were developed. However, since the underlying hardware (in this case a Transputer network) is operating on word lengths of powers of two, Fermat number transforms (FNT) have proven to be best suited.

One transform that has become very popular in recent years in the area of digital picture compression, especially with the advent of HDTV, is the discrete cosine transform (DCT) [Cla85, Rao90]. This is because the DCT compares very closely with the Karhunen-Loève transform (KLT) which is theoretically optimal in compressing typical image data having reasonable inter-element correlation. The DCT is a data independent transform (unlike the KLT) and many fast algorithms exist for its implementation. The DCT is a real transform as is the discrete sine transform (DST).

Section 3.1.2 deals with separable image transforms. The separability is a key idea and provides a basis for simplifying higher dimensional signal transforms. Section 3.2 will give an introduction to the theory of the FFT, the NTT, the discrete cosine transform (DCT) and the discrete sine transform (DST). Section 3.3 provides some graph-theoretical concepts useful for the FFT. The FFT algorithm using the perfect shuffle [Pea68] is discussed in section 3.4. Section 3.5 deals with the parallel implementation of the FFT, FNT, DCT, and DST on a Transputer network and gives some measurements of the execution times.

3.1.2   Separable Image Transforms

A sampled image $f(m, n)$ is a finite, two-dimensional array naturally represented by a matrix of sampled values

$$[f] = \{f(m, n)\} = \{f_{mn}\}.$$

The Kronecker product of a square $(M \times M)$-matrix $\mathbf{A}$ with a square $(N \times N)$-matrix $\mathbf{B}$ is an $(MN \times MN)$-matrix $\mathbf{C}$ of the form

$$\mathbf{C} = \mathbf{A} \times \mathbf{B} = \begin{pmatrix} a_{0,0}\mathbf{B} & \cdots & a_{0,M}\mathbf{B} \\ \vdots & & \vdots \\ a_{M-1,1}\mathbf{B} & \cdots & a_{M-1,M-1}\mathbf{B} \end{pmatrix}.$$

The important simplification introduced by the Kronecker product is that the general vector transformation

$$\mathbf{F} = \mathbf{Cf}$$

may be expressed in the equivalent matrix form

$$[F] = \mathbf{A}[f]\mathbf{B}.$$

This operation is called a separable transform [Hal79] since the matrix $\mathbf{A}$ operates on columns and the matrix $\mathbf{B}$ operates on the rows of the picture matrix $[f]$. If the $\mathbf{A}$ and $\mathbf{B}$ matrices are orthonormal,

$$\mathbf{A}\mathbf{A}^{*'} = I \text{ and } \mathbf{B}\mathbf{B}^{*'} = I,$$

then an inverse transformation may be expressed as

$$[f] = \mathbf{A}^{*'}[F]\mathbf{B}^{*}.$$

Another interesting representation may be developed by expressing the transformation in the slightly different form

$$[F] = \mathbf{A}[f]\mathbf{B}'.$$

If the $\mathbf{A}$ and $\mathbf{B}$ matrices are written in terms of their column basis vectors

$$\mathbf{A} = [\mathbf{a}_0, \mathbf{a}_1, \ldots, \mathbf{a}_{M-1}] \text{ and } \mathbf{B} = (\mathbf{b}_0, \mathbf{b}_1, \ldots, \mathbf{b}_{N-1}),$$

then the transformation may be written in the form of an outer product

$$[F] = \sum_{i=0}^{M-1} \sum_{j=0}^{N-1} f_{ij} \mathbf{a}_i \mathbf{b}'_j.$$

Note that each outer product $\mathbf{a}_i \mathbf{b}'_j$ forms an $M \times N$ rank one matrix. The total set of the MN outer product matrices may be considered as a set of basis matrices which may be used to represent the image matrix. Several important image transforms will be considered in the next sections.

3.2 THE DISCRETE FOURIER TRANSFORM AND RELATED TRANSFORMS

3.2.1 The Discrete Fourier Transform – DFT

This is by no means an attempt to describe the complete story of the ubiquitous Fourier transform (FT). However, it aims to summarize some notations relevant to this report. For an excellent introduction to the FT see Brigham [Bri88].

The continuous two-dimensional Fourier transform is defined by the transform pair

$$F(u, v) = \int_{-\infty}^{+\infty} \int_{-\infty}^{+\infty} f(x, y) \exp[-2\pi j(ux + vy)] dx dy$$

$$f(x, y) = \int_{-\infty}^{+\infty} \int_{-\infty}^{+\infty} F(u, v) \exp[2\pi j[(ux + vy)] du dv.$$

The significance of this transform is enhanced by the physical fact that the Fourier transform of an image field is equal to the far field or Fraunhofer diffraction pattern of the image. This property also provides the basis for the computation of the Fourier transform with optical systems.

In both the continuous and discrete cases, the Fourier transform is a complex function

$$F(u, v) = R(u, v) + jI(u, v),$$

with $R(u,v)$ and $I(u,v)$ as the real and imaginary components, respectively, and $j = \sqrt{-1}$. It is often convenient to represent $F(u,v)$ in terms of its magnitude $|F(u,v)|$ and phase spectrum $\phi(u,v)$, where

$$F(u,v) = |F(u,v)| \exp[j\phi(u,v)]$$

or

$$|F(u,v)| = [R^2(u,v) + I^2(u,v)]^{1/2},$$

$$\phi(u,v) = \arctan[I(u,v)/R(u,v)].$$

Since both photographic film and the human eye respond to the magnitude of an image field, it is difficult to directly observe the phase spectra. Holographic techniques are, however, based upon recording both the magnitude and phase spectra, and either can be easily computed with digital techniques. It is now well known that the phase spectrum contains most of the information about the positions of edges in an image.

The two-dimensional discrete Fourier transform (DFT) is defined as the transform pair

$$F(k,l) = \frac{1}{N} \sum_{m=0}^{N-1} \sum_{n=0}^{N-1} f(m,n) \exp[-2\pi j(km+ln)/N],$$

$$f(m,n) = \frac{1}{N} \sum_{k=0}^{N-1} \sum_{l=0}^{N-1} F(k,l) \exp[2\pi j(km+ln)/N].$$

A square image of size N by N has been assumed for simplicity and the factor of $1/N$ has been distributed between the forward and inverse forms for symmetry.

The Fourier transform is widely used in signal processing and this is because of the importance of the Fourier domain. This corresponds to the frequency spectrum of the signal and each frequency stores a portion of the overall signal energy.

The significance of the discrete Fourier transform is enhanced not only by its use to approximate the continuous transform, but also because it may efficiently be computed via the fast Fourier transform (FFT) algorithm.

The fast Fourier transform (FFT) is a fast method of computing the DFT [Bet84]. It is based on the fact that the roots of unity form a cyclic group C_N. Instead of taking the single group elements (roots of unity) of this large group, first the normal subgroup C_q ($N = pq$) is taken and the DFT is computed for the smaller group C_N/C_q. The cosets are now used instead of the single roots of unity. Thereafter, the same algorithm is applied recursively for the cosets. Substituting the DFTs with FFTs yields an efficient method to do convolutions.

Another important mathematical fact is that the discrete Fourier transform may be used to determine the eigenvalues of a circulant matrix.

The Fourier transform properties of linearity, shift of position, modulation, convolution, multiplication, and correlation are completely analogous to the continuous case with the main differences being due to the discrete, periodic nature of the image and its transform. The other properties — scale change, rotation, differentiation, and integration — require either interpolation or a specific numerical algorithm but can be made at least approximately analogous to the continuous case.

The discrete Fourier transform has the well-known convolution property

$$\mathbf{y} = \mathbf{x} * \mathbf{h} = DFT^{-1}(DFT(\mathbf{x}) \circ DFT(\mathbf{h})),$$

where $\mathbf{x}$, $\mathbf{h}$, $\mathbf{y}$ are two-dimensional signals.

The kernel function of the discrete transform

$$\exp[-2\pi j(km + ln)/N]$$

has several interesting interpretations. First, note that it is separable:

$$\exp(-2\pi jkm/N)\exp(-2\pi jln/N).$$

Each of the factors may be described as solutions to the equation

$$w^N = 1$$

which leads to the interpretation of

$$w_{km} = \exp(-2\pi jkm/N)$$

as a primitive N-th root of unity in the complex number field. Since there are only N distinct roots of unity, the terms w_{km} can take only N distinct values regardless of the integer values of k or m.

The values of w_{km} for the principal values of k and m, i.e.,

$$k, m = 0, 1, \ldots N - 1,$$

may be arranged in a simple $(N \times N)$-matrix, the so-called Fourier matrix.

An interesting property of this matrix is that it is unitary, that is, the inner product of any one column (row) with the conjugate of any other column (row) is equal to zero unless the columns (rows) are identical.

$$\sum_{m=0}^{N-1} w_{mk} w_{ml}^* = \begin{cases} N, & \text{if } k = l, \\ 0, & \text{if } k \neq l. \end{cases}$$

It follows that $\mathbf{W}^{-1} = \mathbf{W}^*/N$. Another non-obvious property was observed: the Fourier matrix can be factored into the product of sparse and diagonal matrices. This observation may be considered to be the basis of the FFT algorithm.

The two-dimensional discrete Fourier transform can be written in matrix notation.

If the series representation is written in the form of two consecutive one-dimensional transforms,

$$NF(k, l) = \sum_{m=0}^{N-1} H(m, l) \exp(-2\pi jkm/N),$$

where

$$H(m, l) = \sum_{n=0}^{N-1} f(m, n) \exp(2\pi jnl/N).$$

Note that each of the above equations can be put into the form corresponding to matrix multiplication. In general, the matrix product for square and diagonal matrices subscripted from 0 to $N-1$

$$\mathbf{A} = \mathbf{BC}$$

is computed by

$$a_{ml} = b_{mn}c_{nl}.$$

Letting

$$a_{m,l} = H(m,l), \quad b_{m,n} = f(m,n), \quad c_{n,l} = \exp(2\pi jnl/N),$$

and using the correspondence leads to the matrix relationship

$$[H] = [f][W]$$

where

$$[H] = [H(m,l)], \quad [f] = [f(m,n)], \quad [W] = [\exp(2\pi jml/N)].$$

Therefore, the computation of the $[H]$ matrix may be considered a postmultiplication of the picture matrix by the $[W]$ matrix or equivalently as computing the DFT of the rows of the picture matrix.

A similar correspondence may be made for the final computation of the discrete two-dimensional Fourier transform. Let

$$a_{k,l} = F(k,l), \quad b_{k,m} = \exp(2\pi jkm/N), \quad c_{m,l} = H(m,l).$$

The matrix multiplication correspondence now leads to

$$N[F] = [W][H],$$

where

$$N[F] = [F(k,l)], \quad [W] = [\exp(2\pi jkm/N)], \quad [H] = [H(m,l)].$$

Therefore, the final transform operation may be considered as premultiplication by the $[W]$ matrix or equivalently as computing the DFT of the columns of the intermediate matrix $[H]$.

Combining the previous matrix equations leads to the well-known two-dimensional transform result

$$[F] = N^{-1}[W][f][W].$$

Since the matrix $[W]$ is unitary and symmetric, its inverse is equal to its conjugate and the inverse two-dimensional transform is

$$[f] = N^{-1}[W^*][F][W^*].$$

3.2.2 Number-Theoretic Transforms – NTT

In real applications the coefficients will often be elements of the ring $\mathbf{Z}$ of integers. Number-theoretic transforms (NTT) were introduced as a generalization of the DFT over residue class rings of integers [Aga74, Nus81, Cre86].

Let $\mathbf{Z}$ be the ring of integers and $m > 1$ an odd integer with prime factorization

$$m = p_1^{r_1} p_2^{r_2} \cdots p_s^{r_s}. \tag{3.1}$$

Then $\alpha \in \mathbf{Z}$ is called a primitive N-th root of unity modulo m if [Aga76]

$$\alpha^N \equiv 1 \bmod m, \tag{3.2}$$

$$\gcd(\alpha^n - 1, m) = 1 \text{ for every } n = 1, \ldots, N-1. \tag{3.3}$$

A necessary and sufficient condition for the existence of such primitive N-th roots of unity modulo m is

$$N \mid \gcd(p_1 - 1, \ldots, p_s - 1),$$

where gcd denotes the greatest common divisor.

The NTT of length N with α as primitive N-th root of unity modulo m and its inverse are defined between N-point integer sequences

$$X_n \equiv \sum_{k=0}^{N-1} x_k \alpha^{nk} \bmod m, \quad n = 0, \ldots, N-1,$$

$$x_k \equiv N' \sum_{n=0}^{N-1} X_n \alpha^{-nk} \bmod m, \quad k = 0, \ldots, N-1,$$

where $NN' \equiv 1 \bmod m$. Note that the components of a signal

$$\mathbf{x} = (x_0, x_1, \ldots, x_{N-1})^T$$

have to be quantized to integers before using the NTT.

The NTT has a similar structure and properties to the DFT, particularly the cyclic convolution property [Aga76, Ree76, McC79, Cre85a, Cre85b, Cre85c, Crc89, Cre91] (see section 3.2.1).

From the numerical point of view the following three essential conditions on the NTTs are required:

- the transform length N has to be large enough and highly factorizable in order to implement fast algorithms such as prime-factor, Winograd, single-radix, and mixed-radix algorithms [Duh82],
- the primitive N-th root α should have a simple binary representation (2, 4, 8, 16, for example), so that the binary arithmetic modulo m is easy to perform,
- the modulus m has to be large enough to avoid overflow but on the other hand small enough so that the machine word length is not exceeded.

For most practical applications α and N are given and a convenient modulus m has to be found.

For instance, the Fermat number transform (FNT) which will be described in the next section is a good compromise between these various conditions [Aga76, Nus81].

3.2.3   The Fermat Number Transform – FNT

A Fermat number F_t has the form

$$F_t = 2^{2^t} + 1 = 2^b + 1, \qquad b = 2^t. \tag{3.4}$$

An NTT with Fermat number modulus is called a Fermat number transform (FNT). Here the element 2 serves as a primitive 2^{t+1}-th root of unity modulo F_t. The FNT and its inverse are defined by

$$X_n \equiv \sum_{k=0}^{2^{t+1}-1} x_k 2^{nk} \bmod F_t, \quad n = 0, \ldots, 2^{t+1} - 1,$$

$$x_k \equiv -2^{2^t-t-1} \sum_{n=0}^{2^{t+1}-1} X_n 2^{-nk} \bmod F_t, \quad k = 0, \ldots, 2^{t+1} - 1,$$

where $-2^{2^t-t-1} \bmod F_t$ is the multiplicative inverse of $N = 2^{t+1} \bmod F_t$.

The FNT uses the well-known radix-2 FFT algorithm for transform lengths of $N = 2^{t+1}$, $t > 0$. Here only binary additions and simple bit-shifting operations are necessary in contrast to complex multiplications in the case of the classical Fourier transform over the field of complex numbers $\mathbb{C}$.

Table 3.1 lists some parameters of the FNT.

t	b	F_t	N for $\alpha = 2$	N for $\alpha = \sqrt{2}$	$N_{\max}$	α for $N_{\max}$
0	1	$2^1 + 1$	2	-	2	2
1	2	$2^2 + 1$	4	-	4	2
2	4	$2^4 + 1$	8	16	16	$\sqrt{2}$
3	8	$2^8 + 1$	16	32	256	3
4	16	$2^{16} + 1$	32	64	65536	3
5	32	$2^{32} + 1$	64	128	128	$\sqrt{2}$
6	64	$2^{64} + 1$	128	256	256	$\sqrt{2}$

Table 3.1   Parameters of the FNT for F_t ($t = 0, 1, \ldots, 6$).

3.2.4   Binary Arithmetics for the FNT

The main advantage of the FNT for VLSI implementation can be found in the number representation. There are two general possibilities for the arithmetics hardware:

- Schönhage's representation [Sch71] requires more bits and chip area, but can be implemented without control circuitry. By this we save the area of several barrel shifters and multiplexers.
- The Leibowitz arithmetic [Lei76] will be described in detail in this section.

3.2.4.1   Schönhage's arithmetic

Let an arbitrary number a be represented as an integer in the range $0, \ldots, 2^{2^{t+1}}$, which is twice as large as necessary. But this is an advantage, since by computing modulo F_t the following equations hold:

$$2^{2^{t+1}} \equiv 1 \quad \mod F_t,$$
$$2^{2^t} \equiv -1 \quad \mod F_t.$$

Thus, a multiplication with 2^{2^t} results in a negation. On the other hand a multiplication with 2^{2^t} is equivalent to swapping the upper and lower bits of the number representation. Since negation is an often used operation in an FFT and since it can be realized by simple wiring, this number representation is advantageous for VLSI [Zer91].

Another frequent operation occurring in FFTs is multiplication with roots of unity. As can easily be checked, roots of unity in a Fermat ring are powers of two. Therefore, multiplication with these can again be done by wiring; the complexity of the wiring is moderately low.

It is quite obvious now that Fermat FFTs are suitable for VLSI implementations.

3.2.4.2   Leibowitz arithmetic

Every integer modulo $2^b + 1$ can be represented using $b + 1$ bits. We will now describe a special coding for integers modulo Fermat numbers F_t. This coding scheme was introduced by Leibowitz [Lei76] and allows an efficient implementation of the arithmetic modulo F_t. Table 3.2 shows a comparison between the standard binary coding and the Leibowitz coding. In this special coding the most significant bit equals 1 if and only if the coding represents the number zero. Three basic operations have to be defined modulo F_t: negation, addition, and multiplication by 2. Other operations can be performed using these standard operations. According to Nussbaumer [Nus81] the coding can be formally described by

$$x = \sum_{i=0}^{b-1} x_i 2^i + x_b 2^b + 1, \qquad x_i x_b = 0; \qquad x_i, x_b \in \{0, 1\}. \tag{3.5}$$

Here x_b is called the carry bit.

The negation $\overline{x}$ of x can be obtained using (3.5):

$$\overline{x} = \sum_{i=0}^{b-1} \overline{x}_i 2^i + \overline{x}_b 2^b + 1, \tag{3.6}$$

where $\overline{x}_i = 1 - x_i$, $i \neq b$ and $\overline{x}_b = x$. The negation of numbers $x \neq 0$ corresponds to a complement of the coded bits except the carry bit.

Example:
  $5 \to 0100 \quad \Rightarrow \quad (-5) \to 1011.$

Number	Binary coding	Leibowitz coding	Number	Binary coding	Leibowitz coding
1	0 0001	0 0000	$9 = -8 \bmod F_t$	0 1001	0 1000
2	0 0010	0 0001	$10 = -7 \bmod F_t$	0 1010	0 1001
3	0 0011	0 0010	$11 = -6 \bmod F_t$	0 1011	0 1010
4	0 0100	0 0011	$12 = -5 \bmod F_t$	0 1100	0 1011
5	0 0101	0 0100	$13 = -4 \bmod F_t$	0 1101	0 1100
6	0 0110	0 0101	$14 = -3 \bmod F_t$	0 1110	0 1101
7	0 0111	0 0110	$15 = -2 \bmod F_t$	0 1111	0 1110
8	0 0000	0 0111	$16 = -1 \bmod F_t$	1 1000	0 1111
			$17 = \ \ 0 \bmod F_t$	1 0001	1 0000

Table 3.2 Binary coding and Leibowitz coding for $b = 4$.

The addition of two numbers $x \neq 0$, $y \neq 0$

$$x = \sum_{i=0}^{b-1} x_i 2^i + 1, \quad y = \sum_{i=0}^{b-1} y_i 2^i + 1 \tag{3.7}$$

is

$$x + y = \sum_{i=0}^{b-1} (x_i + y_i) 2^i + 2 = z_b 2^b + \sum_{i=0}^{b-1} z_i 2^i + 2. \tag{3.8}$$

If $z_b = 1$ then

$$x + y = 2^b + 1 + \sum_{i=0}^{b-1} z_i 2^i + 1 = \sum_{i=0}^{b-1} z_i 2^i + 1 \qquad \bmod F_t. \tag{3.9}$$

For $z_b = 0$ we have

$$x + y = \sum_{i=0}^{b-1} z_i 2^i + 2 = \left(\sum_{i=0}^{b-1} z_i 2^i + 1 \cdot 2^0 \right) + 1. \tag{3.10}$$

The addition of numbers $x, y \neq 0$ corresponds to a binary summation of the coded numbers followed by an addition of the carry bit. If at least one of the numbers x, y equals 0 (for example $x = 0$) then it follows that $x + y = y$.

Example:

```
6  →        0    0101
12 →        0    1011
          ─────────── +
          1    0000
          ─────────── +
                0
18 ≡ 1 →    0    0000
```

The multiplication of a number $x \neq 0$ by 2 gives

$$2x = 2(\sum_{i=0}^{b-1} x_i 2^i + 1) = x_{b-1} 2^b + \sum_{i=0}^{b-1} x_i 2^{i+1} + 1 + 1. \tag{3.11}$$

If $x_{b-1} = 1$ then

$$2x = (2^b + 1) + \sum_{i=0}^{b-1} x_i 2^{i+1} + 1 = \sum_{j=0}^{b-1} x_j 2^j + 0 \cdot 2^0 + 1 \qquad \mod F_t. \tag{3.12}$$

If $x_{b-1} = 0$ then

$$2x = \sum_{i=0}^{b-2} x_i 2^{i+1} + 1 + 1 = \sum_{j=0}^{b-1} x_j 2^j + 1 \cdot 2^0 + 1 \qquad \mod F_t, \tag{3.13}$$

i.e. for the multiplication of a number $x \neq 0$ by 2 we have to shift this number to the left and add the complemented carry bit to the right.

Example:

$(-7) \rightarrow$ 1001
$(-7) \cdot 2 \rightarrow$ 0010

For the remaining operations,

- the subtraction can be performed by means of negation and addition,
- the multiplication by 2^k corresponds to a k-fold shift operation,
- the general multiplication of two numbers $x \cdot y$ $(x, y \neq 0)$ can be performed by repeated additions and shifts and by representing an arbitrary integer factor as a sum of powers of 2.

3.2.5 FFT Algorithms for the FNT

It is known that the method of "divide and conquer" can be used to derive the fast Fourier transform algorithm [Nus81, Bet84]. Since the structure of the FNT is identical to that of the discrete Fourier transform for lengths of powers of two, the same algorithm can be used for the classical radix-2 FFT and the radix-2 fast FNT, respectively [Nus81, Bet84, Cre85b]. The only difference is the substitution of the complex multiplication by complex N-th roots of unity in the Fourier transform case by simple bit shifting operations in the case of the Fermat number transform.

3.2.6 The Discrete Cosine Transform – DCT

The discrete cosine transform pair is defined by

$$C(k) = C_o \sqrt{\frac{2}{N}} \sum_{n=0}^{N-1} x(n) \cos \left\{ k \left(n + \frac{1}{2} \right) \frac{\pi}{N} \right\}, \qquad k = 0 \dots N-1, \tag{3.14}$$

$$x(n) = C_o \sqrt{\frac{2}{N}} \sum_{k=0}^{N-1} C(k) \cos\left\{ k\left(n + \frac{1}{2}\right)\frac{\pi}{N} \right\}, \qquad n = 0 \ldots N-1, \qquad (3.15)$$

$$\text{where } C_o = \begin{cases} \frac{1}{2} & \text{if } n \text{ or } k = 1, \\ 1 & \text{otherwise.} \end{cases}$$

The kernel defines a set of basis functions which can be represented by an $(N \times N)$-matrix. However, this direct method requires an inordinate amount of computation. In order for the DCT to be of any practical use a fast algorithm is needed.

3.2.7   FFT Algorithm for the DCT

The importance of the DCT is due to another one of its properties – that it is easily implemented via the FFT. Hence, all recent developments in the FFT algorithms can immediately be transformed for use with the DCT [Wan85].

Although there are several possible methods for generating a fast transform, the most widely used of these is through the FFT [Ahm74]. By rearranging equation (3.14) and comparing with the FFT of length $2N$ it can be shown [Ell82] that the DCT can be calculated from

$$C(k) = 2\Re e\left\{ \exp\left(-j\frac{\pi k}{2N}\right) \text{DFT}(2N)_k \right\}, \qquad (3.16)$$

i.e. the DCT is given by twice the real part of a rotated DFT of the original signal which has been padded out with zeros. This simple fast algorithm for the DCT has the obvious disadvantage that an FFT of twice the length of the original sequence has to be calculated which means that a lot of processing is wasted. Indeed, most of the total time taken in performing the transform is spent doing the FFT (rather than the phase shift, etc.). Therefore, an algorithm using a shorter FFT would be of considerable advantage.

A further improvement can be achieved by using the approach given by Makhoul in [Mak80]. Here, the DCT is calculated from an N-point DFT using only a re-ordering technique of the original sequence. First the N-point real data sequence $x(n)$ is re-ordered to obtain a sequence $v(n)$,

$$v(n) = \begin{cases} x(2n), & n = 0 \ldots \frac{N}{2} - 1, \\ x(2N - 2n - 1), & n = \frac{N}{2} \ldots N - 1, \end{cases}$$

i.e., the first $(N/2)$ elements of which are the even points of $x(n)$ in order, followed by the odd points of $x(n)$ in reverse order. Makhoul [Mak80] showed that the DCT terms can be calculated from

$$C(k) = 2\Re e\left\{ \omega_{4N}^k \sum_{n=0}^{N-1} v(n)\omega_N^{nk} \right\}. \qquad (3.17)$$

The N-length FFT of $v(n)$ is calculated and the DCT terms can then be computed by shifting the phase of this complex data by the ω_{4N}^k factor and taking the real part. In practice only the first $(N/2) + 1$ terms are multiplied by the correction factor, because due to the Hermitian symmetry of the FFT data all of the required information is contained in these terms.

Both of the above algorithms were implemented and it was found that the insignificant increase in complexity of the N-length method did produce a working DCT procedure almost twice as fast as the $2N$-length method.

3.2.8 The Discrete Sine Transform – DST

The DST shows properties similar to those of the DCT, but is rarely used in image processing applications, generally due to its expected competition with the DCT.

The discrete sine transform pair is defined by

$$S(k) = \sqrt{\frac{2}{N+1}} \sum_{n=0}^{N-1} x(n) \sin\left\{\frac{(k+1)(n+1)\pi}{N+1}\right\}, \qquad k = 0 \ldots N-1, \qquad (3.18)$$

$$x(n) = \sqrt{\frac{2}{N+1}} \sum_{k=0}^{N-1} S(k) \sin\left\{\frac{(k+1)(n+1)\pi}{N+1}\right\}, \qquad n = 0 \ldots N-1. \qquad (3.19)$$

Using this form, the DCT (see (3.14)-(3.15)) and the DST are closely related. However, it can clearly be seen that the first row of coefficients in the transform matrix (corresponding to the dc basis vector) will not be constant as was the case for the DCT and hence it no longer carries out a true N-point transform.

3.2.9 FFT Algorithm for the DST

In analogy to the fast DCT algorithm described in the previous section, it is also possible to derive a fast algorithm for the DST. This is described in detail in [Rao90, Ers85]. The DST can be implemented by taking the imaginary part of the FFT of length $2N + 2$ of an extended sequence. Furthermore, in analogy to the fast DCT algorithm described above an approach using an $(N + 1)$-point FFT for the N-point DST is derived in [Rao90, Ers85].

3.3 GRAPH-THEORETICAL CONCEPTS FOR THE TOPOLOGY

3.3.1 The Perfect Shuffle P_n

The perfect shuffle P_n is a graph of $N = 2^n$ nodes in which a directed edge from the node i to the node j exists if and only if

$$j = \begin{cases} 2i & ; \quad 0 \leq i < N/2 \\ 2i + 1 - N & ; \quad N/2 \leq i < N. \end{cases} \qquad \text{(Shuffle)}$$

Equivalent to this definition is the following: between two nodes i and j with the binary representation $i_{n-1} \ldots i_0$ and $j_{n-1} \ldots j_0$ there exists an edge if and only if $j_{n-1} \ldots j_0 = i_{n-2} \ldots i_0 i_{n-1}$.

The name of this graph originates from shuffling playing cards. The permutation of the data achieved in the first communication step corresponds to the shuffling procedure shown in Figure 3.1 (the numbers represent the original positions of the cards).

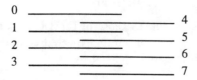

Figure 3.1   The mixing property of the shuffle exchange.

After n shuffle operations the initial position of each element of the input data is reached again. Frequently, the perfect shuffle is completed to a connected graph, the so-called shuffle exchange network, as shown in Figure 3.2. Here some (additional) bidirectional connections exist between the nodes i and j if and only if

$$i \text{ is even and } j = i + 1. \qquad \text{(Exchange)}$$

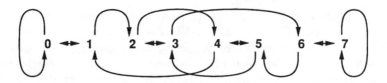

Figure 3.2   Shuffle exchange network.

In analogy to the shuffle there is an equivalent definition utilizing the binary representation: between the nodes i und j there exists an edge if and only if $i_0 = 0$ and $j = j_{n-1} \ldots j_1 1 = i_{n-1} \ldots i_1 1$. The shuffle exchange network with $N = 2^n$ nodes and 3 connections per node has a diameter of $2 \log_2 N - 1 = 2n - 1$.

Among other applications, it is well suited as a topology for [Sto71]

- sorting,
- matrix transposition,
- evaluation of polynomials,
- FFT.

The applications mentioned above have the common property that their input data can be distributed to the 2^n nodes of a hypercube. For the calculation of the solution, all data pairs located on adjacent nodes are subject to the problem specific operation. Exactly these pairs are generated by the shuffle exchange network at the ends of the exchange connections in $(n-1)$ shuffle steps.

3.3.2 The de Bruijn Graph B_m

The de Bruijn graph B_n arises from overlapping all state diagrams of feedback shift registers of the same length, as shown in Figure 3.3 [Gol67].

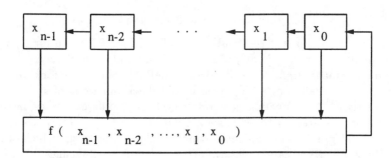

Figure 3.3 Shift register of length n with feedback function f.

The bit sequence $X := x_{n-1}x_{n-2}\ldots x_1 x_0$ will denote the state of a shift register. Possible successors of X are the states

$$x_{n-2}x_{n-3}\ldots x_1 x_0 0 \quad \text{and} \quad x_{n-2}x_{n-3}\ldots x_1 x_0 1.$$

These states differ only in their last bit which is determined by

$$x_0 := f(x_{n-1}, x_{n-2}, \ldots, x_1, x_0), \quad x_i \in \{0,1\}, \quad i = 0\ldots n-1; \quad f: \{0,1\}^n \to \{0,1\}.$$

The de Bruijn graph B_n consists of $N = 2^n$ nodes. The nodes i and j have the binary representations $i_{n-1}i_{n-2}\ldots i_1 i_0$ and $j_{n-1}j_{n-2}\ldots j_1 j_0$. There exists an edge between i and j if and only if

$$j_{n-1}j_{n-2}\ldots j_1 j_0 = i_{n-2}i_{n-3}\ldots i_0 0$$
$$\text{or}$$
$$j_{n-1}j_{n-2}\ldots j_1 j_0 = i_{n-2}i_{n-3}\ldots i_0 1.$$

An example for $N = 2^3 = 8$ is shown in Figure 3.4.

If the edges are defined by

$$[j_{n-1}j_{n-2}\ldots j_1 j_0 = 0 i_{n-2}i_{n-3}\ldots i_0 \text{ or } j_{n-1}j_{n-2}\ldots j_1 j_0 = 1 i_{n-2}i_{n-3}\ldots i_0],$$

then a graph isomorphic to B_n is generated. Equivalent to the above definition is the following: between the two edges i and j there exists exactly one directed edge if and

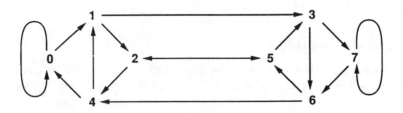

Figure 3.4   The de Bruijn graph B_3.

only if for $0 \leq i < N/2$ one of the relations $j = 2i$ or $j = 2i+1$ and for $N/2 \leq i < N$ one of the relations $j = 2i - N$ or $j = 2i + 1 - N$ is valid, respectively.

The name originates from N. G. de Bruijn [deB46], who in 1946 proved with the help of this graph that from all 2^{2^n} possible feedback functions of shift registers of length n exactly $2^{2^n - n - 1}$ functions generate a cycle of 2^n different states, i.e. functions f such that for all states i, j there exists a k with $0 \leq k < 2^n : f^k(i) = j$.

The de Bruijn graphs have an interesting "doubling" property which states that from B_n the graph B_{n+1} can be determined by identifying the edges of B_n with the nodes of B_{n+1}. There is an edge from the node i to the node j in B_{n+1} if and only if in B_n the end point of the edge i is the same as the starting point of the edge j. (In analogy to the doubling property there is also a "halving" property.)

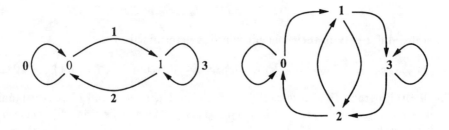

Figure 3.5   The "doubling" of B_1 to B_2.

The de Bruijn graph B_n with $N = 2^n$ nodes and 4 edges per node has a diameter of $\log_2 N = n$. It contains several subgraphs [Sam89], for example rings of N edges, binary trees of $N - 1$ nodes or a 1-step shuffle exchange network. Furthermore, it is 1-fault tolerant: deleting one edge or one node does not change the connectedness of the graph. The de Bruijn graph can also be defined for $M \neq 2^k$ edges [Sch74]: the node i is connected with the node j by an edge if and only if $j = 2i \mod M$ or

$j = 2i + 1 \bmod M$. Here we obtain a diameter of $\lceil \log_2 M \rceil$. Figure 3.6 shows a de Bruijn graph with 7 edges.

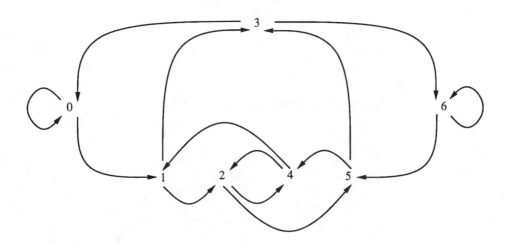

Figure 3.6 A de Bruijn graph with 7 edges.

3.3.3 Homomorphic Relation between P_n and B_m

The mapping

$$h : \begin{cases} \text{nodes in } P_n & \to & \text{nodes in } B_m, \\ \text{node } i & \mapsto & \text{node } (i \bmod 2^{n-m}) \end{cases}$$

can be extended to a surjective graph homomorphism from the perfect shuffle P_n to the de Bruijn graph B_m for $n > m \geq 0$. Using the equivalence relation

$$i \equiv_{n-m} j :\Longleftrightarrow h(i) = h(j)$$

for nodes i, j of P_n we obtain the homomorphism theorem shown in Figure 3.7.

Figure 3.8 contains the graph P_3 and its two homomorphic images generated by $\equiv_1$ and $\equiv_2$.

R. CREUTZBURG *et al.*

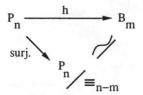

Figure 3.7   Homomorphic relations of P_n and B_m.

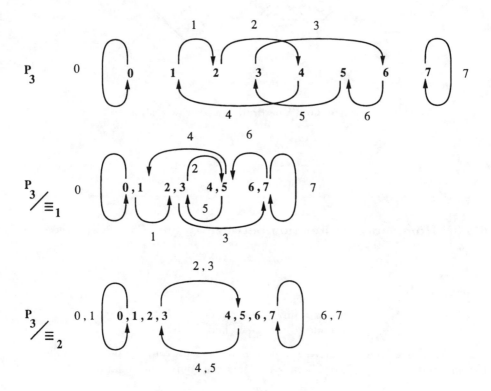

Figure 3.8   Homomorphic relations of Figure 3.7 for $N = 3$.

3.4 FFT WITH THE PERFECT SHUFFLE

The discrete Fourier transform (DFT) over the complex number field $\mathbb{C}$ is defined as the multiplication of a vector $\mathbf{x} \in \mathbb{C}^N$ with a matrix $T_N \in \mathbb{C}^{N \times N}$, where

$$T_N := (\omega^{kl})_{0 \le k, l \le N-1}$$

$$\omega := e^{2\pi i/N} \quad \text{primitive } N\text{-th root of unity,}$$

$$N := 2^n.$$

Some suitable permutations of the rows of T_N yield the fast Fourier transform (FFT) matrix $\bar{T}_N$. The matrix $\bar{T}_N$ can be factorized into the following product of sparse matrices:

$$\bar{T}_N = (\bar{T}_{N/2} \otimes I_2) \cdot D_N \cdot (I_{N/2} \otimes \bar{T}_2), \tag{3.20}$$

where

$$D_N := \begin{pmatrix} I_{N/2} & 0 \\ 0 & K_{N/2} \end{pmatrix}, \quad K_m := \text{diag}(\omega^0, \ldots, \omega^{m-1}), \quad T_2 = \bar{T}_2 := \begin{pmatrix} 1 & 1 \\ 1 & -1 \end{pmatrix},$$

$$I_N := \text{diag}(1, 1, \ldots, 1),$$

and

$$A \otimes B := \begin{pmatrix} A \cdot b_{1,1} & \cdots & A \cdot b_{1,n} \\ \vdots & & \vdots \\ A \cdot b_{n,1} & \cdots & A \cdot b_{n,n} \end{pmatrix}$$

denotes the well-known Kronecker product of $(m \times m)$-matrices A and $(n \times n)$-matrices B.

Expression (3.20) gives the possibility for recursion. For $N = 8$ we get

$$\bar{T}_8 = (\bar{T}_4 \otimes I_2) \cdot D_8 \cdot (I_4 \otimes \bar{T}_2)$$
$$\bar{T}_4 = (\bar{T}_2 \otimes I_2) \cdot D_4 \cdot (I_2 \otimes \bar{T}_2).$$

A substitution yields

$$\bar{T}_8 = ([(\bar{T}_2 \otimes I_2) \cdot D_4 \cdot (I_2 \otimes \bar{T}_2)] \otimes I_2) \cdot D_8 \cdot (I_4 \otimes \bar{T}_2)$$
$$= (\bar{T}_2 \otimes I_4) \cdot \underbrace{(D_4 \otimes I_2)}_{=:Q_1} \cdot (I_2 \otimes \bar{T}_2) \cdot (I_2 \otimes \bar{T}_2 \otimes I_2) \cdot \underbrace{D_8}_{=:Q_2} \cdot (I_4 \otimes \bar{T}_2)$$

$$= (\bar{T}_2 \otimes I_2 \otimes I_2) \cdot Q_1 \cdot (I_2 \otimes \bar{T}_2 \otimes I_2) \cdot Q_2 \cdot (I_2 \otimes I_2 \otimes \bar{T}_2).$$

This results in

$\bar{T}_8 =$

$$
\begin{pmatrix}
1 & 1 & & & & & & \\
1 & -1 & & & & & & \\
& & 1 & 1 & & & & \\
& & 1 & -1 & & & & \\
& & & & 1 & 1 & & \\
& & & & 1 & -1 & & \\
& & & & & & 1 & 1 \\
& & & & & & 1 & -1
\end{pmatrix}
\begin{pmatrix}
1 & & & & & & & \\
& 1 & & & & & & \\
& & \omega^2 & & & & & \\
& & & 1 & & & & \\
& & & & 1 & & & \\
& & & & & 1 & & \\
& & & & & & 1 & \\
& & & & & & & \omega^2
\end{pmatrix}
$$

$$
\begin{pmatrix}
1 & & 1 & & & & & \\
& 1 & & 1 & & & & \\
1 & & -1 & & & & & \\
& 1 & & -1 & & & & \\
& & & & 1 & & 1 & \\
& & & & & 1 & & 1 \\
& & & & 1 & & -1 & \\
& & & & & 1 & & -1
\end{pmatrix}
\begin{pmatrix}
1 & & & & & & & \\
& 1 & & & & & & \\
& & 1 & & & & & \\
& & & 1 & & & & \\
& & & & 1 & & & \\
& & & & & 1 & & \\
& & & & & & \omega & \\
& & & & & & \omega^2 & \\
& & & & & & & \omega^3
\end{pmatrix}
$$

$$
\begin{pmatrix}
1 & & & & 1 & & & \\
& 1 & & & & 1 & & \\
& & 1 & & & & 1 & \\
& & & 1 & & & & 1 \\
1 & & & & -1 & & & \\
& 1 & & & & -1 & & \\
& & 1 & & & & -1 & \\
& & & 1 & & & & -1
\end{pmatrix} .
$$

In general, the decomposition of $\bar{T}_N$ is the following:

$$
\begin{aligned}
\bar{T}_N \;=\; & (\bar{T}_2 \otimes I_2 \otimes \ldots \otimes I_2 \otimes I_2) \cdot Q_1 \cdot \\
& (I_2 \otimes \bar{T}_2 \otimes \ldots \otimes I_2 \otimes I_2) \cdot Q_2 \cdot \\
& \quad\vdots \\
& (I_2 \otimes I_2 \otimes \ldots \otimes \bar{T}_2 \otimes I_2) \cdot Q_{n-1} \cdot \\
& (I_2 \otimes I_2 \otimes \ldots \otimes I_2 \otimes \bar{T}_2).
\end{aligned}
$$

Here Q_r is defined by

$$
Q_r := D_{2^{r+1}} \otimes I_{N/2^{r+1}} .
$$

(It should be noted that for the definition of Q_r another primitive root of unity $\bar{\omega}$ is needed in K_{2^r} defined by $\bar{\omega} := \omega^{2^{n-(r+1)}}$.)

The above example shows the product of matrices for the FFT of length $N = 8$ and the necessary computation steps: the matrices are multiplied consecutively with a column vector, which has been modified by all the previous multiplications. For the diagonal matrices Q_1 and Q_2 this reduces to the multiplication of every vector component by a power of ω. The multiplications with $(\bar{T}_2 \otimes I_2 \otimes I_2)$, $(I_2 \otimes \bar{T}_2 \otimes I_2)$ and $(I_2 \otimes I_2 \otimes \bar{T}_2)$ each require one addition for every resulting vector coefficient. However, the index difference is not the same. In $(\bar{T}_2 \otimes I_2 \otimes I_2)$ the indices are neighbouring, in $(I_2 \otimes \bar{T}_2 \otimes I_2)$ the distance is 2 and in $(I_2 \otimes I_2 \otimes \bar{T}_2)$ it is 4.

In order to work with local data on a Transputer we try to transform the matrix product

$$
I_{2^{r-1}} \otimes \bar{T}_2 \otimes I_{2^{n-r}}
$$

to the form

$$\bar{T}_2 \otimes I_{N/2}.$$

We have $I_2 \otimes A = P(A \otimes I_2)P^{-1}$, where P denotes the permutation matrix describing the perfect shuffle. Thus we can write

$$I_2 \otimes \bar{T}_2 \otimes I_{N/4} = I_2 \otimes (\bar{T}_2 \otimes I_{N/4}) = P((\bar{T}_2 \otimes I_{N/4}) \otimes I_2)P^{-1} = P(\bar{T}_2 \otimes I_{N/2})P^{-1},$$

$$I_2 \otimes (I_2 \otimes (\bar{T}_2 \otimes I_{N/8})) = P(I_2 \otimes (\bar{T}_2 \otimes I_{N/4}))P^{-1} = P^2(\bar{T}_2 \otimes I_{N/2})P^{-2}$$

and more generally (if $\bar{T}_2$ is at the r-th position):

$$I_2 \otimes \ldots \otimes \bar{T}_2 \otimes \ldots \otimes I_2 = P^{r-1}(\bar{T}_2 \otimes I_{N/2})P^{-(r-1)}.$$

Finally, we get

$$\bar{T}_N = \underbrace{(\bar{T}_2 \otimes I_2 \otimes \ldots \otimes I_2 \otimes I_2)}_{=:C} \cdot \ Q_1 \ \cdot$$
$$(I_2 \otimes \bar{T}_2 \otimes \ldots \otimes I_2 \otimes I_2) \cdot \ Q_2 \ \cdot$$
$$\vdots$$
$$(I_2 \otimes I_2 \otimes \ldots \otimes \bar{T}_2 \otimes I_2) \cdot \ Q_{n-1} \ \cdot$$
$$(I_2 \otimes I_2 \otimes \ldots \otimes I_2 \otimes \bar{T}_2)$$

$$= \quad \begin{matrix} & C & Q_1 & \cdot \\ P & C & P^{-1} & Q_2 & \cdot \\ & \vdots & & \\ P^{n-2} & C & P^{-(n-2)} & Q_{n-1} & \cdot \\ P^{n-1} & C & P^{-(n-1)} & \end{matrix}$$

$$= \ C \ Q_1 P \ C \ P^{-1}Q_2 P^2 \ \ldots \ C \ P^{-(n-2)}Q_{n-1}P^{(n-1)} \ C \underbrace{P^{-(n-1)}}_{=P}$$

$$= \ C \ E_1 P \ C \ E_2 P \ \ldots \ C \ E_{n-1}P \ CP.$$

For the matrices Q_r we have

$$P^{-(r-1)}Q_r P^r = \underbrace{P^{-(r-1)}Q_r P^{r-1}}_{=:E_r} P = E_r P.$$

The matrix E_r is a diagonal matrix. Another possibility to get only P_1 in this last formula is to define

$$F_r := P^{-r}Q_r P^r$$

according to [Pea68].

3.5 IMPLEMENTING THE FFT AND FNT ON TRANSPUTER NETWORKS

According to the above considerations one has to provide the following operations for the implementation of the FFT on a Transputer network:

$E_r \mathbf{x}$: multiplication of a vector $\mathbf{x}$ by a diagonal matrix with powers of $e^{2\pi i/N}$ as entries,
$P\mathbf{x}$: permutation of a vector $\mathbf{x}$ by the perfect shuffle,
$C\mathbf{x}$: 2^{n-1} complex additions and subtractions of adjacent vector elements,

where $\mathbf{x} \in \mathbb{C}^N$ and $N = 2^n$.
  The permutation should be implemented using a suitable communication topology. Then the multiplications $E_r\mathbf{x}$ and $C\mathbf{x}$ can be carried out with locally accessible data.

3.5.1 Representation of the E_r

The matrices E_r ($r = 1 \ldots n - 1$) are defined by $E_r := P^{-(r-1)}Q_r P^{(r-1)}$, where P is the perfect shuffle permutation matrix of order N and Q_r is a diagonal matrix. The following example and the Lemma describe the general effects of P on diagonal matrices.

Example: Let $N = 2^3 = 8$. Then

$$P^{-1} \cdot \mathrm{diag}(0,1,2,3,4,5,6,7) \cdot P^1 = \mathrm{diag}(0,2,4,6,1,3,5,7),$$

$$P^{-2} \cdot \mathrm{diag}(0,1,2,3,4,5,6,7) \cdot P^2 = \mathrm{diag}(0,4,1,5,2,6,3,7),$$

$$P^{-3} \cdot \mathrm{diag}(0,1,2,3,4,5,6,7) \cdot P^3 = \mathrm{diag}(0,1,2,3,4,5,6,7).$$

Lemma: Let $P \in \{0,1\}^{2^n \times 2^n}$ be the perfect shuffle permutation matrix. Then for $0 \le r \le n$

$$P^{-r} \cdot \mathrm{diag}(0,1,2,\ldots,2^n - 1) \cdot P^r =$$

$$
\mathrm{diag}\,(\;
\begin{array}{ccccc}
0 \cdot 2^r + \; 0 & , & 1 \cdot 2^r + \; 0 & , & \ldots & , & (2^{n-r} - 1) \cdot 2^r + \; 0, \\
0 \cdot 2^r + \; 1 & , & 1 \cdot 2^r + \; 1 & , & \ldots & , & (2^{n-r} - 1) \cdot 2^r + \; 1, \\
\vdots & & & & & & \\
0 \cdot 2^r + \; 2^r - 1 & , & 1 \cdot 2^r + \; 2^r - 1 & , & \ldots & , & (2^{n-r} - 1) \cdot 2^r + \; 2^r - 1 \;)
\end{array}
$$

The right side of this equation consists of the cosets of the subgroup of $\mathbb{Z}_{2^n}$ that is generated by 2^r.
  The diagonal element $l := 2^{r-1}y + x$ of Q_r is located at position $k = x2^{n-r+1} + y$ ($0 \le y < 2^{n-r+1}$) in the diagonal of $E_r = P^{-(r-1)}Q_r P^{(r-1)}$. This matrix is defined by

$$Q_r := D_{2^{r+1}} \otimes I_{2^{n-r-1}},$$

where

$$D_{2^{r+1}} := \mathrm{diag}(\underbrace{1,\ldots,1}_{2^r \text{ times}}, 1, \bar{\omega}, \ldots, \bar{\omega}^{2^r - 1}) \text{ and } \bar{\omega} := e^{2\pi i/2^{r+1}}.$$

The diagonal matrix Q_r results from concatenating 2^{n-r-1} copies of $D_{2^{r+1}}$ on the diagonal. The value of an entry on the diagonal l in Q_r only depends on its position in a copy of $D_{2^{r+1}}$. This is determined by $\bar{l} := l \mod 2^{r+1}$. Through the definition of $D_{2^{r+1}}$ one can calculate the q_{ll} of Q_r and the e_{kk} of E_r:

$$q_{ll} = \begin{cases} 1 & 0 \le \bar{l} \le 2^r, \\ \bar{\omega}^{\bar{l}-2^r} & 2^r < \bar{l} < 2^{r+1}, \end{cases}$$

$$e_{kk} = \begin{cases} \omega^{\nu} & k \mod 4 = 3, \\ \omega^{\mu} & k \mod 4 = 2 \text{ and } k \ge 2^{n-(r-1)}, \\ \omega^0 = 1 & \text{else,} \end{cases}$$

$$\omega := e^{2\pi i/2^n}, \quad \nu := (2^{r-1} + k \operatorname{div} 2^{n-r+1}) \cdot 2^{n-r-1}, \quad \mu := (k \operatorname{div} 2^{n-r+1}) \cdot 2^{n-r-1}.$$

Example: For $N = 2^4 = 16$ and $\omega = e^{2\pi i/16}$ we have

```
Q₁ = diag (  . . . 4     . . .  4  . . . 4    . . . 4 ),
Q₂ = diag (  . . . .   . 2 4 6  . . . .   . 2 4 6 ),
Q₃ = diag (  . . . .   . . . .  . 1 2 3   4 5 6 7 ),
E₁ = diag (  . . . 4   . . . 4  . . . 4   . . . 4 ),
E₂ = diag (  . . . 4   . . . 4  . . 2 6   . . 2 6 ),
E₃ = diag (  . . . 4   . . 1 5  . . 2 6   . . 3 7 ).
```

(Only the exponents are represented; the dots denote zeros.)

3.5.2 Scalable Topology

The simple idea to use the perfect shuffle directly as a topology is not suitable. Every multiplication of a vector by a matrix would require communication and the number of processors would have to equal the length of the FFT.

However, it is possible to use the de Bruijn graph as a topology. The shuffle operation now splits into two parts: in a first communication step blocks of vector components are exchanged. Then a sorting of all local data in a processor has to be done. The homomorphism described in section 3.3 guarantees that in the second step no exchange between different processors is necessary. The local sorting in each processor can be done in one step combined with the operation $C\mathbf{x}$ and therefore does not lead to more calculation.

3.5.3 Time Measurements

For the implementation the following model was used:

- the original data is provided at a central node,
- it is processed in a processor network which is configurated as a de Bruijn graph and
- the results of the discussed algorithm are expected again at the above mentioned central node.

Figure 3.10 shows that this processor network can be understood as a Transputer-based FFT machine which is connected to a host computer. With the above stated

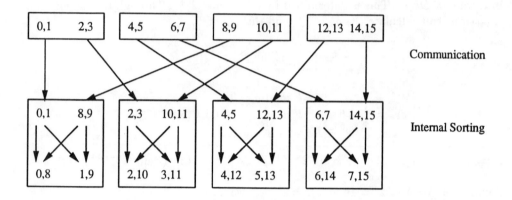

Communication

Internal Sorting

Figure 3.9   A realization of P_4 with B_2.

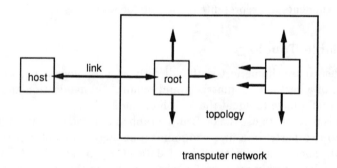

Figure 3.10   Scheme of a Transputer–based FFT machine.

model a new problem arises. The data has to be loaded into the Transputer network via one link and must be distributed to the processor nodes. The results pass through the network the reverse way. To distribute and collect the data in the de Bruijn graph the binary tree with root in node 1 is used. Node 0 serves as root processor for the whole network. It is connected with node 1. Figure 3.11 shows the embedding of the binary tree into the de Bruijn graph B_3. The edges of the binary tree are shown as bold lines; the remaining edges are dotted lines. Since loading and unloading is organized via the binary tree its edges are used bidirectionally.

The algorithm was implemented in the programming language OCCAM on a Parsytec Transputer SuperCluster with 64 processors T800. Randomly generated complex numbers were used for the time measurements. Each data vector consists of $N = 2^n$ components of 2 numbers in the format **REAL 32**.

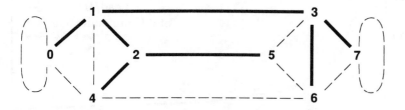

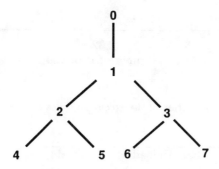

Figure 3.11 Embedding of the binary tree into the de Bruijn graph B_3.

In order to analyse the runtime behaviour of the algorithm in detail, the time consumption of various phases was investigated:

- Phase 1: sending a vector from the host, distribution of the data to the network and collecting the results at the host,
- Phase 2: communication over the edges of the de Bruijn graph,
- Phase 3: arithmetic of the FFT algorithm.

Due to technical constraints three different execution times were measured instead of the phases:

- load/unload (Phase 1),
- total communication (Phase 1 + Phase 2),
- complete FFT (Phase 1 + Phase 2 + Phase 3).

The tables in Figures 3.13, 3.15 and 3.17 summarize the execution times (in ms) for the complex FFT of vector lengths $N = 2^{10}$, $N = 2^{14}$, $N = 2^{18}$, respectively. The results are represented graphically in Figures 3.12, 3.14 and 3.16. (Clearness was the only reason to connect the separate measurement points.) The number of processors used was always a power of 2.

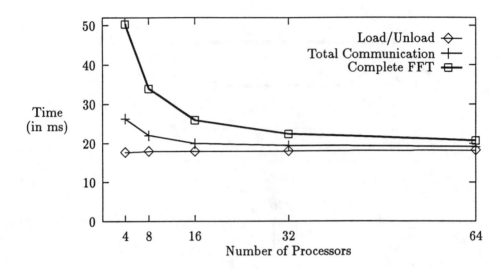

Figure 3.12   Graphical representation of the execution times for the complex FFT of length $N = 2^{10}$.

Number M of Processors	Load/Unload	Total Communication	Complete FFT
4	17.7	26.4	50.3
8	17.9	22.1	33.9
16	17.9	20.0	25.9
32	18.0	19.4	22.3
64	18.3	19.2	20.7

Figure 3.13   Execution times (in ms) for the complex FFT algorithm of length $N = 2^{10}$.

Let N and M denote the vector length and the number of processors, respectively. The theoretical amounts for the different algorithm parts are as follows

- Phase 1: $O(N)$,
- Phase 2: $O(\frac{N}{M} \cdot \mathrm{ld} N)$, i.e. there are $\mathrm{ld} N$ communications where each processor sends and receives N/M vector components,
- Phase 3: $O(\frac{N}{M} \cdot \mathrm{ld} N)$, i.e. there are $\mathrm{ld} N$ computing steps each of N/M additions and $N/(2M)$ multiplications.

In order to compare these theoretical results with the diagrams the vector length N should be considered as a constant in the above formulas. Both the theoretical considerations and the measurements show the same behaviour in all 3 phases.

The time needed by phase 1 is independent of the number of processors M. Transputers can be programmed in such a way that the transmission rate in the network is independent of the number of processors. On the other hand it is clear that phase

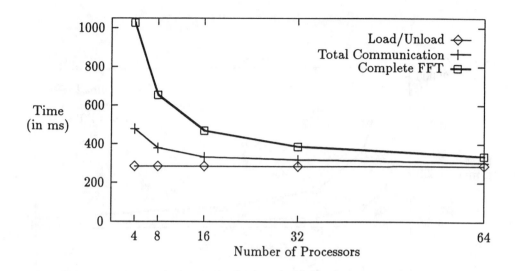

Figure 3.14   Graphical representation of the execution times for the complex FFT of length $N = 2^{14}$.

Number M of Processors	Load/Unload	Total Communication	Complete FFT
4	284.3	476.6	1024.4
8	284.4	378.4	651.2
16	284.4	331.0	467.5
32	284.4	317.0	384.8
64	286.5	302.8	336.3

Figure 3.15   Execution times (in ms) for the complex FFT algorithm of length $N = 2^{14}$.

1 dominates the whole execution time of the algorithm. It cannot be reduced by a greater number of processors.

The time measurements in phase 1 allow one to determine the transmission rate of the link into the network: a value of 0.8 Mbytes/s was achieved. This value[1] differs significantly from the value of 20 Mbits/s which equals 1.8 Mbytes/s given in the INMOS reference book [INM88a, INM88b]. Due to the hierarchical structure of the Parsytec SuperCluster a maximal transmission rate of 0.9 Mbytes/s can be obtained on this system. This value was almost achieved in our implementation.

The communication using the de Bruijn graph as well as the execution times show that the algorithm is optimally parallelized: the resulting speedup is linear with respect to M.

---

[1] In the Transputer link protocol each data byte consists of 11 bits (8 bits data plus 3 bits of control information).

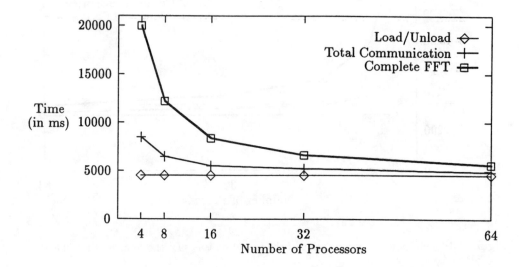

Figure 3.16   Graphical representation of the execution times for the complex FFT of length $N = 2^{18}$.

Number M of Processors	Load/Unload	Total Communication	Complete FFT
4	4548.6	8520.1	20004.7
8	4549.6	6504.2	12214.0
16	4549.6	5525.5	8378.9
32	4546.6	5235.9	6659.8
64	4571.0	4915.6	5625.1

Figure 3.17   Execution times (in ms) for the complex FFT algorithm of length $N = 2^{18}$.

Finally, we think that the realization of the FFT using the de Bruijn graph topology is a very good solution, provided that the time for loading and unloading of the data can be tolerated or is reduced, for example by:

- increasing the data transmission rate using more links to connect the host with the network,
- use of dedicated hardware like the fast pipeline bus proposed in [Lan89].

3.5.4 Implementing the FNT

Since the algorithmic structure of the FNT is exactly the same as for the radix-2 FFT, the topology described above can be applied here as well. The FNT is used for doing convolutions rather than for utilization of the spectrum. Therefore, the inverse FNT has to be calculated. Again the same topology can be used. Unfortunately, the Transputer does not have a separate fixed-point arithmetic unit which could significantly speed up the integer calculations occurring during the computation of the FFT. Only about a 10 percent speed advantage results from doing convolutions with the FNT instead of the FFT. Therefore, in the case of long convolutions a direct fast convolution algorithm should be used. Such a new and very efficient algebraic convolution algorithm was introduced in [Min92].

3.6 CONCLUSION

The fast Fourier transform (FFT) can be well parallelized using the shuffle exchange network. For an implementation on Transputers this algorithm is not well suited due to its imbalance between communication and computation time.

A clever combining of the nodes on the perfect shuffle results in the topology of the de Bruijn graph in which the problem of load balancing of an FFT on a Transputer network can be well regulated [Rog91, Rog92]. This results in a linear speedup of the algorithms.

This chapter describes fast parallel algorithms for the FFT and shows how the optimized parallel FFT kernel can be applied to the calculation of related transforms like the Fermat number transform, the cosine transform and the sine transform. A detailed description of the algorithms as well as the detailed analysis of execution times on a Parsytec SuperCluster with 64 T800 Transputers is given.

Appendix A: OCCAM codes for the FFT

In this appendix we present the main structure of our FFT implementation in OCCAM. The first part shows the overall structure of each processing node.

```
{{{  structure of a processor's program
SEQ
  ...  initialize (compute powers of omega)
  {{{  load
  input ? vector.a  -- read own data
  ...  distribute data to sons
  }}}
  ...  fft algorithm
  {{{  unload
  ...  collect results from sons
  output ! vector.a -- send own data
  }}}
}}}
```

The next program part shows a refinement of the above mentioned `fft algorithm` as it was derived in section 3.4.

```
{{{  structure of the fft-algorithm
...  communication via de Bruijn graph
...  internal sorting combined with C*x
SEQ i=1 FOR n-1
  SEQ
    ...  communication via de Bruijn graph
    ...  multiplication of data with E(n-i-1)
    ...  internal sorting combined with C*x
}}}
```

In the following we give the implementation of the three parts `communication`, `internal sorting` and `multiplication`. The first two of these are described in section 3.5.2, the last one in section 3.5.1.

```
{{{  communication via de Bruijn graph
PAR
  -- use two vectors in order to parallelize
  -- input and output
  -- u = 0.5*length(vector.a)
  in1 ? [vector.b FROM 0 FOR u]
  in2 ? [vector.b FROM u FOR u]
  out1 ! [vector.a FROM 0 FOR u]
  out2 ! [vector.a FROM u FOR u]
}}}
```

```
{{{  internal sorting combined with C*x
-- compute vector.a from values of vector.b
b.low  IS [Vektor.b FROM 0 FOR u]:
b.high IS [Vektor.b FROM u FOR u]:
SEQ j=0 FOR u
  VAL r IS 2*j:
  VAL s IS r+1:
  a  IS b.low [j]:
  b  IS b.high[j]:
  c1 IS vector.a[r]:
  c2 IS vector.a[s]:
  SEQ
    c1[0],c1[1]:= complex.add(a[0],a[1],b[0],b[1])
    c2[0],c2[1]:= complex.sub(a[0],a[1],b[0],b[1])
}}}

{{{  multiplication of data with E(n-i-1)
-- remember: most of the multiplications are by 1
-- so just multiply if necessary!
-- s1, s2[r], omega1[r], omega2[r],
-- number1 and number2[r] were computed in "initialize"
VAL r IS (n-1)-i:
VAL start1 IS ( (s1-1) >> 1) + u:
VAL start2 IS    s2[r] >> 1:
SEQ
  {{{  multiply data in case of "k mod 4 = 3"
  om IS omega1[r]:
  SEQ s=0 FOR number1
    o1 IS om[s]:
    b  IS vector.b[s TIMES 2]:
    b[0],b[1]:=C.mult(b[0],b[1],o1[0],o1[1])
  }}}
  {{{  multiply data in case of "k mod 4 = 2 and ..."
  om IS omega2[r]:
  SEQ s=0 FOR number2[r]
    o2 IS om[s]:
    b  IS vector.b[s TIMES 2]:
    b[0],b[1]:=C.mult(b[0],b[1],o2[0],o2[1])
  }}}
}}}
```

Appendix B: OCCAM codes for the Fermat number transform

The following routines show the calculation for the Fermat number transform. The communication via de Bruijn graph and the internal sorting are the same as for the FFT described in Appendix A.

```
{{{  Arithmetic Fermat (n=32 Bit fixed in diminished-1 representation)

-- The NTT routine doing the short transforms to be calculated locally
-- by a single Transputer.

PROC NTT(VAL INT b, []INT F, []INT f)
  INT omega, omega.k, size, blocks, u, x :
  SEQ
    omega := 64 / b
    size := b >> 1
    blocks := 1
    WHILE (size > 0)
      SEQ
        SEQ h=0 FOR blocks
          SEQ
            omega.k := 0
            SEQ k=(h TIMES (size PLUS size)) FOR size

              {{{ Butterfly using Leibowitz arithmetic

              ...  Abbreviations
              ...  Butterfly calculations

              }}}

              omega.k := omega.k PLUS omega
        size := size >> 1
        blocks := blocks PLUS blocks
        omega := omega PLUS omega
  :

}}}
```

The abbreviations in the next program part just serve to speed up calculations through avoiding having to recalculate the addresses every time. The lower capital variables fk and fks contain the 33rd bit of the number which indicates whether the number is zero or not.

```
{{{  Abbreviations

-- Pointers are set on often used coefficients
-- (speeds up calculation for butterflies)

INT Fk IS F[k] :
INT fk IS f[k] :
INT Fks IS F[k + size] :
INT fks IS f[k + size] :

}}}

{{{  Butterfly calculations

-- The additions are done according to whether one or both of the
-- numbers are zero. The diminished-1 representation of Leibowitz
-- is used here.

SEQ
  u := Fk
  IF
    ((fk \/ fks) = 0)
      SEQ
        x, Fk := LONGSUM(u, (~Fks), 0)
        IF
          (x = 0)
            fk, Fk := LONGSUM(Fk, 1, 0)
          TRUE
            SKIP
        x, Fks := LONGSUM(u, Fks, 0)
        IF
          (x = 0)
            fks, Fks := LONGSUM(Fks, 1, 0)
          TRUE
            SKIP
    ((fk PLUS fks) = 2)
      SKIP
    (fk = 1)
      SEQ
          Fk := (~Fks)
          fk := 0
      TRUE
        SEQ
          Fks := u
          fks := 0
```

```
{{{  Multiplication with roots of unity

--   the multiplication with roots of unity (powers of 2) in
--   diminished-1 rep. is only a complemented cyclic shift.
--   Multiplications with 2^0=1 are skipped.

IF
  (omega.k = 0)
    SKIP
  TRUE
    SEQ
      x, Fk := SHIFTLEFT((-1), Fk, omega.k)
      Fk := Fk \/ (~x)

}}}

}}}
```

Before doing the parallel NTT the input needs to be converted to diminished-1 representation and after the NTT has been calculated, the result is then converted back. These are the needed routines:

```
{{{  convert to diminished-1 representation

-- a number modulo 2^32 + 1 is converted to Leibowitz'
-- diminished-1 representation

PROC encode(INT c, cc)
  SEQ
    IF
      (cc = 1)
        SEQ
          c := (-1)
          cc := 0
      (c = 0)
        cc := 1
      TRUE
        c := c MINUS 1
:

}}}
```

```
{{{  convert back to normal representation

PROC decode(INT c, cc)
  INT x :
  SEQ
    IF
      (cc = 1)
        SEQ
          cc := 0
          c := 0
      (c = (-1))
        SEQ
          cc := 1
          c := 0
      TRUE
        c := c PLUS 1
  :

}}}
```

REFERENCES

[Aga74]   Agarwal, R. C.; C. S. Burrus: *Fast convolution using Fermat number transforms with applications to digital filtering.* IEEE Trans. Acoust. Speech Signal Process. **ASSP-22** (1974), pp. 87-97

[Aga76]   Agarwal, R. C.; C. S. Burrus: *Number theoretic transforms to implement fast digital convolution.* Proc. IEEE **63** (1976), pp. 550-560

[Ahm74]   Ahmed, N.; T. Natarajan; K. R. Rao: *Discrete cosine transform.* IEEE Trans. Comput. **C-23** (1974), pp. 90-93

[Ahm75]   Ahmed, N.; K. R. Rao: *Orthogonal Transforms for Digital Signal Processing.* Springer: Berlin 1975

[Bet84]   Beth, T.: *Verfahren der schnellen Fourier Transformation.* Teubner: Stuttgart 1984

[Bri88]   Brigham, E. O.: *The FFT and its Applications.* Prentice-Hall: Englewood Cliffs (NJ) 1988

[Cla85]   Clarke, R. J.: *Transform Coding of Images.* Academic Press: New York 1985.

[Cre85a] Creutzburg, R.; M. Tasche: *F-Transformation und Faltung in kommutativen Ringen.* J. Inf. Process. Cybern. **EIK-21** (1985), pp. 129-149

[Cre85b] Creutzburg, R.; H.-J. Grundmann: *Die Fermattransformation und ihre Anwendung bei der schnellen Berechnung digitaler Faltungen.* J. Inf. Process. Cybern. **EIK-21** (1985), pp. 35-46

[Cre85c]   Creutzburg, R.; H.-J. Grundmann: *Determination of convenient moduli for 16-bit mixed-radix number-theoretic transforms.* Rostock. Math. Kolloq. **28** (1985), pp. 99-110

[Cre86]   Creutzburg, R.; M. Tasche: *Number-theoretic transforms of prescribed length.* Math. Comp. (USA) **47** (1986), pp. 693-701

[Cre88]   Creutzburg, R.; G. Steidl: *Construction of parameters for number-theoretic transforms in rings of cyclotomic integers.* J. Inf. Process. Cybern. **EIK-24** (1988), pp. 573-584

[Cre89]   Creutzburg, R.; M. Tasche: *Parameter determination for complex number-theoretic transforms using cyclotomic polynomials.* Math. Comp. (USA) **52** (1989), pp. 189-200

[Cre91]   Creutzburg, R.: *Parameters for complex FFTs in finite residue class rings.* Proceed. EUROCODE'90 (Udine, Italy), Lecture Notes in Computer Science **514** 1991, pp. 222-226

[deB46]   de Bruijn, N. G.: *A combinatorial problem.* Koninklijke Nederlandse Academie Van Wetenschapen, Proceed. **49** Part 20 (1946), pp. 758-764

[Duh82]   Duhamel, P.; H. Hollman: *Number-theoretic transforms with 2 as root of unity.* Electron. Lett. **18** (1982), pp. 978-980

[Ell82]   Elliott, D. F.; K. R. Rao: *Fast Transforms: Algorithms, Analyses, Applications.* Academic Press: New York 1982

[Ers85]   Ersoy, O.: *On relating discrete Fourier, sine and symmetric cosine transforms.* IEEE Trans. Acoust. Speech Signal Process. **ASSP-33** (1985), pp. 219-222

[Gol67]   Golomb, S. W.: *Shift Register Sequences.* Holden-Day: San Francisco 1967

[Hal79]   Hall, E. L.: *Computer Image Processing and Recognition.* Academic Press: New York 1979

[INM88a]   INMOS Ltd: *OCCAM 2 Reference Manual.* Prentice-Hall: Englewood Cliffs (NJ) 1988

[INM88b]   INMOS Ltd: *Transputer Development System.* Prentice-Hall: Englewood Cliffs (NJ) 1988

[Lan89]   Lang, B.: *Ein paralleles Transputersystem zur digitalen Bildverarbeitung mit schneller Pipelinekopplung.* Informatik-Fachberichte **219** (1989), pp. 372-379

[Lei76]   Leibowitz, L. M.: *A binary arithmetic for the Fermat number transform.* Naval Research Lab. Report 7971, Washington, D. C., 1976

[Mak80]   Makhoul, J.: *A fast transform in one and two dimensions.* IEEE Trans. Acoust. Speech Signal Process. **ASSP-28** (1980) No. 1, pp. 213-226

[McC79]   McClellan, J. H.; C. M. Rader: *Number Theory in Digital Signal Processing.* Prentice-Hall: Englewood Cliffs (NJ) 1979

[Min92]   Minkwitz, T.; R. Creutzburg. *A new fast algebraic convolution algorithm.* in: *Signal Processing VI: Theories and Applications.* (Eds.: J. Vandewalle; R. Boite; M. Moonen; A. Oosterlinck) Elsevier Science Publ.: Amsterdam 1992, pp. 933-936

[Nus81]   Nussbaumer, H. J.: *Fast Fourier Transform and Convolution Algorithms.* Springer: Berlin 1981

[Pea68]   Pease, M. C.: *An adaption of the fast Fourier transform for parallel processing.* Journal ACM **15** (1968), pp. 252-264

[Rao90]   Rao, K. R.; P. Yip: *Discrete Cosine Transform, Algorithms, Advantages, Applications.* Academic Press: Boston 1990

[Ree76]   Reed, I. S.; T. K. Truong: *Complex integer convolutions over a direct sum of Galois fields.* IEEE Trans. Inform. Theory **IT-21** (1976), pp. 169-175

[Rog91]   Roggenbach, M.: *FFT mit dem Perfect Shuffle.* In: Tagungsband Workshop über Parallelverarbeitung (Eds.: Ecker et al.), Informatik-Berichte 91/1, Technische Universität Clausthal, 1991, pp. 1-11

[Rog92]   Roggenbach, M.; R. Creutzburg; T. Minkwitz; T. Umland: *Implementierung von parallelen FFT-Algorithmen auf Transputern.* In: Tagungsband 4. Transputer-Anwender-Treffen (TAT'92), Aachen 22.-23. September 1992, pp. 94-95

[Sam89]   Samatham, M. R.; D. K. Pradhan: *The de Bruijn multiprocessor network: a versatile parallel processing and sorting network for VLSI.* IEEE Trans. Comput. **C-38** (1989), pp. 567-581

[Sch71] Schönhage, A.; V. Strassen: *Schnelle Multiplikation großer Zahlen.* Computing **7** (1971), pp. 281-292

[Sch74] Schlumberger, M. L.: *De Bruijn communication networks.* Ph. D. Dissertation, Stanford University, 1974

[Sto71] Stone, H. S.: *Parallel processing with the perfect shuffle.* IEEE Trans. Comput. **C-20** (1971), pp. 153-161

[Uml92] Umland, T.; R. Vollmar: *Transputerpraktikum.* B. G. Teubner: Stuttgart 1992

[Wan85] Wang, Z.: *On computing the discrete Fourier and cosine transforms.* IEEE Trans. Acoust. Speech Signal Process. **ASSP-33** (1985), pp. 1341-1344

[Zer91] Zerfowski, D.: *Implementierung des Multiplikationsverfahrens von Schönhage–Strassen.* Diploma thesis, University of Karlsruhe, 1991

4

Parallel Edge Detection and Related Algorithms

STEPHEN MARSHALL

4.1 INTRODUCTION

Edge detection is invariably among the earliest operations to be carried out in any vision task. It involves translation of numeric (pixel) data to symbolic (edge tokens) data. It is a critical operation in that it is very difficult to recover from errors made at this stage.

Edges are essentially surface boundary discontinuities. They are found at places where there is an abrupt change in some visual property. In most applications edges are sought as discontinuities in grey level intensity but there are also texture or colour edges. In this chapter it is assumed that the edges being sought are those of grey level intensity.[1]

Over the past 30 years there have emerged many edge operators and even the most sophisticated available today frequently fail to produce simply connected continuous object boundaries. The earliest operators [Rob65, Prew70] consisted of small mask-like operations which detected changes in only one direction. Since then operators have been modified to include estimates of noise measures within images and to be non-directional [Mar80, Can86].

This chapter provides a brief review of edge detection techniques followed by examples of the implementation of edge detectors on different architectures. It then describes the thinning algorithms and methods closely related to edge detection such

---

[1] To detect discontinuities in different properties such as texture or colour the image would be pre-filtered to convert the property to an intensity value and then standard edge detection techniques would be applied.

Parallel Algorithms for Digital Image Processing, Computer Vision and Neural Networks, ed. I. Pitas

as the Hough transform. Some alternative methods of edge detection such as image reconstruction and neural networks are also covered. Systems containing parallel edge detection are then given. Finally a summary and conclusions are presented.

It should be noted for completeness that not all vision research groups agree that edge detection is the correct way to proceed in early vision. For example Mowforth and Gillespie [Mow87] argue both that edge detection is ill-posed and that those involved in edge detection-based research are unable to provide a consensus for specification. With these objections noted a brief introduction to the edge detection problem is presented.

4.2   THE EDGE DETECTION PROBLEM

Most edge detection algorithms can be summarised by the three basic stages outlined below:

(i) the image is convolved with a derivative mask to produce a measure of intensity gradient,

(ii) a threshold operation is applied in which those locations possessing intensity gradient values greater than a set level are classified as edge tokens,

(iii) a linking or following algorithm is applied in which the edge points arising from the masking operation are gathered together to form coherent edges.

Stages **(i)** and **(ii)** form the main edge detection process. The output from these stages is usually 'noisy' and characterised by

- disjoint fragments of edges rather than continuous boundaries,

- multiple responses from the same edge,

- 'phantom' edge fragments resulting from noise.

These noise artifacts lead to stage **(iii)** in which attempts are made to clean up the response from the edge masks by thinning lines, bridging gaps and eliminating isolated edge points unsupported by neighbouring data.

There have been many variations around these three stages leading to a series of edge detection techniques. Some of the most common ones are described here together with their theoretical justification.

Edge detection techniques

The separation of scenes into object and background is an essential step in image interpretation. The identification of the boundaries (or *edges*) between various parts of a scene is carried out effortlessly by the Human Visual System (HVS). Edges (usually) occur at those places in an image where there is an abrupt change in intensity. In a mathematical sense it therefore involves a derivative operation designed to estimate spatial gradient and hence identify discontinuities in intensity value. This task is complicated in two ways. *Firstly* in a sampled signal such as an image any difference

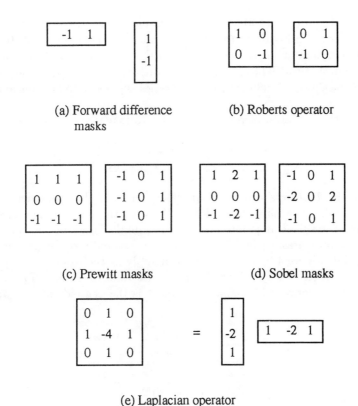

(a) Forward difference
masks

(b) Roberts operator

(c) Prewitt masks

(d) Sobel masks

(e) Laplacian operator

Figure 4.1 Various masks used for edge detection.

in neighbouring pixel values could be interpreted as an edge, i.e. there is no obvious point of distinction between edges and steep gradients. There is instead, a continuum of spatial gradient values which requires the setting of a threshold value to decide how steep a gradient must be before it can be classified as an edge. *Secondly* images are two dimensional and edges have a direction as well as a magnitude measure. Edge detectors must therefore be able to deal with edges occurring at any orientation in the image.

The gradient vector $\nabla f(x, y)$ of a two dimensional function $f(x, y)$ may be expressed in terms of directionally oriented spatial derivatives as follows:

$$\nabla f(x, y) = \left[\begin{array}{c} \delta f(x, y)/\delta x \\ \delta f(x, y)/\delta y \end{array} \right] \tag{4.1}$$

The simplest method to calculate the derivatives of equation (4.1) is the two point *forward difference* approach,

$$\frac{\delta f}{\delta x}(x, y) \approx \frac{f(x + \Delta x, y) - f(x, y)}{\Delta x} \tag{4.2}$$

$$\frac{\delta f}{\delta y}(x, y) \approx \frac{f(x, y + \Delta y) - f(x, y)}{\Delta y} \tag{4.3}$$

The functions of equations (4.2), (4.3) may be implemented by correlating the image with the masks shown in Figure 4.1(a). This approach unfortunately leads to a better estimate of the gradient at the midpoint *between* the points rather than at any point defined on the sampled grid. The error in the derivative approximation using equations (4.2), (4.3) may be shown [Sch89], via a Taylor series expansion to be a linear function of Δx.

A variation of the forward difference operator is to take diagonal differences,

$$\nabla_1 = f(x + \Delta x, y + \Delta y) - f(x, y) \tag{4.4}$$
$$\nabla_2 = f(x, y + \Delta y) - f(x + \Delta x, y) \tag{4.5}$$

which leads to the **Roberts operator** [Rob65]. This may be implemented by the pair of 2×2 masks shown in Figure 4.1(b). As with the previous operator it is a better measure of gradient at points *between* the samples, than of any point on the sample grid. The measures ∇_1 and ∇_2 are, at least, estimates of the gradient at the same spatial point. Figure 4.2 shows the effect of applying the Roberts operator to an image. The image is formed by taking the maximum value of ∇_1 and ∇_2.

A further approximation to the spatial gradient is the *centred* difference approximation,

$$\nabla_1 = \frac{f(x + \Delta x, y) - f(x - \Delta x, y)}{2(\Delta x)} \tag{4.6}$$

$$\nabla_2 = \frac{f(x, y + \Delta y) - f(x, y - \Delta y)}{2(\Delta y)} \tag{4.7}$$

The centred difference approximations give good estimates of the gradient at (x, y) and they may be shown [Sch89] to have an approximation error which is a function of $(\Delta x)^2$. They may be implemented as simple 3×3 masks. Two variations on these approximations which differ only in the weighting given to coefficients orthogonal to the derivative are the **Prewitt** and **Sobel** edge masks [Prew70] which are shown in Figures 4.1(c) and (d).

The quantities ∇_1 and ∇_2 represent measures of the spatial gradient in two orthogonal directions. They are usually combined to produce a magnitude, M, and direction, ϕ, as follows:

$$M = \sqrt{\nabla_1^2 + \nabla_2^2} \tag{4.8}$$

$$\phi = \tan^{-1}\left(\frac{\nabla_2}{\nabla_1}\right) \tag{4.9}$$

When operators such as the Prewitt and Sobel are applied to an area of an image containing a long constant slope they result in very thick edges. This is because they provide a measure of gradient rather than an indication of the peak gradient. Other operators, such as the Laplacian, measure the *second derivative* or the *rate of change of gradient*. Peak spatial gradients are, therefore, located at the zero crossings in the output of such operators. The zero crossing locations are spatially continuous and occur only in closed contours, which means that there should be no gaps in

Figure 4.2   The output of the Roberts operator.

edges produced by this method. In practice a very large number of zero crossings are produced and these must be reduced in some way. The two dimensional Laplacian operator is given in equation (4.10):

$$\nabla^2 f(x,y) = \frac{\delta^2 f(x,y)}{\delta x^2} + \frac{\delta^2 f(x,y)}{\delta y^2} \qquad (4.10)$$

This operator may be approximated by a 3×3 mask which can also be separated into two 3×1 dimensional masks as shown in Figure 4.1(e). These masks may be simply derived from a succession of forward and backward difference operations [Sch89].

The Laplacian operator applied alone tends to be prone to noise effects and it is therefore often preceded by smoothing with a Gaussian mask to reduce noise:

$$G(x,y) = (1/2\pi\sigma^2)\exp(-(x^2 + y^2)/2\sigma^2) \qquad (4.11)$$

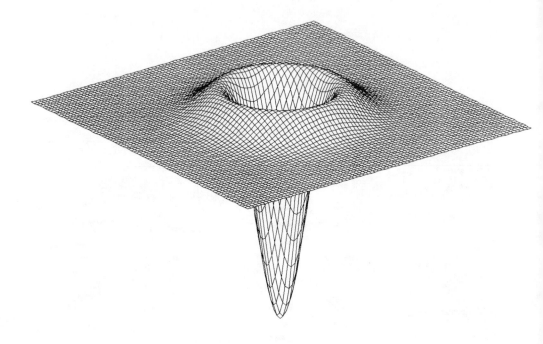

Figure 4.3 The 2D Laplacian of Gaussian operator.

These two stages may be combined into a single mask operation known as the **Laplacian of Gaussian** (LOG) operator which may be shown to equal

$$\text{LOG} = \nabla^2 G(x,y) = (1/\pi\sigma^4)(r^2/2\sigma^2 - 1)\exp(-r^2/2\sigma^2) \tag{4.12}$$

where $r^2 = x^2 + y^2$.

A plot of the LOG operator is shown in Figure 4.3. It is a circular symmetric function which is of infinite extent. In practice the operator would be sampled onto a mask and truncated at a value of r, such that 99% of the area beneath the Gaussian function was included under the curve.

This operator may also be separated and applied as four one-dimensional masks which has the advantage of computational efficiency,

$$\text{LOG} = \nabla^2 G(x,y) = (1/\pi\sigma^4)((x^2 + y^2)/2\sigma^2 - 1)\exp(-(x^2 + y^2)/2\sigma^2) \tag{4.13}$$

$$= (1/\sqrt{2\pi}\sigma^2)(x^2/\sigma^2 - 1)\exp(-x^2/2\sigma^2).(1/\sqrt{2\pi}\sigma^2)\exp(-y^2/2\sigma^2)$$
$$+ (1/\sqrt{2\pi}\sigma^2)(y^2/\sigma^2 - 1)\exp(-y^2/2\sigma^2).(1/\sqrt{2\pi}\sigma^2)\exp(-x^2/2\sigma^2)$$

$$= g''(x).g(y) + g''(y).g(x)$$

Figure 4.4 Zero crossings resulting from application of LOG operator ($\sigma = 2.0$).

where $g(.)$ and $g''(.)$ are one-dimensional Gaussian functions and their respective second derivatives. An example of the zero crossings resulting from the application of the LOG edge detector for $\sigma = 2.0$ is shown in Figure 4.4.

Canny Edge Detector

The **Canny edge detector** which optimises the three criteria of detection, localisation and a single response to a single edge has become established as the most effective edge detector of its type. It is described here briefly; full implementation details are given in [Can86].

Whilst based on a convolution operator the Canny edge detector also incorporates some aspects of stage **(iii)** directly into the algorithm. It consists broadly of five stages:

1. The image is blurred with a two-dimensional Gaussian to lessen the effects of noise.

2. The smoothed image is convolved with directional gradient operators.

3. Non-maximal gradients are suppressed in the direction of the maximum gradient.

4. Adaptive thresholding with hysteresis is used to distinguish 'true edges' from noise.

5. A map of consistent edges from a number of scales is built by 'feature synthesis' involving consideration of the S/N ratio at each scale.

An example of Canny edge detector applied to the earlier test image is shown in Figure 4.5.

The following sections will consider the implementation of edge detection and related algorithms on parallel hardware. Before proceeding to parallel implementations it is worth noting that a recent development in edge tracking across sequences of images has involved the fitting of 'snakes' or B-Spline curves [Kass87] to edge fragments. This has been considered as a separate task following edge detection and is not covered here.

4.3   PARALLEL PROCESSING ASPECTS

It is clearly not possible in a publication such as this to mention every research project or commercial device which is in use for parallel edge detection. The author has attempted to give examples of edge detection implementation for various types of parallel configurations and quote performance results where available.

The objective of parallel processing is to perform a task more quickly by distributing the work over a number of processors. Parallel processing is at its most efficient when the work being carried out by each processor is equal to and independent of the workload of the other processors. There are basically two main types of parallelism and two main types of parallel processor. The two main types of parallelism are:

- Data parallelism

- Task parallelism

Data parallelism involves partitioning of the data, in this case an image, such that each part or sub-image is processed by a different processor.

Task parallelism involves the partitioning of various elements of the task into subtasks such that each processor carries out a different sub-task.

The two main types of multiprocessor systems are:

- Single Instruction Multiple Data (SIMD)

- Multiple Instruction Multiple Data (MIMD)

SIMD machines are those in which all of the processors perform the same task at the same time on a different piece of data. Vector and array processors are machines

Figure 4.5   The output from a Canny edge detector ($\sigma = 2.0$).

of this type; in general each processor is connected only to its neighbours. Generalised information such as sine and cosine tables may be broadcast to all PEs simultaneously but more processor specific information can take a long time to disseminate as it must be propagated from processor to processor in single steps. These machines are well suited to localised operations such as convolution and linear transforms performed over the entire image, but less suited to data dependent operations such as edge tracking and linking. An example of an SIMD machine is the Distributed Array Processor or DAP produced by Active Memory Technology, Reading, England.

    MIMD machines are those in which each processor is able to carry out a different series of instructions. The INMOS transputer [INM89] is a processor of this type. A further classification of MIMD machines is into those which have memory distributed among processors and those which have a shared common memory. MIMD machines may behave in a way similar to SIMD machines simply by arranging that each processor performs the same operation at the same time. The INMOS transputer in particular may be configured to perform 'processor farming' in which a task is broken down into workpackets. The workpackets are allocated to the various processors by a master processor. Each processor carries out its tasks on the workpackets and returns it to the master. Workpackets are sent to the processors as they become free. This is therefore an effective method for load balancing when the amount of processing required for each packet is data dependent and therefore unpredictable at the time of configuration.

The various elements of the task of edge detection are very different in their potential for parallel implementation. They are discussed in the following section.

4.3.1   Parallel Implementation of Edge Detection

The first stage of edge detection involving convolution by a mask is inherently simpler to implement on parallel hardware than the final stage of linking, grouping and thinning operations. This is because the amount of processing required for any sub-image is predictable and equal to all of the others. It is an ideal situation to employ data parallelism.

There now exist commercially available software libraries of routines to implement most of the text book algorithms such as masking operators and thinning algorithms. Active Memory Technology (AMT) of Reading, England have a software image processing library for their DAP, Parsytec of Aachen, Germany have their own software library and the Vision Technology Transfer Centre (VTTC) based at National Engineering Laboratory, East Kilbride, Scotland have developed the IPLIB package for transputer based image processing systems. The following sections give examples of the implementation of edge detection techniques, particularly the Canny edge detector, on various types of parallel processing hardware.

4.3.2   Implementation of Edge Detection on an SIMD Processor

The simpler edge detection techniques such as the Sobel and Prewitt operators involve a convolution of the image with a 3×3 mask and the time taken for this is the same as for any similarly sized convolution. Only the mask weights would differ between these operations. A paper investigating the performance of various computer architectures for these and other benchmarking tasks is given in [Pres89]. Further surveys of the implementation of image processing algorithms on SIMD and MIMD machines are given in [Cha90, Cyp89]

More sophisticated edge detectors such as the Canny also include a convolution stage. There have been several implementations of the Canny operator on SIMD machines particularly the DAP [Mur88]. The DAP is a bit-serial word-parallel machine with an SIMD $n \times n$ processing array where n is either 32 or 64. Images larger than this size are mapped onto the processing array in either 'sheet' or 'crinkled' mapping (see below).

In most practical implementations of the Canny operator two simplifications are made. First the 'feature synthesis' stage is omitted, and secondly integer arithmetic is used wherever possible to speed up the processing.

A specific example of the Canny operator implemented on the DAP is given in [Wys89]. The basic approach is outlined below:

1. The image is first transformed to a 'crinkled mapping', i.e. the image is sampled at

$$\textbf{image\_edge\_size/DAP\_edge\_size}$$

   intervals. The resulting sub-images are referred to as tiles. After crinkle mapping neighbours are generally found at the same coordinates in other tiles. Neighbourhood operations on the image therefore involve memory accesses rather than processor to processor communication.

2. Gaussian smoothing is carried out by exploiting the fact that a two-dimensional Gaussian filter may be decomposed and implemented as two separate one-dimensional convolutions along the X and Y directions [Wei85]. Integer arithmetic is used at this stage.

3. Two versions of the gradient operator are implemented. One of them uses the first derivative of a Gaussian which is a good approximation to the optimum (for a step edge in white noise). The second uses a simpler [−1 0 +1] mask which has been found to be satisfactory for most applications. This stage yields partial derivatives of the image in the x and y directions.

4. Non-maximal values are suppressed in the direction normal to the edge direction. Edge direction is estimated from the partial derivatives in the x and y directions and only the maximum gradient values are retained. This stage is the most computationally complex. The complexity arises from the use of floating point arithmetic and the calculation of tangents to determine edge orientation from partial derivatives. The output from this stage is a sparse set of edgels connected without branching.

5. The final stage involves thresholding at two levels with hysteresis. The upper threshold level is set well above the estimated noise and the lower level is within the noise. An edgel is marked as valid if it either exceeds the upper threshold or exceeds the lower threshold and is connected to a valid edge. This is an iterative process where the connection may exist through several other edgels all of which exceed the lower threshold. In most practical systems a limit is set on the number of iterations with the arbitrary value of 5 being the most common.

The timings achieved by this implementation were in the order of 800 ms for a 256 × 256 image with slight variations for the width of Gaussian smoothing. Unlike the sequential implementations these timings were virtually unchanged with image complexity.

4.3.3   Implementation of Edge Detection on an MIMD Processor

The INMOS transputer has formed the basis for many MIMD image processing systems. The transputer is a small complete Von Neumann computer. A number of transputers may be assembled into a network or array. Each transputer has four bi-directional communication links which may be connected to the links of neighbouring transputers in various topologies to form processing structures such as rings, pipelines or arrays.

The Canny edge detector has been used as an integral part of the TINA [Por87] and MARVIN (Multiprocessor ARchitecture for VIsioN) [Bro89] 3D vision systems developed at the University of Sheffield, England. MARVIN is a transputer based general purpose vision engine capable of employing different types of parallelism within a single overall application. It consists of 25 (T800) transputers firm-wired as a regular, fully connected mesh with 3 rows, 8 columns and an extension for the root processor. A scaled down version of the machine architecture is shown in Figure 4.6. The root processor carries out no vision processing but holds various servers and performs data distribution and collection functions. One row of processors consist of special locally developed transputer cards (named TMAX) provided with 4 frame-rate byte-wide bi-directional video buses and controllers. The buses can be ganged to allow 32 bit wide transfer of data streams. They are used to route large amounts of image data around the system and provide fast data transit. This helps to alleviate the problem of data transfer found in many other systems of this type.

The MARVIN system has its own software infrastructure [Bro90] which allows the programmer to ignore the *physical* topology of the system and to work with a *logical* topology which may be chosen and changed dynamically.

The vision system is derived from the TINA system which may be used for recovery of scene descriptions via stereo matching and the location of modelled objects within such scenes. The output of the vision system may be used to guide a robot arm to pick up objects in a cluttered scene. The stereo matching algorithm employed is known as PMF [Pol85] which is an edge based approach incorporating a disparity gradient constraint. The edges to be matched are derived via a parallel implementation of the Canny edge detector.

Although the overall system follows a modular feedforward approach incorporating edge detection, PMF, 2D and 3D geometry, joining and matching operations, the authors reject a pipeline approach. (This is not to say that the pipeline is rejected by all workers in this area and a pipeline implementation of Canny edge detector is described below.) The authors also reject processor farming techniques as the overheads of data reorganisation are considered to be too high.

The Canny edge detector is implemented by data parallelism with the image partitioned into a number of horizontal strips distributed over 16 transputers. A subsequent joining operation must then be employed to connect together edges which straddle a strip boundary; see Figure 4.7. A quadratic interpolation procedure is introduced to locate the precise edge location to sub-pixel accuracy. The size of the images is 512×512 and the complete matching strategy is implemented in 10 seconds with the Canny edge detector being the most expensive element at 5.5 seconds.

4.3.4   Other Architectures for Edge Detection

In contrast to the TINA and MARVIN approach an alternative method proposes a pipelined structure for the videorate implementation of Canny edge detector [Ruf88]. A block diagram of the pipeline is shown in Figure 4.8. The system exploits the separability property of the Gaussian operator and a series of masks are used to perform the edge growing at the hysteresis stage. The pipeline architecture is highly

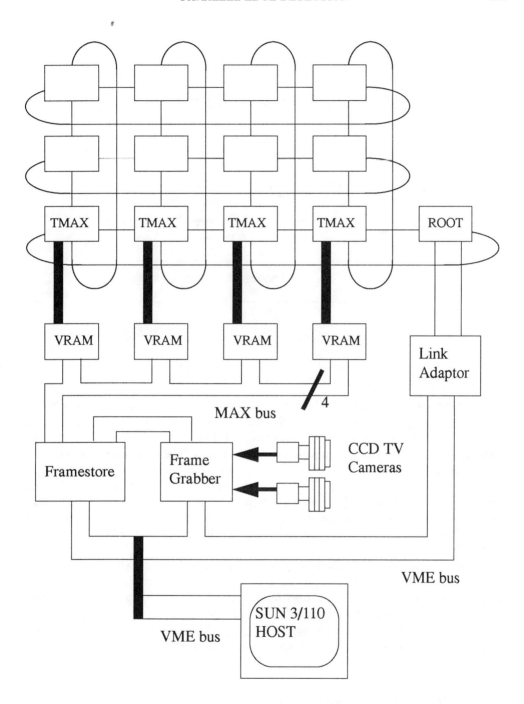

Figure 4.6 MARVIN architecture. Reproduced from Figure 1 of [Ryg91a] by permission of the publishers, Butterworth-Heinemann Ltd. ©.

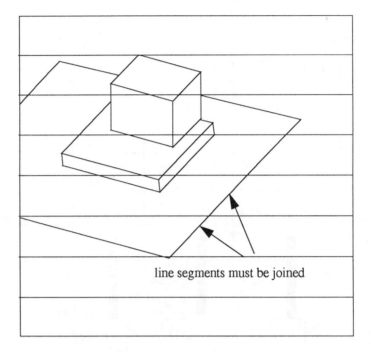

Figure 4.7 Edges which straddle strip boundaries. Reproduced from Figure 7(a) of [Ryg91b] by permission of AIVRU, University of Sheffield ©.

appropriate for an operator at the earlier stages of vision such as the Canny which consists of a sequence of stages, and the data throughput is high. Unfortunately it is not appropriate for higher level vision tasks. This is because a pipeline maximises *data throughput* but fails to minimise *processor latency*. The reason for this is that in the earlier tasks of vision, such as convolution, the data which is passed from module to module is very large (approx 1 MByte). However the later modules pass on data objects such as strings and pointers to data structures which require a very small bit rate. As the overall throughput of a pipeline is determined by its slowest module, many of the processors towards the end of the pipeline can remain idle through work starvation.

What appears to be required to implement a complete vision system is a front end processor performing global operations and employing *data parallelism* with a more sophisticated later stage to implement *task parallelism* for the data dependent higher level vision operations. An early attempt at just such an architecture is the Disputer [Pag88] which employs a combination of a 256 processor SIMD and a 42 processor MIMD machine in order to optimise the strongest properties of both.

4.4   RELATED ALGORITHMS

The related algorithms such as grouping, thinning and linking are by their nature much more complicated to implement in parallel than the convolution mask in the earlier stages. This is because the related algorithms deal with symbolic tokens, i.e. edge

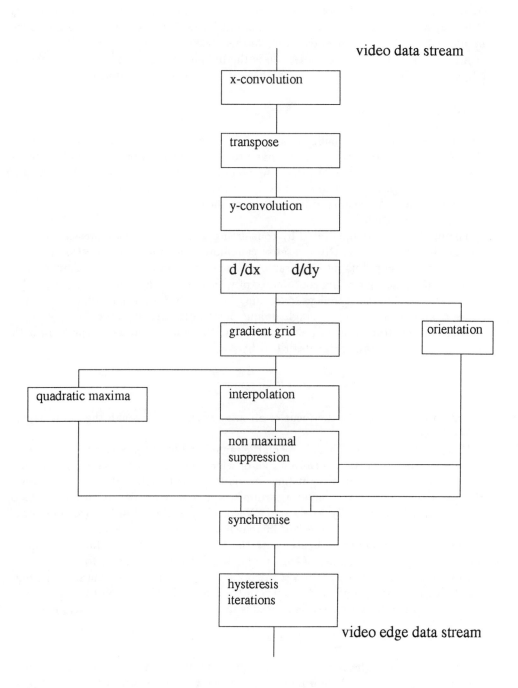

Figure 4.8 Pipelined Canny architecture. Reproduced from Figure 1(a) of [Ruf88] by permission of the publishers, Oxford University Press ©.

fragments, and the number of these arising from any sub-image may vary considerably. When straightforward data parallelism is applied here then many of the processors will be idle waiting for the others to complete their task.

An important task in edge detection is the linking of edge fragments into coherent edges and an important tool to carry this out is the Hough transform.

Hough Transform

The Hough transform [Hou62] is a powerful tool used for the detection of known shapes in images. It is relatively immune to noise and gaps in the boundary but is computationally expensive. For the detection of straight lines it involves the mapping of candidate edge points in the image into a two-dimensional accumulator or Hough parameter space. A brief description of the method is given here and a full description can be found in [Bal82].

The method is best illustrated by considering a slope-intercept representation of a straight line, $y = mx + c$. Given a set of candidate edge points the detection proceeds by mapping these points into a parameter space or accumulator. The accumulator is a two-dimensional space, the coordinates of which are m, slope and c, intercept. Any (infinite) straight line in image space may be described by a pair of values (m, c), hence it may be mapped to a single unique point in the accumulator.

Following on from this, a point (x_1, y_1) in the image may be mapped into the accumulator as a straight line described by

$$m = \frac{-c}{x_1} + \frac{y_1}{x_1} \tag{4.14}$$

Equation (4.14) describes the locus of all lines which pass through the point (x_1, y_1) in the image.

When a set of edge points all lying on the same straight line $y = m'x + c'$ are mapped into the accumulator, they form lines all of which intersect at the same unique point (m', c'). The presence of straight lines in the image is therefore detected as *peaks* in the accumulator. The accumulator is implemented as a number of discrete cells or counters which are initially set to zero. When a line is plotted in the accumulator all of the cells lying along the line are incremented by one. The presence of very large values in the accumulator indicates both the detection of a straight line in the image and a measure of the number of edge points which have contributed to it.

In practice the representation $y = mx + c$ has a number of disadvantages, the most serious being that it must span values of both m and c from $-\infty$ to $+\infty$. A more practical representation for straight lines is in terms of the two parameters ρ and θ,

$$\rho = x \cos \theta + y \sin \theta \tag{4.15}$$

where ρ represents the normal distance from the line to the origin and θ denotes the angular position of the normal. The representation is shown in Figure 4.9, ρ is a positive quantity limited to the length of the image diagonal and θ is bounded by 0 and 2π.

The Hough transform is essentially a voting system in which the coordinates of each edge point are used to increment values of ρ and θ in the accumulator according to

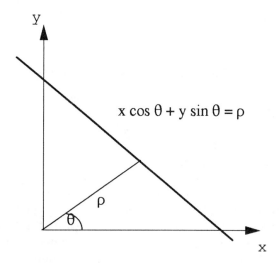

Figure 4.9 Practical ρ, θ representation of a straight line.

equation (4.15). In this representation an edge point maps into the accumulator as a sinusoidal curve but the principle is the same. The sinusoidal curve indicates all of the possible values of ρ and θ which specify straight lines passing through the given edge point. Colinear points in the image all map to curves in Hough space which intersect at a single unique point. The coordinates of this point (ρ_i, θ_i) specify the common line through the colinear points in image space.

The practical implementation of the Hough transform therefore involves two distinct sequential stages:

- Firstly the candidate edge points derived from a convolution operation are mapped into the accumulator space as sinusoidal curves as per equation (4.15).

- Secondly when all of the points have been mapped, the peak values in the accumulator space are detected.

The second operation here is simple and localised and it is the first one which has been the source of much research as to the optimum strategy for parallel implementation. In the earlier convolution operation the input data was an image array and the output data was also an image array. Because of the localised nature of convolution, both arrays could be partitioned into sub-images and there was a clear one-to-one mapping between input and output sub-images. That is, the data in a single input sub-image only influenced the results in a single output sub-image (plus some edge pixels in neighbouring sub-blocks). The implementation of the Hough transform is, however, quite a different matter. The input data is an edge detected image and the output data is a parameter array of approximately the same dimensions. If the input image is partitioned into sub-blocks the edge fragments arising from any one sub-block will contribute to widely spread regions of the Hough space. This requires a global distribution of results which can lead to long propagation delays in SIMD machines

and to memory access conflicts in MIMD machines. The following sections describe
how the Hough transform has been implemented on different types of processing array
and how some of these problems have been overcome.

4.4.1   The Hough Transform on an SIMD Machine

Rosenfeld *et al.* [Ros88] have carried out an analysis of the processing times required
to compute the Hough transform using various strategies on a mesh-connected SIMD
parallel processor. The processor is assumed to have **n** × **n** processing elements with
the image occupying one processor per pixel. The Hough array computed is also of
dimensions **n** × **n** and is superimposed on the mesh such that each PE represents a
unique combination of (ρ, θ) and possesses a counter containing the number of times
that this combination has been incremented. The Hough space is therefore overlaid
on the **n** × **n** image. As might be expected the authors go on to conclude that a mesh
connected processor is not well suited to tasks such as the Hough transform which
require global communication. This is because the summations involved in computing
the transform require that values be shifted to a common location and that this
requires in the order of $O(n)$ operations. The authors derive the computation time for
different strategies in terms of the various timings required to carry out operations
such as a shift, add, comparison, etc. They simplify the problem by making use of
the edge gradient supplied by the edge detector (in their case a Sobel) and update
only those values of θ consistent with this edge orientation. This is carried out by
only updating a narrow band of k angular values centred around the nominal edge
orientation. Three strategies are investigated and these will be described briefly here
together with the timings. Full implementation details are given in [Ros88]. The three
strategies which they explore are as follows:

(i) Computing the transform for one θ at a time: This is the simplest strategy
where values of θ, together with corresponding values of $\cos\theta$ and $\sin\theta$, are successively
broadcast to all PEs. A PE will only respond if it represents an edge pixel and if the
orientation of that edge lies within a narrow band of k values centred around θ. Those
PEs which respond evaluate the corresponding value of ρ from equation (4.15) This
leads to a set of values of ρ (corresponding to a single value of θ) arising at various
PEs scattered across the array. These must be gathered together to increment the
appropriate values of ρ in the Hough accumulator along column θ. This process is
carried out by a series of vertical cyclical operations in which each of the values of ρ
is used to increment a temporary counter of the appropriate value on their original
row. The values of the temporary counters are then shifted horizontally and summed
in column θ. The entire operation must be repeated n times, once for each value of θ.
The total processing time is given approximately as

$$n^2 b(2t_s + t_c + t'_+) \tag{4.16}$$

where
b is the number of bits used to store the values,
t_s is the time per bit for a *shifting* operation,
t_c is the time per bit for a *comparison* operation and

t'_+ is the time per bit for an *increment* operation.

Although many of the PEs are idle at each step, computing the transform for one θ at a time proves ultimately to be the fastest strategy as the communication stage is kept as simple as possible.

(ii) Using different θ's at each PE: This is similar to the previous stage; in principle each PE is only concerned with k values of θ centred around its nominal value. It is therefore possible to compute the algorithm in k stages rather than n. The algorithm does, however, require a large amount of temporary memory at each processor as k sets of results must be stored temporarily. The algorithm proceeds as in the previous section with the values of θ and its sine and cosine being broadcast to all PEs. Each PE element representing an edge pixel computes k sets of (ρ, θ) and stores them in local memory. Now each PE computes ρ for a different value of θ. The values are then cyclically shifted first vertically and then horizontally to increment the appropriate accumulator values for each set of (ρ, θ). Unfortunately it is necessary to count both ρ and θ intermediate values and not just ρ values as in the previous stage. This requires the use of n bit counters in each PE which not only places a large demand on memory but also scales up the shifting time, making this strategy ultimately much slower than the previous one, with a processing time approximately equal to

$$kn^2 b(t_s + tc + t'_+) \tag{4.17}$$

(iii) Sorting the (ρ, θ) values: This algorithm is aimed at moving the set of values of (ρ, θ) around the mesh in a more efficient manner. The values of θ and its sine and cosine are broadcast to all PEs and ρ and θ combinations of values are calculated as in the previous stage at each PE representing an edge.

The values of ρ and θ are then regarded as a concatenation of ρ and θ into a single $2b$ bit number. They are then sorted into ascending order by using a series of comparison and shifting operations. The entire array is then sorted into a 'snake like' pattern. The lengths of 'runs' of the same value of ρ and θ correspond to the final accumulator values of the Hough array. They are hence the number of counts for each point (ρ, θ) in the Hough space. Run lengths may be easily determined by comparison of values of adjacent PEs. As the data is sorted it is mapped into the accumulator array using a series of cyclical shifts which has been shown to be more efficient that the second method described above. A further saving in processing time can be made by packing all of the information from edge pixels into a sub-block in one corner of the image. This cuts down sorting time as the distance between each set of values is reduced. It is also possible to distribute some of the computations to the idle processors and speed up the total processing time. The approximate processing time is estimated as

$$knb(45t_s + 21t_c + t'_+) \tag{4.18}$$

For examples of mesh processors such as NASA's Massively Parallel Processor (MPP) [Pot85] and Martin Marietta Corp.'s Geometric Arithmetic Parallel Processor (GAPP) [Dav84] the number of cycles per bit is 3 for t_s, 3 for t_c and 2 for t'_+. Both the MPP and GAP have a cycle time of 100 ns and therefore according to [Ros88] their performance can be treated identically. The algorithms may be carried out for $n=128$, $b=7$ and k $=10$ in the following times:

(i)   Computing the transform for one θ at a time   130 ms
(ii)   Using different θ 's at each PE   920 ms
(iii)   Sorting the (ρ,θ) values   180 ms

It is, however, pointed out that the second method described is not possible on the GAPP due to lack of local memory. Rosenfeld also points out that whilst algorithms **(i)** and **(iii)** are very different in their approach they lead to similar results.

4.4.2   The Hough Transform on an MIMD Machine

For MIMD machines the main problem concerns the structuring of the memory rather than data propagation. The two main strategies to implement the Hough transform in an MIMD distributed memory system are either to distribute the *image memory* or to distribute the *accumulator memory* array across the PEs. If the image array is partitioned and distributed to a number of processors all of the processors require access to the whole of the Hough accumulator. This can lead to several processors attempting to access the same portion of memory at the same time. To prevent this, mutually exclusive access to the parameter space is necessary and must be implemented via a locking protocol. This clearly increases the overheads and reduces the efficiency of the overall system as some processors must wait in an idle state until the memory becomes free.

Alternatively the parameter space may be partitioned with each sub-array being allocated to a different processor. This prevents conflicts at the output but may well result in processors queuing up to read the same portion of the image at the input. One solution to the second problem is to acquire processing efficiency at the expense of memory by replicating the edge data at every processor (this would normally be done by storing the edge points as a list of their coordinates rather than storing an entire image array).

Thazhuthaveetil *et al.* [Tha91] have carried out a theoretical analysis into the relative efficiencies of distributing the image memory and the transform memory. They consider three cases which are summarised as follows:

Par-row: The edge image is partitioned into horizontal strips with a processor allocated to each strip. Each processor then updates the accumulator according to equation (4.15). This will invariably lead to several processors attempting to update the same area of the accumulator at the same time. Three types of locking protocol are considered. These are known as *fine, medium* and *coarse* grain locking. In coarse grain locking the entire Hough accumulator array is locked as a single shared data object with only one processor gaining access at any one time. Medium grain locking involves the partitioning of the Hough space into a number of segments with each segment being locked independently. In fine grain locking each memory cell is individually locked.

Par-window : This approach is similar to Par-row except that the image is partitioned into rectangular windows rather than strips. A separate processor is allocated to each window which then computes ρ and θ over the entire Hough array. It is a more general case of Par-row which requires a greater overhead to check if a given pixel lies within the window.

Par-θ : In this approach the angle θ is distributed among the processors with each processor being responsible for a different range of θ. The processors access the image in raster scan order with each processor computing the values of ρ and updating the accumulator for those values of θ in its range. No conflict is possible in Hough array access as each processor deals with a different value of θ. There may be a memory contention at the input whilst reading the image and to reduce this a variation on Par-θ is for each processor to begin its scan of the image at a different point.

The relative advantages and disadvantages of these methods were analysed and are summarised as follows:

- Par-row is essentially communication bound and Par-θ tends to be computation bound.

- Par-window performance is sensitive to edge pixel distribution and less efficient for large numbers of windows due to the overheads.

- Lock overheads were not found to be significant except for coarse grain locking.

A point echoed in other papers including the SIMD work was that simple algorithms which took no account of edge point distribution performed best. Crude attempts at load balancing generally increased overheads which made them less effective overall. Two pieces of work which result in very different attempts to improve on these approaches are those of Ben-Tzvi who adopts a synchronised processor approach and Austin who employs processor farming. These are described below.

Synchronised Processors

Ben-Tzvi *et al.* [Ben89, Ben90] have implemented a synchronous MIMD system for Hough transform implementation. It is based on the TMS320C25 digital signal processor and follows their earlier work on transputer arrays [Egh89]. Both the image and Hough accumulator arrays are distributed among the processors as shown in Figure 4.10. Each processor accesses only one part of each array, there is no overlap and therefore there can be no memory contention between processors. Every processor updates its own assigned portion of the Hough space for every (x,y) in the original image. This means that image edge data must be communicated between processors. In order to avoid lengthy communication of coordinate data a synchronous strategy is employed.

The computation of the Hough transform proceeds as follows. The processors scan through their own portion of the image. They are synchronised so that each one accesses the same relative position in its segment of the image at any given time. The processors maintain a count of the number of memory accesses carried out and can therefore determine the precise coordinates of the pixels being accessed by every other processor. The only information which therefore needs to be communicated between processors at this stage is a binary signal (from each processor) indicating the presence (or absence) of an edge pixel at each step. If none of the processors encounters an edge pixel at a given step no action is taken and they all proceed to the next pixel. If a

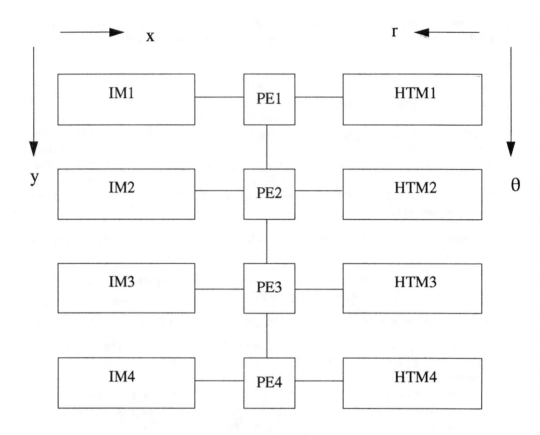

Figure 4.10 Distributed image memory, distributed Hough memory. Reproduced from Figure 1 of [Ben90] by permission of the publishers, Academic Press ©.

processor encounters an edge pixel this information is signalled simultaneously to all of the processors. The signals from all the processors are put into a register which is available to all processors.

Each processor therefore has sent to it two pieces of data at each step: a binary signal indicating if one or more processors has encountered an edge, and a register specifying which processors have encountered the edge. The topology is shown in Figure 4.11. The processors check the first signal and only read the second one if an edge has been signalled. If a given processor signals an edge pixel in its sector the other processors calculate its coordinates (x,y) from their relative position within their own sector and a knowledge of which processors have signalled. Each processor then updates its own portion of the Hough accumulator and proceeds to the next pixel. The process is summarised in Figure 4.12. This algorithm has been implemented on their OSMMA (Overlapped Shared Memory Multiprocessor Architecture) system and for a 256 × 256 image using four PEs the processing time is given as 21.72 ms with a cycle time of 100 ns. The architecture of OSMMA is very flexible and can be used to implement curve detection and edge thinning algorithms (see later).

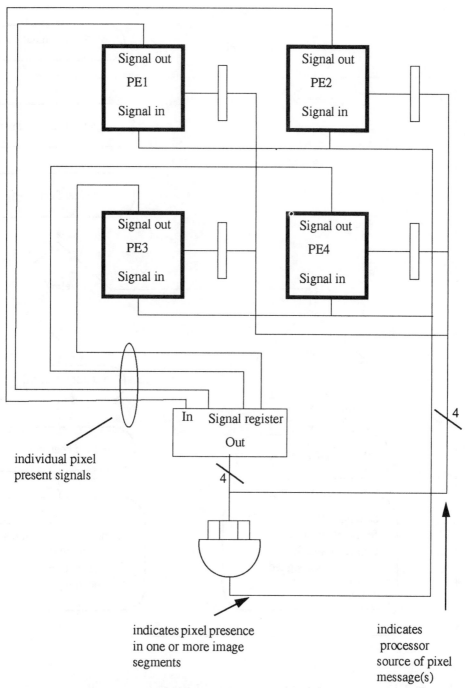

Figure 4.11 OSMMA processor communication. Reproduced from Figure 2 of [Ben90] by permission of the publishers, Academic Press ©.

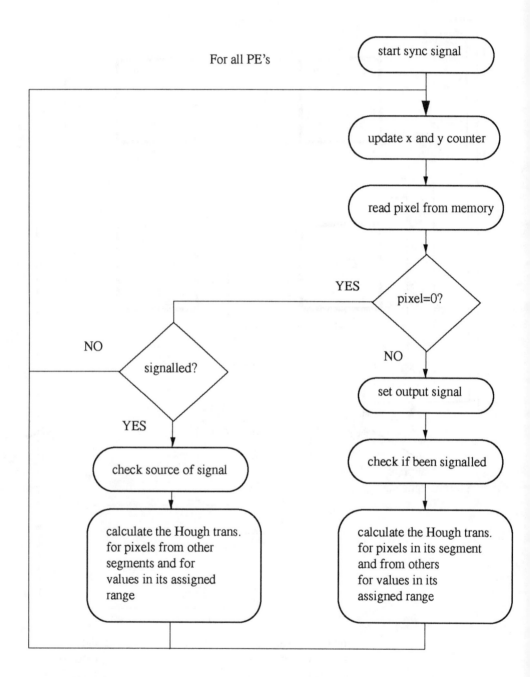

Figure 4.12   OSMMA flow diagram for parallel Hough transform. Reproduced from
Figure 3 of [Ben90] by permission of the publishers, Academic Press ©.

Processor Farming

A novel approach [Aus91] to the parallel implementation of the Hough transform on an MIMD transputer array is based on the Adaptive Hough transform [Ill87]. The adaptive Hough transform (AHT) achieves considerable computational speedup by exploiting the fact that the Hough space is generally sparsely populated and that we are normally only interested in the detail in the neighbourhood of a small number of peaks. The speedup is achieved by computing the Hough space initially to a coarse resolution. A decision is then made as to which areas of the space are likely to contain a peak and these are then computed to a finer resolution. Only limited sections of the accumulator space near to its peaks are computed to a high level of detail. When subject to a parallel implementation the AHT encounters the problem of load balancing as the location at which peaks will arise is not predictable.

The approach adopted by Austin *et al.* [Aus91] is to employ a master–slave architecture utilising a hybrid of geometric parallelism and the processor farm paradigm. The system initially computes a coarsely sampled version of the Hough space by allocating regions of the Hough space evenly across all of the processors. Each slave processor returns its results to the master as they are computed. The master then determines which areas of the Hough space are worthy of further investigation and it allocates these to the slave processors as they become free. The slave processors are given the coarse coordinates of a peak which they attempt to locate to a finer degree of accuracy by a process of *iterative focusing*. This means that they gradually increase the resolution adaptively in a direction where the peak is likely to occur and then pass the coordinates of the significant peaks back to the master processor. The application of [Aus91] is for plane detection which therefore requires a three-dimensional Hough space. Two algorithms are investigated: one makes use of the local surface normal gradient to limit the area of the accumulator which must be updated; the other, the so called naive algorithm, updates all candidate parameters. Results are presented for both toroidal wrap around and ring topologies and for the number of processors used no appreciable difference was noted. The processing time for the surface normal algorithm using 17 transputers is quoted at 111 ms for a 256×256 and at 35 ms for a 64×64 image. This algorithm is, however, prone to noise from the surface normal measurement. Work starvation can also be a problem with the smaller image, and no significant speedup was noted beyond three processors.

For the naive algorithm the processing time exceeds that of the surface normal algorithm by a threefold order of magnitude to 42-48 seconds. This is not really surprising as the Hough space includes an additional dimension. (All timings exclude image reading and display times.) Improvements to the Hough transform have recently been proposed by [Agh92] who obtain super-resolution estimates of line parameters by exploiting a recently developed signal processing technique known as ESPRIT. Such methods will no doubt result in an active area of research into the parallel implementation of such algorithms in future.

4.4.3 Thinning Algorithms

An operation closely related to edge detection is that of edge thinning. Frequently the edges produced from convolution operators such as the Sobel result in fragments which are substantially wider than one pixel. (The problem is not as pronounced with the Canny operator as the non-maximal suppression phase provides its own inherent thinning.)

The objective of the thinning algorithm is to erode the edge fragments by removing pixels in a direction perpendicular to the edge direction. It is important that thinning algorithms preserve the connectivity of edges. The result should be a connected one pixel wide skeletal edge. There are two basic approaches to edge thinning: the first involves deleting unwanted pixels by iteratively applying sets of masks, and the second makes use of logical and arithmetic operations for contour tracing. Only the mask approach is suitable for parallel implementation. There are various parallel implementations of thinning algorithms in the literature including [Zha84, Chi87]. The most recent is [Hay91] which is based on the OSMMA system described earlier. It uses a combination of 38 logical masks which are shown in Figure 4.13. The masks are compared to sections of an edge detected image and the centre pixel beneath the mask is set to zero (i.e. deleted) if the surrounding 3×3 region does not match any of the 38 patterns.

Notice that the centre pixel of the mask is always 1 so that the mask need only be applied at edge locations. The remaining 8 logical pixel values are loaded into the accumulator of the processor in a set order. Of the 256 possible combinations of these pixels, 38 represent a match and the rest do not. The comparison is carried out by indexing a lookup table with the word formed from the 8 pixel values. By this method the number of masks may be increased without changing the processing time. One iteration is therefore sufficient to complete the thinning and the time taken to process a 256×256 image with 8 processors is given as approximately 216 ms, which is an order of magnitude faster than the corresponding times for earlier methods [Zha84]. A comparative evaluation of fast thinning algorithms on a multiprocessor architecture is given in [Hay92].

4.5   OTHER EDGE DETECTION TECHNIQUES

Whilst the strategy outlined above for edge detection is the most common approach there are other techniques which consider the image as the noise corrupted version of an 'ideal' image. The ideal image consists of smooth regions and distinct, continuous step edges. The approach is one of **image reconstruction**. It employs a regularisation method to modify pixel values such that they incorporate general properties expected in an image. These strategies usually involve the optimisation of a global cost function over an entire image. The cost function [Bla86] contains a number of terms such as the mean square error between the original image and the reconstructed image plus a penalty for discontinuities and edge processes. Optimisation techniques such as simulated annealing [Gem84] and graduated non-convexity are used to minimise the cost function over thousands of iterations [Mur86]. The position of edge processes in the final reconstructed image is indicated by the 'detected edges'. These techniques tend to be very computationally expensive and therefore not yet fast enough to be included in real time systems. They have, however, provided the basis for much research. Kashko [Kash87] has implemented reconstruction schemes taking between 5

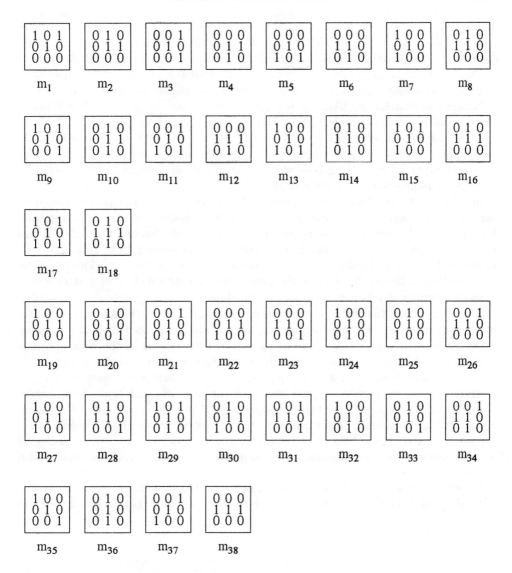

Figure 4.13 Thirty-eight thinning masks. Reproduced from Figure 3 of [Hay91] by permission of the IEE Publishing Department ©.

and 40 seconds (depending on the complexity of line functions) to reconstruct a 256 × 256 image on an AMT DAP.

An interesting point to note here is that in most parallel implementations of serial algorithms the mathematical properties are the same as for the serial case. i.e. the algorithm is essentially working on the same numbers. However, in the case of image reconstruction the parallel algorithm has different properties from the serial approach. The algorithm proceeds by computing new values for each pixel depending on the properties of its neighbours and assuming that the values of neighbouring pixels are held fixed. It is not therefore possible to update all pixel values simultaneously.

The solution to this problem is to apply a system of 'chequerboard' updating where only half the pixels are updated at any one time (those corresponding to the white squares on a chessboard) and the other half (those corresponding to the black squares) are updated at the next cycle. As might be expected the process of 'chequerboard' updating takes longer to converge than corresponding sequential algorithms.

Neural networks are likely to provide a growth area in the near future and a recent example of their application to edge detection is given in [Agh91].

A novel paper on edge grouping is [Sau90] which employs a *symbolic* scale space technique. Edge primitives are aggregated and pruned into meaningful structures. This paper attempts to bridge the gap between low level early descriptors and symbolic data descriptors representing real world objects.

In addition to the hardware implementations described in the previous section, increases in processing speed may be achieved by the exploitation of **software parallelism** [Pac89]. This technique is quite independent of the hardware parallelism and may be superimposed to obtain additional savings in processing time. It may also be introduced with sequential processing machines to realise time savings. The technique is applied when the word length of the processing element's ALU is of greater length than the number of bits used to represent the data.

The idea is that the image data is packed into the ALU such that several image pixels are processed simultaneously during any one arithmetic operation. A processing overhead is introduced in the form of packing and unpacking of the data and it is suggested that this can be most effectively handled by a dedicated coprocessor to convert the data from say a 3×3 neighbourhood mask format into packed form.

The technique appears to be most efficient for applications with limited numbers of grey levels and particularly for binary images. The MACSYM system [Ina84] is an example of a multiprocessor binary image processing system for document reading which exploits this technique. Also the CESARO-2 [Pac87] system is quoted as achieving an eightfold increase in processing speed for binary images in a low cost robot vision system.

Finally no work on parallel image processing would be complete without a mention of CLIP [Duf75, Duf76, Woo80, Woo88] which continues to make a large contribution in this area.

4.6   SYSTEMS

Much of the literature in this area describes complete systems containing a module which implements edge detection algorithms in parallel rather than edge detection for its own sake. As well as the earlier examples of TINA and MARVIN, examples of complete systems containing edge detection implemented in parallel are the ISOR [Mur88] structure from motion system, a real time 3D object tracking system [Ste90], a system for robot road following [Mor90] and a prototype robotic assembly system [Fal89].

4.7   SUMMARY AND CONCLUSIONS

This chapter has reviewed some of the techniques and architectures used for parallel edge detection and related algorithms. The very different nature of the early convolution operation and the later grouping and thinning operations means that no one architecture is ideally suited to both stages. In general SIMD architectures work well for locally connected operations performed uniformly across the entire image. They are not, however, well suited to the later data dependent operations of edge thinning and tracking. The movement of data around the processing elements is a major problem with SIMD architectures. In general it appears to be more efficient to use simple algorithms even if this means that several processors remain idle, rather than attempt to keep them all busy by routing tasks around the array.

The later operations of edge detection are better performed by MIMD architectures as processors may carry out different operations on different parts of the image. The main difficulty with these architectures is that of memory distribution among the processors. This is particularly acute for techniques such as the Hough transform which requires global access by every processor. The operations to be performed are data dependent and are only executed in certain areas of the memory which can lead to work starvation of the processors. Two techniques of edge detection to combat this problem are *processor synchronisation* and *processor farming*. Processor synchronisation removes the need to transmit pixel addresses by arranging for all of the processors to access the same relative position in their memory sector at the same time. Processor farming is used to make the processing array switch smoothly from a data parallelism approach in the early stages of edge detection to task parallelism in the later stages. Only certain areas of the memory are investigated and tasks are allocated to processors as they become free.

A very serious problem in image analysis on MIMD machines is that of getting the image data into and out of the processing array. The MARVIN system employs a number of processors in the form of an image bus to route data rapidly around the array in order to deal with this problem.

Alternative methods of edge detection based on image reconstruction, neural networks and symbolic processing are all areas which should prove to be fruitful over the next few years.

REFERENCES

[Agh91]   Aghajan, H.K., Schaper, C.D., Kailath, T., (1991), Edge detection for optical image metrology using unsupervised neural network learning. *Neural Networks for Signal Processing– Proceedings of 1991 IEEE Workshop* (ed. B.H. Juang, S.Y. Kung, C.A. Kamm), 188-197, IEEE Signal Processing Society.

[Agh92]   Aghajan. H.K., Kailath, T., (1992), A subspace fitting approach to super resolution multi-line fitting and straight edge detection. *IEEE Acoustics, Speech and Signal Processing*, ICASSP-92, San Francisco.

[Aus91]   Austin, W.J., Wallace, A.M., Fraitot, V., (1991), Parallel algorithms for plane detection using an adaptive Hough transform. *Journal of Image and Vision Computing*, Vol. 9, No. 6.

120 S. MARSHALL

S. MARSHALL

[Bal82] Ballard, D.H., Brown, C.M., (1982), *Computer Vision*, Prentice-Hall Inc., 123-128.

[Ben89] Ben-Tzvi, D., Naqvi, A.A., Sandler, M., (1989), Efficient parallel implementation of the Hough transform on a distributed memory system. *Journal of Image and Vision Computing*, Vol. 7, No. 3, 167-172.

[Ben90] Ben-Tzvi, D., Naqvi, A.A., Sandler, M., (1990), Synchronous multiprocessor implementation of the Hough transform. *Computer Vision, Graphics and Image Processing*, Vol. 52, 437-466.

[Bla86] Blake, A., Zisserman, A., (1986), Weak continuity constraints in computer vision. *University of Edinburgh Computer Science Report*.

[Bro89] Brown, C.R., Rygol, M., (1989), MARVIN: Multiprocessor Architecture for Vision. *Applying Transputer Based Parallel Machines* (Proc. OUG-10), IOS Press.

[Bro90] Brown, C.R., Rygol, M., (1990), An environment for the development of large applications in Parallel C. *Applications of Transputers 2*, Proc TA90, IOS Press.

[Can86] Canny, J., F., (1986), A computational approach to edge detection. *IEEE Trans. PAMI, Vol. 8, No. 6*, 679-689.

[Cha90] Chaudhary, V., Aggarwal, J.K., (1990), Parallelism in computer vision: a review. In *Parallel Algorithms for Machine Intelligence and Vision*, (ed. V. Kumar, P.S. Gopalakrishnan), Springer-Verlag.

[Chi87] Chin, R.T., Wan, H, K., (1987), A one-pass thinning algorithm and its parallel implementation. *Computer Vision, Graphics and Image Processing*, Vol. 40, 30-40.

[Cyp89] Cypher, R., Sanz, J.L.C., (1989), SIMD architectures and algorithms for image processing and computer vision. *IEEE Trans. ASSP*, Vol. 37, No. 12, 2158-2173.

[Dav84] Davis, R., Thomas, D., (1984), Systolic array chip matches the pace of high-speed processing. *Electron. Design*, Oct 31, 207-218.

[Duf75] Duff, M.J.B., Watson, D.M., (1975), CLIP3: A Cellular Logic Image Processor. In *New Concepts and Technologies in Parallel Information Processing*, (ed. E.R. Caianello), 75-86, Noordhoff International.

[Duf76] Duff, M.J.B., (1976), CLIP4: A large scale integrated circuit array parallel processor. *Proc. Int. Joint Conf. on Pattern Recognition*, 728-733.

[Egh89] Eghtesadi, S., Sandler, M., (1989), Implementation of the Hough transform for intermediate-level vision on a transputer network. *Microprocessors and Microsystems*, Vol. 13, No. 3, 212-218.

[Fal89] Fallside, F., Jahanbin, M.R., Marsland, T.P., Tabandeh, A.S., Wright, M.W., (1989), A protoype, integrated, CAD-based robotic assembly system. *IEEE Conference on Robotics and Automation*, Arizona.

[Gem84] Geman, S., Geman, D., (1984), Stochastic relaxation, Gibbs Distributions and the Bayesian Restoration of images. *Trans. IEEE PAMI, Vol. 6*, 721-741.

[Hay91] Hayat, L., Naqvi, A., Sandler, M.B., (1991), Parallel implementations of fast thinning algorithm using image compression. *Proc. IEE-I*, Vol. 138, No. 6, 615-620.

[Hay92] Hayat, L., Naqvi, A., Sandler, M.B., (1992), A comparative evaluation of fast thinning algorithms on a multiprocessor architecture. *Journal of Image and Vision Computing*, Vol. 10, No. 4, 210-218.

[Hou62]   Hough, P.V.C., (1962), Methods and means for recognizing complex patterns. *U.S. Patent No. 3069654.*

[Ill87]   Illingworth, J., Kittler J., (1987), The adaptive Hough transform. *IEEE Trans. PAMI*, Vol. 9, No. 5, 690-698.

[Ina84]   Inagaki, K., Kato, T., Hiroshima, T., Sakai, T., (1984), MACSYM: a hierarchical parallel image processing system for event-driven pattern understanding of documents. *Pattern Recognition*, Vol. 17, No. 1, 85-108.

[INM89]   INMOS Ltd., (1989), *Transputer Technical Notes*, Prentice-Hall.

[Kash87] Kashko, A., (1987), A parallel approach to graduated nonconvexity on an SIMD machine. *QMC Computer Science Report 406.*

[Kass87] Kass, M., Witkin, A., Terzopoulos, D., (1987), Snakes: Active contour models. *First International Conference on Computer Vision*, London, June 1987, 259-268, IEEE Computer Society Press, Washington, DC.

[Mar80]   Marr, D., Hildreth, E., (1980), Theory of edge detection. *Proc. Royal Soc. London*, Vol. 207, 187-217.

[Mor90]   Morgan, A.D., Dagless, E.L., Milford, D.J., Thomas, B.T., (1990), Road edge tracking for robot road following: a real time implementation. *Journal of Image and Vision Computing*, Vol. 8, No. 3, 233-241.

[Mow87]   Mowforth, P., Gillespie, L., (1987), Edge detection as an ill-posed specification task. *Turing Institute Research Memoranda*, TIRM-87-026.

[Mur86]   Murray, D.W., Kashko, A., Buxton, H., (1986), A parallel approach to the picture restoration algorithm of Geman and Geman on an SIMD machine. *Journal of Image and Vision Computing*, Vol. 4, No. 3.

[Mur88]   Murray, D.W., Castelow, D.A., Buxton, B.F., (1988), From an image sequence to a recognised polyhedral object. *Journal of Image and Vision Computing*, Vol. 6, No. 2, 107-120.

[Pac87]   Pachowicz, P.W., (1987), Unpacked and packed data processing by the hardware neighbourhood parallel system. *Proc. 5th SCIA*, Stockholm, Sweden, 245-251.

[Pac89]   Pachowicz, P.W., (1989), Image processing by software parallel computation. *Journal of Image and Vision Computing*, Vol. 7, No. 2, 122-128.

[Pag88]   Page, I., (1988), The Disputer: A dual paradigm parallel processor for graphics and vision. In *Parallel Architectures and Computer Vision*, Clarendon Press, Oxford.

[Pol85]   Pollard, S.B., Mayhew, J.E.W., Frisby, J.P., (1985), PMF: A stereo correspondence algorithm using disparity gradient limit. *Perception*, Vol. 14, 449-470.

[Por87]   Porrill, J., Pollard, S.B., Pridmore, T.P., Bowen, J., Mayhew, J.E.W., Frisby, J.P., (1987), TINA: The Sheffield AIVRU vision system. *IJCAI 9*, Milan, 1138-1144.

[Pot85]   Potter, J.L., (Ed), (1985), *The Massively Parallel Processor*, MIT Press, Cambridge, MA.

[Pres89] Preston, K., (1989), The Abingdon cross benchmarking survey. *Computer*, Vol. 22, No. 7, 9-18.

[Prew70] Prewitt, J., (1970), Object enhancement and extraction. *In Picture Processing and Psychopictorics* (ed. B. Lipkin, A. Rosenfeld), 75-149, Academic Press, New York.

[Rob65] Roberts, L. G., (1965), Machine perception of three dimensional solid. *Optical and Electro-optical Information Processing* (ed. J.T. Tippell) 159-197, MIT Press.

[Ros88] Rosenfeld, A., Ornelas, J., Hung, Y., (1988), Hough Transform algorithms for mesh-connected SIMD parallel processors. *Computer Vision, Graphics and Image Processing*, Vol. 41, 293-305.

[Ruf88] Ruff, B.P.D., (1988), Pipeline architecture for video rate Canny operator used at the initial stage of a stereo image analysis system. In *Parallel Architectures and Computer Vision*, Clarendon Press, Oxford.

[Ryg91a] Rygol, M., Pollard, S., Brown, C., (1991), Multiprocessor 3D vision system for pick and place. *Journal of Image and Vision Computing*, Vol. 9, No. 1.

[Ryg91b] Rygol, M., Pollard, S., Brown, C., (1991), MARVIN and TINA: A multiprocessor 3D vision system. *University of Sheffield, Artificial Intelligence Vision Research Unit Report 54*, AIVRU54.

[Sau90] Saund, E., (1990), Symbolic construction of a '2-D' scale space image. *IEEE Trans. PAMI*, Vol. 12, No. 8.

[Sch89] Schalkoff, R.J., (1989), *Digital Image Processing and Computer Vision*, John Wiley and Sons, 147-148.

[Ste90] Stephens, R.S., (1990), Real-time 3DS object tracking. *Journal of Image and Vision Computing*, Vol. 8, No. 1, 91-96.

[Tha91] Thazhuthaveetil, M.J., Shah, A.V., (1991), Parallel Hough transform algorithm performance. *Journal of Image and Vision Computing*, Vol. 9, No. 2, 88-92.

[Wei85] Weijak, J.S., Buxton, H., Buxton, B.F., (1985), Convolution with separable masks for early image processing. *Computer Vision, Graphics and Image Processing*, Vol. 32, 279-290.

[Woo80] Wood, A.M., (1980), The CLIP4: Array processor. *J. British Interplanetary Society*, Vol. 33, 338.

[Woo88] Wood, A.M., (1988), Intermediate-level vision, relations and processor arrays: An application of Clip4 to image sequence analysis. In *Parallel Architectures and Computer Vision*, Clarendon Press, Oxford.

[Wys89] Wysocki, J., (1989), A parallel implementation of the Canny operator for the DAP. *Queen Mary College Technical Report*.

[Zha84] Zhang, T.Y., Suen, C.Y., (1984), A fast parallel algorithm for thinning digital patterns. *Communications of the ACM*, Vol. 27, No. 3, 236-239.

5

Parallel Segmentation Algorithms

M. PROESMANS, A. OOSTERLINCK

5.1 INTRODUCTION

This chapter gives an overview and a general framework for parallel implementation of image processing techniques. The communication strategy and model of parallel computation will be discussed starting from a brief overview. Among the wide range of vision tasks already investigated, we select the most promising and currently less attended vision algorithms. These comprise in general simultaneous suppression of noise, sharpening of discontinuities and labelling of visual cue data. The discussion on parallel architecture naturally involves the popular transputer networks.

5.2 PARALLELISM IN COMPUTER VISION

Computer vision tasks require an enormous amount of computation, especially when the data is in image form, demanding high performance computers for practical real–time applications. In general, however, parallelism appears to be the only economical way to achieve the performance required for vision tasks.

There have been several methods of classifying computer architectures. The most common classification, based on control (Flynn), considers the presence or absence of potential multiplicity in the instruction and data stream of the computer. Given that, four classes of computers result, SISD (single instruction, single data), MISD (multiple instruction, single data), SIMD (single instruction, multiple data) and MIMD (multiple instruction, multiple data).

A SIMD computer is implemented as a set of identical synchronized processing elements capable of simultaneously performing the same operation on different data.

Parallel Algorithms for Digital Image Processing, Computer Vision and Neural Networks, ed. I. Pitas
© 1993 John Wiley & Sons Ltd

Although the processor elements execute in parallel, processor elements may be programmed to ignore any particular instruction. SIMD computers are also called processor arrays. MIMD computers consist of a number of fully programmable processors each capable of executing its own program.

The applicability of an architecture to image processing problems depends upon their nature, ranging from low level image processing to more complex image analysis. Historically, a fundamental bottleneck in processing capability has been perceived to lie with the low level image processing task. Many SIMD and pipeline architectures have been developed for low level image processing applications, whereas special architectures for high level image analysis have received less attention. Considering the low level architectures, algorithms have been suggested for binary array processors [Ree80], pipeline processors [Ste79], and special function processors such as systolic arrays [Kun82, Yen81], or pyramid arrays [Dye82].

In general, low-level vision tasks require computations for each pixel of the image. This is indicative of the amount of computation required. Fortunately, these computations are usually highly regular in the sense that the same computations are performed for all portions of the image. These low level tasks consist of, for example, smoothing operations, convolutions, histogram generation, Hough transforms, clustering algorithms, etc. Thus the key issue in designing parallel algorithms is to distribute the execution of the various parts of the algorithm over a number of communicating processors.

Considering for example the convolution operation, each processor in a SIMD processor array accesses its allocated subimage in an order which eliminates communication with adjacent processors for the calculation at the boundaries of the subimage: the image is divided into overlapping subimages and each processor works on its subimage. Kung and Song [Kun82] present a 2 dimensional convolution algorithm on a 2 dimensional systolic array, and Lee and Aggarwal [Lee87] present a parallel 2 dimensional convolution scheme for a mesh connected array processor consisting of the same number of simple processor elements as the number of pixels in the image. The algorithms for histogram generation are in general machine dependent. Conceptually, the image is divided into equal subimages and histograms are generated for each subimage, which are then combined in a second pass to form the histogram for the entire image (e.g. [Ram86]). In clustering analysis the squared-error clustering technique seems to be the most popular one and being iterative, requires substantial computation ([Ni85, Li86]). Contour extraction caught the attention of several researchers [Gue85, Ber84], as did contour labelling [Lev86].

Unlike low level vision, computations in intermediate or high level vision are not always regular, and thus, parallelism is not always evident. Most of the intermediate level vision tasks are region growing ([Gam85]) or relaxation and segmentation algorithms.

A very popular field in image processing is region labelling. The process of region labelling partitions an image into disjoint subsets which correspond to different objects in the image [Asa81]. Region labelling is one of the basic operations in image processing. Once an image has been partitioned into regions, these regions can be studied, described and possibly identified. Because of its importance in image analysis, much work has been done in the area of region labelling [Asa81]. In an algorithm of Morrin [Mor76], labeling is achieved by a combination of boundary following and raster scanning. Grant and Reid's [Gra81] method records the object boundary and scan line intercepts in an array form. The algorithm of Agrawala and Kulkarni [Agr77] is based on the technique of tracking. The algorithm keeps track of the continuations of all boundaries found in a row scan of the image. There has been a lot of interest in developing parallel architectures and algorithms for the labelling problem. Reisis and Kumar [Rei85] and Alnuweiri and Kumar [Aln89] use a relaxation technique on a mesh connected computer. They achieve an efficient implementation by using a special memory architecture and stack managment. In [Sun87] raster scanning is implemented using a divide-and-conquer strategy. The image is partitioned into a set of subimages which are processed concurrently by multiple processing elements on a hypercube machine. The algorithm can handle a variety of region types including holes, convoluted boundaries, interleaved boundaries, etc. Lim et al. [Lim89] and Cypher et al. [Cyp87] abstract the task of labelling into a special case of the problem of labelling connected components, that is, the problem of assigning labels to connected nodes in a graph. This type of approach typically achieves a time complexity of $O(\log N)$. Wu [Wu89] converts the labelling problem into a search for region boundaries for which chain and crack codes are used to represent the boundaries. Last but not least, many segmentation or labelling algorithms are based on deterministic or stochastic relaxation. The image is then modelled as a Markov random field (e.g. [Der87]).

This small overview describes most of the algorithms that have been investigated for implementation on various parallel structures. The interested reader might find good overviews of these types of vision tasks in [Cha90, Ree84]. However, to give the reader an idea of the true nature of a parallel algorithm, we would like to discuss a very recent class of image analysis techniques, which are based on regularization, and try to combine a number of classical vision tasks such as smoothing or noise suppression, segmentation and labelling, into a unifying concept. The global idea is to extract some feature map, e.g. discontinuities, together with additional maps which try to suppress noise or spurious signals, and on the other hand enhance important local features in the images. Most of these algorithms are in one way or another suitable for parallel implementation. Furthermore, considering the parallel architectures described above, less attention has been paid to a currently very popular processor, the transputer. Transputer networks are in fact very flexible building blocks, which enable the construction of any arbitrary processor topology.

5.3 REGULARIZING FUNCTIONALS

5.3.1 Introduction

Traditional edge detection methods detect discontinuities at a very local scale. In general the local change in amplitude of the original data is estimated by the outcome of some gradient operator, and if a threshold is exceeded somewhere, that locality can be considered to be a discontinuity. A sequential tracking algorithm can be used to link the separate sites.

These methods are in fact very noise sensitive. Several researchers (e.g. [Ter86], [Bla86]) have been investigating more global approaches such as plate or membrane models to recontruct the noisy original data. In that case the solution is to be found using regularizing functionals. Regularization techniques have been proved to be quite suitable for solving ill-posed problems such as optical flow, stereo matching, shape from shading, surface reconstruction and others. For such problems the analytic formulation is not enough for finding a reliable solution on the basis of the data alone. The solution might be non-unique or unstable or may not even exist. Regularizing the solution may render it well-posed in the Hadamard sense [Tik77]. Therefore regularization forms a unifying and sound mathematical basis for the treatment of ill-posed problems. The underlying idea is to make additional assumptions, i.e. to impose some physically plausible constraints on the solution(s). Often one assumes the eventual solution to be smooth (the so-called "smoothness constaint"). Although adding smoothness constraints offers a suitable framework for the solution of ill-posed problems, a number of important problems remain unaccounted for. It was evident from the start that simple smoothing conditions do not yield satisfactory results, especially with jump discontinuities since these are blurred. Some refinements to the original membrane and plate models have therefore been put forward, for example weak continuity constraints [Bla86, Ter86]. Others [Gam87, Gem84] introduced line processes which are guided by intensity data. Intensity also played a crucial role in the discontinuity preserving algorithms proposed by Cornelius and Kanade [Cor83] and Nagel and Enckelmann [Nag86, Nag87].

We will elaborate a scheme for discontinuity propagation that is similar to the above approaches. The idea is to fit the original data with a cracking plate, based on theories of fracture mechanics. In other words, the plate model which regularizes the reconstruction problem will be provided with a mechanism by which the discontinuities propagate very similarly to cracks in solid materials. In fracture mechanics, if a local discontinuity is present as an initial tear or crack, it will influence the local stress field much stronger than in current regularization models, due to large stress concentrations near the crack tip. Of course, from our point of view these are mere analogies. The crucial element is that crack growth shows a facilitation effect in the longitudinal direction and an inhibitory effect in the transverse direction.

5.3.2 Variational Formulation

The representation of visible surfaces has attracted considerable interest as an intermediate goal of computer vision since Gibson made the conjecture that human visual perception amounts to perception of visible surfaces, and this research gained even more momentum since the introduction of ideas about $2\frac{1}{2}D$ sketch by Marr. This section will develop a particular computational approach to intermediate-level vision. The problem itself is a non-trivial inverse problem. The visual field is only known in a limited number of samples. As such the surface will not be determined uniquely everywhere; there remain infinitely many feasible surfaces. Furthermore, the estimates are subject to errors, and high spatial frequency noise can locally perturb the surface radically. From these considerations it is clear that our problem is ill-posed, since they do not guarantee that a solution exists, or that it will be unique or stable.

Regularization provides a systematic approach to reformulating this ill-posed problem as a well-posed and effectively solvable variational principle. The regularized plate bending problem tries to find a surface $w = f(x, y)$ which approximates as well as pos-

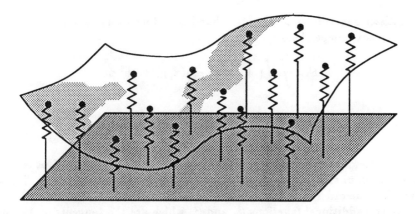

Figure 5.1 Physical interpretation of the plate model.

sible a given set of points (in this case the image intensity data), while the surface itself should possess some degree of "smoothness".

Let K be a linear space of admissible functions. The regularized problem is formulated mathematically as finding $w \in K$ according to the variational principle

$$\Pi(w) = \min_{v \in K} \Pi(v), \quad \Pi(v) = \mathbf{E}(v) + \mathbf{D}(v)$$

where the term $\mathbf{D}(v)$ must ensure that the solution w does not deviate too much from the original measurements c_i (measurements such as intensity values, depth information, etc.), and $\mathbf{E}(v)$ should guarantee some degree of continuity of the function. A physical model is depicted in Figure 5.1. The visual data apply forces in the z-direction which deflect the surface from its nominally planar state. The penalty function $\mathbf{D}(v)$ is the total deformation energy of a set of ideal springs attached to the data.

Experiments carried out by Grimson [Gri81] seem to indicate that second order plate surfaces (C^2) exhibit an appropriate degree of smoothness. From a mathematical point of view, the energy density of a C^2-surface depends upon the principal curvatures of the surface (e.g. [Bla86, Ter86]):

$$e = \frac{A}{2}(\kappa_1^2 + \kappa_2^2) + B\kappa_1\kappa_2$$

In general κ_1 and κ_2 introduce second order derivatives. Originally, Grimson proposed a rather simple functional

$$E = \int\int_\Omega e \, dx dy = \int\int_\Omega (f_{xx}^2 + 2f_{xy}^2 + f_{yy}^2) dx dy$$

Terzopoulos [Ter86, Ter84] suggested the use of additional derivatives in order to cope with discontinuities in zero or first order derivatives:

$$E = \int\int \rho(x, y)(\tau(x, y)(f_{xx}^2 + 2f_{xy}^2 + f_{yy}^2) + (1 - \tau(x, y))(f_x^2 + f_y^2)) dx dy$$

Blake and Zisserman [Bla86] on the other hand introduced some non-linearity in order to gain viewpoint-independence:

$$E = \int \int (\ (f(x,y) - g(x,y))^2 \cos^2 \phi$$

$$+ \mu^2 (\frac{(1 + f_y^2)f_{xx} + (1 + f_x^2)f_{yy} - 2f_x f_y f_{xy}}{(sec^2\phi)^3}) \ )dxdy$$

One of the problems with these expressions is that second order derivatives complicate the discretization of the governing equations and the incorporation of the discontinuities. Therefore the order of the functional should be reduced. This can be achieved by introducing two additional functions β_x and β_y which are the tangents on the surface in the x and y direction respectively. An additional advantage is that we can achieve a greater viewpoint independence. If we write the energy density as a function of the so-called mean and gaussian curvature

$$e = 2A\mathbf{H}^2 + (B - A)\mathbf{K} \tag{5.1}$$

and rewrite these curvatures as a function of β_x and β_y

$$\mathbf{H} = \frac{1}{2}\left(\frac{\partial \beta_x}{\partial x} + \frac{\partial \beta_y}{\partial y}\right) \quad \mathbf{K} = \frac{\partial \beta_x}{\partial x}\frac{\partial \beta_y}{\partial y} - \left(\frac{1}{2}\left(\frac{\partial \beta_x}{\partial y} + \frac{\partial \beta_y}{\partial x}\right)\right)^2$$

the potential energy takes the form (divide equation (5.1) by $\frac{A}{2}$ and define $\nu = \frac{B}{A}$)

$$e = \left(\frac{\partial \beta_x}{\partial x}\right)^2 + \left(\frac{\partial \beta_y}{\partial y}\right)^2 + 2\nu\frac{\partial \beta_x}{\partial x}\frac{\partial \beta_y}{\partial y} + \frac{1 - \nu}{2}\left(\frac{\partial \beta_x}{\partial y} + \frac{\partial \beta_y}{\partial x}\right)^2 \tag{5.2}$$

and ν becomes the well-known Poisson coefficient in elasticity theory. To account for the external forces which are responsible for the bending of the plate, we consider our plate to be connected to the original data by a number of springs. Let $c(i)$ be the value of the i-th sample of the original data and $w(i)$ the corresponding value of the plate that is to be found. The energy involved in stretching those springs can be written as $\mathbf{D} = \sum_{i=1}^{N} \frac{\xi_i}{2}(w(i) - c_i)^2$ where ξ_i denotes the stiffness of a spring at location i, with the linear force–displacement characteristic $F = \xi_i(w(i) - c_i)$ (Hooke's law). The surface will then reach equilibrium as the energy of the whole system is at a minimum. So we have to minimize a functional of the form

$$\int\int_\Omega e(x,y)dxdy + \sum_{i=1}^{N} \frac{\xi_i}{2}(w(i) - c_i)^2$$

The three unknown functions w, β_x and β_y are, however, not independent. In fact the functional should be subjected to some constraints $\beta_x = \frac{\partial w}{\partial x}$, $\beta_y = \frac{\partial w}{\partial y}$ which can be introduced in our functional by the Lagrange multiplier method

$$\int\int_\Omega e(x,y) + kc(x,y)$$

where kc ensures that the constraints are nearly satisfied. The term kc is the *penalty function*. Thus the overall surface response to the given loads can be found by minimizing the functional

$$\int\int_\Omega \left(\frac{\partial \beta_x}{\partial x}\right)^2 + \left(\frac{\partial \beta_y}{\partial y}\right)^2 + 2\nu\frac{\partial \beta_x}{\partial x}\frac{\partial \beta_y}{\partial y} + \frac{1-\nu}{2}\left(\frac{\partial \beta_x}{\partial y} + \frac{\partial \beta_y}{\partial x}\right)^2$$

$$+ k\left(\left(\beta_x - \frac{\partial w}{\partial x}\right)^2 + \left(\beta_y - \frac{\partial w}{\partial y}\right)^2\right)\,dxdy + \sum_{i=1}^N \frac{\xi_i}{2}(w(i) - c_i)^2 \qquad (5.3)$$

5.3.3 Finite Element Discretization

In the finite element method representation, a function is approximated by a linear combination of local support basis functions. In visual applications, a natural tessellation would follow the image sampling pattern, i.e. the domain is tesselated into square subdomains with sides of length h. Within the subdomain or "*element*", the function values depend upon the node values (pixel values) according to an interpolation function.

In order for the finite element approach to converge, the element interpolation functions should be appropriately chosen. In finite element terms, they have to be complete and compatible [Red86]. The order of the interpolation function depends upon the order of derivatives in the functional. The Terzopoulos case would require a quadratic interpolation functional. Non-linear functionals such as Blake's are even more complex to solve. For our plate problem we can restrict ourselves to a very simple bilinear interpolation function. This is not only of computational interest but it will simplify the discussion on parallelizing in this class of algorithms. This function assumes the form:

$$w^e(x, y) = axy + bx + cy + d$$

(where w^e denotes the function values w within an element e). Using these approximations for w, β_x, β_y, we can write the functional as

$$\mathrm{II} = \sum_{e=1}^{n_e} \int_{\Omega_e} \left(\frac{\partial \beta_x^e}{\partial x}\right)^2 + \left(\frac{\partial \beta_y^e}{\partial y}\right)^2 + \frac{1}{2}\left(\left(\frac{\partial \beta_x^e}{\partial y} + \frac{\partial \beta_y^e}{\partial x}\right)^2\right)$$

$$+ k\left(\left(\beta_x^e - \frac{\partial w^e}{\partial x}\right)^2 + \left(\beta_y^e - \frac{\partial w^e}{\partial y}\right)^2\right)\,dxdy + \sum_{i=1}^N \frac{\xi_i}{2}(w(i) - c_i)^2$$

in which each of the terms can be evaluated separately. The number of elements is $n_e = (n-1)^2$, n being the size of the image. This discrete functional can be minimized by setting to zero the partial derivatives with respect to each of the node values $w_{i,j}, \beta_{x,i,j}, \beta_{y,i,j}$.

$$\frac{\partial \mathrm{II}}{\partial w_{i,j}} = 0 \quad \frac{\partial \mathrm{II}}{\partial \beta_{x,i,j}} = 0 \quad \frac{\partial \mathrm{II}}{\partial \beta_{y,i,j}} = 0 \quad i, j = 1, ..., N$$

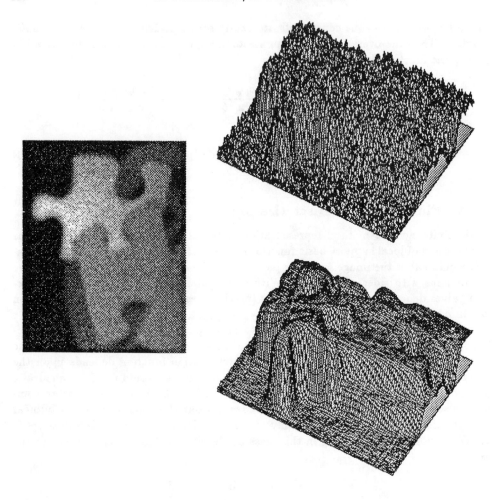

Figure 5.2 Left : original noisy intensity image. Upper right : corresponding intensity surface. Lower right : solution of the plate bending problem.

We omit the details of the calculation of these derivatives. The final result is a linear system of $3n^2$ equations given below by means of computational molecules [Ter84]. This $3n^2$ system of equations can be interpreted as a 3×3 system in which the unknowns are the *images* w, β_x, β_y, and the coefficients convolution masks.

$$\left(\begin{bmatrix} -1 & 0 & -1 \\ -2 & 8 & -2 \\ -1 & 0 & -1 \end{bmatrix} + \tfrac{1}{6}kh^2 \begin{bmatrix} 1 & 4 & 1 \\ 4 & 16 & 4 \\ 1 & 4 & 1 \end{bmatrix} \right) *\beta_x + \tfrac{1}{2} \begin{bmatrix} 1 & 0 & -1 \\ 0 & 0 & 0 \\ -1 & 0 & 1 \end{bmatrix} *\beta_y - \tfrac{1}{3}kh \begin{bmatrix} -1 & 0 & 1 \\ -4 & 0 & 4 \\ -1 & 0 & 1 \end{bmatrix} *w = 0$$

$$\frac{1}{3}\begin{bmatrix} 1 & 0 & -1 \\ 0 & 0 & 0 \\ -1 & 0 & 1 \end{bmatrix} * \beta_\bullet + \left(\begin{bmatrix} -1 & -2 & -1 \\ 0 & 8 & 0 \\ -1 & -2 & -1 \end{bmatrix} + \frac{1}{3}kh^2 \begin{bmatrix} 1 & 4 & 1 \\ 4 & 16 & 4 \\ 1 & 4 & 1 \end{bmatrix} \right) * \beta_y - \frac{1}{3}kh \begin{bmatrix} 1 & 4 & 1 \\ 0 & 0 & 0 \\ -1 & -4 & -1 \end{bmatrix} * w = 0$$

$$kh \begin{bmatrix} -1 & 0 & 1 \\ -4 & 0 & 4 \\ -1 & 0 & 1 \end{bmatrix} * \beta_\bullet + kh \begin{bmatrix} 1 & 4 & 1 \\ 0 & 0 & 0 \\ -1 & -4 & -1 \end{bmatrix} * \beta_y + \left(4k \begin{bmatrix} -1 & -1 & -1 \\ -1 & 8 & -1 \\ -1 & -1 & -1 \end{bmatrix} + 6\xi \right) * w = 6\xi C$$

This system of equations has computationally desirable properties. Its matrix is positive definite, sparse, banded and symmetric, due to the local support of the finite element representation. Its size, on the other hand, may become extremely large, since the number of pixels in typical images can range from 10^4 to 10^5 or more. This combination of properties suggests the application of iterative techniques such as relaxation methods. We used a parallel coupled Gauss–Seidel scheme in which three equations are solved simultaneously for each point (i, j), and the results are immediately exploited in subsequent iterations. Figure 5.2 shows the finite element representation of the plate for the intensity image on the left. The figure clearly shows that the noise is dramatically reduced, at the expense of edges that are blurred.

5.3.4   Discontinuities

As mentioned, the straightforward application of smoothness conditions does not allow for satisfactory results in the neighbourhood of discontinuities. One way to deal with discontinuities is to associate an energy term, i.e. penalizing term, and add it to the functional:

$$\Pi(v) = \mathbf{E}(v) + \mathbf{D}(v) + \nu B$$

B represents the presence of discontinuities within the image. This kind of functional is, however, non-convex and hard to solve. Mumford and Shah [Mum88] investigated the functional, on a purely theoretical basis, and found that only a restricted number of discontinuity configurations could result from minimization. Many researchers tackled the problem by linearizing the functional, using for example non-convex algorithms [Bla86], or subsequent linear approximations [Ter84], while others solved the problem by more stochastic solution methods such as simulated annealing (Kirkpatrick, Maroquin, Geman and Geman [Gem84]).

The introduction of discontinuities can easily be explained by a physical analogue: cracks in solid materials. The presence of cracks in solids has been the subject of intensive research which has led to a new branch in mechanics, namely fracture mechanics [Bro86, Sne69, Law75].

A first observation is that any stress situation can be described by three independent modes of crack growth: the opening, tearing and sliding mode (Figure 5.3). In all three modes it has been found that there is a very large stress concentration in the

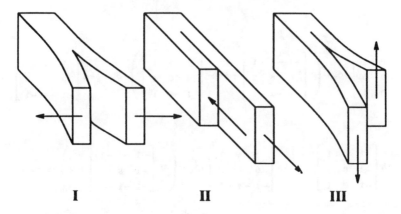

Figure 5.3 The three modes of crack growth for a plate in vertical direction: I. opening mode, II. sliding mode, III. tearing mode.

neighbourhood of the crack tip. Applied mathematics shows us that there exists a singularity in the stress function:

$$\sigma_{ij} = \frac{K}{\sqrt{2\pi r}} f_{ij}(\theta) \tag{5.4}$$

where $f_{ij}(\theta)$ is a function of the geometry of the solid in the neighbourhood of the crack, K is the so-called stress intensity factor [Irw57, Irw58], and crack propagation will occur if K exceeds some critical value k_c.

For a plate model as described above and assuming that the plate is subject only to small vertical displacements (i.e. the pixel coordinates remain fixed), only the tearing mode (III) crack growth has to be considered. For this mode, discontinuities can be placed between the elements of the finite element discretization. In our case, the element mesh being the square image sampling pattern, a discontinuity is supposed to go through the pixels and may thus be considered to be a concatenation of straight linear pieces lying along the sides of the surrounding elements. Since the number of pixel values per pixel exceeds 1 on a discontinuity line, the model should duplicate the pixels in order to use more nodes (i.e. variables) for the same spatial coordinates.

5.3.5 Propagation

Thus far the "crack system" is considered to be static. However, if an unbalanced force acts on any volume element within the cracked body, the element will be accelerated, and thereby acquire kinetic energy, i.e. the crack or discontinuity will propagate [Gri21].

Gamble and Poggio [Gam87] and Geman and Geman [Gem84] introduced a line process by which discontinuity propagation towards neighbouring points is facilitated once an initial discontinuity has originated, with a preference for smooth paths. These schemes are rather *ad hoc*, however, since the various configurations have to be specified in conjunction with a cost assigned to them by the user of the program.

Another approach would be to follow the physical analogue. If we consider an incre-

Figure 5.4 Subsequent step of the crack propagation process.

mental extension δc of some crack, it may logically - not only on a physical, but also on a mathematical basis - be proposed that the favoured direction θ will be the one which maximizes the decrease in total energy. In other words, crack growth will take place in the direction for which the energy release rate is maximum. If we define the energy release rate as $R = \frac{\partial E}{\partial c}$ then this criterion of maximum release rate would be

$$\frac{\partial R}{\partial \theta} = 0 \qquad \frac{\partial^2 R}{\partial \theta^2} < 0$$

Experiments show that the energy distribution of each of the terms is generally concentrated in the neighbourhood of large stress regions. Among these terms, the penalty term $(\beta_x - \frac{\partial w}{\partial x})^2 + (\beta_y - \frac{\partial w}{\partial y})^2$ displays the appropriate behaviour for discontinuity detection which corresponds to the characteristics of the transverse forces in elasticity theory. Furthermore, the energy distribution in the neighbourhood of the crack increases hyperbolically while approaching the crack tip in accordance with fracture mechanics. Figure 5.4 shows some intermediate steps of a propagation process based on these energy functions.

The equations which result from the finite element discretization are highly suitable for iterative implementations on parallel structures. Some important neurophysiological issues fit into this framework, such as cooperative–competitive mechanisms and multi-resolution interactions.

5.4   PARALLEL IMPLEMENTATION

5.4.1   Image Processing and Transputers

There are a number of alternative approaches to the problem of speeding up an algorithm, namely

- hardware acceleration
- design of fast sequential algorithms
- design of parallel algorithms

Since hardware acceleration involves the introduction of dedicated hardware, it has been left out of the scope of this research. Sometimes, the run time can be decreased sequentially by an appropriate control of the relaxation parameters of the iterative scheme. As is the case in this particular problem, the convergence rate can be dramatically improved by using Chebyshev acceleration where

$$\omega = \frac{1}{1 - \frac{\tau^2 . \omega}{4}}$$

(ω being the relaxation parameter). In general, parallelism is the only convenient way of speeding up the algorithm.

Most architectures used for low level vision implementation are of the SIMD type. Lin and Kumar [Lin91], for example, present a $2D$ parallel algorithm for discrete relaxation techniques. Derin and Won [Der87] introduce a segmentation algorithm based on deterministic relaxation with varying neighbourhood structures. Carver Mead [Car89] investigated the possibility of implementing relaxation type algorithms directly in VLSI circuits.

One of the most flexible and currently very popular processors is the *transputers*. A transputer is no more than a microcomputer with its own local memory and with links for connecting one transputer to another (Figure 5.5). The transputer architecture defines a family of programmable VLSI components. The definition of the architecture falls naturally into the logical aspects which define how a system of interconnected transputers is designed and programmed, and the physical aspects which define how transputers, as VLSI components, are interconnected and controlled. A typical member of the transputer product family is a single chip containing processor, memory, and communication links which provide point to point connection between transputers. In addition, each transputer product contains special circuitry and interfaces adapting it to a particular use. A transputer can be used in a single processor system or in networks to build high performance concurrent systems. A network of transputers and peripheral controllers is easily constructed using point-to-point communication. This allows transputer networks of arbitrary size and topology to be constructed.

To provide synchronized communication, each message has to be acknowledged. Consequently, a link requires at least one signal wire in each direction. A link between two transputers is implemented by connecting a link interface on one transputer to a link interface on the other by two one-dimensional signal lines, along which the data is transmitted serially.

The parallel implementation of our plate bending problem supports the realization of an arbitrary communications network. The transputers typically form an $m \times n$

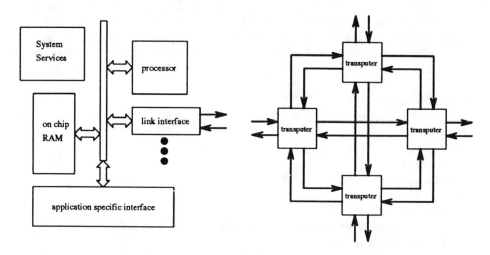

Figure 5.5 Left: transputer architecture. Right: transputer communication links.

topology in which m and n can be chosen. Each of the transputers will have a unique place within the $m \times n$ configuration, which is determined by its row and column.

5.4.2 Divide and Conquer

Many parallel algorithms suggested [Kun82, Lee87] are dedicated to a specific low level vision task. We will try to build a framework which enables an efficient treatment of not only the plate bending problem, but also of general low-level tasks such as convolutions and other relaxation schemes such as diffusion equations. Figure 5.6

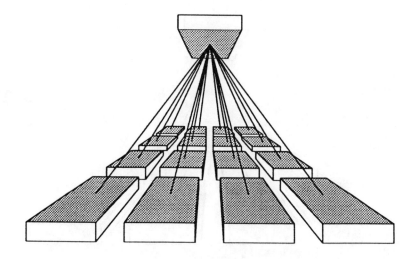

Figure 5.6 Communication between host computer and transputer platform.

depicts the communication channels between the host processor and the transputers. They are used for the division of the original image from the host processor to the working transputers. Each transputer will receive a subimage which will differ by at most one pixel in length and width from other transputer subimages, in order to achieve optimal subdivision of the task. The general idea can be illustrated by the following flow chart.

```
void divide_array() {
  W = W0; H = H0; n = n0; m = m0;
  while (m > 0)
    {
    w = W/m+1;
    while (n > 0)
      {
      h = H/n+1;
      send subimage of size w x h to current transputer
      H = H-h; n = n-1;
      }
    H = H0; n = n0;
    W = W-w; m = m-1;
    }
  }
```

5.4.3   Pipeline

Before any process can be run on the transputer, the host has to send instructions or commands to tell the transputers what operation they have to perform. For low-level image processing tasks the computations on each of the transputers are in general identical or at least very similar. In that case the commands are the same for

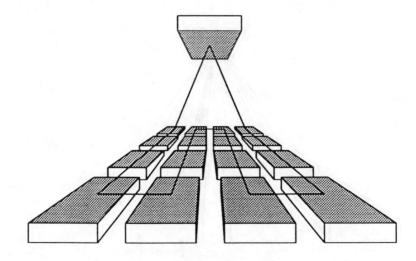

Figure 5.7   Pipeline through $m \times n$ transputer configuration.

each transputer. Within our framework, we create a pipeline communication channel through the $m \times n$ transputer configuration, which guarantees the fastest throughput of the commands to the transputers. An additional advantage of this channel is that it can be used for passing global parameters, entered on the host process, or for gathering global status information.

```
void create_pipeline() {
  link_host_to_proc (0,0)

  if (n mod 2 == 0)
    last_proc = (0,n-1)
  else
    last_proc = (m-1,n-1)

  for (i = 0; i < m; i++)
  for (j = 0; j < n; j++) {
    proc = (i,j)

    if (proc == last_proc)
      link_proc_to_host
    else {
      if (j { mod 2 = 0) {
        if (i == m-1) next_proc = (i,j+1)
        else next_proc = (i+1,j)
      }
      else {
        if (i == 0) next_proc = (i,j+1)
        else next_proc = (i-1,j)
      }
    }
    link_proc_to_next_proc
  }
}
```

5.4.4   Neighbours

Computation at the boundaries of transputer subimages suggests communication with adjacent transputers in order to gather the necessary information. For simple low level tasks, such as convolution, this interaction can be avoided by subdividing the original image into overlapping subimages. For relaxation schemes, however, such an approach would not be appropriate, since at each iteration the boundary values have been changed. Figure 5.8 shows the links which enable the transputers to exchange information (e.g. about the plate's behaviour or existence of discontinuities at their boundaries). Note that the global performance of the transputer configuration will be largely influenced by the timing constraints of these links, since at each iteration the transputers will have to update their boundary values via these channels. It is

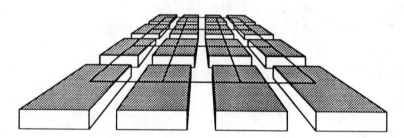

Figure 5.8   Communication between neighbouring transputers.

therefore of crucial importance that the communication should be realized as efficiently as possible.

Figure 5.9 and the flow chart below shows how to gather all information from the eight neighbouring transputers in just four steps. The idea is to allocate enough transputer memory, so that on each side of the actual subimage enough space is provided for additional boundary information. In each step a part of this space is filled and can then be exploited in subsequent steps. The size of the boundary t for the plate bending problem is 1, since the computations require a 3×3 environment at each pixel.

```
void interchange (direction, size) {
  if (i mod 2 == 0) {
    send <size> boundary pixels values to <direction>
    get <size> boundary pixels values from <opposite direction>
  }
  else {
    get <size> boundary pixels values from <opposite direction>
    send <size> boundary pixels values to <direction>
  }
}

void exchange_border_information() {
  interchange (right, $h$)
  interchange (down, $w+t$)
  interchange (left, $h+t$)
  interchange (up, $w+2t$)
}
```

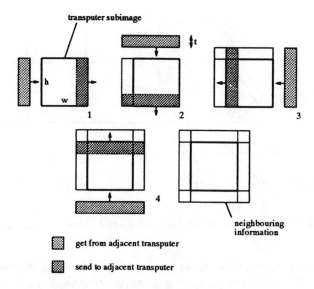

Figure 5.9 Subsequent steps in data transfer between transputers at each iteration.

5.4.5   Parallelization

The communications network has proved successful not only for the plate model but also for similar relaxation schemes. Note that due to the intrinsic sequential nature of the algorithm, i.e. iterations have to be carried out one after the other, parallelization concerns only the space domain. The general outlook of the program is as follows:

```
main(HOST)() {
  divide_array();
  pipeline_command(start);
  while not(converged) pipeline_command(continue);

  pipeline_command(converged);
  collect_results();
}

main(TRANSPUTER)() {
  accept_array();
  pipeline_command(get_status);
  while (continue) {
    for (color = 1; color <= 4; color++) {
      exchange_border_information();
      update_solution();
    }
  pipeline_command(send_error);
  return_results();
  }
```

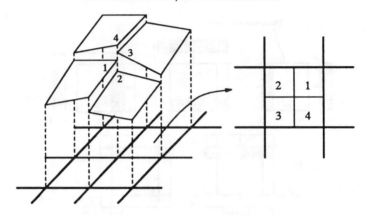

Figure 5.10   Multiple values for same spatial coordinate (i.e. pixel).

The implementation of an algorithm on the parallel network, however, is not always straightforward. The incorporation of discontinuities into the model involves duplication of the pixels in order to represent multiple pixel values per pixel (Figure 5.10). Therefore special arrangements have to be taken for the eventual equations, since the element contributions have now been split apart. Our plate model is capable of handling this kind of discontinuity since the equations only depend on the element contributions of the node under consideration.

For instance, the first computational molecule [Ter86] we encounter in the equations described above, can be written as a summation of the contributions of the 4 surrounding elements (the centre pixel is depicted in bold).

$$
\begin{bmatrix} -1 & 0 & -1 \\ -2 & 8 & -2 \\ -1 & 0 & -1 \end{bmatrix} = \begin{bmatrix} -1 & 0 \\ -1 & 2 \\ -1 & 0 \end{bmatrix} + \begin{bmatrix} \\ -1 & 2 \\ -1 & 0 \end{bmatrix} + \begin{bmatrix} 0 & -1 \\ 2 & -1 \\ \end{bmatrix} + \begin{bmatrix} 2 & -1 \\ 0 & -1 \\ \end{bmatrix}
$$

We only need an additional data structure to keep up with the relation between the elements and the corresponding nodes. As in Figure 5.10, each pixel corresponds to a 2×2 matrix, in which each entry $(1, ..., 4)$ corresponds to a corner value of the pixel element. Note, however, that for such a data structure, we do not need to interchange all four pixel nodes with adjacent transputers: boundary information to be sent to the right, for example, only involves node values 1 and 4. Therefore, the image of 2×2 pixel nodes can readily be treated as an ordinary image of double size.

The Gauss–Seidel scheme as such is not suitable for parallel implementation since new values are immediately exploited in the subsequent computations. If such a scheme were applied separately on each transputer subimage, the global system would not be equivalent to the single processor system and furthermore, its performance would approximate that of the Jacobi relaxation scheme: in the limit where the number of processors reaches the number of pixels the Gauss–Seidel scheme would have degraded to a Jacobi scheme which has proved to be not as effective as the Gauss–Seidel scheme.

However, with an appropriate choice of the order in which the nodes are updated according to the plate equations, the relaxation scheme can be made independent of

Figure 5.11 Four-coloured Gauss–Seidel relaxation scheme.

the number of transputers and/or their configuration. An obvious approach is to divide the collection of nodes in a number of groups, each of which is treated separately. In numerical analysis, this kind of approach is referred to as a "coloured relaxation" scheme, where we associate a colour with each of the groups. For example, the parallel implementation of the classical Poisson equation would require a so-called red–black scheme. In our case a four-coloured scheme would be appropriate, since each pixel requires a 3×3 neighbourhood to calculate its new value. Each transputer will be assigned a code that represents the colour in which it has to operate.

5.5 RESULTS

The algorithms are implemented on a computing surface (MEIKO) consisting of 28 *T800* transputers. The computing surface is mapped onto a host SUN Sparc station. Each of the transputers has a 32 bit processor and internal memory ranging from 1 to 4 Mbytes. The instruction throughput at 30 MHz reaches 30 Mips peak and 15 Mips sustained. The standard INMOS communication links allow networks of transputer family products to be constructed by point-to-point connections with no external logic. The *IMS T800* links support ths standard operating speed of 10 Mbits/s. Each link can transfer data bidirectionally at up to 2.35 Mbytes/sec. Software has been written in a parallel C language (CStools MEIKO).

Figures 5.12 and 5.13 show some results of the plate model. These results have a number of interesting properties compared with other plate models in the literature. By the introduction of the angular functions β_x and β_y, we realized that the finite element representation of the plate could be achieved with smaller support interpolation functions, which nonetheless are complete and compatible. This simplified the integration of discontinuities a great deal. Furthermore, we gain more viewpoint independence and the angular functions allow direct incorporation of surface normals. The plate's functional has the nice characteristic that it explicitly includes a shear deformation term which is responsible for the mode III propagation. This enabled us to implement the scheme for facilitated discontinuity propagation.

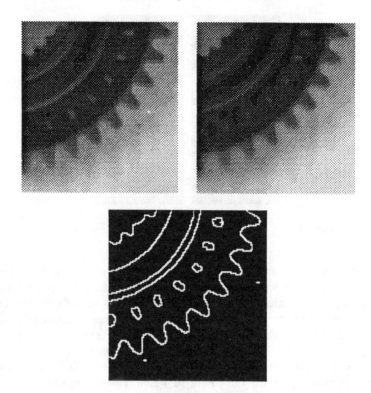

Figure 5.12 The segmentation of a toothed wheel. Upper left: original image. Upper right: plate model. Below: extracted discontinuity line ($\nu = 0$, $k = 0.1$, $h = 1$, $\xi = 1.0$).

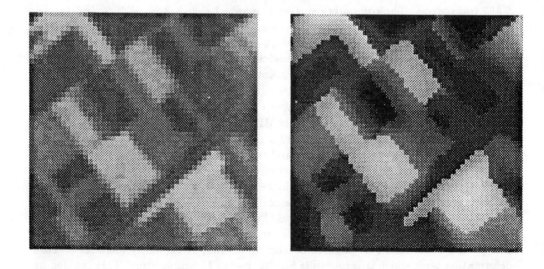

Figure 5.13 Landscape image of a SPOT-satellite. Left: original image. Right: the cracked plate ($\nu = 0$, $k = 0.1$, $h = 1$, $\xi = 1.0$).

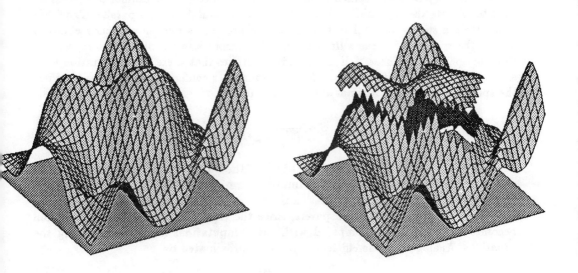

Figure 5.14 Two intermediate steps in the propagation process on the SPOT-image : the blob corresponds to the most central white patch in the original grey value image.

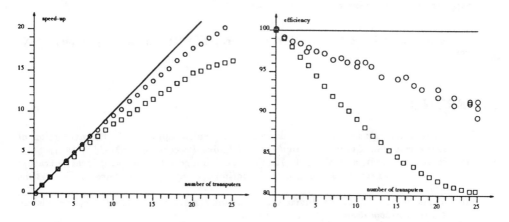

Figure 5.15 Speed-up and efficiency : the squares denote a worst-case simulation, the circles correspond to realistic timing measurements.

The quality of a parallel algorithm is determined by a number of quantities, the most important being the speed-up (Figure 5.15). The *speed-up* is defined as the running time of the sequential algorithm executed on one processor, divided by the running time of the parallel algorithm executed on a number of processors. The *processor utilization* or *efficiency* is defined as the speed-up divided by the number of processors used to execute the algorithm. Clearly, the best one can do with a parallel algorithm is to attain a speed-up equal to the number of processors and an efficiency equal to one. If the speed-up increases linearly with increasing number of processors, we say that the speed-up is linear. A linear speed-up implies that there is no saturation with an increasing number of processors. For the transputer configuration described earlier, the speed-up can be approximated by the formula

$$S \sim \frac{1}{(\frac{1}{\sqrt{x}} + 2f\frac{d}{n})^2}$$

where n is the size of the image, d the width of the boundary information, and x the number of transputers; f reflects the importance of the communication between the transputers in respect to the calculation time. It is clear that saturation does show up with increasing numbers of transputers, since the time necessary for communication becomes relatively larger compared with the computations involved in solving the equations. Analogously, the efficiency can be approximated by

$$\eta = \frac{1}{(1 + 2f\frac{d}{n}\sqrt{x})^2}$$

Clearly, if no communication were necessary ($d = 0$), the efficiency would reach 100%.

ACKNOWLEDGMENTS

We gratefully acknowledge the support of the EC ESPRIT BRA project 3001 "INSIGHT".

REFERENCES

[Agr77]   A. K. Agrawala and A. V. Kulkarni. A sequential approach to the extraction of shape features. *Computer Graphics and Image Processing*, 6:538–557, 1977.

[Aln89]   H. M. Alnuweir, and V. K. P. Kumar. Fast image labeling using local operators on mesh-connected computers. *International Conference on Parallel Processing*, 1989.

[Asa81]   T. Asano and N. Yokoya. Image segmentation scheme for low level computer vision. *Pattern Recognition*, 14(11):173–186, 1981.

[Ber84]   P. Bertolazzi and M. Pirossi. A parallel algorithm for the optimal detection of a noisy curve. *Comput. Vision Graphics Image Processing*, 27:100–113, 1984.

[Bla86]   A. Blake and A. Zisserman. Invariant surface reconstruction using weak continuity constraints. *IEEE conf. on Computer Vision and Pattern Recognition*, 1986.

[Bro86]   D. Broek. *Elementary Engineering Fracture Mechanics*. Martinus Nijhoff Publishers, 4th revised edition, 1986.

[Car89]   Carver Mead. *Analog VLSI and Neural Systems*. Addison-Wesley Publishing Co,

1989.

[Cha90]   V. Chaudhary and J. K. Aggarwal. *Parallelism in computer vision, a review*, in *Parallel Algorithms for Machine Intelligence*. Springer, 1990.

[Cor83]   N. Cornelius and T. Kanade. Adapting optical flow to measure object motion in reflectance and X-ray sequences in *Proc. ACM Siggraph/Sigart Interdisciplinary Workshop on Motion: Representation and Perception*, pages 50–58, 1983.

[Cyp87]   R. E. Cypher, J. L. C. Sanz and L. Snyder. Practical algorithms for image component labeling on SIMD mesh connected computers. *Pattern Recognition*, 1987.

[Der87]   H. Derin and C. Won. A parallel image segmentation algorithm using relaxation with varying neighbourhoods and its mapping to array processors. *Comp. Vision Graphics and Image Proc.*, 40:213–218, 1987.

[Dye82]   C. R. Dyer. A VLSI Pyramid machine for hierarchical parallel image processing, in *Proc. IEEE Conf. on Patt. Recog. and Image Proc.*, pages 381–386, 1982.

[Gam85]   J. P. Gambotto and O. Monga. A parallel and hierarchical algorithm for region growing. *Proc. IEEE Conf. on Comp. Vision Pattern Recognition*, 1985.

[Gam87]   E. Gamble and T. Poggio. Visual integration and detection of discontinuities: the key role of intensity edges. A.I.Memo 970, MIT, October 1987.

[Gem84]   S. Geman and D. Geman. Stochastic relaxation, Gibbs distributions and the Bayesian restoration of images. *IEEE Trans. on Pattern Analysis and Machine Intelligence*, 6(11), 1984.

[Gra81]   G. Grant and A. F. Reid. An efficient algorithm for boundary tracking and feature extraction. *Computer Graphics and Image Processing*, 17:225–237, 1981.

[Gri21]   A. A. Griffith. The phenomena of rupture and flow in solids. *Phil. Trans. Roy. Soc. London* A221:163-197, 1921.

[Gri81]   W. E. L. Grimson. *From Images to Surfaces : A Computational Study of the Human Early Visual System*. MIT press, Cambridge, MA, 1981.

[Gue85]   C. Guerra. A VLSI algorithm for the optimal detection of a curve, in *Proc. of Workshop on Comput. Arch. for Pattern Anal. Mach. Intell.* 1985.

[Irw57]   G. R. Irwin. Analysis of stresses and strains near the end of a crack traversing a plate. *Trans. ASME J. Appl. Mech.*, 1957.

[Irw58]   G. R. Irwin. *Fracture, Handbuch der Physik*, volume 6, Springer, Berlin, 1958.

[Kun82]   H. T. Kung and S. W. Song. A systolic 2-D convolution chip, in *Multicomputers for Image Processing: Algorithms and Programs*. Academic Press, New York, 1982.

[Law75]   B. R. Lawn and T. R. Wilshaw. *Fracture of Brittle Solids*. Cambridge Solid States Science Series, Cambridge University Press, 1975.

[Lee87]   S. Y. Lee and J. K. Aggarwal. Parallel 2-D convolution on a mesh connected array processor. *IEEE Trans Pattern Anal. Mach. Intell.*, 9(4), 1987.

[Lev86]   S. Levialdi and V. Cantoni. Contour labeling by pyramidal processing, in *Intermediate-Level Image Processing* (ed. M. J. B. Duff), Academic Press, 1986.

[Li86]   X. Li and Z. Fang. Parallel algorithms for clustering on hypercube SIMD computers, in *Proc IEEE Conf. on Comp. Vision Pattern Recognition*, 1986.

[Lim89]   W. Lim, A. Agrawal and I. Nekludova. A fast parallel algorithm for labeling connected components in image arrays, *Parallel Processing for Computer Vision and Display* (ed P. M. Den, R. A. Earnshow and T. R. Heywood), Addison-Wesley 1989.

[Lin91]   W. M. Lin and V. K. Kumar. Parallel algorithms and architectures for discrete relaxation techniques. In *Proc. Comp. Vision and Pattern Recognition*, pages 514–515, 1991.

[Mor76]   T. H. Morrin. Chain-link compression of arbitrary black-white images. *Computer Graphics and Image Processing*, 5:172–189, 1976.

[Mum88]   D. Mumford and J. Shah. Optimal approximations by piecewise smooth functions and associated problems. *Comp. Vision*, 1988.

[Nag86]   H. H. Nagel and W. Enckelmann. An investigation of smoothness constraints for the estimation of displacement vector fields from image sequences. *IEEE Trans. Pattern Analysis Machine Intelligence*, 8(5):565–593, 1986.

[Nag87]   H. H. Nagel. On the estimation of optical flow: relations between different approaches and some new results. *Artificial Intelligence*, 8:299-324, 1987.

[Ni85]   L. M. Ni and A. K. Jain. A VLSI systolic architecture for pattern clustering. *IEEE Trans. Pattern Analysis Machine Intelligence*, 7, 1985.

[Ram86]   D. V. Ramanamurthy and N. J. Dimopoulos. Parallel algorithms for low level vision on the homogeneous multiprocessor. In *Proc IEEE Conf. on Comp. Vision Pattern Recognition*, 1986.

[Red86]   J. N. Reddy. *Applied Functional Analysis and Variational Methods in Engineering.* McGraw-Hill, 1986.

[Ree80]   A. P. Reeves. A systematically designed binary array processor. *IEEE Trans. Comput.*, C-29:278–287, 1980.

[Ree84]   A. P. Reeves, Parallel computer architectures for image processing. *Comp. Vision, Graphics and Image Proc.*, 25:68-88, 1984.

[Rei85]   D. Reisis and P. Kumar. Parallel processing of the labeling problem. *International Conference on Parallel Processing*, 1985.

[Ste79]   R. Sternberg. Parallel architectures for Image processing. In *Proc. 3rd Int. IEEE COMPSAC*, Chicago, pages 712–717, 1979.

[Sne69]   I. N. Sneddon and M. Lowengrub. *Crack Problems in Classical Theory of Elasticity.* SIAM Series of Applied Mathematics, 1969.

[Sun87]   M. H. Sunwoo, B. S. Baroody and J. K. Aggarwal. A parallel algorithm for region labeling. *Int. Conf. on Systems, Man and Cybernetics*, 1987.

[Ter84]   D. Terzopoulos. Multilevel reconstruction of visual surfaces: variational principles and finite element representations, in *Multiresolution Image Processing and Analysis* (ed. A. Rosenfeld), Springer-Verlag, New York, 1984, pages 237-310.

[Ter86]   D. Terzopoulos. Image analysis using multigrid relaxation methods. *IEEE Trans. Pattern Analysis Machine Intelligence*, 8(2):129–139, 1986.

[Tik77]   A. Tikhonov and V. Arsenin. *Solutions of Ill-Posed Problems.* Winston, Washington DC, 1977.

[Wu89]   A. Y. Wu, S. K. Bhaskar and A. Rosenfeld. Parallel processing of region boundaries. *Pattern Recognition*, 22(2):165–172, 1989.

[Yen81]   D. W. L. Yen and A. V. Kulkarni. The ESL systolic processor for signal and image processing. In *IEEE Comp. Soc. Workshop on Comp. Arch. for Patt. Anal. and Image Database Management*, pages 273-277, Hot Springs, 1981.

6

MIMD and SIMD Parallel Range Data Segmentation

R. B. FISHER, E. TRUCCO, M. D. BROWN, A. C. HUME

6.1   INTRODUCTION

Model-based object recognition is based on a comparison of models and data. This implies that models and data must be expressed in or converted to a representation which allows easy comparison. Recently, our main research effort has been investigating three-dimensional object recognition, using surface-based geometric model primitives and range data [NAI91]. Hence, one requirement of the project is to compute a description of the surfaces visible in the range data in terms of surface patches. This is a specialised region-finding process, producing image regions that correspond to the distinct surface patches of the object and scene being observed. There are several ways to find these matches, but the main two are based on either parametric surface fitting or use of local shape properties to group pixels belonging to the same patch. Besl [BES87], Grimson and Lozano-Perez [GRI85] and Brady *et al.* [BRA85] give a good overview of the different methods. This chapter considers an algorithm based on the latter approach.

The segmentation module discussed in this chapter is part of Imagine2 [FIS89], a system aimed at model-based recognition of complex 3-D curved objects from range data. In Imagine2, object models are composed of *surface patches* belonging to different *shape classes*, where each shape class is characterised by its curvature properties. Hence, the task of the segmentation module is to describe the input surface in terms of such patches, thus providing the subsequent model invocation and matching stages with a suitable representation of the data.

The **rangeseg** program described here segments range surfaces into homogeneous

---

Parallel Algorithms for Digital Image Processing, Computer Vision and Neural Networks, ed. I. Pitas
© 1993 John Wiley & Sons Ltd

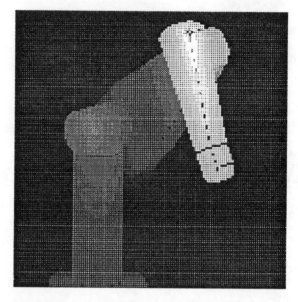

Figure 6.1   Depth shaded raw range image.

patches by developing a local differential representation based on the concept of *local surface curvature*, a technique which has been widely employed in computer vision for segmentation and recognition. Surfaces can be uniquely characterised at every point by two independent curvature measures, and each range image pixel can be classified into one of {planar, positive cylindrical, negative cylindrical, positive elliptical, negative elliptical or hyperbolic}. Grouping adjacent pixels with the same classification provides the regions. An example of a raw range image appears in Figure 6.1 and the patches extracted appear in Figure 6.2.

We have chosen to describe the **rangeseg** program because it requires a number of algorithms with different computational structures:

- many stages require only local neighbourhoods (e.g. 3×3 or 7×7) suggesting a SIMD implementation,

- some stages require only single pixel operations also suggesting a SIMD implementation,

- the global diffusion smoothing stage requires inversion of a large number of 128 (or 256, 512) entry tri-diagonal matrices suggesting a pipeline or MIMD implementation, and

- the final region-finding process is a parallel label-propagation process, which has a more MIMD task-parallel structure.

A consequence of this program structure is that no single model of parallel activity is perfectly suited for the whole program.

In the sections that follow, we describe the full set of algorithms (Section 6.3) and the parallel MIMD (Section 6.4) and the SIMD (Section 6.5) issues that we have explored with respect to these algorithms. The different architectures explored in evaluating the usefulness of parallel execution were the Meiko multi-transputer architecture and the Connection Machine. We will call the ideal set of algorithms the **rangeseg** program, although portions have been implemented in different ways (serial, SIMD, MIMD).

6.2 BRIEF OVERVIEW OF REGION SEGMENTATION ALGORITHMS

While edge-detection has been the major generic feature searched for in images, region finding has also had a long history of research. One reason why regions might be preferred is that regions are more compact than edges, thus are more likely to be a result of a significant scene process. Hence, if image regions can be reliably detected, then reliable information about the scene is likely (based on the assumption of the low likelihood of coincidental image coherence across a large portion of the image). In three-dimensional scenes, coherent regions are strong evidence for distinct surface patches, so much information about the scene can be inferred easily. It is also often the case that there are fewer regions than edge fragments in a scene description, which improves the computational complexity of later stages of processing.

There are several different classes of region-finding algorithms, each of which has potential for specific forms of parallelisation. Parallel processing of image data has been expected for some time, so a number of different approaches have been developed [BRA83], [DUF81], [CHA90], [CYP89].

- **Global classification of pixels and region forming by label propagation**

  Examples of this are in remote sensing or outdoor scene labelling [HAN78] or indoor office region finding [BRI70] where individual pixels are labelled by their multispectral characteristic.

  Each individual pixel can be labelled independently, simultaneously, using a SIMD architecture, or sequentially across separate image subregions in a MIMD architecture. Regions are formed by identifying connected sets of pixels with the same labels. This can be done by marker propagation to connected neighbouring pixels having the same label (SIMD [DUF78], [LIT86]) or by parallel tracking processes (MIMD [EAR91]).

- **Merging connected regions that have similar properties**

  Examples of this are in road region finding for vehicle navigation [GAY89] or indoor scenes [TEN77] where initial seed regions have been previously formed (e.g. by virtue of having identical properties). The merging process selects two (or more) adjacent regions whose characteristics are sufficiently similar for merging. The full set of regions can be best represented as a graph whose nodes are the regions connected by adjacency arcs.

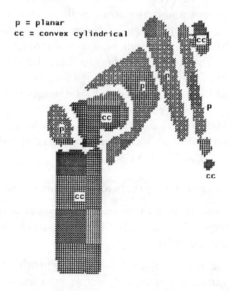

Figure 6.2   Surface patches extracted from the range image.

With this model, pairs of nodes (i.e. regions) connected by an adjacency arc are candidates for merging. These pairs can be tested in parallel by a MIMD task-farming approach (i.e. testing and merging pairs of regions can be delegated by a master processor to a set of worker processors). A successful merge reduces the structure of the graph by relabelling the arcs to the new merged node. The major computational problems are testing the criteria for merging and the recalculation of merged region properties. The task-farm model requires that each worker processor has all needed information. Hence, either the testing and merging must be done using a few properties that can be distributed along with the request for checking, or some form of shared-memory architecture is needed.

Some region merging processes have an intrinsic sequential character, such as choosing to merge only the best pair of regions at each cycle, and then recalculating the new next-best pair to merge based on the properties of the resulting merged region.

- **Recursively splitting regions that are inhomogeneous**

  An example of this approach segments an outdoor scene by splitting the image into regions of compatible pixels using the "red" colour channel, and then further splitting each of these regions into subregions using the "green" colour channel, and so on for the "blue" channel [HAN78].

  A geometric form of splitting is based on the quadtree algorithm [SAM80], which recursively splits inhomogeneous square image regions into four square subregions. Each of these are further split until the resulting subregions are homogeneous in the chosen property. Once all regions are homogeneous, adjacent compatible regions are merged, as in the item above.

  If the quadtree splitting algorithm can test consistency locally, then a SIMD algorithm can be developed that propagates inconsistency flags within regions, thus marking them locally for splitting. The property-based segmentation can use a SIMD algorithm wherein pixels can locally sever links to the neighbours with incompatible properties, and then a label propagation process can link compatible pixels into regions.

- **Iterative growth at region boundaries**

  A special case of region merging starts with core regions whose consistency is certain, and then grows these to form larger regions by adding compatible pixels at the region boundary. A good example of this is in the context of surface finding from 3D data [BES87]. In that work, primitive regions were seeded by the central portion of regions having consistent curvature signs (as in the work described in this chapter). Full region finding starts by fitting a polynomial surface through the core region and then adding adjacent pixels whose 3D distance from the polynomial surface was small. Region growing stops when no more adjacent pixels can be added. (The process also tests for shifting to a higher order polynomial.)

  If each region can be characterised simply (e.g. as a set of polynomial coefficients), then much of the region growing can be executed in a SIMD architecture, with processors at "adjacent" pixels locally testing for consistency and then propagating the testing to successfully merged neighbours. However, as only processors adjacent to those representing region boundaries are active, this approach does not exploit the full potential parallelism. In addition, periodic recalculation of region properties (e.g. a new polynomial fit) can only be parallel amongst the regions, which are much less than the number of pixels.

A MIMD process with one processor per region can also be effective, but requires either shared memory or each processor having a copy of the raw data. While the addition of new pixels to the region is locally sequential, it is not necessary to redistribute processing to recalculate the region parameters (unlike in the SIMD option).

- **Modifying local region labels until agreement is reached**

  This approach assumes that adjacent pixels with identical labels define regions, and the computation involves changing the labels assigned to each pixel until convergence occurs [ROS78]. Each pixel can have one of several labels (i.e. the region can be one of several different types). The calculations are based on both the original properties of the pixel and the labels of adjacent pixels, and the choice of which label to assign to each pixel has some probabilistic basis. Examples of this class of computation are the relaxation labelling processes [ROS78] and image reconstruction using Markov random fields [GEM84].

  The SIMD parallel model is ideal for this class of algorithm, in that only local neighbourhood data is needed. Further, as this algorithm typically iterates until convergence occurs, the SIMD distributed form is also appropriate.

6.3   THE RANGE DATA SEGMENTATION ALGORITHMS

In this section, we describe the mathematical transformations [TRU91] applied to the data at each stage of the process (which also describes the serial implementation). The input to the process is an array of range values (e.g. 128×128) and the output is a list of the regions with an attached list of pixels comprising each region.

In **rangeseg**, the range surface is segmented according to the sign of the *gaussian curvature* (K) and *mean curvature* (H):

$$K = \kappa_1 \kappa_2 \quad H = \frac{\kappa_1 + \kappa_2}{2}$$

where κ_1 and κ_2 are the principal curvatures at a point P. A surface patch $\mathcal{P}$ in the segmented image is an image region where the signs of H and K do not change. Let $\text{sgn}(x)$ be the sign of the real number x: then $\mathcal{P}$ can be qualitatively characterised by the ordered pair $(\text{sgn}(H), \text{sgn}(K))$, which in turn identifies a whole class of surface patches. In order to segment the surface, therefore, an ordered triple $(P, \text{sgn}(H), \text{sgn}(K))$ is computed at each point P. In actual fact, **rangeseg** computes a more exhaustive local representation $\mathcal{D}(P) = (P, d_1, d_2, N, \kappa_1, \kappa_2)$ known as the *augmented Darboux frame* [SAN90], where d_1 and d_2 are the principal directions and N is the normal at P. The patch classes defined by the signs of H and K are discussed in detail in Section 6.3.7.

Given a patchwise differentiable surface $\mathcal{S}$, say the depth image of a cube, H and K

are undefined at singular (e.g. depth discontinuity) points. In a digitally sampled version of $\mathcal{S}$, points corresponding to singularities lead to noisy or unreliable curvature estimates. Unlike most approaches found in the literature (e.g. [CAI91], [BES87], [WAN85], [FER90]), we compute a discontinuity map before estimating the curvatures; then we use the discontinuities to impose boundary conditions on the smoothing and curvature estimation. This limits the rounding effects of smoothing, which bends the true surface into spurious elliptic or cylindrical patches where the surfaces intersect. Limiting this distortion is particularly useful in scale-space analysis [LIN90] where the surface is smoothed by convolution with gaussians of increasing variance and the deformation at discontinuities is propagated and amplified.

In the segmented image, therefore, patches are surrounded by contours which are loci of points belonging to three discontinuity classes: *depth, orientation* and *curvature sign*. The latter means that the sign of either the gaussian or the mean curvatures changes across two adjacent pixels.

6.3.1 Depth and Orientation Discontinuities

At each image point P, the absolute value of the directional derivative

$$d(P, \mathbf{n}) = \frac{\partial u}{\partial \mathbf{n}}(P)$$

is estimated in a 3×3 neighbourhood and for eight directions of $\mathbf{n}$. If this quantity is large enough P is labelled as a depth discontinuity point. An illustration is given in Figure 6.3, which plots $d(P, \mathbf{n})$ taken across an image of five adjacent, parallel cylinders of decreasing radii. In this example the direction $\mathbf{n}$ is perpendicular to the axes of the cylinders. At present, discontinuities are detected by comparing $\frac{\partial u}{\partial \mathbf{n}}$ with a user-supplied threshold τ_d, tuned manually to an optimal value (usually between 10 and 20). Although very simple, this thresholding mechanism worked well in our experiments. It was always possible to reach a value of τ_d giving good results.

Orientation discontinuities are detected as loci of discontinuity points for the tangent plane. Given the parametrisation $s(x, y) = (x, y, h(x, y))$ of surface S and a point $P \in S$, the tangent plane T at P is the plane through P and perpendicular to the normal

$$\mathbf{N}(P) = \frac{(-h_x, -h_y, 1)}{(1 + h_x^2 + h_y^2)^{1/2}}$$

where the subscripts indicate partial differentiation. In order to estimate $\mathbf{N}(P)$, a quadric patch is fitted to a local environment of P using least squares, so that the estimated gradient (h_x, h_y) at P is given by

$$h_x = \frac{\sum_{k \in I(P)} \Delta x_k \Delta h(\Delta x_k)}{\sum_{k \in I(P)} \Delta x_k^2} \qquad h_y = \frac{\sum_{k \in I(P)} \Delta y_k \Delta h(\Delta y_k)}{\sum_{k \in I(P)} \Delta y_k^2}$$

where $I(P)$ is a local neighbourhood of P, Δx_k and Δy_k are the incremental steps in the x and y directions and $\Delta h(\Delta q)$ is the increment of h over the increment Δq. The computation is performed in world coordinates.

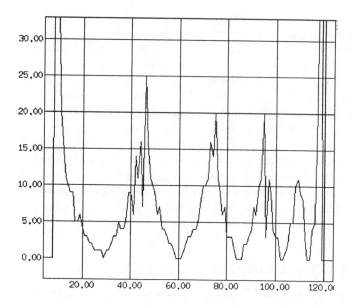

Figure 6.3 Gradient along a scanline of an image of cylinders, plotted against position (in pixel coordinates).

In the continuous case, an orientation discontinuity point for T corresponds to a discontinuity in the normal field $\mathbf{N}$. In the discrete case, an orientation discontinuity is a point P such that at least one point P_1 in a local neighbourhood of P satisfies

$$|\mathbf{N}(P) \cdot \mathbf{N}(P_1)| < \tau_o$$

where τ_o is a user-defined threshold. In our experiments, usual values of τ_o were between 0.75 and 0.9.

6.3.2   Diffusion Smoothing

Diffusion smoothing provides an elegant mathematical framework for gaussian smoothing and scale-space analysis. It subsumes repeated average, gaussian and spline smoothing. We sketch below how it can be implemented with an efficient, implicit numerical scheme guaranteeing unconditional stability suggested by [CAI91].

Intuitively, diffusion smoothing regards the surface $h(x, y)$ as the initial configuration of a heat distribution $u(x, y, t)$ at $t = 0$, which evolves according to the diffusion equation

$$\frac{\partial u}{\partial t} = b\nabla^2 u \tag{6.1}$$

with initial value $u(x, y, 0) = h(x, y)$.

The closed-form solution of this problem is the gaussian convolution

$$u(x, y) = \frac{1}{4\pi bt} \int_{-\infty}^{\infty} \int_{-\infty}^{\infty} h(\xi, \eta) \exp\left[-\frac{(\eta - x)^2 + (\xi - y)^2}{4bt}\right] d\xi d\eta$$

where the relation

$$\sigma = \sqrt{2bt} \tag{6.2}$$

links the time t to the standard deviation σ of gaussian smoothing. Given the same initial values, therefore, the solution of equation (6.1) at time t_k is equivalent to the result of the convolution of the initial surface with a gaussian of variance $\sqrt{2bt_k}$.

Equation (6.1) is solved numerically using Feng's implicit scheme described in [CAI91]:

$$\frac{1}{\tau}(u_{p,q}^{k+\frac{1}{2}} - u_{p,q}^k) - \frac{b}{h^2}(u_{p+1,q}^{k+\frac{1}{2}} - 2u_{p,q}^{k+\frac{1}{2}} + u_{p-1,q}^{k+\frac{1}{2}}) = 0 \tag{6.3}$$

$$\frac{1}{\tau}(u_{p,q}^{k+1} - u_{p,q}^{k+\frac{1}{2}}) - \frac{b}{h^2}(u_{p,q+1}^{k+1} - 2u_{p,q}^{k+1} + u_{p,q-1}^{k+1}) = 0 \tag{6.4}$$

$$u_{p,q}^0 = f_{p,q} \quad p,q = 0,\dots,M \quad k = 0,\dots,\infty \tag{6.5}$$

where τ is the time unit, h the spatial grid unit, M the image size (see [CAI91] for an extended discussion of this scheme), p,q are the pixel positions, $p,q \in [0,M)$ and $k \in [0,\infty)$.

In matrix form, we have

$$AU_q^{k+\frac{1}{2}} = U_q^k \quad AU_p^{k+1} = U_p^{k+\frac{1}{2}}$$

where A is a tridiagonal and diagonal-dominant matrix, U_r^t is the array of u values for constant r (r row or column index as appropriate).

There are several practical advantages which make the diffusion approach attractive. Cai [CAI91] has shown that the scheme (6.3, 6.4) is unconditionally stable and faster than repeated averaging. Moreover, the scheme can be adopted with a variable time step to obtain a scale space representation. The finite scale space produced is denser than that of gaussian smoothing ([CAI91]). We take advantage of such features in our implementation: the image is smoothed at a desired spatial scale σ by calculating the corresponding $t = t(\sigma)$ and solving system (6.3, 6.4) only once. Finally, the diffusion equation form allows an elegant and coherent boundary treatment on the surface being smoothed, as discussed in the next section.

6.3.3   Boundary Treatment

Cai [CAI89] suggested a "small leakage" boundary condition for attenuating the boundary deformation effect in the diffusion approach. Gaussian smoothing is equivalent to diffusion smoothing with "perfectly insulated" boundaries; the typical distortion arising (Figure 6.4) is avoided by allowing the surface to leak into the background.

This is achieved by imposing at each border point

$$b_{in}\frac{\partial u}{\partial \mathbf{n}} = b_{out}\frac{\partial u}{\partial \mathbf{n}} \tag{6.6}$$

where b_{in} is the diffusion coefficient on the surface, b_{out} is the diffusion coefficient of

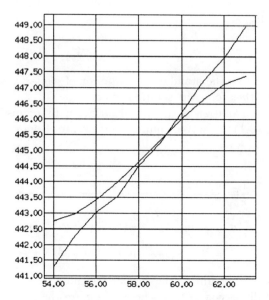

Figure 6.4 Typical distortion of planar profile after gaussian smoothing. The original pro-file is bent at the border: towards the background on the right, away from the background on the left.

a narrow stripe surrounding the background and **n** is the normal at the boundary in the $z = 0$ plane. Cai suggests that b_{out} should be "much smaller" than b_{in}, e.g. 10%.

Condition (6.6) can be simplified by splitting it into two equations along the x and y axis respectively. Discretising at the boundary pixel (p, q) at time $(k + 1/2)$ for x, $(k + 1)$ for y, we obtain

$$\begin{bmatrix} b_{in} & -(b_{in} - b_{out}) & b_{out} \end{bmatrix} \begin{bmatrix} u_{p-1,q}^{k+1/2} \\ u_{p,q}^{k+1/2} \\ u_{p+1,q}^{k+1/2} \end{bmatrix} = 0 \tag{6.7}$$

$$\begin{bmatrix} b_{in} & -(b_{in} - b_{out}) & b_{out} \end{bmatrix} \begin{bmatrix} u_{p,q-1}^{k+1} \\ u_{p,q}^{k+1} \\ u_{p,q+1}^{k+1} \end{bmatrix} = 0 \tag{6.8}$$

There are a few problems with this boundary treatment. In practice, it requires that the gradient immediately inside the border be a certain fraction of the gradient immediately outside the border. In other words, the background pulls the surface rim down; in the common situation of a surface sloping towards the background at the border, the border lifting effect shown in Figure 6.4 will be overcome by a sufficiently small b_{out} and the convexity of the surface (but not its *exact* shape) will be preserved. However, if the original surface is *not* convex near the border, the leakage still pulls the surface border towards the background, thus creating an undesired convexity (Fig-ure 6.5). Moreover, slanted planes will be generally distorted into concave or convex regions by the fixed leakage coefficient.

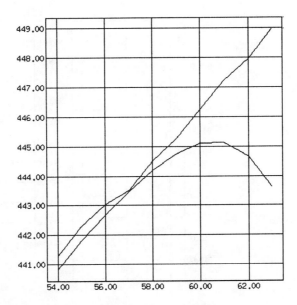

Figure 6.5 Wrong behaviour of leakage with border not sloping towards the background.

It is unlikely that a simple, local boundary condition could preserve completely the sign of the principal curvatures at the boundaries. On the other hand, a complex boundary treatment would spoil the efficiency of scheme (6.3, 6.4). However, condition (6.6) can be at least generalised to accommodate locally convex and concave borders by introducing an *adaptive leakage coefficient* b^a_{out} given by

$$b^a_{out} = b_{in} \left(\frac{\frac{\partial u}{\partial \mathbf{n}}\big|_{in}}{\frac{\partial u}{\partial \mathbf{n}}\big|_{out}} \right) \tag{6.9}$$

The effect of b^a_{out} is to adapt the amount of leakage at the particular border pixel, taking into account the difference between internal and external slope before enforcing the boundary condition (6.6). In our experiments this condition performed better with both planar and curved surfaces. An example is given in Figure 6.6.

6.3.4   Computing the Curvature Images

The principal curvatures at each point P of the smoothed surface are commonly estimated from the coefficients of a regular patch fitted locally to a neighbourhood of P ([FER90], [MON91]). We have adopted an efficient, mixed approach. The idea is to estimate the curvatures from a local spline approximation of the surface, using *cubic B-splines*:

$$\Omega_3(x) = \begin{cases} 0 & \text{if } |x| \geq 2 \\ \frac{1}{2}|x|^3 - x^2 + \frac{2}{3} & \text{if } |x| \leq 1 \\ -\frac{1}{6}|x|^3 + x^2 - 2|x| + \frac{4}{3} & \text{if } |x| \in (1,2) \end{cases} \tag{6.10}$$

Instead of fitting coefficients explicitly — a computationally expensive operation to be

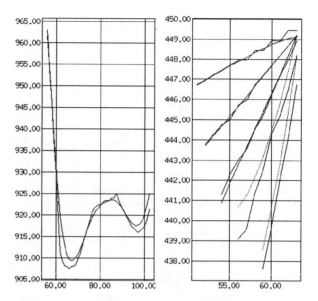

Figure 6.6 Surface cross-section profiles of several different surface orientations with and without the boundary condition. Note the distinct bending of the unsmoothed profiles.

performed at each non-discontinuity point of the surface — we compute the discrete convolution

$$u'_{p,q} = \sum_{i=-1}^{m} \sum_{j=-1}^{m} u_{i,j} \Omega_3(p-i) \Omega_3(q-j) \qquad (6.11)$$

which, when iterated, will converge to a C^2 continuous surface which preserves the concavity–convexity of the original surface ([AHL67], [REI67]). Moreover, for each iteration, the computation can be done in parallel within 3×3 windows.

The gaussian and mean curvature K and H are then given by the relations [DOC76]

$$K = \frac{h_{xx}h_{yy} - h_{xy}^2}{(1 + h_x^2 + h_y^2)^2} \qquad (6.12)$$

$$2H = \frac{(1 + h_x^2)h_{yy} - 2h_x h_y h_{xy} + (1 + h_y^2)h_{xx}}{(1 + h_x^2 + h_y^2)^{3/2}} \qquad (6.13)$$

where the subscripts indicate partial differentiation and we have assumed as usual a surface parametrisation $\mathbf{s}(x, y) = (x, y, h(x, y))$.

6.3.5 Zero Thresholding

A well-known problem in computing a segmentation of a range surface based on curvature signs is how to choose zero thresholds ε_K, ε_H capable of guarding against noise in the H or K images when looking for regions of zero curvature. We adopt Cai's consistent curvature thresholding

$$\varepsilon_K \geq \varepsilon_H{}^2 + 2|H|\varepsilon_H \tag{6.14}$$

which is *consistent* in the sense that a small perturbation ξ in the principal curvatures will still lead to a correct classification of H and K [CAI91].

ε_H is a user-defined parameter. In actual fact, our implementation allows the user to choose between a full classification, using both H and K, and one based on the H image only. This option is useful when all the surfaces in the data are developable (i.e. the gaussian curvature is zero at each point) and avoids the additional exposure to noise induced by estimating K.

The output of the curvature estimation module is the H and K sign images, where each point of the original surface is associated with a label indicating the estimated sign of the curvature. The label can be 0, $+1$ or -1.

6.3.6   Improving the Quality of H, K Sign Images

Small, insignificant spots in the H and K sign images are eliminated by a simple erosion–expansion technique. This is based on the idea that, in discrete mathematics, an invertible transformation T does not always satisfy $f^{-1}f = I$, I identity matrix, as is the case in continuous mathematics. In our case, eroding the regions in the H and K sign images is aimed to make small spots disappear completely, so that nothing of them is left to be grown by the subsequent expansion.

The erosion operation is a *wall-following algorithm* which erodes region contours to a depth specified by the user (generally 1 or 2 pixels). The expansion poses the problem of which regions should be grown first. For each region contour pixel in the H and K images, a local neighbourhood is inspected to decide which label should grow first. The criterion adopted is *local maximum energy*: for each label l a local energy function $E_l = \sum_I \delta_l(i, j)$ is computed in a neighbourhood I of pixel (i, j), where

$$\delta_l(i, j) = \begin{cases} 1 & \text{if } H(i, j) = l \\ 0 & \text{otherwise} \end{cases}$$

The label to be grown is then the one associated with the maximum E_l in I.

6.3.7   Classification and Output Data

The H and K sign images are combined together to give the final surface segmentation into patches belonging to several shape classes. The shape classes are illustrated in Table 6.1.

The case $K > 0$, $H = 0$ makes no geometric sense and has been omitted. Notice also that we group the various possible hyperbolic surface subclasses identified by H when $K < 0$ into one class. The reason is that they do not seem to be perceptually significant for the human vision system. The above classification allows representations of a large number of complex objects which are still a challenge for state-of-the-art recognition systems.

Table 6.1   Surface patches classification scheme.

K	H	shape class
0	0	plane
0	+	negative cylindrical
0	−	positive cylindrical
+	+	negative elliptic
+	−	positive elliptic
−	any	hyperbolic

6.3.8   Overview of Algorithm Structure for Each Process

In order to understand the motivations for the parallel algorithms explored in the next sections, it is useful to know the algorithmic geometry of each of the **rangeseg** subprocesses:

1. **Discontinuity detection:** Depth discontinuities require a 3×3 neighbourhood, and the orientation discontinuities effectively require a 5×5 neighbourhood (3×3 for each surface normal, 3×3 for all of the normals about a point).

2. **Diffusion smoothing:** A single scale of smoothing requires the solution (for an $N \times N$ image) of N tridiagonal systems of linear equations in the column direction and then N tridiagonal systems in the row direction. Each tridiagonal system requires data from three consecutive columns. The coefficients of the tridiagonal system are different for each row and column, depending on the discontinuity structure, so a single matrix inversion is not an option.

3. **Curvature image calculation:** The curvature calculation is done locally and requires a 5×5 neighbourhood to compute the derivatives.

4. **Zero thresholding:** This is done at each pixel independently.

5. **H & K sign image improvement:** This requires multiple passes of a 3×3 neighbourhood algorithm.

6. **Region formation:** This groups pixels with the same classification into global regions by local connectivity, so is a label-propagation type process.

6.4   MIMD IMPLEMENTATION ON A TRANSPUTER (MEIKO) ARCHITECTURE

6.4.1   The Parallel Environment

The transputer implementation was written to run on the Edinburgh Concurrent Supercomputer (a Meiko) using 3L parallel C and the Tiny message passing system. The 3L Toolset for the ECS consists of a C compiler, a linker and a static configurer. The configuration file describes the required placement of user tasks onto the transputers and the connectivity between tasks and the Tiny kernels. The executables produced are loaded and executed on the user's domain using the Alien File Server (afserver) which is also responsible for handling I/O requests from tasks directly connected to the afserver.

Tiny [CLA91] is a message passing system developed at Edinburgh which handles process to process communication and takes care of the storing and forwarding of messages. Tiny is a lightweight system and has lower latencies than alternatives such as CS Tools.

6.4.2 Implementation and Analysis

The architecture of the parallel implementation has a master task on the node attached to the host and a number of slave tasks placed on the remaining processors. The master task reads in the initial data and distributes it to the slave tasks. The slave tasks then perform the processing, occasionally communicating with the master for control and to collate global data. When finished, the slaves return data to the master to be output.

The majority of the **rangeseg** program applies 3×3 masks to a number of arrays and is easily parallelised by partitioning the array between the processors, using a one-layer boundary passing mechanism and occasionally communicating with the master when data relating to the whole image is required. Standard geometric data parallel techniques can therefore be used for the majority of the stages and their implementation is not discussed further.

However, three of the stages — diffusion smoothing, curvature estimation and surface grouping — do not conform to this structure and it was parallelising these stages where the difficulties lay.

6.4.3 Diffusion Smoothing

Performing diffusion smoothing (Sections 6.3.2 and 6.3.3) at a single point requires that the task has access to data corresponding to all other points in its row and column. The method chosen to parallelise this was to distribute the data amongst the tasks so that each task dealt with a number of complete columns, performing the smoothing in the vertical direction and then redistributing the data so that each task could then smooth a number of rows in the horizontal direction. This process of distributing the data between columns and rows would be repeated several times as a number of iterations of the smoothing process were required.

As the data has to be distributed into columns at some stage we concluded that this method would be preferable to the standard method of distributing an array into smaller two-dimensional grids for the whole program as opposed to just for the diffusion smoothing stage. The motivation behind the analysis was that if boundary information is passed in only two directions instead of eight (as shown in Figure 6.7) then code complexity is reduced, and also that there is no need to redistribute the data before the diffusion smoothing stage.

The only difference between the two systems is in the amount of boundary communication which has to take place. Using the columns method, each task has to send and receive two messages, compared to eight sends and receives in the standard grid method. The total amount of information which has to be sent is, however, larger for the columns method.

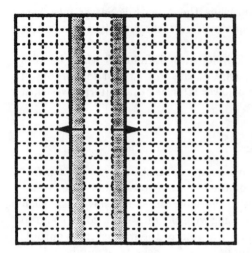 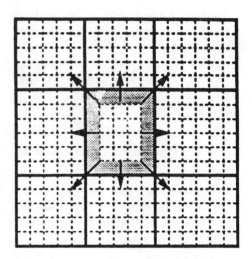

Figure 6.7 The required boundary communication per task using columns method (left) and grid method (right).

The communication costs of the columns method were analysed using the following cost model for Tiny [CLA91]:

$$T(l, b) = \alpha + \beta l + \gamma b + \delta b l$$

which gives the time taken for a message of b bytes to pass over l links. The constants are

- $\alpha = 62.4\ \mu s$, the communication set-up time

- $\beta = 41.0\ \mu s/\text{link}$, the overhead per link

- $\gamma = 0.1\ \mu s/\text{byte}$, time to transfer a byte from user to router and back

- $\delta = 1.3\ \mu s/(\text{byte} \cdot \text{link})$, time to transfer a single byte through a link

6.4.4   Analysis of Boundary Passing Using Columns Method

When data are distributed as a number of complete rows per task, each slice has to transmit and receive two messages each of 128 values (assume 4 bytes per value) over a single link. For a single message,

$$l = 1, \quad b = 128 \times 4 = 512 \text{ bytes}$$

and so:

$$T(l, b) = 820.2\ \mu s$$

Each task has to send and receive two of these, so the total time is:

$$T_{\text{columns total}} = 2 \times 820.2 = 1640.4 \ \mu s$$

This value is invariant to the number of tasks, assuming contention is not a problem when communicating only to immediate neighbours.

The complete program requires approximately 20 boundary passes and so the total communication time for boundary passing with 121 tasks is $20 \times 1640 = 32800 \ \mu s$ when using the columns method.

There are, however, two disadvantages with the columns method. Firstly, the data must be distributed between tasks in complete columns and thus the number of tasks cannot exceed the number of columns of the image. This is not considered a problem since the images are usually either 128×128 or 256×256 and the largest domain on the ECS consists of 131 transputers.

Secondly, the analysis above (and the actual implementation) uses blocking communication for the boundary exchange. A faster implementation would result from using non-blocking communication and overlapping the communication time with processing of the non-boundary points. The number of points which could be processed during the communication is less when using the columns method than when using the grid method and thus the potential for a future speed-up is reduced. The reason for this is that the internal non-boundary area is at a maximum for a square and the grid method partitions the image virtually into squares. Again, this is not considered to be a problem because the small amount of total boundary communication time meant that the speed-up obtained would not be particularly significant.

6.4.5 Redistributing between Columns and Rows

During the diffusion smoothing stage the data has to be redistributed from columns into rows and back again a number of times. This is effectively done by reflecting the image about the line $x = y$. Implementing this reflection in parallel proved to be a bottleneck for the program.

One method requires each task to wait its turn to receive all its new data from each of the other tasks while sending the appropriate portions of its data to the other tasks. Blocking communication must be used for this process due to Tiny's inability to have more than one outstanding event per task per message type. In order to allow a completely non-blocking process on up to 128 tasks 128^2 types would be required.

Unfortunately, when using this method the time to perform a single flip of an image increases rapidly as the number of tasks increases.

An alternative algorithm would use the master task to receive the image from all the slave tasks, perform the flipping and then redistribute the data to the slaves. This would reduce the total number of messages per flip to $2n$ as opposed to $n(n-1)$ as was required by the previous method. Another advantage is that this method could also work using non-blocking communication. However, contention could cause problems with this method because all messages have to be sent to or from the master.

The Tiny equation, however, does not deal with non-blocking communication and so an accurate estimation of the speed of such a method cannot be obtained. The actual time would be somewhere between the time to send just the furthest message (i.e. the time if no contention) and the time which would occur using blocking communication. In order to calculate the lower time bound the following equation is used:

$$T_{lower} = 2T\left(\sqrt{n}+1, \frac{128^2 \times 4}{n}\right)$$

where $\sqrt{n}+1$ is the most number of links a task can be from the master and $\frac{128^2 \times 4}{n}$ is the number of bytes communicated.

To calculate the upper time bound the equation is:

$$T_{upper} = 2nT\left(\frac{\sqrt{n}}{2}+1, \frac{128^2 \times 4}{n}\right)$$

where $\frac{\sqrt{n}}{2}+1$ is the average number of links to the master and $\frac{128^2 \times 4}{n}$ is the number of bytes communicated.

The results of applying these two equations to various numbers of tasks is shown in Table 6.2.

Table 6.2   Bounds for flip times using master task.

number of tasks	T_{lower} (s)	T_{upper} (s)
4	0.131	0.355
16	0.055	0.530
32	0.038	0.709
64	0.025	0.899
128	0.017	1.295

It is anticipated that the actual times would be toward the lower end of this range. However, because of contention as the number of tasks increases the times would vary further from this lower bound. Despite this the results show that this method could be an efficient solution to the flipping problem and thus eliminate the speed-up bottleneck.

6.4.6   Curvature Estimation

As mentioned above the process of estimating the curvature is similar to that for diffusion smoothing in that a two-dimensional problem is split into two one-dimensional problems. The major difference is that for diffusion smoothing, data from the whole row or column is needed, while curvature estimation only requires the three points on each side of the point being considered.

The method which has been implemented is to use the flipping routines as before. This method was chosen because it could be implemented in the time available as the flipping code was already written; however, it requires another eight flip operations and therefore suffers badly from the slowness of the currently implemented flipping operation.

There are two possible solutions to this problem. Firstly, if the flipping operation is implemented efficiently using the master method described above then some extra flips may not be a problem. The other method is to employ some form of three-layer boundary passing instead of the current one-layer method.

This would increase the complexity of the code since boundary points would need to be sent to tasks up to three links away and each task would have to send and receive (either directly or indirectly) boundary information from up to twelve other tasks (three in each of the principal directions). If the flip operation can be efficiently implemented this would probably not be required. Otherwise the method may be faster because it only communicates as much data as is required as oppose to the flipping method which, in the case of curvature estimation, performs some unnecessary work.

6.4.7 Surface Grouping

The surface grouping process is different from all other stages in that there is no locality in those points with can affect the value of another point. The process is similar to edge tracking in that the patches of similar curvature are tracked all over the image until the complete region has been identified. As this is the last stage of the program it may be more efficient to run it sequentially on the master task because the data will have to be returned to the master anyway. For details of how such a stage could be parallelised see [WIL90], [EAR91].

6.4.8 Results

The flipping routine has been shown to be the bottleneck of the MIMD implementation which could prevent it being scaled up to run efficiently using a large number of processors. A number of alternatives to the inefficient method implemented have been suggested and a way of reducing its effect by eliminating the flip calls in the curvature estimation stage has been presented. Alternatively, an implementation based on a pipeline of transputers solving linear systems might be another possibility, but any algorithm would still need to cope with alternately decomposing the dataset in two different ways. A third alternative would be to use a different algorithm, wherein the data was smoothed iteratively in a local 3×3 neighbourhood (e.g. following some ideas by Terzopoulos [TER85]). However, this method does not have the same numerical stability as the linear algebra method.

6.5 SIMD IMPLEMENTATION ON A CONNECTION MACHINE ARCHITECTURE

The Connection Machine 200 is a massively parallel supercomputer that is ideal for applications such as range-data segmentation. The machine consists of a large number of single bit processors connected to each other by a grid type network for nearest neighbour communication and a hypercube network for more general communication. The data parallel approach to programming the Connection Machine is very easy to use and a powerful method for expressing many of the algorithms in low and mid level computer vision problems.

The Connection Machine 200 (CM200) produced by Thinking Machines Corporation consists of up to 64k single bit processors each with up to 1 MByte of memory. The performance of the machine is enhanced through the addition of 2048 (for a 64k machine) Weitek floating point units, which have achieved 8 GFlops performance in real application code. The CM200 processors operate in lock-step with each processor performing the same operation on different data at each cycle. The CM200 is available with 32k, 16k, and 8k processors as well as the full 64k. The Data-Vault, produced by Thinking Machines, is a parallel disk system which can sustain 25 MByte/s data transfer rate with the CM200, and so provides a very high performance I/O route. The CM200 sited at the Edinburgh Parallel Computing Centre has 16k single bit processors and 512 Weitek floating point units. In addition a 10 GByte Data-Vault is connected via a CM IO bus to the machine.

The CM200 is programmed using data parallel extensions to either C or Fortran. The data-parallel C language is C* (pronounced see-star) and is based on ANSI C. The range data segmentation program is written in C so C* was used to port this program to the CM200. The program produced by C* (or cmf) is a Sparc executable which runs on the Sun 4 which is the front-end for the CM200. All the serial code runs on this Sun, while parallel code runs on the CM. The Sparc executable makes calls to the CM in order to instruct it to perform operations on the parallel data. Thus code is developed and tested using the normal Unix utilities on a Sun. In addition there is a parallel debugger, Prism, which is used to examine/visualise parallel data.

6.5.1   C*

The C* language is based on ANSI C and has data-parallel extensions which essentially allow the programmer to manipulate parallel data. The new concept of a parallel variable is introduced which consists of a number of elements each on a separate processor. A parallel variable is like an array except it is stored in parallel memory. These parallel variables can be treated like any other variable in C with regard to arithmetic operations, function calling, etc. A new data type in C* is the shape which is used to define the shape of a parallel variable.

```
shape [128][128]image;

int:image     raw, out;
```

This shape declaration specifies a shape of 128×128 called `image` which can then be used to declare parallel variables. Operations on parallel variables must be performed on variables with the same shape if communication is to be avoided. The C* language is constrained by the size of the underlying machine that the program is running on, since the machine appears to have an arbitrarily large number of virtual processors which are mapped onto the real processors by the run-time system. Thus the same piece of code will run on an 8k machine as well as on a 16k machine, without re-compilation or linking.

```
with(image)
{
```

```
    raw = 2;
    out = raw*2;
}
```

The **with** statement selects the current shape to be **image**, and so all parallel variable assignment operations within that **with** block must be with parallel variables of the shape **image**. Each of the 128 × 128 elements in raw receives the value 2, and these values are multiplied by 2 and assigned to the elements of **out**.

The simplest form of communication is between nearest neighbours, and this is called NEWS communication. This is very efficient since all the processors involved are moving data a constant distance in the same direction, and so there is no contention for communication links.

```
with(image)
{
    [.][. +1]right_shift = raw;
    [.][. -1]left_shift  = raw;
    [. +1][.]down_shift  = raw;
    [. -1][.]up_shift    = raw;

    [. +1][. +1]diagonal = raw;

    /* .... */
}
```

The left index is used to index into parallel variables. The two left indexes provide the address of elements in the receiver to which data is sent from the sender. The left index [.][. +1] specifies that data is sent to the same row, but to the column with index one bigger in the receiver, e.g. the element raw[0][0] is sent to right_shift[0][1].

The last construct to be introduced here is that of context, which is the data-parallel version of **if**. Setting a context effectively switches a sub-set of the current virtual processors off. This is achieved using the **where** statement.

```
with(image)
{
    int:image data, temp;

    /* initialise data */

    where(data<23)
    {
            data = 0;
            temp = 100;
```

```
        }
        else
        {
                data = 1;
                temp = temp/2;
        }
}
```

The **where** statement is used to set a context where only the processors with elements of data whose value is less than 23 are switched on. The remainder are switched off, and do not take part in operations. The context once set remains for the entirety of the block and is not restricted to the parallel variable used in the condition. The **else** construct simply flips the active state and so the on processors become inactive and the off ones become active.

6.5.2   Porting the Range Data Segmentation Code

The previous section introduced the basic C* constructs which are needed to port most of the range data segmentation code to the CM. The porting process was carried out routine by routine maintaining serial and parallel versions of all the data so that the results of the parallel operations could be compared with the serial results. The parallelisation task basically involves searching for loops over arrays and then changing these arrays to be parallel variables and then encoding the operations on the arrays using parallel variable assignment and context. The conditional **if** operations on array elements in the serial code are changed into **where** statements in the parallel code. The sequential code can be left unaltered.

The following paragraphs describe the parallelisation of one routine.

This is the code for serial initialisation of the array recording discontinuities:

```
void findddiscontinuities(int rimage[IMSIZE][IMSIZE],
    int dimage[IMSIZE][IMSIZE])
{
    register int x, y;
    register int i, size, *dptr;

    dptr = &dimage[0][0];
    size = IMSIZE*IMSIZE;
    for (i=0; i<size; i++) *dptr++ = RBNONE;
```

The parallel version of the initialisation code is:

```
void findddiscontinuities(int:current *rimage,int:current *dimage)
{
    int:current rimage1,rimage2,dimage1,dimage2,t1;
    *dimage = RBNONE;
```

In the above example the **for** loop is replaced by a parallel variable assignment.

The following serial loop over the image is part of the **findddiscontinuities** routine.

```
for (x=0; x<IMSIZE-1; x++)
    for (y=0; y<IMSIZE-1; y++)
    {
        /* search for 4-connected depth discontinuities
           (only need look on 1 side of a boundary */
        if ((abs( rimage[y][x] - rimage[y][x+1] )
                    > params.d_threshold)
            || ((rimage[y][x] == 0) && (rimage[y][x+1] != 0))
            || ((rimage[y][x] != 0) && (rimage[y][x+1] == 0)))
        {
            /* record discontinuity */
            dimage[y][x] = RBDEPTH;
            dimage[y][x+1] = RBDEPTH;
        }
        if ((abs( rimage[y][x] - rimage[y+1][x] )
                    > params.d_threshold)
            || ((rimage[y][x] == 0) && (rimage[y+1][x] != 0))
            || ((rimage[y][x] != 0) && (rimage[y+1][x] == 0)))
        {
            /* record discontinuity */
            dimage[y][x] = RBDEPTH;
            dimage[y+1][x] = RBDEPTH;
        }
    }
```

The parallel version uses auxiliary arrays **rimage1** and **rimage2** to store the image shifted vertically and horizontally one pixel.

```
where((pcoord(0) < (IMSIZE-1)) && (pcoord(1) < (IMSIZE-1)))
{

  where((abs(*rimage - rimage1) > params.d_threshold)
        || ((*rimage == 0) && (rimage1!=0))
        || ((*rimage != 0) && (rimage1==0)))
    {
      *dimage = RBDEPTH;
      dimage1 = RBDEPTH;
    }
```

```
where((abs(*rimage - rimage2) > params.d_threshold)
      || ((*rimage == 0) && (rimage2!=0))
      || ((*rimage != 0) && (rimage2==0)))
  {
    *dimage = RBDEPTH;
    dimage2 = RBDEPTH;
  }
}
```

The pattern to the parallelisation procedure should be apparent in these two code examples. The array index operations become parallel variable assignments, and the `if` statements become `where` statements.

The results of parallelising some of the routines from the range segmentation program are shown below. The time for the serial machine is for a Sun4/370, while for the CM200 it is for half the machine (8k processors) and includes the time for the non-parallelisable serial code.

Routine	Serial time	Parallel time
Initial noise smoothing	2.04	0.021
Find depth discontinuities	0.877	0.00388612
Make initial range image	0.311	0.213204
Create xyz and normals	3.9	1.91636
Find orientation discontinuities	0.832	0.259058

At this point the algorithm enters the diffusion smoothing stage, which, by its non-data parallel structure (i.e. requiring linear equation solving), is hard to parallelise using the same data-parallel structure as the rest of the process.

These results show that it is possible to achieve a great improvement in some stages of the process (e.g. 200+ times); however, other stages have a large sequential element and show hardly any improvement (e.g. 1.5 times).

6.6   CONCLUSIONS

In this chapter, we have investigated the parallelisation of a program that computes a curvature-based segmentation of a discrete range surface. The segmentation generates a description of the original data which can be used conveniently for matching against surface-based models.

While the problem seems to be a classically data-parallel problem, the crucial stages are the smoothing and label propagation algorithms. The latter process can be viewed as locally data parallel, with the regions then stitched together globally later. However, the smoothing is based on the solution of linear equations, which must occur in two orthogonal passes through the data array. Consequently, no single image distribution is adequate for the current algorithms, and hence there must be a major data redistribution in the midst of the processing. The communication overheads involved in doing this thus limit the performance achievable; in fact, in the worst case, the communication costs increase as the number of processors increases, thus reducing the value of increasing the parallel data processing performance available.

In looking at both a MIMD and a SIMD implementation, we found that neither architecture is ideal for this particular problem — both implementations required some essentially sequential processes, and there were also stages whose intrinsic computational structure was not well matched to the parallel architecture used in the other stages. We were surprised that this straightforward, although large, program with such obvious data-parallelism was not easy to adapt to the two architectures, and that it was not possible to achieve better performance on such powerful and expensive architectures without much more algorithmic reformulation.

REFERENCES

[AHL67] J. Ahlberg, E. Nilson and J. Walsh. *Theory of Splines and its Applications.* Academic Press, 1967.

[BES87] P. Besl. *Surfaces in Range Image Understanding.* Springer-Verlag. 1987.

[BRA83] M. Brady. Parallelism in Vision. *Artificial Intelligence* Vol. 21, pp. 271–283, 1983.

[BRA85] M. Brady, J. Ponce, A. Yuille and H. Asada. *Describing Surfaces.* MIT AI Memo No. 822, 1985.

[BRI70] C. R. Brice and C. L. Fennema. Scene Analysis Using Regions. *Artificial Intelligence* Vol. 1, pp. 205–226, 1970.

[CAI89] L. D. Cai. A "Small Leakage" Model for Diffusion Smoothing of Range Data. *Proc. 11th Int. Joint Conference on Artificial Intelligence,* Detroit, pp. 1585–1590, Morgan-Kaufman, 1989.

[CAI91] L. D. Cai. *Scale-Based Surface Understanding Using Diffusion Smoothing.* PhD dissertation, Department of Artificial Intelligence, University of Edinburgh, 1991.

[CHA90] V. Chaudhary and J.K. Aggarwal. Parallellism in Computer Vision: a Review. In V. Kumar, P.S. Gopalakrishnan (eds), *Parallel Algorithms for Machine Intelligence and Vision.* Springer Verlag, 1990.

[CLA91] L. J. Clarke and G. V. Wilson. Tiny: An Efficient Routing Harness for the Inmos Transputer. *Concurrency Practice and Experience,* Vol. 3, No. 3 June 1991.

[CYP89] R. Cypher and J.L.C. Sanz. SIMD Architectures and Algorithms for Image Processing and Computer Vision. *IEEE Trans. on ASSP,* Vol. 37, No. 12, pp. 2158-2173, Dec. 1989.

[DOC76] M. P. do Carmo. *Differential Geometry of Curves and Surfaces.* Prentice-Hall, 1976.

[DUF78] M. J. B. Duff. Review of the CLIP Image Processing System. *Proc. AFIPS National Computer Conference,* pp. 1055, 1978.

[DUF81] M. J. B. Duff and S. Levialdi. *Languages and Architectures for Image Processing.* Academic Press, London, 1981.

[EAR91] J. Earl. *Extensions to a Distributed Blackboard System for Vision Applications.* Honours Dissertation, Department of Artificial Intelligence, University of Edinburgh, 1991.

[FER90] F. Ferrie, J. Lagarde and P. Whaite. Recovery of Volumetric Object Descriptions from Laser Rangefinder Images. *Proc. First European Conference on Computer Vision*, pp. 387–396, 1990.

[FIS89] R. B. Fisher. *From Surfaces to Objects: Computer Vision and Three Dimensional Scene Analysis.* John Wiley and Sons, Chichester, 1989.

[GAY89] M. Gay. Segmentation Using Region Merging with Edges. *Proc. 5th Alvey Vision Conference*, pp. 115-119, 1989.

[GEM84] S. Geman and D. Geman. Stochastic Relaxation, Gibbs Distributions and the Bayesian Restoration of Images. *IEEE Trans Pattern Analysis and Machine Intelligence* Vol. 6, No. 6, pp. 721–741, Nov 1984.

[GRI85] W. Grimson and T. Lozano-Perez. Finding Cylinders in Range Data. *Proc. IEEE Conference on Computer Vision and Pattern Recognition*, pp. 202–207, 1985.

[HAN78] A. Hanson and E. Riseman. Segmentation of Natural Scenes. in A. Hanson, E. Riseman (eds), *Computer Vision Systems*, 1978.

[KOE82] J. Koenderink and A. van Doorn. The Shape of Smooth Objects and the Way Objects Ends. *Perception* 9, 1982, pp. 129–137.

[LIN90] T. Lindeberg. Scale-Space for Discrete Signals. *IEEE Trans Pattern Analysis and Machine Intelligence* 12, 1990, pp. 234–254.

[LIT86] J. J. Little. *Parallel Algorithms for Computer Vision on the Connection Machine.* MIT AI Memo No. 928, 1986.

[MON91] O. Monga, N. Ayache and P. Sanders. Modeling Uncertainty for Estimating Local Surface Geometry. *Proc. 7th Scandinavian Conference on Image Analysis*, Aalborg, pp. 403–410, 1991.

[NAI91] D. K. Naidu and R. Fisher. A Comparative Analysis of Algorithms for Determining the Peak Position of a Stripe to Sub-pixel Accuracy. *Proc. British Machine Vision Conference*, Glasgow, 1991.

[REI67] C. Reinsch. Smoothing by Spline Functions. *Num. Math.* 10, 1967, pp. 177–183.

[ROS78] A. Rosenfeld. Iterative Methods in Image Analysis. *Pattern Recognition*, Vol. 10, pp. 181, 1978.

[SAM80] H. Samet. Region Representation: Quadtrees from Boundary Codes. *Communications of the ACM*, Vol. 23, No. 3, pp. 163–170, March 1980.

[SAN90] P. T. Sander and S. Zucker. Inferring Surface Trace and Differential Structure from 3-D Images. *IEEE Trans Pattern Analysis and Machine Intelligence* 12, 1990.

[TEN77] J. M. Tenenbaum and H. G. Barrow. Experiments in Interpretation Guided Segmentation. *Artificial Intelligence*, Vol. 18, pp. 241–274, 1977.

[TER85] D. Terzopoulos. *Computing Visible-Surface Representations.* MIT AI Memo No. 800, 1985.

[TRU92] E. Trucco and R. Fisher. Computing Surface-Based Representations from Range Images. *Proc. IEEE International Symposium on Intelligent Control, Glasgow, pp 275–280, August 1992.*

[WAN85] Y. Wang and J. Aggarwal. Construction of Surface Representation from 3-D Volumetric Scene Description. *Proc. IEEE Conference on Computer Vision and Pattern Recognition*, 1985, pp. 130–135.

[WIL90] A. J. S. Wilson, J. G. Mills and M. G. Norman. *Experiments in Tracking and Rendering Surfaces in 3D Seismic Images*. Edinburgh Parallel Computing Centre Technical Report EPCC-TN90-05, 1990.

7

Parallel Stereo and Motion Estimation

M. HOLDEN, M. J. ZEMERLY, J.-P. MULLER

7.1   INTRODUCTION

In 3D computer vision 2D views of the world are captured as images which are composed of 8-bit pixel arrays that are proportional to the brightness of incident radiation. The general goal of computer vision is the recognition of various types of objects present in the scene [Ros88]. Objects can be recognised from fundamental properties of images (e.g. grey levels, texture, shape, scale). Numerous image processing techniques have evolved over the last few decades for applying mathematical transformations to 2D images; these can be used as low-level operators for computer vision. For object recognition the most important techniques are segmentation, feature extraction and template matching. Implicit in these approaches is the assumption that the scene is approximately 2D. However, it can be extended to cover 3D scenes if the orientation of the object is known. Varying illumination conditions, particularly in the case of close range vision, can cause complications because of the shape and the varying texture of the surface. Object recognition within a scene can be much simplified if the surface topography is known, i.e. if the orientation of the surface normal is available for each image point corresponding to a point in the scene. Hence the extraction of 3D coordinates or derivation of range information is central to computer vision.

There are two main approaches to solving the ranging problem: the use of either active or passive sensing of the 3D scene. For active ranging a source is required to irradiate the scene at selected wavelengths. A sensor designed to be sensitive to selected wavelengths is positioned so as to receive the radiant flux. Reflected signals from objects are detected and registered in image form; this is the principal behind

---

Parallel Algorithms for Digital Image Processing, Computer Vision and Neural Networks, ed. I. Pitas
© 1993 John Wiley & Sons Ltd

the operation of laser, radar, sonar and ultrasonic ranging devices [Pin86, SA91]. Passive ranging depends on the radiant energy either emitted by the scene or reflected from its ambient environment (e.g. sunlight). Imaging devices may be sensitive to one or more spectral bands. Passive ranging can be achieved through an analysis of either monocular or stereo (binocular) images. Monocular techniques include shape from shading, shape from contour, shape from motion or shape from texture and depth measurement by focusing [Ros88]. Stereo techniques require the determination of corresponding points by a matching operation. Stereo matching is an attractive method because it leads to a more direct, unambiguous and quantitative derivation than is the case with monocular techniques. Compared with active methods, passive methods can derive a much greater density of surface coordinates [DA89, Lem88] as well as avoiding the problems associated with specular surfaces. Because of the difficulty in arriving at a general analytic solution to the stereo matching problem most researchers have focused on particular application domains. Algorithms are continuously evolving and are able to achieve greater accuracy and a wider domain of applicability often at the expense of computational complexity. In the case of image sequences taken from a moving sensor it is possible (in principle) to derive both the sensor motion and the relative range of points in the scene [Ros88]. Because of the close relationship between stereo and motion it is natural to group them together. For real-time vision upwards of 10^{11} operations per second need to be carried out and this problem can only be addressed by the use of parallel computers [CR92, MCOR88]. This issue is of key importance to real-time stereo for vehicle navigation, robot vision, machine inspection systems and for the processing of satellite imagery with very large array sizes. The approach taken here is to provide a basic introduction to the underlying theory and a review of the main work on algorithms for stereo and motion with particular emphasis being placed on the domain of application. A principal aim is to lay a foundation to the subject and to describe the evolution of different techniques. The first section, 7.2, deals with basic theory and gives an analytical foundation for stereo and contrasts the case when the cameras are aligned on the same horizontal axis with the case when they are not. Section 7.3 reviews stereo algorithms; it starts with the Marr-Poggio 3D scene analysis paradigm based on a model of human perception [MP79]. This provided an impetus for a large body of research into edge based stereo algorithms. Because of the limitations associated with noisy edges other researchers investigated the use of mathematical interest operators to extract alternative features for match primitives. Early work on template matching evolved into a class of sophisticated techniques for correlating individual pixels, collectively known as area based matching algorithms. All these three main classes — edge, interest operator and area based matching algorithm — are described in detail in sections 7.3.1, 7.3.2 and 7.3.3 respectively. The section concludes with illustrations of example imagery and surfaces derived from various matching algorithms. Motion estimation is discussed in section 7.4; it involves calculating a velocity field from a time sequence of images. Two of the most common approaches are feature based and optical flow, both of which are described in detail in sections 7.4.1 and 7.4.2. Both orthographic and perspective projections are considered. In general moving bodies are assumed to be rigid. However, the optic flow approach allows for a relaxation in the rigidity constraint. The section concludes with a number of examples of the results of motion estimation algorithms. Section 7.5 discusses multi-resolution approaches to stereo and motion; this is included because of its relevance to the three main areas covered by the chapter. Analysis at multiple scales both improves the accuracy and reduces computational complexity of stereo and motion algorithms. In addition the technique can be naturally implemented on parallel computers. The final section, 7.6, discusses the issues involved in the parallelisation of stereo and motion algorithms. It begins by describing the two most important classes of parallel architecture: SIMD and MIMD. Next standard paradigms for the design of parallel algorithms are discussed. Finally a number of examples of the most important and recent work on parallel algorithms for stereo and motion are given. The objective here is to give an account of the wide variety of different classes of algorithm and how they have been implemented on each of the two main classes of parallel architectures. The fundamental nature of the subject has led to its use in a wide range of challenging application areas including remote sensing and photogrammetry, terrain modelling, climate modelling, medical imaging, robot vision and vehicle navigation, animation, microscopy and industrial inspection, etc.; see [MT89, BF82, DA89].

7.2 BASIC STEREO THEORY

Fundamental to all frame imaging systems is the principle of perspective transformation. These transformations deal with the projection of points within a 3D scene through a lens onto a 2D plane (typically a photographic film, CCD or other storage media). Points within the scene lie in 3D world space, whilst those in the image plane are 2D representations of the real 3D world. Using the same approach as [GW87] an illustration of perspective view is shown in Figure 7.1. Here two Cartesian coordinate systems (x, y, z) and (X, Y, Z) are chosen to represent the camera and the scene (or world space) respectively. These coordinate systems are chosen so that they are coincident. The lens is situated at a position perpendicular to the centre of the image plane at its focal length, f, i.e. at position $(0, 0, f)$. Assuming that most points of interest are located far from the imaging system so that $Z \gg f$, it is possible to derive a simple relationship between points in 3D world space (X, Y, Z) and those within the image plane. By considering similar triangles, it can be shown that [GW87]:

$$\frac{x}{f} = \frac{X}{f - Z}, \qquad \frac{y}{f} = \frac{Y}{f - Z} \qquad (7.1)$$

These equations can be put into matrix form, and converted from cartesian coordinates where the point is represented by a vector (X, Y, Z) to a homogeneous form whose analogue is defined as (kX, kY, kZ, k), where k is an arbitrary constant > 0 [GW87]. By applying a perspective transformation a 3D scene point can be mapped into an image point. Tracing the ray in the opposite direction is equivalent to applying an inverse perspective transformation from the camera coordinate system back into 3D world coordinates. Notice that a point in the image plane maps into a collinear set of 3D points in world space. This problem can be solved by treating z as a free variable, and leads to Equation (7.2):

$$X = \frac{x}{f}(f - Z), \qquad Y = \frac{y}{f}(f - Z) \qquad (7.2)$$

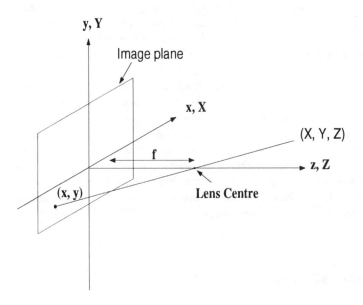

Figure 7.1 Image formation process: the camera coordinate system (x, y, z) is coincident with the world scene coordinate system (X, Y, Z).

Notice that no depth information is included here. This can be recovered through stereoscopic imaging techniques.

7.2.1 Parallel Axes Stereo

Stereo vision involves recovering 3D structure from a pair (or sets of pairs) of images of a scene taken from different viewing points. Because the viewing points are at different positions relative displacements or disparities occur between corresponding items. These disparities enable depth information to be calculated. Figure 7.2 illustrates this schematically with the same scene point being viewed at two different positions. Here left and right camera coordinate systems (x_1, y_1, z_1) and (x_2, y_2, z_2) are perfectly aligned, i.e. the xy planes are coincident with each other and the plane of the world coordinate system XY. This very much simplifies the calculations. Given two image points (x_1, y_1) and (x_2, y_2) of the corresponding scene point, the aim is to find the world coordinates of the scene point. Since the two camera xy planes are aligned, the scene point has the same z coordinate in each case. Translating the two camera coordinate systems so that they are aligned with the world coordinate systems, denoted by subscripts 1 and 2, and using Equation (7.2) gives:

$$X_1 = \frac{x_1}{f}(f - Z), \qquad X_2 = \frac{x_2}{f}(f - Z) \qquad (7.3)$$

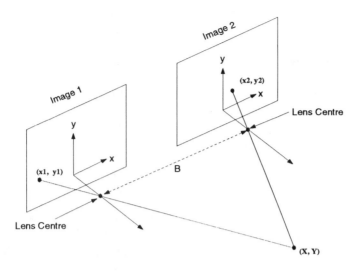

Figure 7.2 Stereo image formation with parallel axes.

Subtracting X_2 from X_1 above gives:

$$X_2 - X_1 = \frac{(x_2 - x_1)}{f}(f - Z)$$

(7.4)

The separation between cameras $X_2 - X_1$ is the baseline (or interocular distance), B; substituting for this and rearranging leads to a formula relating range to disparity:

$$Z = f - \frac{fB}{(x_2 - x_1)}$$

(7.5)

Since the camera system is rigid the baseline and focal length are fixed; for distant objects the second term is dominant, hence the range, Z, is approximately inversely proportional to the range. The difference in position $(x_2 - x_1)$ or displacement is termed the x-disparity, and enables the range to be easily derived. To find the disparity corresponding points must be found, and the most usual method of finding these is to stereo match the two images. Parallel axes (or epipolar) stereo is illustrated in Figure 7.2 and applies when the camera systems are rigid as is the case for close-range applications involving framing cameras such as those in robotics and those which are modelled on human stereo perception. For detailed information on camera imaging systems the reader is referred to [STH80].

7.2.2 Non Parallel Axes Stereo

In contrast to close range applications, remote sensing ones are long-range and the camera coordinate systems are not perfectly aligned, typically differing by at least a rotation and translation. Figure 7.3 illustrates the situation. A line in world coordinates maps to two different vectors in the camera coordinates. This is known as the condition of non-epipolarity and leads to an increase in the search space from 1 to 2

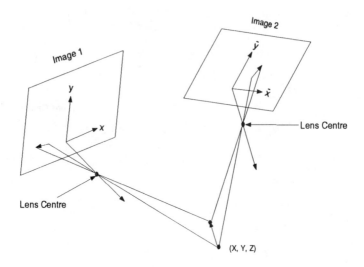

Figure 7.3   Non-epipolar stereo image formation.

dimensions when searching for corresponding points. Once disparities are found they must be translated into ground coordinates by using a camera model. This involves modifying equation (7.5) to allow for the misalignment of the two coordinate systems. Alternatively, if the camera orientation is known it is possible to transform the non-epipolar images into epipolar ones. Two methods are described in [LZ88]; both involve one dimensional resampling of epipolar lines in the original imagery. One method uses linear and the other neighbourhood based interpolation.

7.3   REVIEW OF STEREO MATCHING ALGORITHMS

One of the most popular methods for deriving 3D structure is by finding corresponding points by stereo matching. This operation involves searching image data for a set of homologous matches [DA89]. The lack of a comprehensive theory of stereo matching has resulted in a plethora of techniques each aimed at slightly different application domains. Most algorithms assume that the two images are epipolar aligned and are based on a computational model of human stereo stereopsis first suggested by Marr and Poggio [MP79]. This is based on the results of physiological, clinical and psychophysical experiments. The model assumes that the eyes are located at the same horizontal height and scan the 3D scene horizontally; the brain receives both images and extracts a set of symbolic features from them. Typical features are surface markings, shadows and surface discontinuities such as edges, which correspond to intensity variations in the imagery. The set of features constitute a primal sketch of the scene. Figure 7.4 illustrates a pair of primal sketches; see Figure 7.12 for the original images. Two constraints are imposed on matches: (1) each surface point in one image has at most one unique corresponding point in the other, thus each point has at most one disparity value; (2) the scene is composed of objects whose surfaces are generally smooth when viewed from a distance, resulting in a smooth disparity gradient. Marr

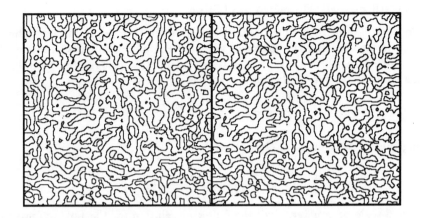

Figure 7.4 Illustration of left and right pair of primal sketches: edges extracted with a LoG filter from SPOT images of Kamchatka.

and Poggio [MP79] suggested that images should be filtered using a series of masks for filtering at different spatial resolutions and orientations. Matching is then performed on the pair of sketches. The locations of the intensity changes are found from the positions of peaks of the gradient of the intensity function or zero-crossings in the second derivative [Gri85]. Zero-crossings are extracted for each orientation and spatial resolution and the pairs are matched. Large scale matching can be used to guide finer grain matching. This is an example of a multi-resolution approach (see later). The set of derived match points is termed a $2\frac{1}{2}$D sketch.

Barnard and Fischler [BF82] classified stereo matching algorithms into two categories.

- Feature based: These extract semantic features from the scene and use them as match primitives. Two common methods are used: edge and interest operator based matching.

- Area based (signal) matching algorithms: Apply a correlation operation to raw or normalised pixel data. For example, given two images, a reference and a search against which to match, a small area is extracted from the reference and used as a template with which to match against a slightly larger window from the search image.

Lemmens [Lem88] considers a further category of relational matching; in this approach structures within images and the relationship to neighbouring structures are represented symbolically. The epipolar condition reduces the search space, so that a 2D correlation is replaced by a 1D one [BF82]. A further classification in terms of epipolar and non-epipolar was proposed by Muller *et al.* [MCOR88].

7.3.1 Edge Based Matchers

Most edge based matchers use a simple operator to extract edge points for match primitives; alternatively sets of edges can be assembled into edge segments for match primitives.

7.3.1.1 MARR-POGGIO-GRIMSON MATCHER

Grimson [Gri85] implemented the Marr-Poggio model [MP79]. In his algorithm edges
are extracted by locating the peaks of the gradient of the intensity function based
on zero-crossings of the Laplacian of a Gaussian (LoG) as suggested by [MP79]. In
cartesian coordinates the Laplacian operator is represented by:

$$\nabla^2 = \frac{\partial^2}{\partial^2 x} + \frac{\partial^2}{\partial^2 y} \tag{7.6}$$

Applying this to the Gaussian, $G(x, y)$:

$$G(x, y) = \frac{1}{2\pi\sigma^2} \exp\left(-\frac{x^2 + y^2}{2\sigma^2}\right) \tag{7.7}$$

where σ is a scale parameter, gives the following relation for the LoG operator:

$$\nabla^2 G(x, y) = \frac{1}{2\pi\sigma^4} \left(\frac{x^2 + y^2}{\sigma^2} - 2\right) \exp\left(-\frac{x^2 + y^2}{2\sigma^2}\right) \tag{7.8}$$

which can also be approximated using the difference of two Gaussians. Zero-crossings
of the filtered imagery represent profound changes in the intensity function.

In the Marr-Poggio model the imagery is assumed to be epipolar aligned, and so
they are scanned horizontally from left to right for zero-crossings. A multi-resolution
(see later) control strategy is used, match estimates at coarse resolution being used
to guide those at a finer one, hence reducing the search space and execution time.
Feature points are matched by taking a point from the left image at position (x, y)
and searching a horizontal window for the corresponding point in the right (x', y). The
window is defined by the following inequality:

$$x + d_i - w_c \leq x' \leq x + d_i + w_c \tag{7.9}$$

where d_i is the disparity in that region and w_c is the central width of the filter. Zero-
crossings in left and right images must have the same contrast sign and approximately
the same orientation. Most of the match errors occur at depth discontinuities, typically
at occluding boundaries. Geometric distortions in the sensors, perspective distortions
in the imaging geometry, noise and local photometric effects introduce displacements
in the positions of zero-crossings and cause a breakdown of the horizontal epipolar
condition which results in unmatched points. Grimson [Gri85] made the following
improvements to the implementation to deal with these effects:

- Convolutions: The left and right images are convolved with a LoG filter at different widths.

- Zero-crossings of the second derivative are extracted from both images and labelled with the following contrast signs: positive, negative, horizontal or all zero.

- The search window is extended to 2D to allow for a small amount of vertical
  disparity (about 2 lines), i.e.:

$$x + d_i - w_c \leq x' \leq x + d_i + w_c; \qquad y - \epsilon \leq y' \leq y + \epsilon \tag{7.10}$$

- Like contrast signs are matched with like.

- Ambiguities are resolved by figural continuity, i.e. matches are restricted to extended zero-crossing contour segments.

Grimson [Gri85] carried out a number of experiments on the algorithm using imagery derived from different scenes: (1) close range (1500 mm) stereo pairs of a laboratory scene, and reported error in disparity estimates of about 15 mm or 1%; (2) aerial photographs of natural terrain: two 512 × 512 pixel stereo pairs of Phoenix, Arizona and Fort Sill, Oklahoma with a disparity range of 41 and 51 pixels respectively; 31403 and 32907 zero-crossing points were extracted from each and 76% and 49% of these were matched with a matching error of 0.3% and 1.8% respectively; (3) aerial photographs of man-made terrain each with a disparity range of 13 pixels: two 320 × 320 pixel stereo pairs of a number of buildings (UBC) and a highway interchange; 16801 and 10642 zero crossings were extracted from each and 73%, 62% of these were matched with a matching error of 0.07% and 2.5% respectively. The algorithm was implemented in LISP on an MIT LISP machine (with optimised microcode) and a special purpose device was used for the convolutions. For a single channel at the original resolution of the UBC images matching was reported to take 5 minutes and with 3 levels 10 minutes.

7.3.1.2 NISHIHARA'S PRISM

Nishihara [Nis84] extended the Marr-Poggio matcher for robotic applications and called the algorithm PRISM. Nishihara experimented with the Grimson implementation and reported that it was sensitive to small misalignments. He sought to improve it and established four principal design goals: (1) noise tolerance, for moderate levels of noise; (2) satisfactory performance for volume occupancy, range measurement and detection of depth discontinuities; (3) practical speed for robotics applications; (4) algorithm simplicity so that it can easily be analysed. Because algorithms that match zero-crossing contours tend to be sensitive to noise, Nishihara based matching on zero-crossing sign representation. To increase the amount of texture the scene is artificially illuminated with an unstructured texture pattern. A stereo pair was captured and filtered at three scales of resolution by convolution with the LoG operator. Each is then clipped to produce coarse, medium and fine scale sign representations that are matched pairwise to produce coarse, medium and fine scale disparity maps. The matching at coarse scales is propagated to those at finer ones to help guide matching. Signals from a pair of vidicon cameras were digitised to provide a stereo pair of 576 × 454 pixel images. These were fed through a high speed digital convolver to produce filtered images at three resolution scales. The matching algorithm is applied to each scale, to produce 8 × 6, 17 × 13 and 36 × 26 disparity maps. The disparity estimates at each level are used to guide the matching at the next finer one. Matching all 3 levels to produce a 36 × 26 disparity map is reported to take 30-40 seconds. The final elevation is modelled using a 36 × 26 grid of square prisms.

7.3.1.3 PMF

Pollard *et al.* developed an edge-based matcher which is also based on the Marr-Poggio model [PMF85]. A surface continuity constraint was used to establish a matching rule based on figural continuity. Figural continuity has the benefit of allowing for a certain amount of surface roughness. This constraint provides a method of disambiguating false matches by limiting the disparity gradient that can exist between correct matches. A disparity gradient of 1 was suggested and should be satisfactory for almost all surfaces (e.g. planar surfaces with maximal slopes of up to 74%). Three constraints are used in PMF:

- The disparity gradient constraint.

- The epipolar constraint.

- The uniqueness constraint: for any feature in the reference image only one match is accepted.

These constraints help solve the stereo disambiguation problem. The choice of matching primitive is left to the discretion of the user, since the efficiency of feature extraction is domain dependent. For natural imagery the zero-crossing Marr-Hildreth operator is used, whilst for synthetic scenes a Canny edge operator was used. PMF has two main stages: (1) to identify a number of possible matches within a circular search area of 7 pixel radius and store them; (2) to calculate their matching strength (potentially in parallel) and apply a relaxation labelling technique so that those with the highest matching strength can be selected. When applying the disparity-gradient-limit all possible matches within the neighbourhood are considered. There are difficulties in handling horizontal edge segments, but these can be overcome by introducing a 2D search for nearly horizontal edges. A limitation of the algorithm is that long segments are particularly difficult to match using disparity gradient information. Pollard *et al.* evaluated the performance of PMF for a number of different types of imagery each of 128 × 128 pixels. The scenes included random dot stereograms, a close range office scene and aerial imagery of a rocky terrain. Three tests with random dot stereograms were carried out. The first showed that for disparity gradients of less than 1 match coverage was about 98%, with a steady decrease to about 50% coverage with a disparity gradient of 1.5. For the second a square wave was encoded and 95% of points were correctly matched with 0.5% unmatched and 4.5% matched incorrectly. For the third, superimposed transparent planar surfaces posed greater difficulties and gave 64% match coverage, 0.5% unmatched and 35.5% incorrectly matched. No match percentages were given for the natural scenes. Day and Muller [DM89] carried out tests on PMF with real 1500 × 1500 pixel extracts from SPOT satellite images of mountainous terrain in the south of France. A sparse match coverage of only 8380 points was observed with a RMS error of 45 m in ground coordinates. The error value should be considered as an upper limit because no allowance is made for errors arising from the camera modelling software required to convert images from non-epipolar to epipolar.

7.3.1.4 DYNAMIC PROGRAMMING

Dynamic programming is a non-linear optimisation technique that was originally applied in control theory and speech recognition. It is based on Bellman's principle of optimality [Bel57] which states that *the optimal path between two given points is also optimum between any two points lying on that path*. This means that the global optimisation of a multistage problem can be split into a series of single stage optimisations involving only two variables. It has the advantage of reducing the number of searches for an N stage optimisation problem with L possible values from $O(L^N)$ to $O(NL^2)$ [Jai89]. As well as providing an optimal solution it also gives several graded suboptimal alternatives. Figure 7.5 illustrates the principle; here nodes marked A-K and the numbers represent the costs associated with particular paths. The optimum path (the one with lowest cumulative cost) between A and B can be found by splitting the graph into two subgraphs A-E and E-B and calculating the optimal paths between them. By applying this principle paths ACE, ACDE and ADCE are immediately eliminated; in a similar way so are EGH and EFGH; by repeated application of the principle the optimal path ADEFJB (shown in bold) is found.

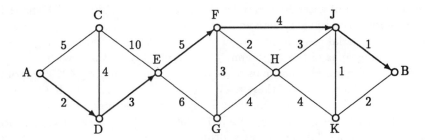

Figure 7.5   Dynamic programming.

Maitre and Wu [MW87] have applied dynamic programming to the registration of NOAA-7-AVHRR images of the Normandy coastline to a reference consisting of digitised map segments. This problem is complicated by clouds that introduce noise and distortion in the imagery. Maitre and Wu adapted classical dynamic programming methodology to handle graph entry, maintaining the optimal path to the end, and breaks in the graph due to occlusions, etc. Costs are calculated as the differences between successive vectors $(i - 1, j)$ and (i, j) which are derived from the absolute difference of translation vectors in the x and y directions. For an exact match this is zero, for an elastic one it is a positive integer and when the path is broken it blows up to infinity. When a break is detected, a virtual node is created in an extended area of the graph. Compatibility with the reference map is maintained according to a rigorous translation of the reference map to the image contour. A Sobel operator is used to detect edges and a logical filter is applied to remove transmission noise. Then the first 400 (approximately) highest definition edges are retained. Tests carried out on 16 different 256 × 256 pixel images of the same coastline were reported to result in 15 correct registrations. The average processing time on a Bull DPS7 (50 KWords of RAM) was 6 minutes per image.

Ohta and Kanade [OK85] designed a stereo matcher based on dynamic programming for epipolar aligned images. The search for correspondences is split into two stages: a 2D search along a pair of scanlines (intra-scanline) and a search between scanlines (inter-scanline). The 2D intra-scanline search is implemented by placing left and right scanlines on the vertical and horizontal axes of a cartesian graph and searching for correspondences between edge-delimited intervals. The inter-scanline search finds correspondences between vertically connected edges in left and right images.

Both searches are performed using dynamic programming and can take place simultaneously, with the latter providing consistency constraints for the former. For dynamic programming to be applied two conditions must be satisfied: (1) decision stages must be ordered so that all results required at a given stage are already available; (2) the behaviour of the process at any stage must depend only on the current state and not on previous ones (i.e. Markovian behaviour). For the intra-scanline search, nodes are taken as edges and costs are derived from the similarity of intensity (mean and variance) between left and right intervals. The ordering scheme simply orders edges from left to right on each scanline. For the inter-scanline search nodes are taken as pairs of connected edges and costs based on intra-scanline costs. Ordering requires leftmost nodes to be processed first. Edges are detected using several operators at different scales and orientations. Edges are then linked together to form connected edges which are ordered in terms of ascending maximum number of arcs. Ohta and Kanade have tested the algorithm on imagery derived from synthesised, urban aerial and close range block scenes. The aerial scene is composed of a pair of 512×512 pixel images derived from aerial photographs of the Pentagon. These are highly textured with a high concentration of buildings and other man-made objects. Approximately 40000 edges have been extracted and about 1% of these are connected. For the 2D search 372 inconsistencies were detected and these were reduced by an order of magnitude to 27 for the 3D search. The CPU time taken on a VAX 11/780 was 52 minutes for the 2D search and 858 minutes for the 3D one. The performance could be significantly improved by parallelising this algorithm, its uniform nature making it easy to parallelise.

Baldwin [BY90] applied dynamic programming to resolve local ambiguities in disparity estimates produced by a set of different match primitives. Baldwin argued that conventional dynamic programming is limited to a 1D search space and that match primitives tend to be limited to specific domains. Most matching strategies impose geometric constraints (usually epipolar) to decrease the search space and reduce the number of ambiguities. The difficulty with these is that the constraints are corrupted as a result of noise and distortion that is introduced during image capture. Baldwin therefore suggested optimising a set of local cost functions, each one of which is associated with a particular match primitive applied to a pair of features or set of pixels. The optimisation is carried out by dynamic programming in disparity space which uses a hypothetical "cyclopean" image space located between the perspective centres of the two images. This approach has the benefit that the global optimisation need no longer be restricted to epipolar scanlines. Baldwin used the following match primitives: (1) Sobel operator to extract edge magnitude and orientation; (2) Laplacian of a Gaussian; (3) Zero crossings of a Laplacian of a Gaussian. First each image is smoothed with a Gaussian filter. Then a Sobel operator is applied to the smoothed image to extract intensity gradient magnitude and orientation images. Finally a Laplacian of a Gaussian is applied to the original image to produce the second derivative. For 800×800 pixel aerial imagery these calculations took 16 hours on a Sun 3/260.

7.3.2 Interest Operator Based Stereo Matchers

Instead of using edges, lines or other vector-like features, interest points such as corners [ZH83, HS88], line crossings or high variance points [Han74, Han88, Mor77, Foe86, FG87] or local extrema of Gaussian curvature [Dre81, LA88] can be used. The advantage here is that the extraction of interest points is more straightforward because edges and lines need further thresholding, thinning and sometimes grouping. Various types of interest operators are reported in the literature but the most widely used are Foerstner and Moravec. Comparisons between different interest operators can be found in [LA88, AZM91].

7.3.2.1 THE MORAVEC INTEREST OPERATOR

The Moravec interest operator [Mor77] is based on the sum of squares of 4 directional variances of the grey levels of pixels in a window. The interest value, I, for a point at the centre of a window is equal to the minimum of four $k \times k$ directional variances. Interest points are selected so that their interest value is higher than a threshold t.

$$I = \min \left(\sum_{x=i-k}^{i+k} \sum_{y=j-k}^{j+k} \left[\begin{array}{c} (g(x, y) - g(x, y + 1))^2 \\ (g(x, y) - g(x + 1, y))^2 \\ (g(x, y) - g(x + 1, y + 1))^2 \\ (g(x, y) - g(x + 1, y - 1))^2 \end{array} \right] \right) \tag{7.11}$$

where k is the size of the operator window and $g(i, j)$ is the grey level value at image point (i, j). A non-maximal suppression operator is applied to prevent clustering of local maxima within a selected window. A limitation of the Moravec operator is that it cannot locate features to sub-pixel accuracy. Some improvements were made to this operator in [AZM91].

7.3.2.2 THE FOERSTNER INTEREST OPERATOR

Interest points are selected so they meet five requirements: distinctness, invariance, stability, seldomness, and interpretability [Foe86, FG87]. Foerstner [Foe86] developed an algorithm based on the error ellipse of the covariance matrix C which gives a direct measure of the curvature of the 2D-autocovariance function within a window.

$$C = \sigma^2 \left[\begin{array}{cc} \sum g_x^2 & \sum g_x g_y \\ \sum g_x g_y & \sum g_y^2 \end{array} \right]^{-1} = \sigma^2 N^{-1} \tag{7.12}$$

where σ^2 is the variance, g_x and g_y are the partial derivatives in x and y directions respectively and N is the normal equation matrix. The sums are calculated in a user specified window size, typically 7×7 pixels.

First, the interest windows are selected from an image so that the error ellipse satisfies the following requirements:

- It should be small.

- It should be as close as possible to a circle.

The size or weight, w, and the shape, q, of the error ellipse are determined from the determinant and trace of the normal equation matrix, N, as follows:

$$w = \frac{\det(N)}{\operatorname{trace}(N)} \tag{7.13}$$

$$q = \frac{4\det(N)}{\text{trace}^2(N)} \tag{7.14}$$

q is equivalent to the ratio of semiaxes of the error ellipse. In the case of a circle q is equal to 1 (for more details see [FG87, STH80]). Both measures can be calculated directly from the grey level intensities. Interest windows are selected so they satisfy thresholds for w and q as follows:

$$w = \begin{cases} w & \text{if} \quad q > q_{lim} \quad \text{and} \quad w > w_{lim} \\ \\ 0 & \text{else} \end{cases} \tag{7.15}$$

where $0.5 \le q_{lim} \le 0.75$ and w_{lim}:

$$w_{lim} = \begin{cases} k.w_{mean} & (0.5 \le k \le 1.5) \\ \\ c.w_{med} & (c = 5) \end{cases} \tag{7.16}$$

where w_{mean} is the average of the weights of all the windows and w_{med} the median of the weights taken over the whole image; k and c are constant values that can be found by experiment.

To prevent clustering of local maxima, a non-maximal suppression operation of the value $w \times q$ is applied within windows of user selected size. Interest points are then located on the basis of one of the following:

1. Centre pixels of the interest windows.

2. Centres of gravity of the interest windows.

3. Centres of circular objects in the interest windows.

Cases 2 and 3 above have the advantage of locating features to sub-pixel accuracy because floating point calculations can be used. For more details see [Foe86, FG87]. For an extension to this operator which allows one to select the best n interest points and distribute them uniformly across the image see [AZM91].

7.3.2.3   SURVEY OF INTEREST OPERATOR BASED STEREO MATCHING METHODS

Many feature-based stereo matching algorithms use interest operators for match primitives. Some of these can be used as initial disparity estimates for other stereo [AZM91, OC88, HZM92] and motion estimation techniques [TSB91, AN88]. Most use either Moravec or Foerstner or variations of these. Some researchers have designed their own operator [HS88]. This section briefly describes some of the most well known stereo matching techniques used with Moravec and Foerstner. These techniques can be classified into two types: correlation matching and relaxation labelling matching.

Correlation Matching

Digital image correlation is a powerful matching technique capable of very high sub-pixel precision [Gru85, FG87, Li90]. Foerstner [Foe86] developed an operator to extract interest points from synthetic image pairs of size 70×70 pixels. Interest points from both images are first extracted. A list of corresponding candidate pairs is drawn up from the two sets of interest points based on a similarity measure governed by four requirements: invariance (e.g. the interest operator allowing for geometric distortion such as scale and rotation), seldomness (e.g. extra weight for seldom points), heuristics (e.g. *a priori* knowledge of maximum disparity) and metric (e.g. correlation of the sum of squares of grey level differences). Next, a consistency operation is performed on the list to reduce the number of candidate match pairs. This is achieved by robust estimation (correlation with an affine transformation between pair patches):

$$\left[\begin{array}{c} px_i + v_{px_i} \\ py_i + v_{py_i} \end{array} \right] = \left[\begin{array}{cc} a & b \\ d & e \end{array} \right] \cdot \left[\begin{array}{c} x_i \\ y_i \end{array} \right] + \left[\begin{array}{c} c \\ f \end{array} \right] \qquad (7.17)$$

where px_i and py_i are the parallaxes in x_i and y_i respectively, v_i is the weighted sum of squares of residuals and $a, \ldots, e$ are the affine transformation parameters. This procedure is iterated with a slower convergence function, e.g. $\tau(v_i) = \frac{v_i}{2}$, that is minimised to reduce the number of ambiguities. The experimental results for synthetic images did not conclude its applicability to real world scene.

Li [Li90] used the same technique to determine the relative orientation of stereo pairs of photographs for digitisation on an analytical plotter. For a real aerial stereo model the accuracy in terms of standard deviation is 3.83 μm (≈ 0.06 pixel).

Zong et al. [ZLS91] used a simple correlation technique with the Foerstner interest points in a multi-resolution (4 levels) matching for guiding the matching of zero crossing points at finer resolutions. This can resample 4096×4096 pixel digitised aerial images to an epipolar geometry; 23 interest points out of 145 are rejected whilst others have a standard deviation of 4.4 μm (0.07 pixel).

Li and Schenck [LS91] used the Foerstner interest operator to find interest points in both images and use stereo matched zero-crossing segments to constrain the search space to find corresponding candidates. Grey level correlation in 5×5 windows is used for matching candidate pairs. Corresponding points are selected when the correlation value exceeds a threshold and the difference between the disparity value of the interest points and the original matched zero-crossing points is less than 5 pixels. No sub-pixel accuracy for the interest points was used here. Instead, a 3×3 correlation value matrix centred on the pixel with maximum correlation value between a pair of corresponding points is approximated by an orthogonal polynomial in order to obtain the sub-pixel accuracy. Multi-resolution matching is also used for matching zero-crossings (only the highest level) and the interest points. Results for a pair of digitised aerial photographs of 4096×4096 pixels indicated that 81 corresponding points are extracted. Finally the relative orientation was calculated and the Y parallax was equal to about 5 μm (0.1 pixel).

Holm [Hol91] proposed a method for automatic registration of satellite images (SPOT) based on the Foerstner interest operator. A small number (30-50) of interest points (or features) are extracted from the left and right images. Correspondences are found using a modified Foerstner correlation method. Large numbers of interest points can be extracted in a second pass, the original one being used to limit the search areas.

Hannah [Han88] developed 2 area-based correlation techniques for aerial image matching. In both techniques a modified Moravec interest operator is used to extract interest points from left and right images. The first does not require epipolar geometry. Normalised (by both mean and variance) cross-correlation is applied in an unconstrained multi-resolution way. The top level of the pyramid is approximately equal to the size of the correlation window. Matches from the top level are propagated down and refined in the next finer level until the lowest level is reached. Matches at all levels are accepted only if their correlation value exceeds a certain threshold. Matches are then verified by back-matching from right to left. The second technique requires camera model information for calculating the epipolar geometry to constrain the search. The same multi-resolution matching strategy is used here together with the epipolar constraint. Matched points with the assumption of a continuous disparity surface are used to obtain a digital disparity surface with a specified grid size for the whole scene. Hannah applied both of these techniques to match a variety of 12 types of images, and in most cases reported visually reasonably correct coverages with a small percentage of noticeable errors.

Allison *et al.* [AZM91, AM92] used modified versions of the Foerstner and Moravec interest operators to extract automatically features from stereo pairs of satellite images such as SPOT and various types of aerial imagery (digitised from photographs on a Leica DSR 11 analytical plotter or taken by airborne sensors such as ATM and ASAS). A comparison between Foerstner and Moravec operators showed the Foerstner operator to be more suitable. Allison *et al.* designed automated techniques for generating corresponding points for each type of imagery.

- For SPOT imagery the camera geometry (provided with the images) is needed to limit the disparity search. A geometric consistency check reduces the number of possible match candidates. Then an adaptive least squares correlation technique (ALSC) is applied to each candidate pair where a precision measure (eigenvalue) is obtained. To select seedpoints a threshold on the precision is used to filter out pairs. Holden *et al.* [HZM92] used this technique to generate hundreds of uniformly spaced initial match estimates for matching full 6000 × 6000 pixel SPOT pairs with GPSM (see the parallel section).

- For digitised aerial imagery the geometric constraint used to guide the search in the right image is provided by the camera model obtained from the analytical plotter (when photographs are digitised). The same matching procedures as SPOT were then used here. Zemerly *et al.* [ZHM92] used this technique to generate seed points for matching 2229 × 2520 pixel aerial images.

- For other types of imagery with no camera information two methods for disparity filtering can be used: relaxation labelling and maximum expected disparity. For the first an improved Barnard and Thompson relaxation labelling method (see next section) is used. For the second a maximum expected disparity filter using *a priori* knowledge of the images possible by manually measuring a few seed points is used. Matching is done using ALSC in both cases. The relaxation labelling technique generated only a few seed points due to distortion of the test images. In the second method a quadratic surface was adaptively fitted to the range of disparities whilst iteratively removing those pairs with standard deviation exceeding 2.5. This method generated for a few test cases 100% accurate points and was used to provide control points for other application areas such as resampling distorted sensor data to digitised aerial photographs of the same area (see [AM92]).

Results of these methods on various types of imagery show the robustness of the techniques developed. Reliability ranging between 80% and 100% is claimed from thousands of initial interest points generated. Reliability is measured as the percentage of the number of seedpoints from which an area-based stereo matcher (Otto-Chau) is able to grow.

Relaxation Labelling Matching

Relaxation labelling processes are standard image processing techniques which are often applied to segmentation [RHZ76, HZ83]. These techniques are mainly used to deal with ambiguities and noise in vision systems. However, they have far broader potential applications and implications. Although technical details of the design and implementation for different applications may vary, the general structure is based on two concepts: (1) the decomposition of complex computation into a simple local one; (2) the requisite use of context to resolve ambiguities.

Barnard and Thompson [BT80] applied relaxation labelling to automatically determine corresponding points for stereo and monocular motion images. First the Moravec operator is used to derive interest points for the two images, then a global match network containing all possible correspondences is reconstructed. The network consists of local match sub-networks for every point in the left image with all possible points in the right within a maximum disparity range. For each correspondence pair for point i in the left with disparity l an initial probability $p_i(l)$ based on a weight $w_i(l)$ is generated:

$$w_i(l) = \frac{1}{(1 + c + s_i(l))} \qquad l \neq l^* \qquad (7.18)$$

where c is a constant (in this case 10), and $s_i(l)$ is a similarity measure derived using the sum of squares of grey level differences of pixels in corresponding 5×5 windows centred on the pair.

$$p_i(l^*) = 1 - \max(w_i(l)) \qquad (l^* = \text{undefined disparity}) \qquad (7.19)$$

$$p_i(l) = p_i(l \setminus i) \times (1 - p_i(l^*)) \qquad l \neq l^* \qquad (7.20)$$

where $p_i(l \setminus i)$ is the probability that point i has label l, given by:

$$p_i(l \setminus i) = \frac{w_i}{\sum_{l' \neq l^*} w_i(l')} \qquad (7.21)$$

where l' is the set of disparities that might be assigned to point i. Note that the sum of probabilities for all sub-networks is unity. A rule of consistency with neighbouring pairs is used to update probabilities. The probability of a pair, i, with disparity l is increased if there exist neighbouring (Neighbourhood of i, $N(i)$) pairs j ($i \neq j$) with high probability of having similar (similarity, θ) disparities l'. N and θ are two thresholds that can be optimised for a certain application (Barnard and Thompson choose 15 and 1 respectively). The new probability $p_i^{k+1}(l)$ is computed from the following set of equations:

$$p_i^{k+1}(l) = p_i^k(l) \times (A + B \times q_i^k(l)) \qquad l \neq l^* \qquad (7.22)$$

$$p_i^{k+1}(l^*) = p_i^k(l^*) \qquad (7.23)$$

where

$$q_i^k(l) = \sum_{j \in N(i)} \left[\sum_{\|l-l'\| \leq \theta} p_i^k(l') \right] \qquad l \neq l^* \qquad (7.24)$$

The new normalised probabilities are then obtained by:

$$p_i^{k+1}(l) = \frac{p_i^{k+1}(l)}{\sum_{l' in L_i} p_i^{k+1}(l')} \qquad (7.25)$$

L_i is the set of disparities that might be assigned to a point. A and B are positive constants which influence the convergence characteristics of the model (Barnard and Thompson used A = 0.3 and B = 3). After a few iterations most of the possible matches have very low probability and setting them to zero if their probability is less than 0.01 increases the efficiency of the algorithm. Probabilities are updated until the network reaches a steady state. In practice this can be achieved by terminating the procedure after only a few iterations (e.g. 10). Then the network is thresholded at a suitable probability level (0.7) and those disparities with probabilities higher than the threshold are selected as the matched output. This technique has been applied to three sets of data: an epipolar stereo pair, a monocular sequence pair of a truck in motion (horizontal disparity known to be about 7) and a monocular sequence pair of aerial urban area. Neither the size of the images nor the number of interest points extracted is given although by visual inspection of the results there are about 50 points. The results presented indicated errors in the second and third pairs due to either the presence of an edge or a dense cluster of interest points. Improvements of this algorithm have been reported by Allison *et al.* and Collins *et al.* [AZM91, CRAM87] with varying success.

7.3.3 Area Based (Signal) Matchers

Given stereo images, a reference (target) and another against which to match (search), the area surrounding the target point is extracted from the target and correlated with an area surrounding the search position in the search image (see Figure 7.6). This technique can be improved by allowing for geometric distortion and noise differences between the images. If the grey level value or intensity function in the target area is $g_t(x_t, y_t)$ and the corresponding one in the search area is $g_s(x_s, y_s)$, it is possible to allow for additive noise $n(x, y)$ as follows:

$$g_t(x_t, y_t) = g_s(x_s, y_s) + n(x, y) \qquad (7.26)$$

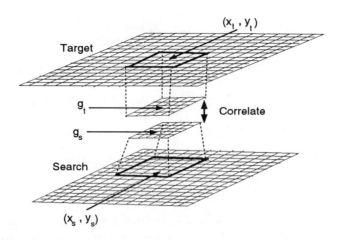

Figure 7.6   Grey level correlation.

7.3.3.1   GREY VALUE CORRELATION

This method uses a statistical measure of similarity, i.e. a covariance measure, the simplest one being the discrete correlation $\sum_{i=1}^{n} g_{ti}.g_{si}$, or by normalising using sample means:

$$\sum_{i=1}^{n}(g_{ti} - \bar{g}_t)(g_{si} - \bar{g}_s) \tag{7.27}$$

There are a number of others based on second moments, Gaussian and Laplacian variance, and ones for weighting the centre of the sample; see [Lem88].

7.3.3.2   LEAST SQUARES CORRELATION

Here we assume an incremental shift (typically ≤ 3 pixels) between target and search areas:

$$\begin{aligned}
x_s &= x_t + \mathrm{d}x \\
y_s &= y_t + \mathrm{d}y
\end{aligned} \tag{7.28}$$

Using equation (7.26) above with the noise term moved to the left hand side gives:

$$g_t(x_t, y_t) + n(x_t, y_t) = g_s(x_t + \mathrm{d}x, y_t + \mathrm{d}y) \tag{7.29}$$

Now taking the partial derivative gives:

$$\Delta g + n = \frac{\partial g_s}{\partial x}\Delta x + \frac{\partial g_s}{\partial y}\Delta y \tag{7.30}$$

Denoting $\frac{\partial g_s}{\partial x}$ by g_x and $\frac{\partial g_s}{\partial y}$ by g_y and multiplying the above first by g_x and then by g_y and summing over the search area yields two equations:

$$\sum g_x \Delta g + n = \sum g_x \frac{\partial g_s}{\partial x} \Delta x + \sum g_x \frac{\partial g_s}{\partial y} \Delta y$$
$$\sum g_y \Delta g + n = \sum g_y \frac{\partial g_s}{\partial x} \Delta x + \sum g_y \frac{\partial g_s}{\partial y} \Delta y \qquad (7.31)$$

which under rearrangement and conversion to matrix form results in:

$$\begin{bmatrix} \Delta x \\ \Delta y \end{bmatrix} = \begin{bmatrix} \sum g_x^2 & \sum g_x g_y \\ \sum g_x g_y & \sum g_y^2 \end{bmatrix}^{-1} \begin{bmatrix} \sum g_x \Delta g \\ \sum g_y \Delta g \end{bmatrix} \qquad (7.32)$$

This approach allows for shifts between the search and target areas.

7.3.3.3 ADAPTIVE LEAST SQUARES CORRELATION

The approach taken above can be extended to allow for more general geometric differences that arise through perspective and sensor distortions. An affine transformation between two planar regions in the images [GB87] is used. Such a model allows for a deformation of a planar region (patch) in the search image in terms of the one in the right. Such a transformation will model rotation and skew as well as translations and can be represented as follows:

$$x_s = a_{11} + a_{12}x_t + a_{21}y_t$$
$$y_s = b_{11} + b_{12}x_t + b_{21}y_t \qquad (7.33)$$

where a_{11} is x shift, a_{12} is change in x scale, a_{21} is shearing in x, b_{11} is shift in y, b_{12} is shearing in y, b_{21} is change in y scale. Gruen and Baltsavias [GB87] model the geometric transformation on a bivariate polynomial. The intensity function $g_s(x_s, y_s)$ in equation (7.26) is first linearised using the Taylor expansion around an initial estimate $g_s^0(x, y)$ which gives:

$$g_s(x_s, y_s) = g_s^0(x, y) + \frac{\partial g_s^0(x, y)}{\partial x} dx_s + \frac{\partial g_s^0(x, y)}{\partial y} dy_s \qquad (7.34)$$

Taking differentials of (7.33):

$$dx_s = da_{11} + da_{12}x_t + da_{21}y_t$$
$$dy_s = db_{11} + db_{12}x_t + db_{21}y_t \qquad (7.35)$$

Dropping the s and t subscripts, converting to the g_x and g_y notation as above and substituting for the differentials leads to:

$$g(x, y) = g^0(x, y) + g_x^0 da_{11} + g_x^0 x da_{12} + g_x^0 y da_{21} + g_y^0 db_{11} + g_y^0 x db_{12} + g_y^0 y db_{21} \qquad (7.36)$$

Converting these equations into matrix form, combining the parameters in a vector X and their coefficients into a design matrix A:

$$X^T = (da_{11}, da_{12}, da_{21}, db_{11}, db_{12}, db_{21}) \qquad (7.37)$$

$$A = (g_x^0, xg_x^0, yg_x^0, g_y^0, xg_y^0, yg_y^0) \qquad (7.38)$$

Denoting the vector difference as l,

$$l = g_t(x, y) - g^0(x, y) \qquad (7.39)$$

Replacing n by an error vector e in equation (7.26) and converting to matrix form gives the following equation:

$$l - e = AX \qquad (7.40)$$

Now we wish to minimise the sum of the squares of the differences. Equation (7.40) forms a system of grey level correlation equations. They are orthogonal to each other and do not have any joint parameter. This is equivalent to solving n sets independently of each other using a standard least squares technique [GB87]. Assuming that the error is random and uniformly distributed with a zero mean, its expectation value, $E(e)$, satisfies $E(e) = 0$. So the variance of the error is:

$$E((e - E(e))(e - E(e))^T) = E(ee^T) = \sigma_0^2 P^{-1} \qquad (7.41)$$

which is the covariance of residuals with P the weight matrix. Applying the least squares estimation model, X can be estimated by its minimum variance unbiased linear estimator with the solution vector $\hat{x}$:

$$\hat{x} = (A^T P A)^{-1} A^T P l \qquad (7.42)$$

The equations above can be used as the basis for an iterative mechanism for refining match estimates by allowing a patch in the search image to deform during each iteration. The algorithm has been found experimentally to converge within a radius of 3 pixels of the correct solution. This scheme is known as Adaptive Least Squares Correlation (ALSC) and leads to high-precision (sub-pixel) match estimates. It has the unique property of returning a match quality measure (the maximum eigenvalue of the covariance matrix).

7.3.3.4   THE OTTO-CHAU STEREO MATCHER

Otto and Chau [OC88] implemented the ALSC matcher and extended it in two ways: (1) by allowing for radiometric shifts and gain in the geometric transformation; (2) by adding a control layer so that whole images can be matched rather than selected patches. Experiments with the original implementation of ALSC using SPOT satellite images indicated poor performance for areas of the imagery affected by atmospheric distortion due to haze. To mitigate against this, ALSC was extended to allow for radiometric shift and gain. This can be achieved by modifying the intensity function in the search image as follows:

$$g_s \rightarrow r_g g_s + r_s \qquad (7.43)$$

where r_g is the multiplicative radiometric gain and r_s is the radiometric shift. This leads to the following modification to the design matrix A and to X:

$$X^T = (da_{11}, da_{12}, da_{21}, db_{11}, db_{12}, db_{21}, r_s, \Delta r_g) \qquad (7.44)$$

$$A = (r_g g_x^0, r_g x g_x^0, r_g y g_x^0, r_g g_y^0, x r_g g_y^0, y r_g g_y^0, 1, g^0) \qquad (7.45)$$

When implementing equation (7.42) Otto and Chau replaced P by the identity matrix and the terms $(A^T A)^{-1}$ and $(A^T l)$ are calculated separately. $(A^T A)^{-1}$ is solved by Cholesky inversion and $A^T l$ is just a straightforward multiplication. To match patches over the whole images a control strategy is required to coordinate the matching over the image domain. Because the disparity surface is almost always continuous for spaceborne stereo imagery Otto and Chau decided to apply a region growing technique similar to those used for image segmentation. The essence of the algorithm is simple: start with a match estimate (seed point) and apply ALSC to refine and predict a set of distortion parameters. Then use these to predict new match estimates in the neighbourhood of the original one [OC88]. Rather than applying ALSC to every image pixel it is most often sufficient to find match points every 3 to 10 pixels and estimate the intervening ones by interpolation. Match estimates are found at the points of intersection of a regularly spaced grid in the left hand image. Otto and Chau carried out experiments to determine the most reliable strategy for growth; it was found that the "best-first" strategy (the next point to be grown from being determined from the best existing match) was optimum. In tests using 240 × 240 pixel SPOT images of Aix-en-Provence matches were obtained for over 99% of matchable points (at 3 pixel grid spacing). Further experiments have also indicated satisfactory match coverage. Otto and Chau determined the number of arithmetic operations required to match a patch. With a Sun 3/180, this translated into an execution time of 0.5 seconds per iteration or about 6 days for a full 6000 × 6000 pixel SPOT scene. Also they predicted an execution time of about 2 hours for 30 T800 transputers assuming a perfect linear speedup and ignoring synchronisation and I/O overheads.

7.3.3.5 SUMMARY OF AREA BASED MATCHERS

Area-based techniques have a number of advantages and disadvantages when compared with other techniques which can be summarised as follows:

- There must be a discernible level of texture; areas which lack texture will not be matched.

- Periodic texture can result in multiple matches.

- Sharp surface depth discontinuities cannot be handled.

- There may not be a corresponding match point due to occlusion.

- In general they are accurate; ALSC for instance has sub-pixel accuracy.

- They are combinable with multi-resolution coarse-to-fine control strategies, match estimates at the higher levels being used to reduce the search space and thus the execution time.

- They are computationally intensive. However, the execution time can be reduced by decreasing the search space either by imposing an epipolar geometry or by using previous matches to constrain it.

- They can be easily parallelised (see later).

7.3.4   Stereo Image Capture

Slama [STH80] discussed a range of different sensors which have been used for the acquisition of stereo-optical views of an area. Traditionally, metric aerial photographs are used; the amount of overlap between the stereo pair is dependent on the velocity of the aircraft and the film rewind. Metric cameras (i.e. those containing calibrated fiducial marks) have also been adapted from the 230 mm × 230 mm standard aircraft format down to 70 mm × 70 mm for close range. The digital pixel equivalent of these systems (at 2 μm per pixel a metric camera photograph digitised with 8-bit quantisation is equivalent to 13 GBytes) by present-day standards is too much data to process in a sensible time frame. The largest CCD arrays are 4096×4096 with 7.5 μm pixels so the precision and field-of-view are still considerably less (approximately 20%) than those of even a 70 mm photograph scanned at the same pixel resolution.

For robotic applications, a small field-of-view may be compensated by multiple CCDs with different focal lengths and/or multiple camera stations [MAB+88]. However, this relies on the real-time computation of inter-camera orientation parameters.

For spaceborne (also increasingly for airborne) systems, a linear "pushbroom" array is used in the across-track direction to maintain fixed geometry whilst the motion of the spacecraft can be used to build up image rows. Two types of stereo can be produced. The first utilises on-board mirrors in the focal plane to point the sensor across-track whilst the second works by using multiple along-track pushbroom elements at different angles [DBM+89].

7.3.5   Example Stereo Image Pairs and Derived Digital Elevation Models

In this section some examples of stereo images are given. Many researchers use synthetic images for work on stereo; these provide a range of texture frequency that is useful for test purposes. The most common type, developed originally for psychological experiments, is the random dot stereogram. Figure 7.7 shows an example of one with a pair of centred pyramidal planes.

Real images are generally more difficult to match; the examples shown here have been carefully chosen to illustrate different characteristics which depend on the range. Stereo matching plays a crucial role in obtaining a Digital Disparity Model (DDM).

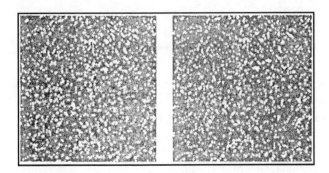

Figure 7.7   Example of a random dot stereogram of pyramidal planes.

For all examples shown here the Otto-Chau stereo matcher [OC88] was used to obtain a very dense gridded DDM. A camera model (see for example [NM92]) is used to convert the DDM into a Digital Disparity Elevation Model (DDEM) which has elevation estimates on an irregular grid. After applying a localised interpolation procedure, Kriging [Dav86], [DM89], a regular grid is obtained. Unmatched areas in the grid or "holes" are the result of occlusions, shadows, lack of texture or discontinuities. Small "holes" can be interpolated; for larger ones monocular techniques (e.g. shape from shading) can be applied.

Close range scenes contain a greater number of discontinuities compared with long range ones. Figure 7.8 shows an example of a close range stereo pair; here an experimental model of a Porsche car is used. In this case a projected random texture pattern is used to provide texture for the stereo matcher. Figure 7.8(a) shows the original image in natural illumination; the pair (b) and (c) are illuminated by artificial texture; (d) shows the DDM (dark is low disparity and light is high). Figure 7.9 shows a visualisation of the DDM of the car shown in Figure 7.8(d). Readers who are interested in the visualisation techniques used here are referred to [MKD+88]. Notice

Figure 7.8 Example of a close range stereo pair and its digital disparity map: Porsche car. Top left (a) original image; top right (b) left textured image; bottom left (c) right textured image; bottom right (d) resultant disparity map.

that the "hole" in the car bonnet is due to a severe distortion of the texture pattern. Three-dimensional xerography can be used to reproduce industrial components with surface models transformed into CAD models. Figure 7.10 shows an example of digitised aerial stereo photographs of Gwydyr Forest area (Snowdonia, UK) on a

Figure 7.9 Visualisation of the disparity map of the car ©UCL 1989.

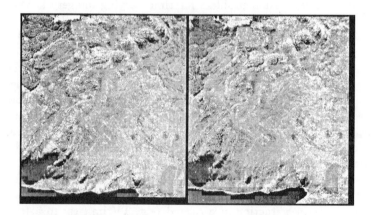

Figure 7.10 Example of a digitised aerial stereo pair: 2229 × 2520 pixels, Gwydyr Forest, Snowdonia, Wales ©NERC 1983.

Leica DSR 11 analytical plotter (with resolution of 0.8 m/pixel). Figure 7.11 shows a static visualisation of the ortho-image texture map superimposed on an automatically derived DEM. Height is exaggerated by a factor of 3. Satellite images contain more high frequency texture than airborne ones. Figure 7.12 shows an example of a SPOT stereo pair of a remote region of the earth (volcano in the Kamchatka area, Russia) where few, if any, unclassified maps exist. The original stereo pair are shown in (a) and (b) and the DDM in (c) (dark=low and bright=high); a visualisation of these results with height exaggeration of 10 is shown in (d). Very little work on the quantitative assessment of either the accuracy or reliability of stereo matchers has been done [DM89, Mul89, DABM91, Gul88]. So no consensus yet exists on which type or hybrid is suitable for any particular application domain. More work is needed in this area.

Figure 7.11 Visualisation of Gwydyr Forest images ©UCL 1992.

7.4 MOTION ESTIMATION

Solving the motion estimation problem for time varying imagery is very important in a diverse range of application areas: (1) industrial: for monitoring industrial processes involving moving objects and robotics; (2) medical: for cell and heart monitoring; (3) meteorological: for tracking clouds and other atmospheric disturbances; (4) oceanographic: for determining currents and tracking sea-surface temperatures; (5) transportation: for highway traffic monitoring and automatic tracking of vehicles; (6) commercial: for compression of TV pictures; (7) military: for automatic target detection (segmentation), recognition, and tracking; There are other time varying imagery applications not explicitly concerned with motion estimation, but rather change estimation for environmental monitoring; these include change detection of land use, deforestation, and mapping.

Time varying images are usually captured using one camera (monocular). Series of snapshots at successive intervals are taken. The interval period depends only on the application itself, from a fraction of a second (e.g. TV images) to a few hours (e.g. weather satellite images). Three types of motion images can be distinguished in the literature:

- A stationary camera with sets of moving objects in a scene, as used for transportation, medical and industrial applications.

- A moving camera with static objects, used for some experimental robot vision applications.

- Both the camera and the objects are moving, used for military and meteorological applications.

No distinction is drawn between the three types since here we are concerned with the relative motion between camera and objects. The motion observed is the apparent motion of a set of features in the images. Binocular time varying images can also be

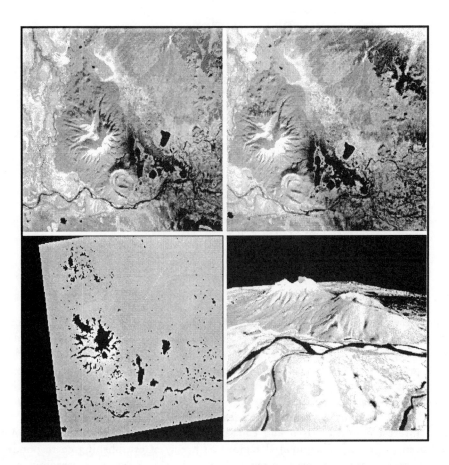

Figure 7.12 Example of a 3000 × 3000 pixel extract from a SPOT stereo pair, DDM, and visualisation of a volcano in Kamchatka, Russia ©UCL 1988. Top left (a) left image; top right (b) right image; bottom left (c) DDM; bottom right (d) visualisation ©UCL 1988. SPOT images ©CNES 1987.

used to help derive the structure of objects and detect their 3D motion. Although structure can be obtained solely from either stereo pairs or a sequence of monocular images, the extra information provided by stereo sequences aids in the extraction of corresponding points from the estimated motion, thus enabling structure to be better determined. Binocular sequences will not be discussed here since they are mostly covered in the stereo section. Those readers particularly interested in this are directed to a good survey of various techniques in [SA91]. Both motion estimation and stereo matching are concerned with the determination of the displacement vector or disparity field. Stereo matching techniques use the disparity field to derive the range given an appropriate camera model. In contrast, motion estimation techniques use the disparity field to determine the velocity of apparent motion of objects.

Motion estimation techniques fit into two categories: feature-based and optic flow (see Figure 7.13). However, early work on motion estimation such as the differential method does not fit into either category (see for example [HT81, Ros83]).

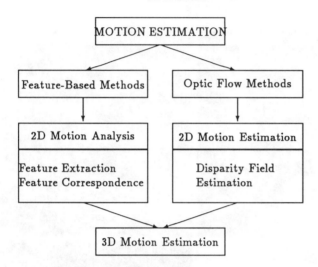

Figure 7.13   Classification of motion estimation algorithms.

7.4.1   Feature-Based Methods

Feature-based methods use features extracted from the sequence of images such as interest points, corners, lines, edges, zero crossings or regions to determine a motion field. Other methods such as the Fourier, Hartley and Hough Transform are also considered as feature-based as they identify certain features within the transformed images. For examples of these see [HT81, YH91, Mah91a, Mah91b]. Establishing feature correspondence between consecutive frames is either assumed or done automatically using some of the techniques described in the feature-based stereo matching section. These include interest operator-based and edge-based matching. Other researchers [AB86, KS91] used matching of segmented regions as a way of establishing correspondence. Some researchers refer to these as region-based [Ros83, KS90] or correspondenceless methods [AB86], However, these lead to additional calculations and thus increased computational complexity of the matching process, although more robustness can be achieved. This method requires image segmentation to extract moving regions which is normally a difficult task. The displacement field (2D translation) is then determined between all frames and used to compute the 3D motion using constraints such as rigid body motion, i.e. the 3D distance between two points on an object remains the same after the motion. These constraints lead to a system of non-linear equations in terms of the 3D motion. They can be solved by calculating the 2D displacement field so that the motion parameters for the objects in the scene can be obtained. The number of motion parameters must at most be equal to the number of equations for the system to be solvable. Early motion estimation work concentrated on the analysis of just two frames, partly due to the lack of multi-frame image sequences and partly because of the similarity with stereo which also uses two frames. This approach is normally restricted to 2D motion estimation because only the transformation between the two views is determined. Line correspondence, for example, requires three views to compute the 3D motion. Point correspondence requires at least four points in three views for every moving object in the scene. In general, there is a trade-off between the number of points and the number of views required to compute the motion parameters. Orthographic or parallel as well as perspective projection images have also been used. Although an orthographic (parallel) projection model is adequate in some cases, it is not appropriate for most applications which require central perspective projections [AN88]. However, the use of these models again leads to increased computational complexity.

7.4.1.1   REVIEW OF FEATURE-BASED MOTION ESTIMATION METHODS

Feature-based methods are a popular way of estimating the motion of objects from a sequence of monocular images. Aggarwal and Nandhakumar [AN88] classified these into three categories: direct formulations, explicit use of rigidity and extended sequences of monocular images. In the following sections feature correspondence between images is assumed to be known.

Direct Formulations

Rigid body motion is assumed in these methods. The rigidity constraint is manifested in single rotation and translation matrices for all observations. Ullman [Ull79] uses an orthographic projection model and then extends it to a perspective one. The following rigidity assumption is made: *Any set of elements undergoing a 2D transformation which has a unique interpretation as a rigid body moving in space, should be interpreted as a body in motion.*

Then rigidity tests are devised and incorporated into a model which leads to a structure from motion theorem: *Given three distinct orthographic views of four non-coplanar points in a rigid configuration, the structure and motion compatible with the three views are uniquely determined.* In the derivation it is assumed that four corresponding points between consecutives frames have been found. Let O, A, B, and C be the four points and assume that the motion of the object is composed of translation and rotation. The orthographic projection of these points on three distinct planes Π_1, Π_2 and Π_3 is known. To determine the 3D configurations of these points a fixed coordinate system with origin at O is chosen. Let **a**, **b**, and **c** be the vectors OA, OB, and OC respectively as in Figure 7.14. Each view has a 2D coordin/te system $(\mathbf{p}_i, \mathbf{q}_i)$ with O as its origin so that $\mathbf{p}_i$ and $\mathbf{q}_i$ are orthogonal unit vectors on Π_i.

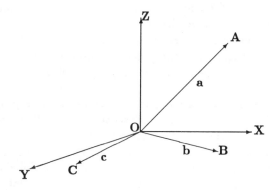

Figure 7.14   Orthographic projection coordinate system.

The image coordinates of (A,B,C) on Π_i, $(x_{ai}, y_{ai}, x_{bi}, y_{bi}, x_{ci}, y_{ci})$, are given by the dot products:

$$
\begin{aligned}
x_{ai} &= \mathbf{a}.\mathbf{p}_i, & y_{ai} &= \mathbf{a}.\mathbf{q}_i \\
x_{bi} &= \mathbf{b}.\mathbf{p}_i, & y_{bi} &= \mathbf{b}.\mathbf{q}_i \\
x_{ci} &= \mathbf{c}.\mathbf{p}_i, & y_{ci} &= \mathbf{c}.\mathbf{q}_i
\end{aligned}
\tag{7.46}
$$

Let $\mathbf{u}_{ij}$ be the unit vector along the intersection line of planes Π_i and Π_j. Vector $\mathbf{u}_{ij}$ lies on Π_i which is spanned by $(\mathbf{p}_i, \mathbf{q}_i)$ and hence it is given by:

$$
\mathbf{u}_{ij} = \alpha_{ij}\mathbf{p}_i + \beta_{ij}\mathbf{q}_i \qquad \text{where} \quad \alpha_{ij}^2 + \beta_{ij}^2 = 1
\tag{7.47}
$$

The vector $\mathbf{u}_{ij}$ also lies on Π_j which is spanned by $(\mathbf{p}_j, \mathbf{q}_j)$ and hence:

$$
\mathbf{u}_{ij} = \gamma_{ij}\mathbf{p}_j + \delta_{ij}\mathbf{q}_j \qquad \text{where} \quad \gamma_{ij}^2 + \delta_{ij}^2 = 1
\tag{7.48}
$$

From equations (7.47) and (7.48) we obtain:

$$
\alpha_{ij}\mathbf{p}_i + \beta_{ij}\mathbf{q}_i = \gamma_{ij}\mathbf{p}_j + \delta_{ij}\mathbf{q}_j
\tag{7.49}
$$

Taking the dot product of equation (7.49) with $\mathbf{a}$, $\mathbf{b}$, and $\mathbf{c}$ gives:

$$
\begin{aligned}
\alpha_{ij}x_{ai} + \beta_{ij}y_{ai} &= \gamma_{ij}x_{aj} + \delta_{ij}y_{aj} \\
\alpha_{ij}x_{bi} + \beta_{ij}y_{bi} &= \gamma_{ij}x_{bj} + \delta_{ij}y_{bj} \\
\alpha_{ij}x_{ci} + \beta_{ij}y_{ci} &= \gamma_{ij}x_{cj} + \delta_{ij}y_{cj}
\end{aligned}
\tag{7.50}
$$

These equations are linearly independent and have two solutions that are equal in magnitude but of opposite signs [Ull79]. Choosing one solution, the vector $\mathbf{u}_{ij}$ can be determined in terms of $(\mathbf{p}_i, \mathbf{q}_i)$ and $(\mathbf{p}_j, \mathbf{q}_j)$. The distances, d_n, are next computed:

$$
\begin{aligned}
d_1 &= \|\mathbf{u}_{12} - \mathbf{u}_{13}\| \\
d_2 &= \|\mathbf{u}_{12} - \mathbf{u}_{23}\| \\
d_3 &= \|\mathbf{u}_{13} - \mathbf{u}_{23}\|
\end{aligned}
\tag{7.51}
$$

The reader is referred to [Ull79] for more details on how a unique triangle with sides d_1, d_2 and d_3 can be obtained. The vertices of this triangle are known to lie at a unit distance from the origin. The three vertices and the origin thus define two possible tetrahedra, one being the reflection of the other. For each tetrahedron, a unique 3D configuration can then be determined from the projections of A, B and C on the three planes.

Roach and Aggarwal [RA80] use a sequence of two perspective projections to determine the structure of rigid objects in a static scene and the 3D motion of a moving camera. Here the camera orientation information (f=focal length, θ=rotation about the x-axis, ϕ=rotation about the y-axis, ψ=rotation about the z-axis and the 3D coordinates of the lens centre (X_0, Y_0, Z_0)) are needed to extract the global 3D coordinates from the 2D camera coordinates. The equations that govern the relation between the 2D image coordinates (x, y) and 3D world coordinates (X, Y, Z) of a point are given by:

$$x = f\frac{a_{11}(X-X_0)+a_{12}(Y-Y_0)+a_{13}(Z-Z_0)}{a_{31}(X-X_0)+a_{32}(Y-Y_0)+a_{33}(Z-Z_0)}$$

$$y = f\frac{a_{21}(X-X_0)+a_{22}(Y-Y_0)+a_{23}(Z-Z_0)}{a_{31}(X-X_0)+a_{32}(Y-Y_0)+a_{33}(Z-Z_0)}$$

(7.52)

where the parameters a_{ij} are functions of (θ, ϕ, ψ).

Roach and Aggarwal showed that five corresponding points in two views are required to recover 3D structure and motion parameters, a total of 27 (the world coordinates of the 5 points, 15 parameters, and the camera position and orientation for 2 views, 12 parameters). By setting the camera orientation angles and coordinates (6 parameters) to zero and the z-component of any of the five points to an arbitrary positive constant, they make the number of unknowns and equations even, each point producing two projection equations (from equation (7.52)) for each view which results in 20 non-linear equations.

Nagel [Nag81] and Huang and Tsai [HT81] showed that this system of non-linear equations can be decomposed. Nagel eliminated the translation vector and solved the rotation matrix separately. Huang and Tsai decomposed the problem into two steps: (1) a set of linear equations determined from two views are solved to obtain eight "pure parameters"; (2) the motion parameters are obtained from these pure parameters by solving a bi-cubic polynomial.

Liu and Huang [LH88] use line correspondences in three views to determine the motion of rigid bodies. The motion is decomposed into a rotation and a translation. Six lines in three views are used to calculate the rotation matrix. First the rotation matrix is calculated, then the translation matrix is derived by an iterative method. Results on synthetic data showed that this method is sensitive to noise and initial estimates.

Explicit Use of Rigidity

The rigid body constraint is used explicitly for all formulations here. Mitchie *et al.* [MSA85] propose a method for calculating the structure and motion based on the principle of conservation of distances in rigid objects regardless of the relative orientation position of the viewing system. This approach leads to a simpler set of non-linear equations which can be solved using iterative numerical methods. For this five known points in two frames are required.

Figure 7.15 shows two perspective projection systems S_1 and S_2. Their centres of projection and the image planes are C_1, C_2 and I_1, I_2 respectively. To ease the description two cameras are assumed here instead of two views from the same camera.

A point P_i in 3D world coordinates (X_i, Y_i, Z_i) in S_1 and (U_i, V_i, W_i) in S_2 is imaged as p_i in I_1 and q_i in I_2. The coordinates of p_i and q_i in I_1 and I_2 are (x_i, y_i) and (u_i, v_i) respectively. Using the principle of conservation of length, i.e. the distance between two points P_i and P_j in S_1 is the same in S_2, gives:

$$\begin{aligned}(X_i - X_j)^2 + (Y_i - Y_j)^2 + (Z_i - Z_j)^2 &= \\ (U_i - U_j)^2 + (V_i - V_j)^2 + (W_i - W_j)^2 &\end{aligned}$$

(7.53)

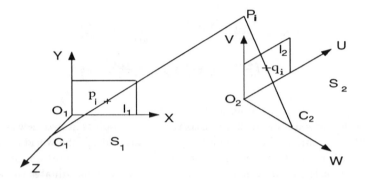

Figure 7.15 Perspective projection coordinate system.

Because P_i lies on the lines $C_1 p_i$ and $C_2 q_i$ the system coordinates in equation (7.53) can be expressed in terms of the image coordinates, (x_i, y_i) and (u_i, v_i), and the focal length of the camera, f (the distance from the centre of projection C to the image plane). This yields a second order non-linear equation with four unknowns λ_i, γ_i, λ_j and γ_j:

$$
\begin{aligned}
(\lambda_i x_i - \lambda_j x_j)^2 + (\lambda_i y_i - \lambda_j y_j)^2 + (\lambda_i - \lambda_j)^2 f_1^2 &= \\
(\gamma_i u_i - \gamma_j u_j)^2 + (\gamma_i v_i - \gamma_j v_j)^2 + (\gamma_i - \gamma_j)^2 f_2^2 &
\end{aligned}
\tag{7.54}
$$

Five points contribute 10 unknowns and 10 equations (every pair contributes one equation). This system can be solved by using iterative least-squares analysis. Once the position of the points has been determined, the motion parameters (translation and rotation) can be obtained by decomposing the motion into a rotation, R, around an axis passing through the origin followed by a translation, see [HT81]:

$$
\begin{bmatrix} U \\ V \\ W \end{bmatrix} = R \begin{bmatrix} X \\ Y \\ Z \end{bmatrix} + \begin{bmatrix} \Delta X \\ \Delta Y \\ \Delta Z \end{bmatrix}
\tag{7.55}
$$

Solutions for equation (7.55) can be found in [HT81, MSA85, AN88].

This method was tested on both synthetic and real images. Results for the real images showed a relative error between the measured and computed distances of about 8%. For noisy synthetic images the error is about 10%.

Tan *et al.* [TSB91] propose an algorithm based on the distance invariance property of the rigidity constraint used in [MSA85]. Tan *et al.* assume that rigid objects are moving and the camera is static. Three corresponding points in two frames are required to calculate the structure and motion parameters. The resulting constraint can be expressed as second-order polynomial equations each involving two unknowns. Camera relative orientation parameters are assumed known. First the structure parameters are determined, then the motion parameters are found non-iteratively. This method is applied to both noisy synthetic and real images and results showed that: (1) the error in motion estimation parameters is proportional to noise; (2) the accuracy of the algorithm improves by using more corresponding points.

Other methods used lines or points and lines [WHA92, AW87] to estimate motion of rigid bodies. Weng *et al.* [WHA92] use long straight lines in three views to compute structure and motion parameters. Here the camera is fixed and the scene is moving. If there are several moving rigid bodies, segmentation is required for each. This method is more complicated than the case with points in two frames. However, the location of lines and their orientation are determined by fitting a line along a sequence of edges. This provides long lines with more edge points and improves the accuracy of measurement of the line position. The basic strategy here is similar to that used for point-based linear algorithms [HT81]. A set of intermediate parameters are first estimated by solving linear equations. The motion parameters are then derived from those intermediate parameters. The uniqueness of the solution and the effects of noise are also studied. Non-linear optimisation methods can be applied to reduce the number of spurious solutions in the system in the presence of noise. Simulation results showed that increasing the number of lines reduces the relative error.

Aggarwal and Wang [AW87] also use points and lines to compute the structure and motion parameters for rigid bodies. Here the camera is assumed to be moving whilst the scene is static. Four points and a line in two views are needed. This method is based on the principle of invariance of lines with respect to motion. This principle states that *certain measurements (e.g. distance between points, angles between lines) are invariant with respect to rigid motion.* This allows for the structure and motion computation to be decomposed. First structure is determined and then the motion parameters of the object are obtained. This decomposition has the benefit of limiting the size of the search space and reducing the number of features required. Both distance and angular invariance are used to construct a set of non-linear equations to determine the structure and motion parameters. Simulation results showed that the algorithm is sensitive to noise if only a minimal number of features are extracted.

Solutions from Long Monocular Image Sequences

These methods require four or more views to determine motion parameters. Shariat and Price [SP90] proposed a method requiring one corresponding point in five frames (two points in four frames or three in three frames) to determine the motion parameters for rigid objects moving in a scene. The algorithm is divided into four modules: (1) initial guess estimator, (2) pure translation estimator, (3) pure rotation estimator and (4) general motion estimator. The pure translation or rotation modules assume that the motion represents a pure translation or rotation and estimate the motion parameters that best fit the data. A Gauss-Newton non-linear least squares method is applied to solve iteratively the set of non-linear equations generated by the method. Given an initial guess generated automatically by the first module the method converges to a solution of the general motion equations. The reader is referred to the original paper for details of each of these modules. Errors are calculated for each parameter along with a measure of confidence of the estimated errors. Results for synthetic and real monocular image sequences are given. Two real data sets of a car moving horizontally and turning are used. In general, the results indicated that the convergence of the solution depends on the noise in the images, the corresponding features selected and the amount of rotation of the objects between two consecutive frames. A brief survey of motion estimation techniques and a comparison with other methods is also provided.

Broida and Chellapa [BC86] assume that the rigid body undergoes both constant translational and constant rotational motion. This avoids the number of unknown parameters increasing with the number of frames. The structure of the object is needed and is assumed to be known. The corresponding points on the object are also assumed known. A Kalman filter is applied recursively to determine the motion parameters. The Kalman filter accumulates knowledge of the object's position and its motion parameters and predicts its positions and motion vectors in subsequent frames. Only simulation results are provided; these indicate reasonable accuracy.

Karmann [Kar90] proposes a similar approach using dynamic models for object motion with a Kalman filter. This is claimed to have been successfully applied to simulations of multi-object tracking (e.g. traffic monitoring), but no results are given. Weng et al. [WHA87] proposed a method for estimating 3D motion of rigid bodies from long image sequences. First, the structure and motion parameters are extracted from two views of eight points. Then, the trajectory of the centre of the mass or a fixed point of the object is calculated based on the assumption that the angular momentum of the object is locally constant and the object possesses an axis of symmetry. Weng et al. approximate the trajectory of the centre of mass by a polynomial and apply this model to the subsequent images for estimating the trajectory and predicting the new location of object points. No results for real image sequences are reported but results of simulations of 3D point sets are provided.

Iu and Wohn [IW90] pointed out that the assumption of the translation and rotation being constant is not generally valid when determining the 3D motion from a long image sequence. Iu and Wohn propose a new state estimation formulation for the general motion in which the 3D translation and rotation are modelled as polynomials of an arbitrary order. An extended Kalman filter is applied recursively to estimate the motion parameters from the non-linear state estimation formulation. The assumptions made here include: (1) the projection of the rotational centre is visible, (2) the motion is smooth and (3) the order of translation and rotation are known. Results presented for a simulation of a noisy image sequence indicated that the errors in the estimate are proportional to the amount of noise and also inversely proportional to the number of frames used. One limitation is that abrupt changes in motion cannot be modelled by a polynomial and thus lead to a decrease in accuracy of the algorithm.

7.4.2   Optic Flow

Optic flow, originated by Gibson [Gib50], is defined as the 2D field of instantaneous velocities of brightness values (caused by motion of either objects or sensor) in the image plane [HS81, AN88]. This approach differs from the feature-based approach in that (1) it computes the velocities of all pixels in the image rather than a sparse set of features, and (2) it does not require inter-frame correspondences.

The movement of an object in a scene manifests itself by temporal changes in intensity values in the image. The velocities of image pixels can be viewed as a function of the motion and the location of the pixel in 3D space. To avoid variations in intensities due to shading a few assumptions are made: (1) the viewed surface is flat, (2) the incidence illumination is uniform across the surface and (3) the reflectance of a point (proportional to its intensity value) varies smoothly and has no spatial discontinuities. In the following treatment it is assumed that the camera is static and objects move in the scene relative to a static background. The 3D motion from a sequence of monocular images of a pixel in 3D space can be estimated with a function that can be represented by a Taylor expansion, assuming the moving object to be a rigid body and the image intensity $g(x, y, t)$ to be a locally continuous and differentiable function [HS81]:

$$g(x + dx, y + dy, t + dt) = g(x, y, t) + g_x dx + g_y dy + g_t dt + \mathcal{O}^2 \qquad (7.56)$$

where $g_x = \frac{\partial g}{\partial x}, g_y = \frac{\partial g}{\partial y}, g_t = \frac{\partial g}{\partial t}$ and $\mathcal{O}^2$ contains second and higher order terms in dx, dy, and dt. If the object undergoes pure translation (dx, dy) after a time interval dt then equation (7.56) becomes a linear equation with two unknowns:

$$g_x u + g_y v + g_t = 0 \qquad (7.57)$$

where $u = \frac{dx}{dt}$ and $v = \frac{dy}{dt}$ are the velocities in x and y directions respectively and are to be determined. g_x, g_y and g_t can be found from the image. Equation (7.57) is usually referred to as the *motion constraint equation*. The collection of velocities u and v for the entire image constitutes the optic flow. The two components of the motion in equation (7.57) cannot be determined without introducing new constraints such as that optic flow is constant or smooth.

Horn and Schunck [HS81] add an error term, ϵ_a, to equation (7.57) and introduce a *smoothness constraint* to solve equation (7.57) by assuming that the objects are undergoing rigid motion or deformation. This constraint can be expressed as minimising either (1) the square of the magnitude of the gradient of the optic flow velocities or (2) the sum of squares of the Laplacians of their components. Horn and Schunck choose the first option:

$$\epsilon_b^2 = \left(\frac{\partial u}{\partial x}\right)^2 + \left(\frac{\partial u}{\partial y}\right)^2 + \left(\frac{\partial v}{\partial x}\right)^2 + \left(\frac{\partial v}{\partial y}\right)^2 \qquad (7.58)$$

Horn and Schunck determine the partial derivatives of the intensity function g_x, g_y and g_t at a point (i, j) from the average of the first four differences taken over adjacent measurements as shown in Figure 7.16. The minimisation of errors in equation (7.57)

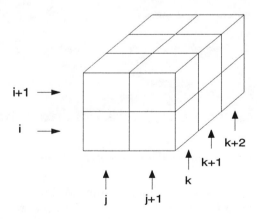

Figure 7.16 Relationship in space and time of the frames: j is the direction of x, i is the direction of y and k is the time direction.

in the rate of change in image intensity, ϵ_a, and in smoothness of the velocity flow constraint, ϵ_b^2 (equation 7.58), results in optimum values for the optical flow velocities u and v. Results for a noisy (1%) four frame sequence of 32×32 pixel images using different patterns of motion gave errors of between 7% and 10% after 32 iterations. The worst case occurred when either the intensity gradient was small or the noise was high. Convergence of the algorithm is provided in the form of diagrams of the velocity vector field after 1, 4, 16 and 32 iterations. A limitation of this algorithm is that it cannot handle large discontinuities because of the smoothness constraint.

Stow [Sto85] and Muller [Mul88] described the application of optic flow to the measurement of fluid flow velocities. Stow showed the relationship between the Horn and Schunck constraint equation and the fluid flow equations for a conservative passive tracer. Muller gave a practical example of its application to sea-surface temperature using area-based template correlation as an input to the solution of the optic flow tangential component. Figure 7.17 shows an example of this method applied to the retrieval of Eulerian velocities from a time sequence of *Voyager* images of Jupiter's Red Spot [Mul82]. The original images are shown in (a) and (b). The optic flow (v(a) and v(b)) is superimposed on the original images in the form of velocity vectors.

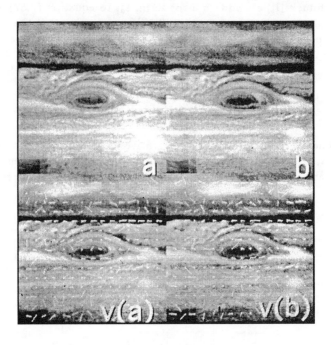

Figure 7.17   Example of a motion pair: Red Spot on Jupiter.

Schunck [Sch85b] proposes another more complicated motion constraint equation. Schunck argues that the original one does not hold for either rotational motion or for non-perspective projections. This is because it does not allow for abrupt changes in either the velocity field due to occlusion or the sharp changes in image intensity. To account for these Schunck applied a theory taken from fluid dynamics, in particular the continuity equation. Schunck's new constraint equation is expressed as:

$$g_x u + g_y v + g_t + g(u_x + v_y) = 0 \qquad (7.59)$$

where $u_x = \frac{\partial u}{\partial x}$, and $v_y = \frac{\partial v}{\partial y}$. This equation is similar to the original one (7.57) except for the additional term containing the divergence of velocity field.

Schunck [Sch85a, Sch89] also extended the algorithm to deal with discontinuities. This work is motivated by evidence from psychology suggesting that the human vision system can estimate the image flow velocity field without blurring the motion boundaries. The constraint equation of Horn and Schunck (7.57) models the relationship between the velocity field and changes in image intensities in space and time. Schunck uses the constraint equation in polar form:

$$d = \rho \cos(\alpha - \beta) \qquad (7.60)$$

where ρ and β are the speed and direction of motion, and d and α are the displacement of the constraint line from the origin and the orientation of the constraint line respectively. The image in space and time $g(x, y, t)$ is transformed into the intrinsic image array $d(x_i, y_i)$ and $\alpha(x_i, y_i)$ using the formulas:

$$d = \frac{|g_t|}{\sqrt{g_x^2 + g_y^2}} \qquad (7.61)$$

$$\alpha = \begin{cases} \arctan g_x, g_y & \text{if } g_t \geq 0 \\ \arctan -g_x, -g_y & \text{otherwise} \end{cases} \qquad (7.62)$$

An algorithm called *constraint line clustering* which works within a specified neighbourhood (e.g. 5 × 5 pixels) is used for estimating the image flow field that is represented by the speed $\rho(x_i, y_i)$ and the direction $\beta(x_i, y_i)$ of motion. Experimental results for noisy synthetic images (random dot stereograms) showed that velocity field estimates are not improved by increasing the neighbourhood size and produced typical error magnitudes. Results for a real noisy image pair showed poor motion constraint data even after smoothing with a Gaussian filter. This is because the scatter plot of d against α showed severe errors forming a random plot. This plot should instead form a cosine pulse with ρ as its amplitude and β as the centre of the pulse [Sch89]. When the d and α arrays are reduced by a factor of 4 the results improved but errors are still present. When a surface-based iterative smoothing algorithm is applied to the velocity field estimates the results are much improved without any blurred motion boundaries important to motion perception.

Nagel [Nag89] noticed that the motion constraint equations (7.57) and (7.59) can only be justified by assumptions which are far too restrictive for image sequences of real world scenes. Nagel argues that the geometrical properties of 3D scenes and perspective projections should be used more explicitly to derive a constraint equation to estimate the displacement rate. Nagel uses a combination of perspective projection and notions from differential geometry to derive a new constraint equation. This equation is given by:

$$g_x u + g_y v + g_t = 4g \left(\frac{\hat{z}^T \mathbf{R}_t}{\hat{z}^T \mathbf{R}} - \frac{\mathbf{R}^T \mathbf{R}_t}{\mathbf{R}^T \mathbf{R}} \right) \qquad (7.63)$$

where $\hat{z}$ is the unit vector in the z direction, $\mathbf{R}$ is the location in space of image point (x, y), T denotes transpose and $\mathbf{R}_t$ is the instantaneous velocity vector of point $\mathbf{R}$.

Willick and Yang [WY91] evaluated the constraint equations proposed by Horn and Schunck, Schunck, and Nagel for a sequence of synthetic images of patterned spheres produced by a ray tracer. Preliminary results showed that the original Horn and Schunck constraint equation was generally more accurate than the proposed alternatives. These results also showed where the constraint equations break down as predicted by Schunck and Nagel, i.e. at the boundaries of objects and where the intensity values change sharply. Willick and Yang suggested that the optic flow method could be improved and also that future research should be directed at proving the existence as well as discovering the correct constraint equations.

Wahl and Simpson [WS91] compared optic flow methods with LoG based ones using the Marr-Ullman technique [MU81] and concluded that the latter technique is less sensitive to noise and time step errors.

7.5   MULTI-RESOLUTION TECHNIQUES

Multi-resolution control strategies, also known as multi-scale, coarse-to-fine and pyramidal, are applicable to a large number of image processing applications including stereo matching and motion estimation. Resolution is of primary importance because three basic physical properties are directly related to it: edges, shape and texture. The position of intensity variations determines the resolution with which edges are perceived. Edges can occur physically for a number of possible reasons:

- When there is a change in the illumination, i.e. at the boundary of shadows [Dye87].

- When an object's surface is perpendicular to the line of sight.

- When there is a change in albedo of the surface, i.e. when the reflectance properties change over the surface.

Certain features in an image may only be significant at a particular scale. A good example of this is when viewing a painting. At close range the subject of the painting can be difficult to understand; only brush strokes are discernible. However, when viewed from further back it becomes much clearer. In general there is no *a priori* basis for selecting an appropriate resolution. For this reason the use of multi-resolution image representations is a powerful tool for the examination of image features at multiple resolution. In particular two approaches are of particular significance:

- The use of coarse-to-fine search strategies for detecting features first at a coarse scale and then using these to converge on features at a finer scale.

- The use of a combination of properties at multiple resolution as a means of disambiguating image features [MP79].

Figure 7.18 illustrates the data representation model used for coarse-to-fine control strategies.

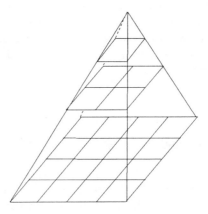

Figure 7.18   Three levels of data in a pyramidal hierarchy.

7.5.1   Pyramidal Data Representations

An image is transformed into a set of representations, each one containing features at a different resolution. These are often referred to as image pyramids. Significant effort has been put into creating and analysing these representations. Two widely used representations are:

- Gaussian Pyramids: Intensity values are smoothed or blurred over successively larger areas, so reducing the effects of noise. Linear smoothing by convolution is equivalent to applying a low pass filter. The size of the filter is determined by a Gaussian point spread function, $G(x, y)$ which takes the form of equation (7.7).

- Laplacian Pyramids: These can be created by applying a Laplacian operator to a Gaussian filtered image (i.e. LoG). This is equivalent to differentiating the smoothed intensity values to produce a set of bandpass filtered copies of the original. The LoG operator can be approximated by the difference between two Gaussians (DoG). Zero crossing pyramids can be constructed by extracting the points where the Laplacian changes sign [Dye87].

There are a number of methods for subdividing images into subimages. Subdividing by quadrants is a particularly useful method because it can be applied repeatedly until a single pixel is reached: see Cantoni *et al.* [CL88].

7.5.2   Multi-Resolution and Parallel Architectures

Multi-resolution techniques naturally map onto parallel architectures. A simple technique is to dedicate a layer of processors to each resolution level. Two pyramidal structures are described by Cantoni *et al.* [CL88]; they are known as bin and quad pyramids. Both have layers of mesh connected processors but differ in the number of processors in successive layers and their vertical connections. The bin-pyramid has 2^N processors per layer and each processor has one upward connection to the previous layer and a pair of down connections to the next layer. The down connections alternate between neighbouring pairs of processors in the same row and the same column.

The quad-pyramid has 4^N processors per layer, and each processor has one upward connection to the previous layer and four downward ones to the next layer. Each processor in the bin-pyramid requires a connectivity of 7, whilst one in a quad-pyramid requires 9. A multi-resolution system may also be simulated by using a flat array and embedding the subimages within it.

7.5.3   Application of Multi-Resolution to Stereo and Motion

A multi-resolution template matching algorithm is described in [RV77]. It starts by matching a coarse template against a coarse search image which reduces the search space, and then proceeds to match at finer resolutions only when there is a small degree of mismatch. Displacement estimates of pixels at the highest (coarsest) level are used as initial estimates when calculating disparities in the subsequent lower (finer) levels of the pyramid. Chang *et al.* [CC90] use a multi-resolution approach to improve stereo matching based on simulated annealing. Starting at the topmost level, optimal solutions can easily be found due to the small search window. The general principle is to propagate disparity estimates to the next (lower) level as an initial state, where they are used to constrain the search space and substantially accelerate convergence. This is called constraint propagation between layers of the pyramid and can lead to a substantial reduction in the number of operations when compared with a single layer approach. The reduction is particularly significant when large images need to be processed and therefore has good potential for both real-time matching and processing very large arrays. Figure 7.19 illustrates the principle of multi-resolution stereo matching and shows disparity estimates being propagated down each level of the pyramid.

7.6   PARALLELISATION OF STEREO AND MOTION ALGORITHMS

Computer vision tasks are highly computationally complex, demanding high performance computers to achieve practical real-time solutions. Parallel computers are currently the only way of achieving the required level of performance [CA90]. Image processing applications inspired the original development of SIMD parallel processing architectures principally designed for low-level operations (see later) [Duf78, Fou87]. A close relationship between image processing and parallel architectures has increased over the last few decades. In contrast to earlier low-level processing applications, surface coordinate extraction by stereo matching and motion estimation involve a higher level of control and organisation and are categorised as intermediate level vision tasks. The control strategies and complex data dependencies mean that there is no simple way of mapping algorithms onto parallel architectures. The 1980s saw the emergence of high performance microprocessors. These have been the driving force behind an alternative, more general purpose MIMD architecture. It is the belief of the authors that this class of architecture provides the best target engine for implementing intermediate and high-level vision tasks. This section describes these architectures in more detail and the issues involved in restructuring algorithms. A number of examples of

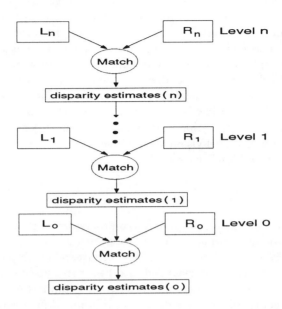

Figure 7.19 Illustration of multi-resolution stereo matching.

parallel stereo and motion algorithms implemented on SIMD and MIMD architectures are discussed.

7.6.1   SIMD and MIMD Architectures

Flynn [Fly66] first proposed a classification scheme for parallel computers based on the multiplicity of instruction and data streams. More recently extensions to the original scheme have been proposed [Fou87, MLL88]. For a comprehensive taxonomy of architectures for vision see [MLL88]. The two most important parallel architectures for computer vision applications are SIMD and MIMD.

7.6.1.1   SIMD

These machines are characterised by a large number (upwards of 10^3) processors. Each processor is relatively simple, often bit serial with a small amount of local memory (typically 10 - 10^3 bytes) for storing a small neighbourhood of image data. There is a single program controller which broadcasts the same instruction to all processing elements. Most modern SIMD machines have the ability to mask out individual instructions so that these are only executed on a particular subset of processors. These machines are traditionally used by employing a programming paradigm whereby the same sequence of instructions is executed on every processing element. There has been a gradual evolution towards making them more general purpose; in particular there has been a steady improvement in flexibility of inter-process communication.

Cantoni *et al.* [CL88] have classified image processing systems into successive generations. The first generation was essentially sequential processors with specialised memory interfaces for array manipulations. The second generation have a special function unit that is able to process a small sub-array of the image. The third generation provided multiplicity of processing elements, each with its own local memory for data storage (SIMD). These machines evolved into larger and more flexible systems with additional concurrent computational units and greater autonomy between processing elements. In particular operation, addressing and connection autonomy and extra flexibility of inter-process communication connectivity was introduced [Fou87, MLL88]. They are primarily used for low-level vision problems where pixel data is independent. The fourth and current generation is aimed at being more general purpose and therefore applicable to higher-level vision tasks; these architectures include modern MIMD computers and SIMD/MIMD hybrids.

7.6.1.2   MIMD

These are networks of general purpose micro-processors as processing elements. They are interconnected by a message routing system which can be either dedicated communications hardware, e.g. a bus, or included as integral on-chip hardware, e.g. transputers. These architectures are classified into two main types: shared and distributed memory. Shared memory machines are easier to program in the sense that no explicit message passing is needed to access data since it is stored in global memory. The main disadvantage here is the limited throughput of the memory interface which becomes saturated as the number of processors are scaled up. More recently, attention has focused on distributed memory machines where processing and store are distributed throughout a network. The inter-connection network is of critical importance and has gradually evolved from a fixed connection scheme to a statically switchable one to one that provides message routing by specialised communication hardware. In advanced designs (e.g. transputers), communications is supported on-chip. Other examples of distributed memory machines are the Intel Hyper-cube and the NCube. MIMD machines have a number of advantages over SIMD architectures: (a) they can support a distributed operating environment; (b) it is possible to use an abstract model of parallelism rather than a low level mapping of algorithm onto architecture; (c) they can support higher level programming environments that remove the need for explicit communication; (d) it is possible to arrive at an efficient solution by applying a much coarser grain of parallelism; (e) each processor can be completely autonomous and able to execute its own sequence of instructions.

MIMD parallel computers enable the design parallel algorithms to be based on abstract models. This is in contrast to SIMD programming where relatively low-level instructions that operate at a pixel level are directly mapped onto the hardware. As such, MIMD machines are much more general purpose [MLL88, CR92] than their SIMD counterparts. Recent research in computational models for parallel machines has focused on Parallel Random Access Machines, PRAMs, where a global shared memory is simultaneously accessible to all processors [Val75, Val82, Sto88]. Some researchers [WRH92, CR92] have recently proposed hybrid architectures, organised in a pyramid hierarchy with MIMD processors at the topmost layer for high-level processing and lower layers of SIMD processors for low-level processing. A number of different communication paradigms are provided, including broadcast communications and shared memory. The main weakness of MIMD machines over conventional serial ones at present is their operating environment. In light of this a considerable amount of effort is being directed into improving system software, particularly operating system kernels and higher-level programming languages such as C++; some programming tools aimed at directly supporting the SPMD model (defined later) are currently under development.

7.6.2 Parallel Programming Paradigms for MIMD Computers

Parallel algorithms can be classified according to two broad categories: data parallelism where data is distributed, and algorithmic parallelism where functional subunits are distributed. These can be further divided into three programming models: geometric parallelism, task parallelism (processor farm) and algorithmic decomposition (e.g. pipelines and systolic arrays) [CL88]. The choice of programming model has a profound influence on the performance of parallel algorithms [Sto88]. Geometric parallelism is useful for applications which are data intensive and data independent. Since data is stored locally there is no extra overhead involved in fetching it from a remote location which leads to good efficiency. This is an analogous model to the one used for programming SIMD machines with the difference that a set of instructions rather than the same one are executed in parallel. Many researchers have coined the acronym Single Program Multiple Data (SPMD) to describe this model. The main difficulty with the geometric data parallel model arises when the processing load per unit area of data is not uniform. This results in a degradation in performance due to load imbalance. Processor farms overcome this by implicitly providing load balancing. However, if the application is data intensive this results in an excessive communications overhead. Algorithmic parallelism can be applied to algorithms that can be decomposed into several stages with a continuous stream of data flowing through; a good example is a compiler. Systolic arrays can be considered as a set of identical processes with data flowing through a number of pipelines (possibly in different directions).

Higher level tools are required to make the task of parallelisation more productive. Over the last decade there has been a wide uptake in the use of high-level programming interfaces and sophisticated operating environments. C, C++ and UNIX are now in widespread use. This has led to improved programming efficiency and reusable source code. Image processing libraries and standard graphical interfaces are commonplace in the distributed workstation environment and analogues are required for parallel systems.

7.6.3 Parallel Stereo Matching

This section begins with a short discussion of the issues involved in designing parallel stereo matching software. Then a brief review of work on parallel implementations on SIMD type architectures, with an example of each of the two main categories (area-based and feature-based) is given. Next attention is focused on MIMD architectures and here also examples of each category are given. Because there is not much literature in this field parallel template matching is also discussed, although this can be considered as a subproblem of area-based stereo matching.

7.6.3.1 SOFTWARE ISSUES

The matching operation can be considered as being composed of two stages: low-level operations for extracting match primitives, and higher level control operations for coordinating the search for possible matches and managing potentially large data sets. This leads to a requirement for support at two levels of operation:

- Low Level Match Primitives: Typically for feature extraction or correlation, this involves applying linear operators to perform linear algebraic transformations on pixel data [CL88]. These are usually data intensive and require intensive 32-bit floating point operations.

- High Level Control: Typically this involves resolving data dependencies (possibly at a pixel level) and introduces data dependent graphs [MLL88]. This leads to complex communication requirements when data is distributed and has a direct impact on the inter-process communication (IPC) model [CL88].

The low-level operations are quite straightforward to implement; often there are specialised high performance components available that can implement these directly. Difficulties arise, however, when addressing higher level control requirements. Most area-based matchers, for instance, are data intensive and therefore need a strategy for partitioning and distributing data. This must take into account data dependencies and data should be located where it is inexpensive to access. Inter-process communications are required to resolve dependencies on remotely stored data. Research on compiler design and dynamic scheduling environments for automatic process/data placement may one day provide assistance; however, because in general these involve abstract models they are difficult to analyse automatically to achieve anything approaching optimum efficiency.

7.6.3.2 SIMD TEMPLATE MATCHING

Kumar and Krishnan [KK89] have designed a parallel algorithm for matching an $M \times M$ pixel template against an $N \times N$ pixel image. The algorithm is targeted to a SIMD nested hypercube architecture consisting of a large number of $N \times N$ processors, where $N = 2^n$ and $M = 2^m$. The processors are arranged into a hypercube topology with $\frac{N^2}{M^2}$ sub-hypercubes each of size $M \times M$. A window in the image $g(i, j)$ is matched against the template $T(s, t)$ as follows:

$$C(i, j) = \sum_{s=0}^{M-1} \sum_{t=0}^{M-1} g((i + s) \bmod N, \, (j + t) \bmod N) \times T(s, t) \qquad (7.64)$$

An analysis of the computational complexity for a single processor showed that the template can be matched against the image in $O(N^2 \times M^2)$ time. For the parallel implementation each processor, $p(i, j)$, initially stores the corresponding image pixel, $g(i, j)$, and the template $T(p, q)$ is stored on the control processor. The algorithm involves three steps, as follows. (1) Each processor $p(i, j)$ accumulates a column of image data $g(i, j)...g(i, j + M - 1)$. The data redistribution can be achieved in M shift operations which takes $O(M \times \log N)$ time. However, this can be improved by buffering blocks of data up to $M - 1$ pixels and shifting these in one operation. This technique reduces the complexity to $O(M \times \log M + \log N)$ time. (2) Next the partial sums are calculated, M rows of the template are broadcast to each processor and multiplied with M image values $g(i, j)...g(i, j + M - 1)$. The M multiplications take $O(M)$ time; these must be repeated M times so the total computation takes $O(M^2)$ time. (3) Next the partial products need to be added; the time for M such operations with a hypercube size N^2 with $O(M)$ memory/processor is $O(M * \log M + \log N)$. In summary analysis shows that the template can be matched in $O(M^2 + \log N)$ time.

7.6.3.3 SIMD EDGE BASED MATCHING

Laine *et al.* [LR91] proposed a feature based matcher for a pipelined SIMD machine with 512×512 bytes of image memory. The matcher was based on a model of human perception which includes the following steps: (1) identify features and extract them from each view independently; (2) match features so they are projections of the same world coordinate; (3) use the disparity between matched features together with the camera model to determine the depth of the matched features. The approach assumes an epipolar camera model and extracts edges along horizontal scanlines. The algorithm is divided into two phases. In the first a loose geometric constraint and the ordering of previous matches are used to filter out unlikely matches. The remaining match candidates are then evaluated using a similarity measure. Matches at this stage can contain ambiguities; these are sorted and truncated to the three best matches. In the second phase the probability of each possible match is calculated based on an individual evaluation and a classification of its set. A relaxation process applies a consistency rule to adjust the probability on the basis of the similarity in the disparity of neighbouring points. The algorithm proceeds iteratively with accepted matches being used to provide a context for the accumulation of new matches. Laine *et al.* gave a detailed description of the various steps involved in the algorithm and an analysis of the complexity of each [LR91]. The algorithm has been applied to synthetic models of an urban scene and digitised stereo aerial photographs of an urban area. Both image pairs are 512×512 pixels. For synthetic and urban aerial images 81% and 79% of edges extracted from the left images were matched (using a search space of 32 pixels). The algorithm has been implemented on various machines; timings are reported for a Gould/DeAnza IP-8500 image processor equipped with a Digital Video Processor (DVP). The synthetic images were matched in 54 seconds and the real urban ones took 62 seconds.

7.6.3.4 MIMD TEMPLATE MATCHING

Ranka and Sahni [RS90] developed and simplified Kumar and Krishnan's algorithm for SIMD architectures. It has the same $O(M^2 + \log N)$ complexity as the original but is claimed to be faster by a constant factor. The algorithm was further developed and simplified for a MIMD hypercube machine (NCUBE/7), its performance again being improved by a constant factor. The SIMD algorithm makes use of the broadcast facility available on these machines; this facility enables messages to be transmitted from the host to all processors in about the same time as a basic arithmetic operation. Messages can be transmitted between processors in about the same time that it takes to perform a 2-byte integer addition (4.3 μs). In contrast to this the NCUBE takes $447 + 2.4b$

μs to communicate a message of length b bytes between neighbouring processors. The algorithm matches an $m \times m$ pixel template against an $n \times n$ pixel image. It is designed to be implemented on a hypercube configuration with p processors such that $\sqrt{p}$ is an integer factor of n. The general approach is to divide the image into a number of square blocks and allocate each of these to a different processor. The template is broadcast and stored locally on each processor. If minimum size blocks, i.e. $\frac{n}{\sqrt{p}} \times \frac{n}{\sqrt{p}}$ bytes, are used then extra inter-process communications are needed for matching the template against pixels at the block boundary. To avoid the additional overhead associated with this, an extra overlapping area of width $m - 2$ pixels is included around the boundary of each. Hypercube-to-hypercube timings for 64×64 pixel images and an 8×8 pixel template on a 64 processor NCUBE/7 shows that the template can be matched in 0.086 seconds (a speedup of 59.2 over a single processor). By comparison, a Cray 2 can perform the same operation in 0.023 seconds, so the NCUBE is only 3.7 times slower, for larger 512×512 pixel images. With a 32×32 pixel template the NCUBE is about 4.2 times slower than the Cray. However, the overhead involved in transferring data between the NCUBE and host must also be taken into consideration. For small sized imagery this can be very significant. However, for larger ones it amounts to an extra overhead of 10%.

7.6.3.5 MIMD AREA BASED MATCHING: PARALLEL OTTO-CHAU AND GPSM

A processor farm implementation of the Otto-Chau region growing algorithm [OC88] was designed for UNIX implementation. It uses special extensions to the UNIX fork and pipe system calls to enable processes to be placed on different processors with interprocess communications provided by interconnecting pipes. Despite the restricted nature of UNIX pipes a processor farm is easy to implement: a pair of pipes connect a central control process with each of the worker processes. An outgoing pipe from the controller provides a channel with which to despatch work packets to each of the worker processes; when a result has been calculated it is returned to the controller through an incoming pipe. Otto and Chau designed the farm with a global region growing algorithm as the controller and ALSC patch matchers as the workers. Holden *et al.* [HZM92] investigated its performance with a T800 Transputer array and observed a good speedup with up to 8 processors for small 240×240 pixel images. However, analysis of the memory requirements indicated that the data structures used for controlling region growing are proportional to the area of the image. This led to the controller requiring large amounts of memory, and so limited the image size that could be processed. Further studies of the communications requirement between controller and workers also indicated that a large bandwidth was needed which resulted in limited scalability. To overcome these limitations a geometrically parallel approach (termed GPSM) employing uniform data partitioning was investigated by Holden *et al.* [HZM92]. Here the left hand image is divided into a number of equally sized rectangular tiles with the corresponding right hand ones determined from the seed points (see Figure 7.20). To allow for local data dependencies at the perimeter of tiles, overlapping regions from neighbouring tiles are included. This overcomes the need for data to be moved around during matching. The process organisation is shown in Figure 7.21; a modified Otto-Chau stereo matching process is created and loaded onto each processor by a special control process referred to as "gpsm". Each match-

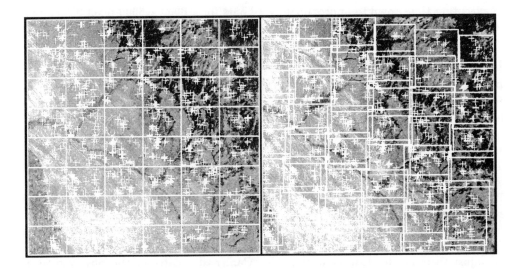

Figure 7.20 GPSM data partitioning scheme for Wyoming: regular in the left (overlap not shown) and irregular in the right with seed points superimposed. Images ©CNES 1988.

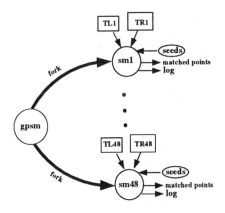

Figure 7.21 GPSM process organisation.

ing process operates on a single corresponding pair of tiles without interacting with any other process. Because each matching process is independent and because of the nature of the ALSC technique initial match estimates or "seed points" are required for each pair of corresponding tiles. Special seed point generating tools have been developed to extract uniformly spaced sets of them; see section 7.3.2.3. Rigorous quality assessments have been carried out with elevation models produced by serial matching and against ground measurements. Comparisons between serial and parallel versions indicated an insignificant difference in match coverage. Performance measurements for an array of 48 T800 Transputers indicated a speedup of about 40 with a reduction in execution time down to approximately 3 hours for a 6000 × 6000 pixel SPOT pair [HZM92].

7.6.3.6   MIMD EDGE BASED MATCHING: PARALLEL PMF

PMF is part of a software suite called TINA, an image processing and scene interpretation system to guide a robotic arm for pick-and-place operations. TINA captures images from a pair of video CCD cameras and processes them to build up a 3D edge-based representation of the scene. TINA consists of four main stages: edge detection; stereo matching (PMF); connect and classify connected edges; and model matching. TINA is implemented on a hybrid architecture consisting of a transputer array and dedicated frame rate hardware: a MaxBus bus and video RAM for fast I/O [BD91, RPB91]. The images are geometrically (spatially) partitioned for the feature extraction stage using a Canny edge detector. Two partitioning schemes have been investigated: one with horizontal raster scans and the other with a 2D mesh. Raster strips were found to be more flexible than a square mesh from the point of view that it is easier to adjust their size for load balancing. The Canny edge detector was observed to be relatively insensitive to signal content. However, other edge extractors are much more sensitive and require partitioning adjustments to be carried out *a priori* to provide good load balancing. The impact of load balancing on execution time is discussed by [BD91] and its effect on performance is compared for 2, 4, and 8 processors. A 13% and 27% reduction in execution time is reported for 4 and 8 processors respectively. For feature matching both geometric and task type parallelism (processor farm) are considered. The data is pre-partitioned by allocating equal numbers of edgels to each transputer. This is reported to reduce the execution time of the slowest processor by one half to less than 6 seconds for 256 × 256 pixel images. Because of the relatively small amount of unevenly distributed data the processor farm (with implicit load balancing) will most probably provide the most efficient solution. A further layer of algorithmic parallelism can be introduced by pipelining the four stages, each stage being placed on a different group of processors. Model matching is parallelised on a task basis using a hierarchical control strategy. For the full TINA system consisting of 24 processors a speedup of 80% per processor was reported [RPB91].

7.6.4   Parallel Motion

7.6.4.1   SIMD OPTIC FLOW MOTION ESTIMATION

Buxton *et al.* [BMBW85] investigated the implementation of a feature based optic flow motion estimation system for monocular image sequences on a SIMD architecture: 64 × 64 pixel images are mapped directly onto a DAP [Red79] with one pixel per processor. First the grey level intensity function is smoothed in both space and time with a Gaussian filter. Then edgels (zero-crossings) are extracted which satisfy a motion constraint equation. From these the average value of the optic flow normal to edgels or the so-called vernier velocity is determined. Next a least squares fit of the vernier velocity field to the image is performed. Then the surface and motion parameters are calculated and the motion interpreted. Results for 64 × 64 pixel images on a 64 × 64 processor array show that frames can be processed every 100 ms which is about half video rate.

7.6.4.2 MIMD FEATURE BASED MOTION ESTIMATION

Choudhary and Ponnusamy [CP92] investigated parallel feature motion estimation systems for sequences of stereo images. Such systems are composed of a number of separately identifiable stages (tasks) that can be pipelined. Figure 7.22 illustrates the process organisation with stereo image sequences at successive time frames (t_i, t_{i+1}) being analysed. The first stage is feature extraction (FE): a LoG operator is con-

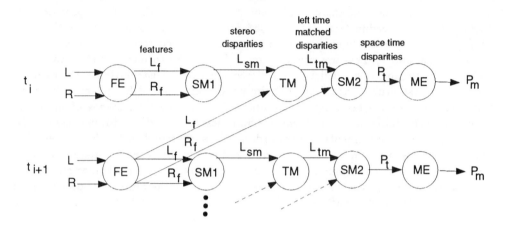

Figure 7.22 Tasks involved in motion estimation: feature extraction (FE), stereo matching (SM), time matching (TM), motion estimation (ME).

volved with the images to extract zero-crossing edge representations $(L_f$ and $R_f)$. Stereo matching (SM1) is first applied to images in the same time frame to derive corresponding points in the usual way. Disparities relative to the left hand image (L_{sm}) are derived and passed to another feature based matcher (TM). This is similar to stereo matching but this time the same left image is matched in different time frames. A heuristic of limited displacement is applied to constrain the horizontal (w) and vertical (l) displacements to within a window of size $l \times w$. Temporal feature displacements in the left image are found and passed to a second stereo matcher (SM2). This matcher establishes correspondences between features from images at time frame t_{i+1} after time point correspondences have been calculated between images at t_i and t_{i+1}. Finally the space–time matches, P_t, are passed to a motion estimation process which calculates the motion parameters (P_m). Each task exhibits a different set of characteristics; each is computationally intensive and involves different types of processing (numerical, symbolic, graph algorithms) that are both data independent and data dependent (with dependencies either local or global). Different data decomposition and load balancing strategies are therefore required for efficient parallelisation. Choudhary and Ponnusamy propose a preprocessing task present in the current stage which can determine load redistribution in the next, and suggested that this task itself could be executed in parallel. Different methods were used for data decomposition and remapping: uniform partitioning where data is divided into partitions of equal size; first order scheduling where data is divided into domains of equal numbers of symbolic features; second order scheduling where data is divided on the basis of both the number of features in the domain and their spatial distribution; dynamic scheduling requiring fine grained parallelism, i.e. splitting the processing into a large number of subtasks (much greater than the number of processors) which are dynamically rescheduled to ensure uniform load balancing. Choudhary and Ponnusamy undertook a series of experiments to measure the speedup for processing 512×512 pixel images; all timings were carried out on an Encore Multimax 520, a shared memory machine with 16 processors. Feature extraction by zero-crossings of the LoG operator is data independent and therefore can be efficiently implemented in parallel with uniform partitioning. This results in a speedup factor of 13 for 16 processors: see Table 7.1 (note that this table gives approximate figures; readers who want detailed results are referred back to the original paper). Features are not evenly distributed throughout the imagery so uniform partitioning is not efficient for stereo matching. Distributing features more evenly with first order scheduling, FO, improves performance by a factor of about 2 and with dynamic scheduling, D, by about 2.5. For the later stages of matching there is a much smaller number of features and these are distributed much less evenly. As a result the improvements of first order, FO, and second order, SO, scheduling schemes over the uniform one become more noticeable. In general dynamic scheduling performs best but not much better than first or second order schemes and this is expected to diminish as scheduling overheads increase as the number of processors is scaled up. Table 7.2 summarises the data partitioning and load balancing strategies

	U	FO	SO	D
FE	13	-	-	-
SM1	4.7	11	11	15
TM	3	11.5	13	14
SM2	2.5	4.5	5	5.5
Overall	5.3	12.1	12.4	12.6

Table 7.1 Speedup of tasks on 16 processors for different data decomposition schemes: uniform partitioning (U), first order partitioning (FO), second order partitioning (SO) and dynamic partitioning (D).

for the various tasks involved in stereo and motion estimation.

ACKNOWLEDGEMENTS

The authors would like to thank Tim Day (Dept. of Photogrammetry, UCL) for the imagery and visualisation of Kamchatka and David Allison (Dept. of Photogrammetry, UCL) for his help in providing aerial stereo imagery. Thanks are also due to the Leverhulme Trust for supporting the work on parallel stereo matching.

Data dependencies	Task	Partitioning	Load balancing
Data-independent local operations	Template matching	Uniform 1D or 2D blocks	Equal size partitioning
	Sobel, LoG, DoG edge extraction	Uniform 1D or 2D blocks	Equal size partitioning
Data-independent global operations	2D FFT	Uniform 1D or 2D blocks	Equal size partitioning
Data-dependent local operations	Feature-based SM	Load balanced 1D or 2D blocks	Equal no. of features
	Area-based SM	Load balanced 1D or 2D blocks	Equal no. of pixels
	Feature-based time matching	Load balanced 1D or 2D blocks	Equal no. of features
Data-dependent global operations	Hough transform	Uniform 1D or 2D blocks	Static: spatial equal no. edges
	Region growing (segmented)	Uniform 1D or 2D blocks	Equal feature density
	Model matching	Non-uniform	Dynamic

Table 7.2 Data-dependencies, partitioning and load balancing for stereo matching (SM) and motion estimation tasks.

REFERENCES

[AB86] J. Aloimonos and A. Basu. Shape and 3-D Motion from Contour without Point to Point Correspondences: General Principles. In *Proc. IEEE Computer Society Conf. on Computer Vision and Pattern Recognition*, pages 518–527, Miami Beach, Florida, 22-26 June 1986.

[AM92] D. Allison and J.-P. Muller. An Automated System for Sub-Pixel Correction and Geocoding of Multi-Spectral and Multi-Look Aerial Imagery. In *Proc. XVII Congress, Int. Soc. for Photogrammetry and Remote Sensing*, Washington, DC, 2-14 August 1992.

[AN88] J. K. Aggarwal and N. Nandhakumar. On Computation of Motion from Sequences of Images—A Review. *Proc. of the IEEE*, 76(8):917–935, 1988.

[AW87] J. K. Aggarwal and Y. F. Wang. Analysis of a Sequence of Images Using Point and Line Correspondences. In *Proc. IEEE Int. Conf. on Robotics and Automation*, pages 1275–1280, Raleigh, NC, 31 March - 3 April 1987.

[AZM91] D. Allison, M. J. Zemerly, and J.-P. Muller. Automatic Seed Point Generation for Stereo Matching and Multi-Image Registration. In *Proc. Int. Geoscience and Remote Sensing Symposium (IGARSS 91)*, volume 4, pages 2417–2421, Espoo, Helsinki, Finland, 3-6 June 1991.

[BC86]   T. J. Broida and R. Chellapa. Estimation of Object Motion Parameters from Noisy Images. *IEEE Trans. on Pattern Analysis and Machine Intelligence*, PAMI-8(1):90–99, 1986.

[BD91]   C. R. Brown and C. M. Dunford. Parallel Architectures for Fast 3D Machine Vision. In J. E. W. Mayhew and J. P. Frisby, editors, *3D Model Recognition from Stereoscopic Cues*, pages 67–75. MIT Press, 1991.

[Bel57]   R. E. Bellman. *Dynamic Programming*. Princeton University Press, Princeton, NJ, 1957.

[BF82]   S. T. Barnard and M. A. Fischler. Computational Stereo. *Computing Surveys*, 14(4):553–572, 1982.

[BMBW85] B. F. Buxton, D. W. Murray, H. Buxton, and N.S. Williams. Structure-from-Motion Algorithms for Computer Vision on an SIMD Architecture. *Computer Physics Communications*, 37:273–280, 1985.

[BT80]   A. T. Barnard and W. B. Thompson. Disparity Analysis of Images. *IEEE Trans. on Pattern Analysis and Machine Intelligence*, PAMI-2(4):333–340, 1980.

[BY90]   R. Baldwin and K. Yamamoto. Digital Superimposition and Automatic DEM Production by Dynamic Programming in Disparity Space. *Int. Archives of Photogrammetry and Remote Sensing*, 28(4):259–272, 1990.

[CA90]   V. Chaudhary and J. K. Aggarwal. Parallelism in Computer Vision: A Review. In V. Kumar, P.S. Gopalakrishnan, and L. N. Kanal, editors, *Parallel Algorithms for Machine Intelligence and Vision*, pages 271–309. Cambridge University Press, 1990.

[CC90]   C. Chang and S. Chatterjee. Multiresolution Stereo - A Bayesian Approach. In *10th Int. Conf. on Pattern Recognition*, volume B, pages 908–912, Atlantic City, NJ, 16-22 June 1990.

[CL88]   V. Cantoni and S. Levialdi. Multi-Processor Computing for Images. *Proc. of the IEEE*, 76(8):959–969, 1988.

[CP92]   A. N. Choudhary and R. Ponnusamy. Parallel Implementation and Evaluation of a Motion Estimation System Algorithm Using Several Data Decomposition Schemes. *IEEE Journal of Parallel and Distributed Computing*, 14:50–65, 1992.

[CR92]   A. N. Choudhary and S. Ranka. Parallel Processing Computer Vision and Image Understanding. *Computer*, 25(2):7–10, 1992.

[CRAM87] K. A. Collins, J. B. G. Roberts, A. Anthony, and J.-P. Muller. Transputer Arrays for Real-Time Feature Point Stereo Matching. In *Proc. ISPRS Intercom. Conf. on Fast Processing of Photogrammetric Data*, pages 419–431, Interlaken, Switzerland, 2-4 June 1987.

[DA89]   U. R. Dhond and J. K. Aggarwal. Structure from Stereo—A Review. *IEEE Trans. on Systems, Man, and Cybernetics*, 19(6):1489–1510, 1989.

[DABM91] A. T. Deacon, A. G. Anthony, S. N. Bhatia, and J.-P. Muller. Evaluation of a CCD-Based Facial Measurement System. *Medical Informatics*, 16(2):213–228, 1991.

[Dav86]   J. C. Davis. *Kriging*. John Wiley & Sons, Inc., New York, 2nd edition, 1986.

[DBM⁺89]   D. J. Diner, C. J. Bruegge, J. V. Martonchik, T. P. Ackerman, R. Davies, S. A. W. Gerstl, H. R. Gordon, P. J. Sellers, J. Clark, J. A. Daniels, E. D. Danielson, V. G. Duval, K. P. Klaasen, G. Lilienthal, D. I. Nakamoto, R. J. Pagano, and T. H. Reilly. MISR: A Multiangle Imaging Spectro-Radiometer for Geophysical and Climatological Research from EOS. *IEEE Trans. on Goescience and Remote Sensing*, GRS-19:200–214, 1989.

[DM89]   T. Day and J.-P. Muller. Quality Assessment of Digital Elevation Models Produced by Automatic Stereomatchers from SPOT Image Pairs. *Image and Vision Computing*, 7(2):95–101, 1989.

[Dre81]   L. Dreschler. *Ermittlung Markanter Punkte auf der Bildern Bewegter Objekte und Berechnug einer 3-D Beschreibung auf dieser Grundlage*. PhD thesis, University of Hamburg, Germany, 1981.

[Duf78]   M. J. B. Duff. Review of CLIP Image Processing System. In *Proc. 1978 AFIPS National Computer Conf.*, pages 1055–1060, 1978.

[Dye87]   C. L. Dyer. Multiscale Image Understanding. In L. Uhr, editor, *Parallel Computer Vision*, pages 171–213. Academic Press, 1987.

[FG87]   W. Foerstner and E. Gulch. A Fast Interest Operator for Detection and Precise Location of Distinct Points, Corners and Centres of Circular Features. In *Proc. ISPRS Intercom. Conf. on Fast Processing of Photogrammetric Data*, pages 281–305, Interlaken, Switzerland, 2-4 June 1987.

[Fly66]   M. Flynn. Very High-Speed Computing Systems. *Proc. IEEE*, 54:1901–1909, December 1966.

[Foe86]   W. Foerstner. A Feature Based Correspondence Algorithm for Image Matching. *Int. Arch. of Photogrammetry and Remote Sensing*, 26(3):150–166, 1986.

[Fou87]   T. Fountain. *Processor Arrays: Architecture and Applications*. Academic Press, New York, 1987.

[GB87]   A. W. Gruen and E. P. Balsavias. Geometrically Constrained Multiphoto Matching. In *ISPRS Intercom. Conf. on Fast Processing of Photogrammetric Data*, pages 204–230, Interlaken, Switzerland, June 2-4 1987.

[Gib50]   J. J. Gibson. *The Perception of Visual World*. Houghton and Mifflin, Boston, MA, 1950.

[Gri85]   W. E. Grimson. Computational Experiments with a Feature Based Stereo Algorithm. *IEEE Trans. on Pattern Analysis and Machine Intelligence*, PAMI-7(1):17–34, 1985.

[Gru85]   A. W. Gruen. Adaptive Least Squares Correlation: A Powerful Image Matching Technique. *S. Afr. Journal of Photogrammetry Remote Sensing and Cartography*, 14(3):175–187, 1985.

[Gul88]   E. Gulch. Results of Test on Image Matching of ISPRS WG III/4. *Int. Archives of Photogrammetry and Remote Sensing*, 27(3):254–271, 1988.

[GW87]   R. C. Gonzalez and P. Wintz. *Digital Image Processing*. Addison-Wesley, 2nd edition, 1987.

[Han74]   M. J. Hannah. *Computer Matching of Areas in Stereo Images*. PhD thesis, University of Stanford, 1974.

[Han88]   M. J. Hannah. Digital Stereo Image Matching Techniques. *Int. Archives of Photogrammetry and Remote Sensing*, 27(3):246–267, 1988.

[Hol91]   M. Holm. Towards Automatic Rectification of Satellite Images Using Feature Based Matching. In *Proc. Int. Geoscience and Remote Sensing Society Symposium (IGARSS 91)*, pages 2439–2442, Espoo, Helsinki, Finland, 3-6 June 1991.

[HS81]   B. K. P. Horn and B. G. Schunck. Determining Optical Flow. *Artificial Intelligence*, 16:185–203, 1981.

[HS88]   C. Harris and M. Stephens. A Combined Corner and Edge Detector. In *Proc. of the 4th Alvey Vision Conf.*, pages 147–142, University of Manchester, UK, 31 August - 2 September 1988.

[HT81]   T. S. Huang and R. Y. Tsai. Chapter 1: Image Sequence Analysis: Motion Estimation. In T. S. Huang, editor, *Image Sequence Analysis*, pages 1–18. Springer-Verlag, 1981.

[HZ83]   R. A. Hummel and S. W. Zucker. On the Foundations of Relaxation Labelling Processes. *IEEE Trans. on Pattern Analysis and Machine Intelligence*, PAMI-5(4):267–287, 1983.

[HZM92]   M. Holden, M. J. Zemerly, and J.-P. Muller. Application of Transputers to Stereo Matching. In *Proc. European Workshops on Parallel Computing*, pages 40–51, Barcelona, Spain, 24-25 March 1992.

[IW90]   S.-L. Iu and K. Wohn. Estimation of General Rigid Body Motion from a Long Sequence of Images. In *10th Int. Conf. on Pattern Recognition*, volume A, pages 217–219, Atlantic City, NJ, 16-22 June 1990.

[Jai89]   A. K. Jain. Chapter 9: Image Analysis and Computer Vision. In A. K. Jain, editor, *Fundamentals of Digital Image Processing*, pages 359–362. Prentice Hall, 1989.

[Kar90]   K. P. Karmann. Time Recursive Motion Estimation Using Dynamical Models for Motion Estimation. In *10th Int. Conf. on Pattern Recognition*, volume A, pages 268–270, Atlantic City, NJ, 16-22 June 1990.

[KK89]   V. K. P. Kumar and V. Krishnan. Efficient Parallel Algorithms for Image Template Matching on Hypercube SIMD Machines. *IEEE Trans. on Pattern Analysis and Machine Intelligence*, 11(6):665–669, 1989.

[KS90]   D.S. Kalivas and A.A. Sawchuk. A 2-D Motion Estimation Algorithm. In *10th Int. Conf. on Pattern Recognition*, volume A, pages 271–273, Atlantic City, NJ, 16-22 June 1990.

[KS91]   D.S. Kalivas and A.A. Sawchuk. A Region Matching Motion Estimation Algorithm. *CVGIP: Image Understanding*, 54(2):275–288, 1991.

[LA88]   T. Luhmann and G. Altrogge. Interest-Operator for Image Matching. *Int. Archives of Photogrammetry and Remote Sensing*, 26(3):459–474, 1988.

[Lem88]   M. J. Lemmens. A Survey on Stereo Matching Techniques. *Int. Archives of Photogrammetry and Remote Sensing*, 27(3):11–23, 1988.

[LH88]   Y. Liu and T. S. Huang. A Linear Algorithm for Determining Motion and Structure from Line Correspondences. *Computer Vision, Graphics and Image Processing*, 44(1):35–57, 1988.

[Li90]   M. Li. High-Precision Relative Orientation Using Feature-Based Matching Tech-
            niques. *ISPRS Journal of Photogrammetry and Remote Sensing*, 44:311–324,
            1990.

[LR91]   A. F. Laine and G.-C. Roman. A Parallel Algorithm for Incremental Stereo
            Matching on SIMD Machines. *IEEE Trans. on Robotics and Automation*, RA-
            7(1):123–134, 1991.

[LS91]   J. C. Li and T. Schenck. Stereo Matching with Subpixel Accuracy. In *Technical
            Papers of ACSM-ASPRS Annual Convention*, volume 5: Photogrammetry and
            Primary Data Acquisition, pages 228–236, Baltimore, 1991.

[LZ88]   Y. Lu and Z. Zhang. Fast Implementation for Generating Epipolar Line Images
            with One-dimensional Resampling. *Int. Archives of Photogrammetry and Remote
            Sensing*, 27(3):511–520, 1988.

[MAB+88]   J.-P. Muller, A. Anthony, A. T. Brown, A. T. Deacon, S. A. Kennedy, P. M.
            Montgomery, G. W. Robertson, and D. M. Watson. Real-Time Stereo Matching
            Using Transputer Arrays for Close-Range Applications. In *Proc. Joint IAPR
            Workshop on Computer Vision - Special Hardware and Industrial Applications*,
            pages 45–49, Tokyo, Japan, 12-14 October 1988.

[Mah91a]   S. A. Mahmoud. Motion Analysis of Multiple Moving Objects Using Hartley
            Transform. *IEEE Trans. on Systems, Man, and Cybernetics*, SMC-21:280–287,
            1991.

[Mah91b]   S. A. Mahmoud. Motion Estimation Based on a Modified Fourier Spectrum.
            Information Processing Letters, 37:311–313, 1991.

[MCOR88]   J.-P. Muller, K. A. Collins, G. P. Otto, and J. B. Roberts. Stereo Matching
            Using Transputer Arrays. *Int. Archives of Photogrammetry and Remote Sensing*,
            27(3):559–586, 1988.

[MKD+88]   J.-P. Muller, J. Kolbusz, M. Dalton, S. Richards, and J. C. Pearson. Visualisation
            of Topographic Data Using Video Animation. *Int. Archives of Photogrammetry
            and Remote Sensing*, 27(4):602–616, 1988.

[MLL88]   M. Maresca, M. A. Lavin, and H. Li. Parallel Architectures for Vision. *Proc. of
            the IEEE*, 76(8):970–981, 1988.

[Mor77]   H. P. Moravec. Towards Automatic Visual Obstacle Avoidance. In *Proc. 5th
            Joint Int. Conf. on Artificial Intelligence*, page 584, Cambridge, 1977.

[MP79]   D. Marr and T. Poggio. A Computational Theory of Human Stereo Vision. *Phil.
            Trans. Royal Society, London*, B-204:301–328, 1979.

[MSA85]   A. Mitchie, S. Seida, and J. K. Aggarwal. Determining Position and Displace-
            ment in Space from Images. In *Proc. IEEE Computer Society Conf. on Computer
            Vision and Pattern Recognition*, pages 504–509, San Francisco, CA, 19-23 June
            1985.

[MT89]   S. B. Marapane and M. M. Trivedi. Region-Based Stereo Analysis for Robotic
            Applications. *IEEE Trans. on Systems, Man, and Cybernetics*, SMC-19(6):1447–
            1464, 1989.

[MU81]   D. Marr and S. Ullman. Directional Selectivity and Its Use in Early Visual
            Processing. *Phil. Trans. Royal Society, London*, B-211:151–180, 1981.

[Mul82]   J.-P. Muller. *Studies of Jovian Meteorology Using Spacecraft and Earth-Based
            Images*. PhD thesis, University of London, 1982.

[Mul88]   J.-P. Muller. Key Issues in Image Understanding in Remote Sensing. *Phil. Trans. Royal Society, London*, A-324:381–395, 1988.

[Mul89]   J.-P. Muller. Real-Time Stereo Matching and Its Role in Future Mapping Systems. In *Surveying and Mapping*, University of Warwick, UK, 17-21 April 1989. 15 pages.

[MW87]   H. Maitre and Y. Wu. Improving Dynamic Programming to Solve Image Registration. *Pattern Recognition*, 20(4):443–462, 1987.

[Nag81]   H. H. Nagel. Chapter 2: Image Sequence Analysis: What Can We Learn from Applications. In T. S. Huang, editor, *Image Sequence Analysis*, pages 19–228. Springer-Verlag, 1981.

[Nag89]   H. H. Nagel. On a Constraint Equation for the Estimation of Displacement Rates in Image Sequences. *IEEE Trans. on Pattern Analysis and Machine Intelligence*, PAMI-11(1):13–30, 1989.

[Nis84]   H. K. Nishihara. Practical Real-Time Imaging Stereo Matcher. *Optical Engineering*, 23(5):536–545, 1984.

[NM92]   A. G. Nwosu and J.-P. Muller. Technical Specification for a Camera Model for the NASA—Advanced Solid-State Array Spectroradiometer (ASAS). In *Proc. American Soc. of Photogrammetry and Remote Sensing (ASPRS) Convention - Monitoring and Mapping Global Change*, volume 4, pages 364–373, 3-7 August 1992.

[OC88]   G.P. Otto and T.K. Chau. A Region-Growing Algorithm for Matching of Terrain Images. *Image and Vision Computing*, 7(2):83–94, 1988.

[OK85]   Y. Ohta and T. Kanade. Stereo by Intra- and Inter-Scanline Search Using Dynamic Programming. *IEEE Trans. on Pattern Analysis and Machine Intelligence*, PAMI-7(2):139–154, 1985.

[Pin86]   L. J. Pinson. Chapter 2. In A. Pugh, editor, *Robot Sensors*, volume 1—Vision, pages 15–66. IFS, 1986.

[PMF85]   S. B. Pollard, J. E. Mayhew, and J. P. Frisby. PMF: A Stereo Correspondence Algorithm Using a Disparity Gradient Limit. *Perception*, 14:449–470, 1985.

[RA80]   J. W. Roach and J. K. Aggarwal. Determining the Movement of Objects from a Sequence of Images. *IEEE Trans. on Pattern Analysis and Machine Intelligence*, PAMI-2(6):554–562, 1980.

[Red79]   S. F. Reddaway. The DAP Approach. *Supercomputers: Infotech State of the Art Report*, 2:311–329, 1979.

[RHZ76]   A. Rosenfeld, R. Hummel, and S. Zucker. Scene Labelling by Relaxation Operations. *IEEE Trans. on Systems, Man and Cybernetics*, 6(5):420–430, 1976.

[Ros83]   A. Rosenfeld. Motion: Analysis of Time-Varying Imagery. In O. D. Faugeras, editor, *Fundamentals of Computer Vision*, pages 173–183. Cambridge University Press, 1983.

[Ros88]   A. Rosenfeld. Computer Vision: Basic Principles. *Proc. of the IEEE*, 76(8):863–868, 1988.

[RPB91]   M. Rygol, S. B. Pollard, and C. R. Brown. A Multiprocessor 3D Vision System for Pick and Place. In J. E. W. Mayhew and J. P. Frisby, editors, *3D Model Recognition from Stereoscopic Cues*, pages 75–80. MIT Press, 1991.

[RS90]   S. Ranka and S. Sahni. Image Template Matching on MIMD Hypercube Multi-
           computers. *Journal of Parallel and Distributed Computing*, 10(1):79–84, 1990.

[RV77]   A. Rosenfeld and G. J. VanderBrug. Coarse-to-Fine Template Matching. *IEEE
           Trans. on Systems, Man and Cybernetics*, 7:104–107, 1977.

[SA91]   B. Sabata and J. K. Aggarwal. Estimation of Motion from a Pair of Range
           Images: A Review. *CVGIP: Image Understanding*, 54(3):309–324, 1991.

[Sch85a]   B. G. Schunck. Image Flow: Fundamentals and Future Research. In *Proc. IEEE
           Computer Society Conf. on Computer Vision and Pattern Recognition*, pages
           560–571, San Francisco, CA, 19-23 June 1985.

[Sch85b]   B. G. Schunck. The Motion Constraint Equation for Optical Flow. In *Proc. Int.
           Conf. on Pattern Recognition*, pages 20–22, Montreal, 1985.

[Sch89]   B. G. Schunck. Image Flow Segmentation and Estimation by Constraint Line
           Clustering. *IEEE Trans. on Pattern Analysis and Machine Intelligence*, PAMI-
           11(10):1010–1027, 1989.

[SP90]   H. Shariat and K. E. Price. Motion Estimation with More Than Two Frames.
           IEEE Trans. on Pattern Analysis and Machine Intelligence, PAMI-12(5):417–
           434, 1990.

[STH80]   C. C. Slama, C. Theurer, and S. W. Henriksen. *Manual of Photogrammetry*.
           American Society of Photogrammetry, 4th edition, 1980.

[Sto85]   D. Stow. Eulerian Velocity Measurements of Hydrodynamic Surfaces Using Op-
           tical Flow Methods. *Int. Journal of Remote Sensing*, 6(12):1855–1860, 1985.

[Sto88]   Q. F. Stout. Mapping Vision Algorithms to Parallel Architectures. *Proc. of the
           IEEE*, 76(8):982–995, 1988.

[TSB91]   T. N. Tan, G. D. Sullivan, and K. D. Baker. Structure from Constrained Motion
           Using Point Correspondences. In P. Mowforth, editor, *Proc. of the British Ma-
           chine Vision Conf.*, pages 301–309, University of Glasgow, UK, 24-26 September
           1991. Springer-Verlag.

[Ull79]   S. Ullman. The Interpretation of Structure from Motion. *Phil. Trans. Royal
           Society, London*, B-203:405–426, 1979.

[Val75]   L. G. Valient. Parallelism in Comparison Problems. *SIAM J. of Computing*, 3,
           1975.

[Val82]   L. G. Valient. A Scheme for Fast Parallel Communication. *SIAM J. of Comput-
           ing*, 11, 1982.

[WHA87]   J. Weng, T. S. Huang, and N. Ahuja. 3-D Motion Estimation, Understanding
           and Prediction from Noisy Image Sequences. *IEEE Trans. on Pattern Analysis
           and Machine Intelligence*, PAMI-9(3):370–389, 1987.

[WHA92]   J. Weng, T. S. Huang, and N. Ahuja. Motion and Structure from Line Corre-
           spondences: Closed-Form Solution, Uniqueness and Optimization. *IEEE Trans.
           on Pattern Analysis and Machine Intelligence*, PAMI-14(3):318–336, 1992.

[WRH92]   C. C. Weems, E. M. Riseman, and A. R. Hanson. Image Understanding Architec-
           ture: Exploiting Potential Parallelism in Machine Vision. *Computer*, 25(2):65–68,
           1992.

[WS91]   D. D. Wahl and J. J. Simpson. Satellite Derived Estimates of the Normal and Tangential Components of Near-Surface Flow. *Int. Journal of Remote Sensing*, 12(12):2529–2571, 1991.

[WY91]   D. Willick and Y.-H. Yang. Experimental Evaluation of Motion Constraint Equations. *CVGIP: Image Understanding*, 54(2):206–214, 1991.

[YH91]   Q. Yang and D. C. Hodgson. Real-Time Motion Tracking Using the Hough Transform. In T. S. Durrani *et al.*, editor, *Applications of Transputer 3: Proc. of Transputer Applications*, pages 548–553, Glasgow, UK, 28-30 August 1991. IOS Press.

[ZH83]   O. A. Zuniga and R. M. Haralick. Corner Detection Using the Facet Model. In *Proc. IEEE Computer Society Conf. on Computer Vision and Pattern Recognition*, pages 30–37, Washington, DC, 1983.

[ZHM92]   M. J. Zemerly, M. Holden, and J.-P. Muller. A Multi-Resolution Approach to Parallel Stereo Matching of Airborne Imagery. In *Proc. XVII Int. Soc. of Photogrammetry and Remote Sensing Congress*, page 8, 2-14 August 1992.

[ZLS91]   J. Zong, J.-C. Li, and T. Schenk. Application of Forstner Interest Operator in Automatic Orientation System. In *Technical Papers of ACSM-ASPRS Annual Convention*, volume 5: Photogrammetry and Primary Data Acquisition, pages 440–448, Baltimore, 1991.

8

Parallel Implementations of the Backpropagation Learning Algorithm Based on Network Topology

STEFANOS KOLLIAS, ANDREAS STAFYLOPATIS

8.1 INTRODUCTION

Two performance measures are important when using a neural network learning algorithm for classification or recognition purposes: *learning speed* and *generalization efficiency*. Learning speed is a crucial factor for training a network in non-excessive time periods, especially in cases of large network architectures and large training data sets. Generalization refers to the ability of the network to provide correct responses, when it is presented with patterns that have not been included in its training data set.

It is well known, for example, that backpropagation has a rather slow rate of convergence. Many backpropagation variants have been, therefore, proposed to improve its learning speed and its convergence properties [Jac88, Kol89, Le89a]. Some of these variants replace the gradient-descent optimization technique used in backpropagation by a more efficient Newton scheme; this can, however, increase the complexity of the algorithm. Thus, deriving parallel implementations for these schemes is important in order to effectively reduce the execution time of the algorithm [Ste90].

Recent results [ANN91, Bau89, Le89a] indicate that good generalization is a result of appropriate network design; a small number of interconnection weights (i.e., free parameters during training) should be generally used for this purpose, and any a priori

Parallel Algorithms for Digital Image Processing, Computer Vision and Neural Networks, ed. I. Pitas
© 1993 John Wiley & Sons Ltd

knowledge about the problem should be built in the network architecture. Structured networks of small size are, therefore, likely to generalize better than fully connected networks.

Two types of approaches are mainly used to design backpropagation networks with a small number of free parameters. The first includes weight elimination [Wig91] or simple weight decay, in which the complexity of the network is penalized, by letting each weight decay towards zero at a rate that is proportional to its magnitude. The second includes receptive field architectures and weight sharing [Le89b, Le89c]. In dynamic environments, where the network input is time-varying, time-delay networks, i.e., networks which take into account both the current and previous input presentations, are typical paradigms of this approach. Receptive fields, weight sharing and time-delay networks have proved very effective, especially for speech and image recognition problems, where huge amounts of still or time-varying data have to be used for network training. Even for these variants of backpropagation the need for faster parallel implementation is a very crucial problem.

We will be interested in the parallelization of backpropagation based on network topology. As already mentioned, network topology is a very crucial factor in learning strategies, especially for convergence and generalization purposes, because it poses various constraints on the parallelization of the algorithm. The types of parallelism which are suitable for the different structured network architectures are investigated using various transputer implementations.

Section 8.2 gives a short description of the backpropagation algorithm and its variants, which are used to improve its learning speed or to reduce the size of the network; also, the use of backpropagation as a building block for other training schemes, such as reinforcement learning techniques, is discussed. The types of parallelism that can be applied when implementing the algorithm are introduced in section 8.3, which also includes a brief overview of existing parallel implementations of schemes based on backpropagation. Section 8.4 examines structured network architectures, including receptive fields, shared weights and time-delay networks. Section 8.5 investigates the parallel implementation of backpropagation for the different structured network architectures; the cases of training and spatial parallelism are examined in detail. Experimental results concerning the performance of the proposed parallel implementations of the backpropagation algorithm are given in section 8.6 and the main conclusions are summarized in section 8.7.

8.2   EFFICIENT LEARNING TECHNIQUES BASED ON BACKPROPAGATION

8.2.1   The Basic Algorithm

Backpropagation is an iterative supervised learning procedure that has been developed for the training of feedforward multilayer networks consisting of an input and an output layer and any number of intermediate, or hidden, layers [Par85, Rum86, Wer74].

Let us assume that the output of each unit i in a feedforward multilayer network is a non-linear function of its total input:

$$y_i = f(\sum_j w_{ij} x_j) \tag{8.1}$$

where w_{ij} is the weight of the link connecting unit j to unit i, y_i is the neuron output, x_j the neuron inputs and f is the sigmoid function. In the forward pass of the backpropagation algorithm, each unit of the network computes its output as a function of a linear combination of its inputs which come from the outputs of the neurons of the previous layer. The same procedure is used after training, when testing the generalization abilities of the network. At the end of forward propagation, during training, the network computes the activation y_i for each output neuron and compares it with the desired output d_i, defining an error by:

$$E = \frac{1}{2} \sum_k (y_k - d_k)^2 \tag{8.2}$$

where k indexes the output units of the network. The backward pass of the algorithm during training involves the adjustment of the weights so that the total error E is minimized. In particular, backpropagation uses the gradient-descent optimization technique to update the interconnection weights, using the partial derivative δ_i of the error associated with each neuron i:

$$\Delta w_{ij}(t) = \eta \delta_i x_j + \beta \Delta w_{ij}(t-1) \tag{8.3}$$

where η is the learning rate parameter, t denotes the number of input presentations and β is the momentum term. In the case of an output neuron, δ_i is computed as follows, where d_i is the desired response:

$$\delta_i = (d_i - y_i) \frac{\partial f}{\partial w_{ij}} \tag{8.4}$$

while in the case of a hidden or input neuron it has the following form:

$$\delta_i = \frac{\partial f}{\partial w_{ij}} \sum_k \delta_k w_{ki} \tag{8.5}$$

for all units k of the upper layer. If *off-line weight updating* is used, the increments Δw are computed for each training pattern, but are not used immediately to update the weights. Weight updating is performed after the presentation of the whole training set, using the accumulated weight increments. If, however, *on-line weight updating* is used, the network interconnection weights are updated after processing each training example.

8.2.2   Efficient Variants of the Algorithm

It is known that gradient-descent backpropagation converges slowly, even for medium sized networks. This fact results from the usually large dimension of the weight space and from the particular shape of the error surface at each iteration point. Oscillation between the sides of deep and narrow valleys, for example, is a well known case where gradient-descent provides poor convergence rates. The search for faster and more robust training methods must meet two requirements: simplicity, in order to reduce the total computational load, and locality, in order to maintain compatibility with distributed hardware architectures.

A simple technique that is used for speeding up the learning rate lets each synapse have its own learning rate parameter, increasing or decreasing its value according to the number of sign changes observed in the partial derivative of the error function with respect to the corresponding weight [Jac88]. The basic idea of this technique is that, if the sign of a certain component of the gradient remains the same for several iterations, it corresponds to a smooth variation of the error surface; the learning rate for this component should, therefore, be increased. On the other hand, if the sign of some component changes in several consecutive iterations, the learning rate parameter should be decreased to avoid oscillation.

An effective way of implementing this idea [Alm90] is to adapt the learning rate parameter at each iteration step. Consider the weight update equation:

$$w_{ij}(t) = w_{ij}(t-1) + \eta_{ij}(t)\partial_{ij}E(t) \tag{8.6}$$

where $\eta_{ij}(t)$ is the specific learning rate parameter of the ij-th synapse at iteration t. Then the learning rate is updated according to the following rule:

$$\eta_{ij}(t) = d_l\eta_{ij}(t-1) \tag{8.7}$$

for $l = 1, 2$, where $l = 1$ if the derivative of E has the same sign in the t and $t-1$ iterations and $l = 2$ otherwise. In general d_1 is slightly greater than unity (between 1.1 and 1.3) and d_2 slightly below $1/d_1$. The above equations imply an exponential increase and decrease of the learning rate parameter.

Other backpropagation variants have been proposed to improve the convergence properties of gradient-descent backpropagation. Conjugate-gradient or Newton-type methods, using approximations of the Hessian matrix of the error in the minimization process, are among these variants. One such algorithm is second-order least squares backpropagation based on the Marquardt-Levenberg optimization technique [Kol89]. Due to the inclusion of second-order information, the algorithm in its general form is more complex than gradient-descent [Kar90]. However, it is more amenable to parallel implementation than simple gradient descent [Ste90]. Both least squares backpropagation and the variant described by equations (8.6) and (8.7) are considered and used in the following.

Other techniques for reducing the size of the network are based on deleting 'useless' connections dynamically during training. Various methods have been proposed for this purpose, which add a constraint term (i.e., a function of the network complexity) to the minimized error criterion penalizing big networks with many parameters [Cha89, Han89, Ish89]. The simplest case is to add the constraint term $\sum_i \sum_j w_{ij}^2$ (which is equivalent to weight decay, since a penalty is introduced for weights with large values [Ish89]) to the minimized error criterion E, but other, more complex, constraints are also possible.

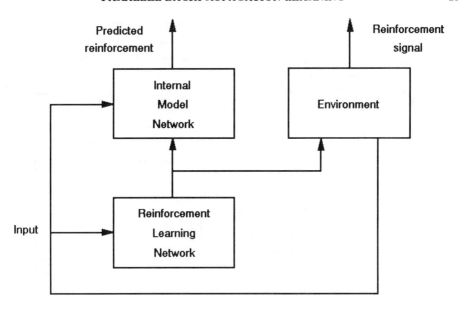

Figure 8.1   Backpropagating through a model of environmental reinforcement.

8.2.3   Reinforcement Learning Based on Backpropagation

Another issue of interest refers to the use of backpropagation variants as building blocks for implementing other learning strategies. In order to demonstrate this aspect, we will briefly consider reinforcement learning approaches exclusively based on the use of backpropagation.

Reinforcement learning could be included in supervised learning algorithms, since external information about the network's performance is provided by the environment. However, due to the particular form of the external information provided to the network, it can be distinguished from both supervised and unsupervised learning, forming a third main learning category [Bar83, Mil90, Wil87]. External information to the network is a scalar signal called *reinforcement*. This signal is provided to every single network unit and evaluates the performance of the network. The reinforcement signal may take on just two values, indicating success or failure, or it may take on a continuum of values, indicating a graded degree of success. The objective of learning is the maximization of some function of this reinforcement signal.

In supervised learning, the network is provided with the exact desired response to every input. So, it can be said that the feedback provided to the system by the teacher (or external environment) is purely 'instructive' [Wil88a]. In reinforcement learning, the network's response is evaluated by the external environment using the scalar reinforcement signal which indicates the appropriateness of this response. This kind of feedback can then be thought of as 'evaluative'.

One approach for incorporating backpropagation into reinforcement learning is to train a second network, to serve as an internal model of the process by which the

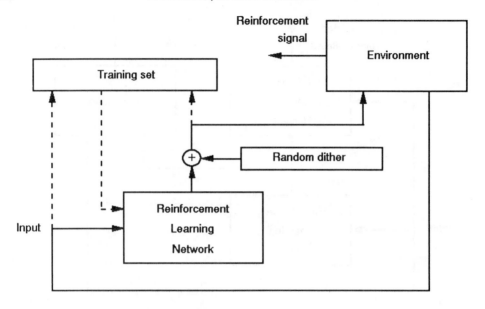

Figure 8.2   Using reinforcement to create training set for backpropagation network.

environment evaluates actions [Mun87, Wil88b]. The internal model can be viewed as a feedforward network undergoing supervised learning. The objective of the internal model is to learn to duplicate the environmental reinforcement signal, by minimizing the prediction error. The weights of this network are thus trained using backpropagation. After training the internal model, the original learning network is trained by backpropagating partial derivative information through the internal model network into the learning network without changing the weights of the internal model network. The objective is now to maximize the predicted reinforcement value. Thus, the weights in the two networks are trained differently using appropriate adaptations of backpropagation (Figure 8.1).

Another approach involving backpropagation is presented in [Mil91]. The network facing the associative reinforcement learning task is also trained using backpropagation. The reinforcement signal provided by the environment is used to create training pairs for this network as follows. The network receives an input and produces an output, which is adjusted by adding a random component. The adjusted output is evaluated by the environment and, if an improved performance is indicated, the output is combined with the corresponding input to form a new entry to the training set of the network (Figure 8.2). This procedure provides a training set containing data of gradually improved quality. In fact, this technique transforms evaluative feedback into instructive feedback, thus allowing direct application of supervised learning.

In both the above learning schemes, backpropagation is used as the basic block for network training. In any case, knowledge about the problem may imply constraints on the network topology that can lead to improved network capabilities.

8.3 PARALLELISM IN BACKPROPAGATION

8.3.1 Types of Parallelism

The implementation of learning schemes based on backpropagation can exploit parallelism in several manners.

A first type of parallelism is *algorithmic parallelism*; algorithmic parallelism refers to possibilities intrinsically related to the algorithm itself. This is the case, for example, with the second-order least squares backpropagation [Kol89] presented in Section 8.2. As a matter of fact, the algorithm is particularly suitable for parallel implementation due to its numerical formulation [Ste90]. In particular, the algorithm uses second-order information of the error, thus requiring matrix computations in each iteration; this augments the complexity of the algorithm to about ten times that of gradient-descent backpropagation. It has been shown that parallel computation of the above mentioned matrix elements provides a great reduction of the complexity of the algorithm, resulting in a similar complexity to that of gradient-descent. This fact, together with the fast convergence properties of the algorithm, provide an efficient parallel implementation of the backpropagation variant.

Other types of parallelism concern partitioning of the job among processors in accordance with the network architecture and ignore any specific numerical properties of the algorithm.

During the forward pass of the backpropagation algorithm, activities propagate sequentially through successive layers, but in parallel within a given layer, assuming that there are no connections between neurons of the same layer. Similarly, the error signals propagating backwards during the backward pass, as well as the weight increments, are computed in parallel within a given layer. This kind of parallelism is characterized as *spatial parallelism*.

As already discussed, weight updating can be performed either off-line or on-line. The former approach implies a 'batch' updating technique making possible a separation of the training patterns into sets that can be processed in parallel within an iteration of the algorithm through the whole training data set; this procedure is defined as *training parallelism*. If on-line updating is used, the application of training parallelism may require a large number of communications between the processors handling different partitions of the data. Both on-line and off-line training are considered in the following, depending on the type of parallelism being exploited in the implementation of the algorithms.

Training parallelism can be viewed as a general principle allowing parallel execution of supervised learning tasks and is generally not affected by peculiarities of the network topology. Also, it is closely related to the idea of off-line weight updating on the basis of a given training set. On the other hand, the implementation of spatial parallelism is strongly dependent on the structure of the network since it involves partitioning of nodes, which in turn implies specific communication patterns. Spatial and training parallelism can be combined to provide hybrid implementations. Also, algorithmic parallelism can be combined with spatial and/or training parallelism in a large multiprocessor environment to yield very efficient implementations.

8.3.2   Parallel Implementations

Exploiting parallelism is an increasingly common approach to improve the performance of neural network systems [Cho88, Dep89, Erc91, DiZ90, Kun88, Sin90]. The development of parallel computers makes it possible to consider efficient implementations of neural network learning algorithms, which take advantage of parallelism in order to reduce large execution times. This is particularly interesting in complex problems, such as speech and image recognition [Pao89], where simulation times can become excessively long. Several implementations of algorithms based on backpropagation have been developed on different parallel architectures.

A programmable systolic array has been proposed in [Kun88], as a means of using intensive and pipelined computing, also circumventing the limitation on communication. This is achieved by first expressing neural processing in terms of iterative matrix operations, which are in turn expressed in terms of dependence graphs, and by finally mapping dependences onto systolic arrays.

In [Pom88], a fast backpropagation algorithm for a linear array of processors is described. Results are reported of the implementation of this algorithm on Warp, a 10-processor programmable systolic array computer. The results imply that linear systolic array machines can be very efficient neural network simulators.

The Connection Machine provides a unique test-bed for the exploration of neural network models. In [Sin90], training set parallelism is exploited as a means of efficiently implementing backpropagation using a Connection Machine. This is performed by placing a complete copy of the nodes of the network along with a single training pattern in each processor of the Connection Machine; results are given which indicate that the speed of implementation has a constant or linear time dependence with respect to the size of the network. Other implementations of neural computational paradigms related to backpropagation on the Connection Machine are reported in [Dep89].

Various experimental speedup results from implementation of backpropagation on a hypercube parallel processor, such as an 8-processor Intel iPSC/2, are presented in [Erc91]. Speedup values of 6 to 7 fold are reported, exploiting training, as well as sorts of spatial parallelism, in cases where large training sets were available. Other fundamental work regarding implementation of backpropagation on grid and hypercube parallel processors is presented in [Zha90].

In [Sij92], a software parallel implementation of backpropagation is proposed, which can provide considerable speedup, when implemented not only on special purpose VLSI circuits or parallel MIMD machines, but also on networks of workstations.

A network of transputers represents a suitable parallel environment for the implementation of neural network learning strategies. In particular, transputers can be combined in a variety of network configurations and have been successfully applied to the implementation of fully connected backpropagation networks [Bey87, Mil89, Ern88, Mur91, Pau91, Pet91]. In general, the performance of such systems depends on the number of transputers in the network, the speed of communication between transputers and the performance of each individual transputer.

An extension of Hoare's Communicating Sequential Processes (CSP) programming model and the Occam programming language is presented in [Cho88], defining a new specification and programming language which offers comfort in writing programs based on connectionist concepts. The features of the language are semantically coherent with the behaviour of entities related to neural computing, and can support efficient transputer implementations.

The parallel implementation of the backpropagation algorithm on a 16-transputer architecture is presented in [Ern88]; the implementation is evaluated by means of a pattern recognition application and the role of various parameters is analysed.

An efficient systolic array algorithm for implementing backpropagation on a transputer system is developed in [Mil89]. A pipelined implementation of backpropagation based on the parallelization of matrix products on a torus of transputers is proposed in [Pet91]; both analytical and experimental results indicate that the performance of pipelined parallel learning algorithms is almost independent of the neural network architecture.

An interesting technique for improving the efficiency of parallel implementations of feedforward networks is based on the notion of a 'spy' process [Pau91]. The spy has been implemented on a 32-transputer system and represents a powerful tool for evaluating the performance of a model and selecting the best network architecture and set of parameters, as well as for comparing the efficiency of various parallel implementations.

In [Mur91], it is stated that for fully or randomly connected networks, the specific topology of the transputer network used to implement a neural architecture (i.e., grid, line, hypercube) has only a small, constant effect on the achieved speedup. It is also concluded that modular neural networks are better suited for such parallel implementations.

An investigation of several issues related to the efficient exploitation of transputers in simulating neural networks can be found in [Vuu92], where several parallelization schemes and communication patterns are examined in conjunction with the mechanisms provided by the Helios distributed operating system.

8.4   STRUCTURED NETWORK ARCHITECTURES FOR IMAGE RECOGNITION

The problem of what constitutes a sufficiently large training sample and a suitable network architecture for backpropagation networks has been a subject of recent research [Hau89, Bau90, Bau91, ANN91, Pea91]. Results indicate that the likelihood of correct generalization depends on the size of the hypothesis space, i.e., the total number of networks being considered, on the size of the solution space, i.e., the set of networks which give good generalization, and on the number of training examples. In general, if good generalization is aimed, the size of the network should be kept as small as possible, using at the same time a sufficient number of training examples.

8.4.1   Receptive Fields - Weight Sharing

The size of the network can be reduced by imposing constraints on the network topology. A technique that is frequently used in image recognition problems restricts each neuron to have as input only a small portion of the input pattern, called a *receptive field*. Thus, each hidden or output unit is connected to a subset of the units of the previous layer, as shown in Figure 8.3, for non-overlapping fields. It should be men-

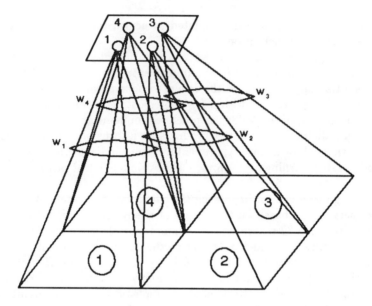

Figure 8.3   Receptive fields.

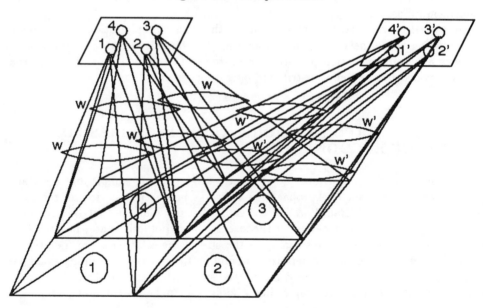

Figure 8.4   Weight sharing.

tioned that this technique results in a network with fewer interconnections, which is also in accordance with the properties of human vision and understanding.

Another technique in this category is weight sharing. As shown in Figure 8.4, this technique imposes equality constraints among the connection strengths, in the sense that several interconnections in the network are controlled by a single weight. In this way, the number of free parameters in the network is reduced, leading, therefore, to better generalization properties and avoiding overfitting problems. Weight sharing can be used for shift-invariant feature extraction and is generally used in many pattern recognition problems. However, it should be mentioned that, when implementing weight-shared backpropagation, the most frequently used technique in imposing weight equality constraints is the following: the increment of each weight shared by different neurons is computed independently by all corresponding neurons; the weight is then updated by the average of all computed increments. As will be shown in the following, this technique may require a significant amount of communications among different processors, when implementing in parallel on-line forms of the weight-shared backpropagation algorithm.

The shared weights–receptive fields technique is an extension of backpropagation used in many applications involving shift invariant image recognition. Each hidden unit of these networks receives its inputs from a receptive field on the previous layer, while receptive fields of neighbouring units may overlap by a number of rows or columns. Weight sharing is performed by defining groups of neurons within each hidden layer and by letting all hidden units of each group use the same set of weights. Finally, the output layer is generally fully connected to the last hidden layer of the network.

8.4.2 Time-Delay Networks

Another structured network architecture, that is similar to weight sharing, concerns time-delay neural networks (TDNN). Such networks have the ability to represent relationships between events in time and can learn features or abstractions that are invariant under translation in time. To do this, a time-delay unit differs from a conventional unit in that it receives not only the current input elements, but also delayed replicas of them, as shown in Figure 8.5. As a result, a time-delay unit has the ability to relate and compare its current input to the past history of events.

A time-delay network is composed of many such units, forming a multilayer structure that receives sequences of input patterns. Such networks have been used for speech recognition [Wai89] and can also be applied in moving image monitoring or recognition. An equivalent way of investigating such networks is by using a spatially expanded input pattern [Wai89], as shown in Figure 8.6, plus some constraints on the weights. In particular, each collection of time-delay units is duplicated for each one frame shift in time. In this way, the whole history of activations is available at once. Moreover, the weights of the corresponding connections in the time shifted copies are the same.

Figure 8.6 displays a time-delay network, fed by a sequence of 12 input frames, each consisting of 16 units (representing either a set of coefficients extracted from a speech signal, or a 4×4 window in a frame of an image sequence). A group of eight units is used in the first hidden layer, each unit of which is fully connected to the first three input frames (using 48 weights). As shown in Figure 8.6, this group is duplicated nine times, so that hidden units view all frames of the input sequence. Moreover, the next hidden layer is similarly composed of a group of four units, each of which is connected to four frames of the first hidden layer. Six duplications of this group are used in this layer, while the output layer is fully connected.

It can be easily understood from the above that time-delay networks would be equivalent to receptive fields–shared weights networks, if spatial weight equality constraints

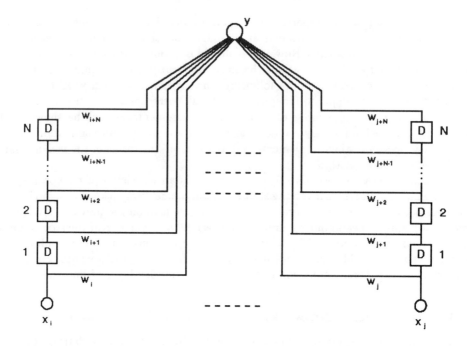

Figure 8.5 A time-delay unit.

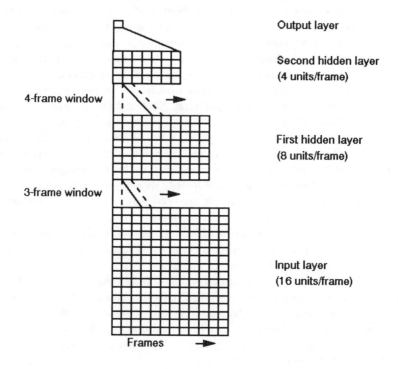

Figure 8.6 A TDNN architecture.

were replaced by temporal ones. As a consequence, time-delay and weight sharing backpropagation networks have similar performance, when implemented in parallel.

8.5 PARALLEL IMPLEMENTATIONS OF STRUCTURED NETWORKS

In the following, we shall investigate parallel implementations of structured networks, using training and spatial parallelism. As the former constitutes a general approach, we will restrict ourselves to a description of the method, which is directly applicable to the different network architectures. As far as spatial parallelism is concerned, we will address in detail the parallel implementation of the different schemes.

The implementation of parallelism will be treated in a general manner, in order to provide an understanding of the issues involved, independently of the particular multi-transputer architecture. A nine-transputer system will comprise the basis for our investigation. Our discussion, however, can be easily projected to parallel architectures of higher dimension in all the considered cases of structured networks.

8.5.1 Training Parallelism

As already stated, training parallelism can be obtained if the presentation of the training examples is performed in parallel on different processors. Therefore, the set of associated input-output patterns is partitioned, so that every transputer processes a subset of them. However, each transputer executes the same algorithm, i.e., the network of transputers operates as a single instruction multiple data (SIMD) machine. The implemented algorithm may be any variant of backpropagation applied to a general fully connected network, or to some particular network structure. At the beginning, the copies of the neural network on each transputer are identical, which means that the same architecture, parameters and initial set of weights are distributed to each processor, prior to the start of the learning process.

A multiprocessor architecture based on nine transputers, which can be used to implement the learning algorithms, is depicted in Figure 8.7. This is a tree architecture, having the minimum depth among all possible topologies that could be configured. This is of major importance, because it reduces the communication cost, caused by the exchanges of messages between transputers. In general, since each transputer is provided with four links, the least communication cost is obtained when transputers are connected so as to form a ternary tree of minimum length. This will become apparent from the description of the learning process in relation to the nine-transputer case.

Training parallelism should be generally applied, when updating of weights is performed after the presentation of the whole training data set (off-line strategy), since on-line updating would require a prohibitively large amount of communication. The distribution of training samples among the transputers is managed, so that each transputer keeps a similar number of data. After the transputers have finished one pass of the training examples they contain, the weights of the interconnection links should be updated.

Referring to the nine-transputer case of Figure 8.7, after the end of a training

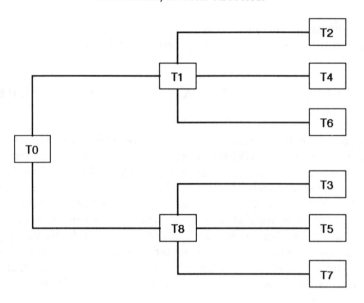

Figure 8.7 A 9-transputer architecture for training parallelism.

cycle, the weight increments computed by T2, T4, T6 are transmitted to T1 and then added to the increments that have been computed by T1. At the same time, T8 receives the weight changes computed by T3, T5, T7, and adds them to its own. Finally, T0 receives from T1 and T8 the partial weight changes that are added to its locally computed changes to yield the global weight increments. Then T0 computes the updated weights, which are broadcast to all transputers, in order for a new training cycle to start. It should be noted that the decision whether the training of the system should be terminated or not is taken by transputer T0. This is achieved by comparing the current global error to the maximum acceptable error, defined by the user at the beginning of the learning process. In order to compute the global error of the system, transputer T0 receives the locally computed errors, together with the computed weight changes from transputers T1–T8.

The description of the algorithm reveals that the computed weight increments, as well as the local errors, are transmitted from the leaves of the tree (T2, T4, T6, T3, T5, T7) to the root (T0), whereas the updated weights move in the opposite direction. Therefore, at each step of the algorithm, the tree of transputers must be traversed twice. Consequently, the smaller is the depth of the tree, the faster is the implementation of the algorithm.

We have used the nine-transputer architecture as a basis for addressing issues related to the implementation of training parallelism. The above discussion applies to all neural network structures considered and carries over to the case of larger transputer architectures.

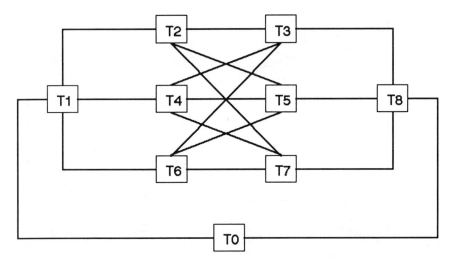

Figure 8.8   A 9-transputer architecture for spatial parallelism.

8.5.2   Spatial Parallelism

8.5.2.1   RECEPTIVE FIELDS

Consider again a nine-transputer architecture. A possible configuration, which is well suited to spatial parallelism, is the one depicted in Figure 8.8 in planar representation. This configuration is a cube with its diagonals interconnected and is characterized by low communication cost, since distances between nodes are kept to a minimum. We can observe that each one of transputers T2, T4, T6 communicates directly with transputers T3, T5, T7. However, transputers T2, T4, T6 (T3, T5, T7) can communicate with each other only through transputer T1 (T8). Thus, transputers T1 and T8 are used not only as computing elements, but also as nodes for communication and synchronization of the other transputers. Transputers T1 and T8 communicate with each other through transputer T0. Communication between transputers is ensured by a router designed in accordance with this architecture.

To exploit spatial parallelism inherent in the backpropagation algorithm, the network is divided into vertical 'slices' and uniformly distributed among the transputers, as shown in Figure 8.9. In particular, each layer of the network is partitioned into equal parts, each part to be handled by one of the existing transputers. Moreover, each transputer contains the connection weights between its neurons and the neurons of the next layer, the outputs and the error signals for each one of its neurons.

Different types of messages are exchanged between transputers during the forward and backward transmission of information. During the first phase, the outputs of all neurons belonging to each layer are computed and sent, together with the corresponding weights, to every neuron of the next layer to which these neurons are connected. To reduce the number of exchanged messages, each transputer computes the weighted averages of the outputs of the neurons that it contains and sends the results to the corresponding neurons of the next layer. During the second phase, the errors are computed at the neuron outputs of each layer, starting from the upper one, and are then

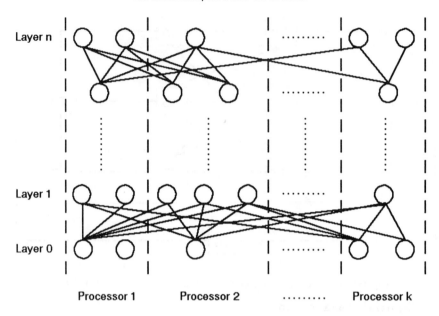

Figure 8.9 Partitioning of neurons in spatial parallelism.

transmitted to the lower layers, to be used for updating the network weights. Updating is performed using the on-line strategy.

The above described general approach applies equally to fully connected neural networks, in which each neuron is connected to all neurons of the lower and upper layer, and to structured networks with a reduced number of connections. Considering the receptive fields topology we could observe several points that improve the efficiency of the above parallel implementation. The small number of interconnections in receptive fields structured networks allows us to reduce the number of exchanged messages by distributing among the transputers 'windows', instead of neurons. These 'windows' correspond to the receptive fields, defined on the input and on each hidden layer of a neural network with the above architecture.

Considering the transputer architecture shown in Figure 8.8, we can propose an allocation of tasks that is well suited to the receptive field structure. This allocation gives emphasis to simplicity and efficiency of communication rather than to maximizing the exploitation of computing power, and provides helpful insight into the mechanisms related to receptive fields. Transputers T2, T3, T4, T5, T6 and T7 are used for computations related to the input nodes, and generally, in the case of a multi-hidden layer network, they are responsible for the computations from the input layer up to the last hidden layer. Among these transputers we distribute the windows of the input layer and of all hidden layers, except for the last one which is fully connected to the output layer. Each transputer contains the windows which correspond to its geometrical position, so that all transputers handle a similar number of windows. For example, T2 handles the upper-left windows of the groups contained in a layer, T3 handles the upper-right windows, etc.

Transputers T1 and T8 handle the last hidden layer. In particular, T1 undertakes the left-hand part of all groups of this layer, while T8 undertakes the right-hand part.

This stems from the fact that T1 is connected directly to transputers T2, T4 and T6, which handle the left windows of all groups of the previous layer. Similarly, T8 is connected directly to transputers T3, T5 and T7, which handle the right windows of all groups of the previous layer. Finally, T0 is responsible for the computation of the neuron outputs at the output layer.

During the forward pass of the learning process, each one of transputers T2-T7 first computes the outputs of all neurons in a specific layer, that belong to windows handled by this transputer. Following that, each of the above transputers computes the activations of all neurons in the next layer that receive their inputs from windows assigned to this transputer. The aforementioned process is iterative, in the sense that it starts from the input layer and concludes at the last hidden layer. It should be pointed out that, for one-hidden layer networks, transputers T2-T7 do not need to exchange any messages during the forward pass. However, for multi-hidden layer networks, exchange of messages between neighbouring transputers may be required. To what extent this exchange is needed depends on the sizes and the overlaps between the windows defined on each layer. The outputs of the neurons belonging to the last hidden layer are sent by T2, T4, T6 to T1 and by T3, T5, T7 to T8. Transputers T1 and T8 compute the partial inputs to the neurons of the output layer. The actual neuron outputs of the output layer are computed by T0 through summation of the partial inputs.

During the backward pass, the errors are computed at the neuron outputs of each layer, starting from the upper one, on transputer T0. Then the errors are transmitted to the lower layers, which are handled by T2-T7. The transmission is performed through T1 and T8. Each transputer T2-T7 computes the weight changes of the interconnection links assigned to that transputer.

8.5.2.2   WEIGHT SHARING AND TIME-DELAY NETWORKS

The above described approach for implementing receptive fields is general and can be used with both on-line and off-line updating in an efficient manner. An adaptation of this technique can be easily obtained in the case where receptive fields are combined with weight sharing. A major problem that has to be taken into account, when implementing such a technique in parallel, is the requirement for satisfaction of weight equality constraints between groups of neurons. To achieve this, each one of transputers T2-T7 in Figure 8.8 must exchange the computed weight increments with the other transputers; updating of the weights is performed by averaging all collected weight increments within each group of neurons that share the same weights. If on-line updating is used, weight equality in each group of neurons sharing the same weights is obtained at the expense of additional communication cost. This additional cost is mainly due to the fact that, in order to take advantage of receptive fields, neurons sharing the same set of weights must be assigned to different processors. If, however, off-line updating is adopted, it is obvious that the overhead on the proposed simple receptive fields parallel implementation due to weight sharing is rather negligible. If such a scheme is used for image recognition, a hybrid approach is the most appropriate solution; this approach can include both training parallelism (through partitioning of the training data set over disjoint subsets of the available processors/transputers) and spatial parallelism (by using the proposed receptive fields–shared weights implementation on each one of the above subsets); in spatial parallelism, each transputer stores and uses appropriate windows of the input and hidden node configurations. If a large multiprocessor environment is available, algorithmic parallelism can also be implemented, replacing gradient-descent backpropagation by the proposed second-order variants.

Another point related to the above implementation is that, in all cases, transputers T2–T7 remain idle for a period of time, during both the forward and backward passes. The performance of the system can be improved by applying *pipelining* simultaneously with spatial parallelism. This can be achieved as follows. In the period between transmission to the last hidden layer and receipt of the computed error, transputers T2–T7 can perform the forward computations needed for the next training example. To realize this, there is a need for some additional variables to store the neuron activations, which have been computed in the previous forward pass. As a consequence, updating of weights should be performed off-line in this case. In what follows, when we refer to spatial parallelism, we mean the joint application of spatial parallelism and pipelining.

As discussed in section 8.4, time-delay neural networks constitute a specific type of structured networks, that can be viewed as receptive fields–weight sharing architectures, if the requirement for weight equality refers to temporal translation instead of spatial. As was shown in Figure 8.6, each hidden time-delay unit has a receptive field consisting of a small number of frames of the previous layer. Thus, although the nature of problems addressed in each case can be different, the issues involved in parallel implementations of receptive field and time-delay networks are quite similar. As a consequence, parallelism based on receptive fields also applies to time-delay networks; additional communication costs are, however, introduced, as in the above-described case of weight-sharing, when implementing in parallel the weight equality constraints.

8.6   EXPERIMENTAL RESULTS AND PERFORMANCE ISSUES

As reported in [Ste90], the execution time of a parallel implementation of the least squares backpropagation on the INTEL IPSC/2 multiprocessor has been compared to that of a serial implementation of the gradient-descent algorithm, for a network with 111 neurons and 2778 interconnections. It was observed that, using 16 processors, the execution times of both algorithms are comparable; a decrease in the complexity of the least squares backpropagation algorithm by a factor of 10 has been, therefore, achieved through its parallel implementation. Experiments [Kol89, Ste90] show that the least squares algorithm is about 100 times faster than gradient-descent based backpropagation. Consequently, algorithmic parallelism can be used to provide an efficient learning scheme.

A parallel version of the backpropagation variant described by equations (8.6) and (8.7) was experimentally implemented on a 9-transputer FAST9 board, as well as on a 16-transputer Multicluster system. The FAST9 network was controlled by an IBM compatible PC AT equipped with the TDS2 software to allow programming in OCCAM, while the Multicluster was connected to a SPARC-Station and was programmed in OCCAM under the Multitool 5.0 environment. Extensive evaluation of the algo-

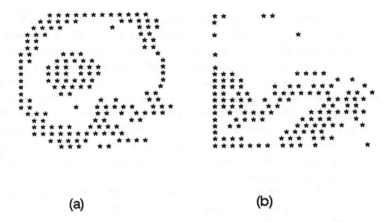

(a)   (b)

Figure 8.10   Binary images for the two classes of solder joints.

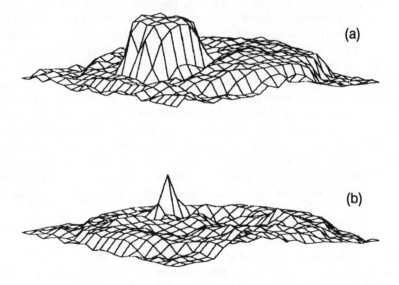

Figure 8.11   Grey level images for the two classes of solder joints.

rithms was mainly performed on the FAST9 system and the results reported in the following concern the 9-transputer case.

The 9-transputer parallel system, on which the backpropagation receptive fields–shared weights algorithm has been implemented, was used for classification in the problem of inspection of solder-joints in printed circuit board manufacturing. Each solder-joint data set was described as a set of two-dimensional images of size 20 × 20 pixels. Local averaging was used for size reduction, to obtain data sets of 15×15, 10×10 and 5 × 5 pixel two-dimensional images. In the presented examples, both binary and grey scale images were used. Two classes of solder joints had to be recognized; the first class contained sufficient solder, while the second contained insufficient or excessive solder. Figures 8.10 and 8.11 display binary and grey scale images, respectively, that represent characteristic examples of the first (a) and second (b) class of solder joints.

To evaluate the performance of the multi-transputer architecture, *speedup* was considered as a measure of particular interest. The speedup S_p is defined, for each number of transputers p, as $S_p = T_1/T_p$, i.e., the ratio of the time needed to complete the algorithm on a single transputer to the execution time when p transputers are available. Speedup typically increases with the number of processors dedicated to the problem. However, as more processors are assigned to the execution of an algorithm, the total amount of processor idle time can be expected to increase, due to factors such as the time required for communication and synchronization. As a consequence, the *efficiency* E_p, defined as the average utilization of the p allocated processors, decreases as the number of available processors increases. In general, the relationship between efficiency and speedup is given by $S_p = pE_p$.

To analyze the performance of the multi-transputer architecture, experiments were designed to investigate how the speedup attained by the parallel system is affected by various parameters.

Figure 8.12 shows the relationship between the number of training samples and the achieved speedup, in the case of training parallelism using the configuration of Figure 8.7. The implemented algorithm is the receptive fields–shared weights version of backpropagation. According to the diagram, speedup is improved as the number of training samples increases. In fact, speedup approaches the maximum value of 9 when a large number of training patterns is used. Results are presented for three different neural network architectures. Each architecture constitutes a one-hidden-layer network with two output units. The size of the input images, which are solder-joint examples, is either 5×5 or 10×10 pixels, while each hidden unit receives its input from a receptive field on the input layer. Receptive fields are 2×2 or 3×3 pixels wide. Furthermore, receptive fields corresponding to neighbouring hidden units overlap by one row or one column. For example, the architecture designated in Figure 8.12 as 10×10 (2×2), represents a network receiving 10×10 pixel images at its input and having receptive fields of size 2×2 on its input layer. This results in a hidden layer composed of 9×9 units.

As can be deduced from Figure 8.12, for a given number of training samples, the larger is the size of the network, the higher is the obtained speedup. This is due to the fact that an increase in the size of the neural network stored in each transputer results in a larger amount of computations performed by the transputers, before they communicate to exchange the weight changes. Although in this case the communication cost increases as well, the number of computations per unit of communication rises, leading to an improved efficiency of the transputers. Similarly, for a given architecture, when the number of training examples increases, then for each transputer the ratio of computation time to communication time also increases. As a consequence, the efficiency of the transputers, and therefore the speedup, is improved.

In general, the application of training parallelism is limited only by the memory size of each transputer. In such a case, the combination of training and spatial parallelism can provide a good solution. However, various factors such as the image size, the number of training samples and the size of the receptive fields have to be taken into account.

Figure 8.13 shows the behaviour of speedup as a function of the image size, in the case of spatial parallelism using the configuration of Figure 8.8. To obtain that behaviour, the parallel implementation of the receptive fields–shared weights version

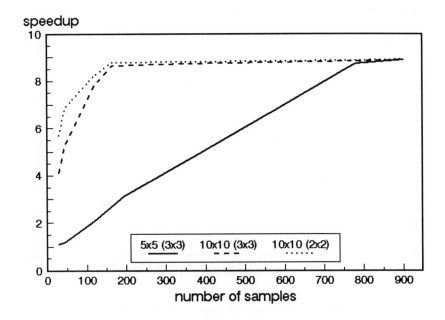

Figure 8.12 Speedup in training parallelism.

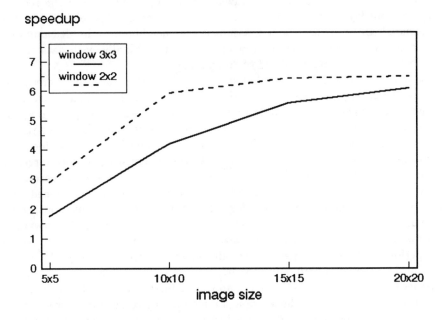

Figure 8.13 Speedup in spatial parallelism.

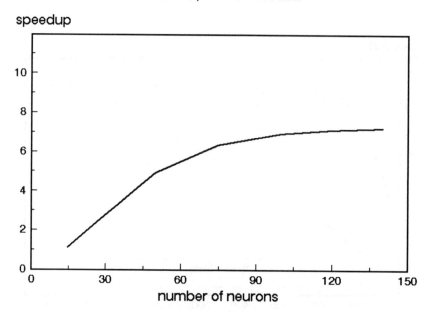

Figure 8.14   Fully connected network (spatial parallelism).

of backpropagation was considered. The implemented architectures were one-hidden-layer networks, receiving as input image planes of size 5×5, 10×10, 15×15 and 20×20 pixels. Each network had two output units for determining the class of each solder-joint pattern. Two parametric curves were drawn, depending on the size of the receptive fields on the input layer. Specifically, the cases of 2×2 and 3×3 pixel receptive fields were considered. In both cases, it was assumed that neighbouring hidden units have receptive fields which overlap by one row or one column. Finally, each data set used throughout the experiments consisted of 30 training examples.

Observation of Figure 8.13 reveals that speedup rises as the image size increases and approaches a value slightly higher than 6. Higher values of speedup cannot be achieved due to the synchronization constraints imposed by the implemented pipelining. As a matter of fact, according to the adopted allocation of tasks, only six out of the nine transputers attain a high degree of utilization. The rationale for the above mentioned rise of speedup can be formulated as follows. As the image size becomes larger, the size of the neural net (number of windows and interconnections) also increases. Since the network (windows and the corresponding interconnections) is partitioned to the transputers, each processor now undertakes a larger amount of computations. In fact, the communication load related to the exchange of information during the forward and backward pass also becomes heavier. However, the computations per unit of communication performed by each transputer are also increased. Consequently, the speedup attained by the parallel system is improved.

To further investigate the validity of the above argument, we considered the parallel implementation of conventional backpropagation on a fully connected network. To this goal, the architecture of Figure 8.8 was used to exploit the spatial parallelism inherent in the algorithm through partitioning of neurons on the nine transputers. Neural networks of different sizes were implemented, each one trained to classify 30 solder-joint images of size 5 × 5 pixels. Figure 8.14 presents the speedup attained for each network size. It is interesting to note that speedup rises as the number of neurons in the network increases. As was argued above, the reason lies in the fact that a network of larger size leads to an increased utilization of the allocated processors.

As far as the recognition of solder joints is concerned, both the conventional backpropagation and the receptive fields–shared weights version, which were used for the classification of solder-joint images, achieved an excellent success rate of 100% during training. Moreover, the receptive fields–shared weights algorithm showed better generalization properties, providing the best performance (96%) during testing.

8.7 CONCLUSIONS

An investigation of the parallel implementation of neural-network learning algorithms based on network topology has been presented. Specific interest was given to the receptive fields, shared weights and time-delay network implementations, since these structured architectures are widely used in pattern recognition applications for shift, or time, invariant feature extraction. Moreover, structured networks exhibit better generalization properties, avoiding overfitting problems. Various approaches for parallelizing neural network learning strategies have been presented, including algorithmic, training and spatial parallelism. Also, hybrid parallelism and pipelining have been considered.

In training parallelism, a copy of the neural network is stored on each processor, while each processor works with a subset of the training set. Thus, memory requirements per processor are dependent on the size of the network, which sometimes may be too large. Moreover, communication cost depends on the number of interconnection weights that have to be exchanged. Spatial parallelism is based on the distribution of neurons and connection weights among the available processors. Therefore, memory requirements are not as heavy as in the case of training parallelism. However, the partitioning of the network results in an increased need for communication among neurons that belong to different processors. Thus, a major issue of concern when devising an efficient implementation is the distribution of load, which minimizes the number of exchanged messages. We have proposed an efficient way for implementing the receptive fields and shared weights or time-delay network training algorithms, based on the assignment of 'windows' to the processors instead of neurons.

The evaluation of the parallel algorithms has been achieved through implementation on transputer-based multiprocessor systems. Real solder-joint data have been applied to test the system performance and certain measures, such as speedup, have been used to evaluate the efficiency of the parallel implementation.

The presented results have been obtained using a network of nine transputers, configured in specific topologies, while extensions to larger transputer networks were also considered. Some of the main results regarding parallelism are the following. In training parallelism, speedup increases as the number of training patterns increases. The same holds as the size of the network increases, the rise being more significant in the case of small sized training sets. In spatial parallelism, speedup also rises as the size of the network increases. An issue of current investigation is the combined use of training and spatial parallelism, which can lead to further improvement of the performance of the learning algorithm.

REFERENCES

[Alm90]   L. Almeida, and F. Silva. Acceleration Techniques for the Backpropagation Algorithm. *Lecture Notes in Computer Science*, number 412, pages 110–119, 1990.

[ANN91]   ANNIE Handbook. Application of Neural Networks for Industry in Europe. ESPRIT Project 2092, 1991.

[Bar83]   A.G. Barto, R.S. Sutton, and C.W. Anderson. Neuronlike Elements that Can Solve Difficult Learning Control Problems. *IEEE Transactions on Systems, Man and Cybernetics*, 13:835–846, 1983.

[Bau89]   E. Baum, and D. Haussler. What Size Net Gives Valid Generalization? *Neural Computation*, 1:151–160, 1989.

[Bau90]   E. Baum. When Are n-Nearest Neighbor and Backpropagation Accurate for Feasible Sized Sets of Examples? *Lecture Notes in Computer Science*, number 412, pages 2–27, 1990.

[Bau91]   E. Baum, and K. Lang. Constructing Hidden Units Using Examples and Queries. In *Advances in Neural Information Processing Systems*, number 3, pages 904–910, San Mateo, CA. Morgan Kaufman, 1991.

[Bey87]   T. Beynon, and N. Dodd. The Implementation of Multi-Layer Perceptrons on Transputer Networks. In *Proc. 7th International Workshop on Parallel Programming of Transputer-Based Machines*, Grenoble, September 1987.

[Cha89]   Y. Chauvin. A Backpropagation Algorithm with Optimal Use of Hidden Units. In D. Touretzky, editor, *Advances in Neural Information Processing Systems*, number 1, pages 519–526, Palo Alto, CA. Morgan Kaufman, 1989.

[Cho88]   P. Chol, and T. Muntean. NEURAL: Towards an OCCAM Extension for Neurocomputers. In *Proc. nEuro'88*, pages 653–662, Paris, June 1988.

[Dep89]   E. Deprit. Implementing Recurrent Back-Propagation on the Connection Machine. *Neural Networks*, 2(4):295–314, 1989.

[DiZ90]   E. Di Zitti, M. Chirico, M. Paganini, and G.M. Bisio. Partitioning Large Neural Computations on 2-D Meshes of Transputers. In *Proc. ESPRIT PCA Workshop*, ISPRA, Italy, Dec. 1990.

[Erc91]   D. Ercoscun, and K. Oflazer. Experiments with Parallel Backpropagation on a Hypercube Parallel Processor System. In *Proc. ICANN-91*, pages 1465–1468, Espoo, Finland, June 1991.

[Ern88]   C. Ernoult. Performance of Backpropagation on a Parallel Transputer-based Machine. In *Proc. Neuro-Nimes '88*, pages 311–324, 1988.

[Han89]   S. Hanson. Comparing Biases for Minimal Network Construction with Backpropagation. In D. Touretzky, editor, *Advances in Neural Information Processing Systems*, number 1, pages 177–185, Palo Alto, CA. Morgan Kaufman, 1989.

[Hau89]   D. Haussler. Generalizing the PAC Model for Neural Nets and Other Learning Applications. Technical Report, UCSC-CRL-89-30, 1989.

[Ish89]   M. Ishikawa. A Structural Learning Algorithm with Forgetting of Weight Link Weights. In *Proc. IJCNN 89*, number 2, Washington DC, June 1989.

[Jac88]   R. Jacobs. Increased Rates of Convergence through Learning Rate Adaptation. *Neural Networks*, 1(4):295–308, 1988.

[Kar90]   N.B. Karayiannis, and A.N. Venetsanopoulos. Efficient Learning Algorithms for Single-layered Neural Networks. In R. Eckmiller, G. Hartmann, and G. Hauske, editors, *Parallel Processing in Neural Systems and Computers*, pages 173–176. North-Holland, 1990.

[Kol89]   S. Kollias, and D. Anastassiou. An Adaptive Least Squares Algorithm for the Efficient Training of Artificial Neural Networks. *IEEE Transactions on Circuits and Systems*, 36:1092–1101, 1989.

[Kun88]   S.Y. Kung, and J.N. Hwang. Parallel Architectures for Artificial Neural Nets. In *Proc. IEEE Second International Conference on Neural Networks*, number II, pages 165–172, 1988.

[Le89a]   Y. LeCun. Generalization and Network Design Strategies. In *Connectionism in Perspective*, pages 143–155. North Holland, Switzerland, 1989.

[Le89b]   Y. LeCun. A Theoretical Framework for Backpropagation. In D. Touretzky, G. Hinton, and T. Sejnowski, editors, *Proc. 1988 Connectionist Models Summer School*, pages 21–28, CMU, Pittsburgh, PA. Morgan Kaufman, 1989.

[Le89c]   Y. LeCun, L.D. Jackel, B. Boser, J.S. Denker, H.P. Graf, I. Guyon, D. Henderson, R.E. Howard, and W. Hubbard. Handwritten Digit Recognition: Applications of Neural Network Chips and Automatic Learning. *IEEE Communications Magazine*, 41–46, November 1989.

[Mil89]   J. del R. Millan, and P. Bofill. Learning by Backpropagation: a Systolic Algorithm and its Transputer Implementation. *Int. J. Neural Networks — Research and Applications*, 1(3):119–137, 1989.

[Mil90]   W.T. Miller, R.S. Sutton, and P.J. Werbos, editors. *Neural Networks for Control*. MIT Press, 1990.

[Mil91]   P.M. Mills, and A.Y. Zomaya. Reinforcement Learning using Back-Propagation as a Building Block. In *Proc. IJCNN 91*, pages 1554–1559, Singapore, 1991.

[Mun87]   P. Munro. A Dual Back-propagation Scheme for Scalar Reward Learning. In *Proc. Ninth Annual Conference of the Cognitive Science Society*, pages 165–176, Hillsdale, NJ. Erlbaum, 1987.

[Mur91]   J.M.J. Murre. Transputer Implementations of Neural Networks: An Analysis. In *Proc. ICANN-91*, pages 1537–1540, Espoo, Finland, June 1991.

[Pao89]   Y.H. Pao. *Adaptive Pattern Recognition and Neural Networks*. Addison-Wesley, 1989.

[Par85]   D. Parker. Learning Logic, Technical Report TR-47, MIT, Center for Computational Research and Management Sciences, 1985.

[Pau91]   H. Paugam-Moisy. Parallelizing Multilayer Neural Networks. In *Proc. ESPRIT PCA Workshop*, Bonn, May 1991.

[Pea91]   B. Pearlmutter, and R. Rosenfeld. Chaitin-Kolmogorov Complexity and Generalization in Neural Networks. In *Advances in Neural Information Processing Systems*, number 3, pages 925–931, San Mateo, CA. Morgan Kaufman, 1991.

[Pet91]   A. Petrowski, G. Dreyfus, and C. Girault. Performance of a Pipelined Backprop-agation Algorithm on a Parallel Computer. In *Proc. ESPRIT PCA Workshop*, Bonn, May 1991.

[Pom88]   D.A. Pomerleau, G.L. Gusciora, D.S. Touretzky, and H.T. Kung. Neural Network Simulation at Warp Speed: How We Got 17 Million Connections per Second. In *Proc. IEEE Second International Conference on Neural Networks*, number II, pages 143–150, 1988.

[Rum86]   D. Rumelhart, and J. McClelland, editors. *Parallel Distributed Processing : Explorations in the Microstructure of Cognition*, number 1. MIT Press, 1986.

[Sij92]   F. Sijstermans. A Parallel Backpropation Algorithm. In W. Joosen, and E. Milgrom, editors, *Parallel Computing: From Theory to Sound Practice*, IOS Press, 1992.

[Sin90]   A. Singer. Exploiting the Inherent Parallelism of Artificial Neural Networks to Achieve 1300 Million Interconnects per Second. In *Proc. INNC*, pages 656–660, Paris, 1990.

[Ste90]   J. Steck, B. McMillin, and K. Krishnamuthy. Parallel Implementation of a Recursive Least Squares Neural Network Training Method on the INTEL IPSC/2. In *Proc. IJCNN-90*, San Diego, CA, 1990.

[Vuu92]   L.G. Vuurpijl, and Th.E. Schouten. Suitability of Transputers for Neural Network Simulations. In W. Joosen, and E. Milgrom, editors, *Parallel Computing: From Theory to Sound Practice*, IOS Press, 1992.

[Wai89]   A. Waibel *et al.* Phoneme Recognition Using Time-Delay Neural Networks. *IEEE Transactions on ASSP*, 37:328–339, 1989.

[Wer74]   P. Werbos. *Beyond Regression: New Tools for Prediction and Analysis in the Behavioral Sciences*. PhD Thesis, Harvard University, 1974.

[Wig91]   A. Wigend, D. Rumelhart, and B. Huberman. Generalization by Weight Elimination with Application to Forecasting. In *Advances in Neural Information Processing Systems*, number 3, pages 875–882, San Mateo, CA. Morgan Kaufman, 1991.

[Wil87]   R.J. Williams. A Class of Gradient-Estimating Algorithms for Reinforcement Learning in Neural Networks. In *Proc. First Annual International Conference on Neural Networks*, number II, pages 601–608, San Diego, CA, 1987.

[Wil88a]   R.J. Williams. Toward a Theory of Reinforcement Learning Connectionist Systems. Technical Report, NU-CCS-88-3, College of Computer Science, Northeastern University, 1988.

[Wil88b]   R.J. Williams. On the Use of Backpropagation in Associative Reinforcement Learning. In *Proc. Second Annual International Conference on Neural Networks*, number I, pages 263–270, San Diego, CA, 1988.

[Zha90]   X. Zhang, M. McKenna, J.P. Mesirov, and D.L. Waltz. The Backpropagation Algorithm on Grid and Hypercube Architectures. *Parallel Computing*, 14:317–327, 1990.

9

Parallel Neural Computation Based on Algebraic Partitioning

ALAIN PETROWSKI, HELENE PAUGAM-MOISY

9.1 INTRODUCTION

The artificial neural network paradigms implement many elementary interconnected simple automata which run simultaneously. However, most actual implementations are simulations on sequential computers, and neural networks need extensive computation, especially for the learning phase. Research in the field of massively parallel implementations of neural networks on loosely coupled machines will enable the study of the behavior of large networks and will give rise to powerful neural chips.

There are many ways of parallelizing neural algorithms. When an algorithm is parallelized, programs and data have to be distributed among the processors. For example, a neural network can be partitioned into "small" subnetworks which are placed on several processors [GH89, HOE90]. At most, several processors are needed to simulate a neuron or a connection between two neurons [DEP89]. A widespread variant of this parallelization method for a multilayer neural network is the vertical slicing that consists in partitioning every layer into as many parts as the number of available processors. This method is described for example in [RW89, YNM90]. These parallelizations can be classified as "parallelization based on neural network partitioning". A different kind of parallelization is based on the duplication of a neural network on all available processors. A typical example is given in [WZ90]. The parallelizations presented in this chapter are based on the parallelization of matrix products which are involved in most neural models. Several authors have addressed this point of view such as [KH89, NF89, PPD89, PDG91].

Parallel Algorithms for Digital Image Processing, Computer Vision and Neural Networks, ed. I. Pitas
© 1993 John Wiley & Sons Ltd

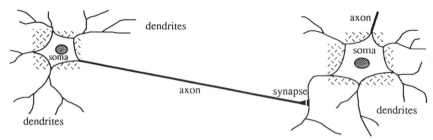

Figure 9.1   Biological neurons (simplified scheme).

Sections 9.2 to 9.4 are a tutorial presentation of neural networks. Some paralleliza-tions on MIMD machines of supervised learning algorithms, such as back-propagation and Hopfield networks, are presented in sections 9.5 and 9.6. Section 9.7 deals with parallelizations of Kohonen self-organizing feature maps.

9.2   ARTIFICIAL NEURAL NETWORKS

9.2.1   Artificial Neuron and Neural Network

In 1943, McCulloch and Pitts [MCP43] build a mathematical abstraction of the bio-logical nerve cell. The *artificial neuron* is a binary threshold unit (Figure 9.2), which simulates a simplified scheme of a nerve cell functioning in brain (Figure 9.1). The average human brain contains about 10^{11} neurons, each of them being connected to approximately 10^4 other cells. When a cell is sufficiently excited from its inputs, an electrical activity is sent away along its output fiber, called the *axon*. This excitation is then transmitted towards the *dendrites* of many other cells, via contact points called *synapses*.

The neuron model computes a weighted sum of its inputs coming from other cells, and generates a zero or a one according to whether this sum is above or below a given threshold. Since they represent the biological synapses, coefficients w_j are often named *synaptic weights*. Like synapses, weights can be either excitatory (positive value) or inhibitory (negative value). This very simple automaton is computationally a powerful device.

The threshold function of the historical model can be changed into other transition functions: identity function, for a linear associator; sigmoid function, when derivability is requested; etc. (Figure 9.3).

An *artificial neural network*, or *neural network*, is a set of *units*, or artificial neurons, which are connected by a network of weighted links, according to various architectures. Weights and transition functions have to be adjusted such that the network realizes a suited relation between the input space and the output space. This relation depends on the network architecture, the nature of its dynamics, the threshold and weight values, and so on. From the computer scientist viewpoint, the art of *connectionism* is to find networks which realize functions as close as possible to those, generally unknown, of the applications.

Let w_{ij} be the weight of the connection between the input of neuron i and the output of neuron j; w_{ij} is a postsynaptic weight of neuron i, and also a presynaptic weight

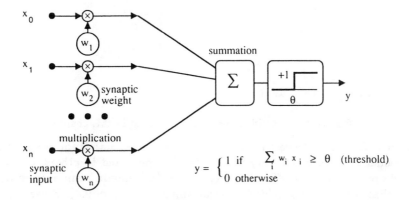

$$y = \begin{cases} 1 & \text{if} \quad \sum_i w_i x_i \geq \theta \quad \text{(threshold)} \\ 0 & \text{otherwise} \end{cases}$$

Figure 9.2   The McCulloch and Pitts model.

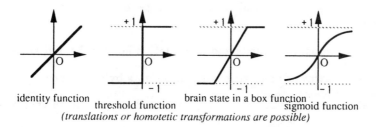

identity function   threshold function   brain state in a box function   sigmoid function
(translations or homotetic transformations are possible)

Figure 9.3   Usual transition functions.

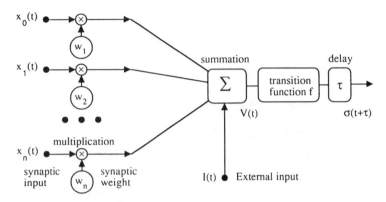

Figure 9.4 Artificial neuron model used in this chapter.

of neuron j. It belongs to row i, column j of the *weight matrix* (or *synaptic matrix*). In the model that we used, every neuron can be connected to others. Consequently, the weight matrix is square. The input of the network should be performed by special neurons that own a non-weighted external input I_i (Figure 9.4). However, in order to simplify analysis, we will consider that every neuron owns an external input I_i. If the external input of a neuron is useless, it will be discarded by keeping $I_i(t) = 0$, whatever time t is.

The evolution of state of such a neuron is given by the following expressions:

$$V_i(t) = I_i(t) + \sum_{i=1}^{n} w_j.x_j(t) \tag{9.1}$$

$$\sigma_i(t + \tau) = f(V_i(t)) \tag{9.2}$$

9.2.2 Connectionist Models

For describing a connectionist model, the following features have to be specified:

- *architecture*: a valued graph of connections between neural units, where values are synaptic weights,

- *dynamics*: a computation mode and an evolution law for the unit states,

- *learning rule*: a way of modifying synaptic weights by experience.

Several notations will be fixed as below. They will be used in further algorithm descriptions.

1. S is the training set. When the problem is a dichotomy, let S^+ and S^- be the training subsets belonging to each of the two classes. $\{S^+, S^-\}$ is a partition of S.

2. X is the input vector of a given pattern. It is indexed from 1 to s, in order to distinguish the various patterns of S, where s is the number of patterns of the training set.

3. **W** is the weight matrix.

4. **C** is the adjacency matrix. If a connection exists between neurons i and j, $C_{ij} = 1$, otherwise $C_{ij} = 0$. **C** indicates the network *connectivity*.

The state of a neural network can be evaluated in many ways: in parallel, sequentially, by blocks, etc. As far as the parallel evaluation is concerned, the states of all neurons simultaneously change at a time defined by an external synchronization signal. The dynamics of such a network are *synchronous*. With *asynchronous dynamics*, only one neuron changes its state at a given moment. The order of the state evaluations is arbitrary. This mode is closer to biological reality because there is no global synchronization signal in a nervous system. In this chapter, the "sequential evaluation mode" refers to the mode that corresponds to asynchronous dynamics, so that a given arbitrary order of state evaluations is kept during the lifetime of the network.

With block-sequential dynamics, the state of neuron subsets can change simultaneously. There is an intermediate situation between synchronous and asynchronous dynamics. The dynamics of a network have implications on its stability [KH90], its learning algorithm [PIN87, RF87], and the efficiency of computation as shown below.

Many models are studied in connectionist literature. After a short presentation of the two famous historical models, Perceptron and Adaline, the most used algorithms will be described: back-propagation learning and Kohonen maps. Various parallel implementations of back-propagation and Kohonen maps will be further addressed in detail.

9.2.3 Learning and Retrieving Phases

Solving a problem with a neural network essentially means determining values of these synaptic coefficients. Unlike computers, which need an explicit programming of the calculations in order to solve a class of problems, the synaptic coefficients of a neural network adjust themselves automatically from a subset of problems that are submitted to it. The phase of computation of synaptic coefficients is called the *"training phase"*. The problems that are submitted to the network during its training are the *"training patterns"*. During learning, not all weights of the synaptic matrix are modified. For example, if coefficient C_{ij} of the adjacency matrix **C** is equal to zero, that corresponds to a missing connection. Consequently, the corresponding weight w_{ij} is forced to zero during learning.

The quality of learning depends on the *generalization* ability of the resulting network, i.e. its ability to give correct responses for numerous similar problems, even though a small part of them have been used for its training. The quality of the training will be better the greater the number of training patterns in comparison with the number of free synaptic coefficients of the network. The quality of generalization also depends on the architecture of the network. The *"spy"*, which is described in the next chapter, is an attempt to find a suitable neural architecture for a given training problem.

In these two chapters, the learning algorithms that we will study are of two types: supervised learning and unsupervised learning.

Supervised learning needs a teacher: while training, every problem presented to the neural network is accompanied by the expected response. The network must modify its free parameters in order to give an output that matches at best the desired response. For example, for a handwritten numeral recognition problem, images of digits are presented to the network; the desired responses could be binary codes of these numerals. Supervised learning allows the training of a neural network to associate a given stimulus with an appropriate action. Learning rules are based on techniques from various scientific domains, such as numerical analysis, (least mean square, gradient, Newton method), statistical physics (simulated annealing: Boltzmann machine), algorithmics (decision trees, Voronoï diagram), or biology (cortical columns, genetic algorithms). In this chapter, we will consider the well-known learning rule, the back-propagation algorithm, which is a gradient method, and we will remark that most of other known learning rules are particular cases of this algorithm.

Unsupervised learning allows a neural network to extract useful information only from the redundancy of the patterns which are presented to it: there is no teacher. This kind of learning issues from observation of animal behavior and is based on biological knowledge of the organization of the brain [BAR89]. In this chapter, self-organizing Kohonen maps are presented as an illustration of unsupervised learning.

9.3 SUPERVISED LEARNING ALGORITHMS FOR NEURAL NETWORKS

A pattern of the training set presented to a network is a vector, the components of which are applied to the inputs of a network. To each pattern is associated a desired response, supplied by a "teacher". This desired response is a vector as well, the components of which correspond to output neurons. Supervised learning consists of presenting to the network a set of patterns to its inputs. For every training pattern, a distance between the desired state vector and the actual state vector computed by the network is defined. The learning algorithm modifies the synaptic weights in order to reduce this distance to an acceptable value. The computation of the weights can sometimes be direct; for example, a Hopfield network can be trained with the pseudo-inverse rule [PGD85]. More often, the computation of weights is iterative. In this case, a gradient method is generally used. An iterative method is preferred because of its generality and because of the simplicity of the computations. However, when possible, a direct computation is often more efficient than iterative methods.

9.3.1 Historical Models: Perceptron and Adaline

In the sixties, Rosenblatt [ROS58], Minsky and Papert [MP69] designed and studied a learning machine, the *Perceptron* (Figure 9.5). This machine was a network of threshold automata that was composed of a "retina" on which patterns to recognize were presented, a collection of associator cells, and a decision cell. Fixed preprocessing is performed from the retina to associator cells. The decision cell is a linear automaton, the output of which is thresholded:

$$\phi\left(x_1, ..., x_n\right) = H\left(\sum_{i=1}^{n} w_i x_i - \theta\right)$$

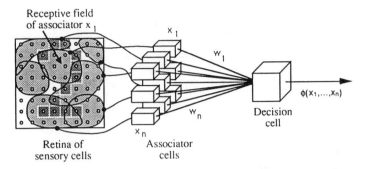

Figure 9.5 Rosenblatt's Perceptron.

where weights w_i and threshold θ are adaptive. x_i are outputs of the n associator cells. H is the threshold function: $H(a) = 1$ if $a > 0$, otherwise, $H(a) = 0$.

Such a device allows the separation of training patterns into two classes on both sides of hyperplane $\sum w_i \xi_i = \theta$. In practice, threshold θ is identified as an additional weight $w_0 = -\theta$, called *bias*, associated with a fixed input $x_0 = 1$. That defines the architecture and the activation propagation rule of this model.

By putting down $\mathbf{X} = (x_0, ..., x_n)$ and $\mathbf{W} = (w_0, ..., w_n)$, $\phi(\mathbf{X}) = H\left(\mathbf{W}^T\mathbf{X}\right)$ can be written in vectorial form. It is assumed that $\phi(\mathbf{X})$ must be equal to $d(\mathbf{X})$, the desired state for pattern $\mathbf{X}$. $d = 1$ if $\mathbf{X}$ belongs to S^+, otherwise $d = 0$ for every pattern in S^-. Then, the Perceptron learning rule can be written as follows:

Perceptron algorithm:

$\mathbf{W}$ is randomly initialized
While some patterns $\mathbf{X}$ are misclassified
      For every pattern $\mathbf{X}$ of the training set:
          $\mathbf{W} = (d - \phi)\,\mathbf{X} + \mathbf{W}$
      End-for
End while

In plain words: there is modification of $\mathbf{W}$ only if pattern $\mathbf{X}$ is misclassified.

Convergence theorem of the Perceptron algorithm:

Let S be an indifferent set of unitary vectors; if there exists a vector $\mathbf{W}^*$ and a real number $\delta > 0$ such that $\mathbf{W}^{*T}\mathbf{X} > \delta$ for every $\mathbf{X}$ in S^+, and $\mathbf{W}^{*T}\mathbf{X} < \delta$ for every $\mathbf{X}$ in S^-, then the Perceptron algorithm converges after a finite number of presentations of the training set.

In other words, the theorem indicates that, if both pattern classes are linearly separable, the Perceptron converges towards a correct solution, i.e. it will determine a separator hyperplane after a finite number of steps.

At the same epoch, Widrow studied a model of a quite similar cell, called *Adaline* (ADAptive LINear Element) [WH60, WL90] (Figure 9.6).

This cell is a linear automaton, like the decision cell of the Perceptron. It has

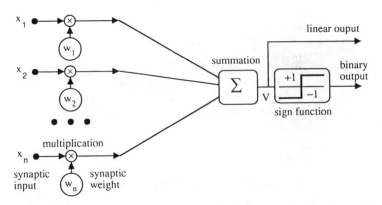

Figure 9.6 Widrow's Adaline (ADAptive LINear Element).

two outputs: a linear one and a binary one as a result of thresholding. The essential difference in comparison with the Perceptron concerns the learning rule: the error is evaluated with the linear output, before thresholding. This learning rule was derived from the *least mean square (LMS)* algorithm by Widrow and Hoff, in 1960.

Widrow–Hoff rule, or delta-rule:

At time t, presentation of pattern $\mathbf{X}(t)$:
computation of the Adaline linear output:

$$V(t) = \sum_{i=0}^{n} w_i(t)x_i(t) = \mathbf{W}^{\mathrm{T}}(t)\mathbf{X}(t)$$

presentation of the desired output $d(t)$ for pattern $\mathbf{X}(t)$:
weight update: $\forall i \in \{0, ..., n\}$

$$w_i(t+1) = w_i(t) + \eta\left(d(t) - V(t)\right)x_i(t)$$

which can be rewritten:

$$\Delta\mathbf{W}(t) = \eta\left(d(t) - \mathbf{W}^{\mathrm{T}}(t)\mathbf{X}(t)\right)\mathbf{X}(t)$$

If $J(t) = \frac{1}{2}(d(t) - V(t))^2$ is the contribution to the quadratic cost generated by the cell for a pattern presented at time t, it may be noticed that the gradient:

$$-\frac{\partial J}{\partial w_i}(t) = (d(t) - V(t))\,x_i(t) \qquad (\forall i \in \{0, ..., n\})$$

is proportional to $\Delta w_i(t)$ The updating of weights tends to decrease the quadratic cost $J(t)$: it is an adaptation of the least mean square method. The proportionality factor η is frequently called the *gradient step* or *learning rate*.

It can be shown [WS85] that this algorithm tends to minimize the global quadratic cost J defined as the sum of the contributions $J(k)$ of every pattern $X(k)$ of the training set: $J = \sum_{k=1}^{s} J(k)$ where s is the number of patterns in the training set.

This algorithm is often more efficient than the total gradient method applied to the minimization of cost J. The Widrow–Hoff algorithm is also known as the *LMS algorithm* or *stochastic gradient algorithm*.

In these two cases, Perceptron and Adaline, only one layer of synaptic weights was modifiable by training. Applications of these kinds of networks were limited to linearly separable problems. More complex architectures cannot be trained by these algorithms because they need the assignment of a "desired state" for every trainable neuron in the network, even for neurons that are not outputs of the network. This difficulty is known as the *"credit assignment problem"*.

9.3.2 Feedforward Neural Networks

An adjacency graph can be associated with a neural network so that the nodes represent the neurons and the arcs represent the synapses. The arcs are directed from the output of a neuron towards the input of another and they are weighted by synaptic coefficients. The graph associated with a feedforward network is a graph without circuits. In such a network, there are neurons without postynaptic connection(s) which are necessarily input neurons and there are neurons without presynaptic connection(s) which are necessarily output neurons.

The neurons of a feedforward network can always be indexed so that the output of a neuron j can be connected to an input of a neuron i subject to the condition that $j < i$. The synaptic matrix of this kind of network is lower triangular.

In a feedforward network, when the environment applies a constant state to the input of the network, the state of the output reaches a constant state after some evaluation steps. This output state only depends on the input state and on the synaptic matrix, whatever the dynamics are: the network has no memory. Then, the dependence with time of the expressions (9.1) and (9.2) can disappear, being replaced by a dependence defined by the adjacency graph: the state of a neuron is correctly evaluated only if all the states of the "predecessor" neurons have been evaluated. In order to minimize the computation time, according to the numeration convention of neurons of the network, the state of a neuron i can be updated when the states of all neurons j, with $j < i$, are updated. However, this order of evaluation may be a partial order. In order to specify an optimum evaluation mode in a feedforward network, the concept of *"layer"* is defined below.

Layer λ_i of neuron i depends on the layers λ_j of the neurons connected to its inputs as follows:

$$\lambda_i = \max_j (\lambda_j) + 1$$

The neurons that do not have synaptic inputs belong to layer 0 (Figure 9.7). The way of partitioning a network into layers is not generally single and the above definition is arbitrary; for example, another way to define layers could be a recursive definition, similar to the one above, from neurons without presynaptic connection(s) up to neurons without postsynaptic connection(s).

Let L be the greatest value λ_i, for every neuron i of the network. All the neurons

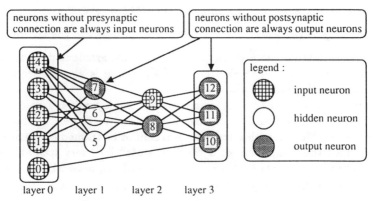

Figure 9.7 An example of partition into layers of a feedforward neural network.

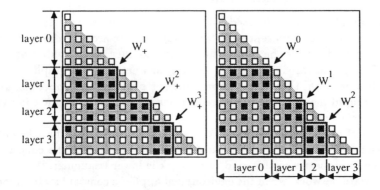

Figure 9.8 Synaptic matrix of the above network: two block decompositions.

of layer L are output neurons, but not all output neurons are on layer L. The number of network layers is $L + 1$. Figure 9.7 shows the partition into layers of a network of 13 neurons according to the above rule.

The indices of layers specify an order for evaluating the states of all the neurons of the network. But inside a layer, the evaluation order is indifferent. Now, it is possible to formally describe the evaluation mode of the state of a feedforward network.

Let $\mathbf{W}_+^\lambda$ be the rectangular matrix block whose synaptic coefficients w_{ij} are related to connections between neuron i of layer λ and the output of neuron j of any lower layer. In the same way, let $\mathbf{W}_-^\lambda$ be the block whose coefficients w_{ij} are related to connections between neuron j of layer λ and neuron i of any upper layer (Figure 9.8).

Below are some additional notations:

$\mathbf{V}^\lambda$	: sub-vector "potential" restricted to layer λ
σ^λ	: sub-vector "state" restricted to layer λ
$\sigma^{0..\lambda-1}$	: sub-vector "state" restricted to layers 0 to $\lambda - 1$
$\mathbf{I}^\lambda$	: sub-vector of the inputs of layer λ
.	: matrix product operator
$f()$	: vectorial extension of the transition function

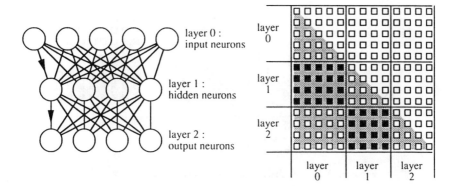

Figure 9.9 A simple three-layer network. On the right, the adjacency matrix is shown: a black square indicates the existence of a synaptic connection.

$\times$: vectorial extension of the multiplication,
i.e.: let A_i, B_i, C_i be the coefficients of vectors $\mathbf{A}$, $\mathbf{B}$, $\mathbf{C}$; $1 \le i \le n$:
$\mathbf{C} = \mathbf{A} \times \mathbf{B}$ if $C_i = A_i \times B_i \; \forall i \in [1, n]$

The state of the neurons of a given layer λ depends on the state of the neurons of lower layers, these states having been computed before. Expressions (9.1) and (9.2) relating to neurons of layer λ can be written in matrix notation:

$$\mathbf{V}^\lambda(t) = \mathbf{W}_+^\lambda \cdot \sigma^{0..\lambda-1}(t) + \mathbf{I}^\lambda(t)$$

$$\sigma^\lambda(t + \tau) = f\left(\mathbf{V}^\lambda(t)\right)$$

The states of all neurons of a layer can be simultaneously evaluated.

For a feedforward network, it is preferable to express the state of the neurons in accordance with the k-th input $\mathbf{I}(k)$ presented to the network, instead of time, because time does not convey any useful information:

$$\mathbf{V}^\lambda(k) = \mathbf{W}_+^\lambda \cdot \sigma^{0..\lambda-1}(k) + \mathbf{I}^\lambda(k) \tag{9.3}$$

$$\sigma^\lambda(k) = f\left(\mathbf{V}^\lambda(k)\right) \tag{9.4}$$

Among the architectures of feedforward networks, some of them are widely used, like the simple multilayer network, where only adjacent layers are interconnected. Figure 9.9 shows a three-layer network composed of an input layer, a hidden layer and an output layer. The layer structure of such a network is consistent with intuition.

On the other hand, the intuition adapts itself with more difficulty to the layer structure of the fully connected feedforward network (Figure 9.10). As a matter of fact, each layer of such a network owns only one neuron. Its synaptic matrix is fully lower triangular. For a given number of neurons, this network has the greatest "computing power".

Let $n(\lambda)$ be the number of neurons on layer λ. If $n(\lambda) > 1$, the synaptic matrix is block lower triangular (Figures 9.8 and 9.9).

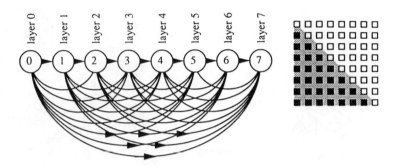

Figure 9.10   A fully connected feedforward network.

9.3.3   Recurrent Neural Networks

As opposed to feedforward networks, the synaptic matrix of a recurrent network cannot be organized as a lower triangular matrix by permuting rows and columns: there are circuits in the graph associated with the network. First, we will consider the most famous type of recurrent network: the Hopfield network. Then, more general architectures will be taken into consideration.

AN EXAMPLE OF A FULLY CONNECTED RECURRENT NETWORK: THE HOPFIELD NETWORK

Each neuron of a Hopfield network [HOP82] is both input and output of the network: there is no hidden neuron. The network is used as follows. An initial state having been applied to the network, it freely evolves until it reaches a steady state. The certainty of the stability arises from constraints imposed on the synaptic matrix that depend on the dynamics of the network. Explaining the Hopfield network theory would be beyond the purpose of this chapter. The interested reader could refer to [KH90].

Synchronous dynamics: The synaptic matrix must be symmetric, positive definite in order that the network evolves until reaching a steady state [KH90]. When an external synchronization signal arises, the state of all the neurons is evaluated. It is possible to write expressions (9.1) and (9.2) in matrix form:

$$\mathbf{V}(t) = \mathbf{W}.\sigma(t) + \mathbf{I}(t) \tag{9.5}$$

where symbol "." represents the product of a matrix with a vector. $\mathbf{V}(t)$, $\mathbf{I}(t)$ and $\sigma(t)$ are n component vectors, where n is the number of neurons in the network. Vector $\mathbf{I}(0)$ of external inputs is the initial network state. During its free evolution, $\mathbf{I}(t)$ is zero, for $t \neq 0$. The next state of the neural network is:

$$\sigma(t + \Delta t) = f(\mathbf{V}(t)) \tag{9.6}$$

where Δt is the time needed to update the state of all neurons of the network. Let τ be the time for updating the state of any neuron. For synchronous dynamics, $\Delta t = \tau$. The transition function $f()$ is chosen as the sign function.

Asynchronous dynamics: Now, in order for the network to evolve toward a steady state, whatever the initial state is, the synaptic matrix has to be symmetric, with a zero or positive diagonal [KH90]. This condition of stability is less restrictive than in the case of synchronous dynamics. If the numbering of neurons of the network is such that it indicates the chosen evaluation order, the potential and state of each neuron are given by the following expressions:

$$V_i(t) = \sum_{j=1}^{i-1} (w_{ij} \ \sigma_j(t)) + \sum_{j=i}^{n} (w_{ij} \ \sigma_j(t - \Delta t)) + I_i(t) \tag{9.7}$$

$$\sigma_i(t + \tau) = f(V_i(t)) \tag{9.8}$$

These expressions cannot be written in matrix form.

The time interval for updating the whole network is $\Delta t = \sum \tau$.

Thus, the behavior of a neural network depends on the type of its dynamics. Moreover, related computations will be more or less efficient. As a matter of fact, matrix computations of expressions (9.5) and (9.6) are easy to implement efficiently on a parallel machine, but this is not the case for expressions (9.7) and (9.8).

"UNFOLDING" A RECURRENT NETWORK INTO A FEEDFORWARD NETWORK.

In order to make the study of a recurrent network easier, it is possible to transform it into a feedforward network by considering time as an additional way to number a neuron [RHW86]. It is as though neuron i at time t was different from neuron i at time $t + k\Delta t$, where k is an integer: neurons of the network are replicated as many times as there are elementary time intervals Δt in a sequence.

In fact, the way to unfold a recurrent network into a feedforward network depends on its dynamics. Figure 9.11 shows how to replicate a network of five neurons to observe its synchronous evolution during a time interval of four time units. Part (a) of the figure symbolizes lower and upper triangular parts of the recurrent network synaptic matrix. Part (c) shows the synaptic matrix of the resulting feedforward neural network. The latter is obtained from one-layer networks connected in succession. Delay devices are inserted between each layer in order to represent evolution in time of the recurrent network.

Figure 9.12 is related to a recurrent network of five neurons, the state of which is sequentially evaluated (asynchronous dynamics). The feedforward network obtained is composed of fully connected feedforward networks connected in succession. The number of layers of the resulting network is 20; it has only one neuron per layer. Parts (a), (b) and (c) of this figure are similar to those of Figure 9.11.

The computational complexity performed during a time unit Δt depends on the chosen dynamics. Δt corresponds to the duration needed for computing the state of all the neurons of the network. For synchronous dynamics, the function that gives the new state at time $t + \Delta t$ from the state at time t is linearly separable because the recurrent network is transformed into a feedforward network which owns only one layer between times t and $t + \Delta t$. This limitation disappears when the recurrent network is asynchronous because it is unfolded into a feedforward network that possesses several layers between times t and $t + \Delta t$.

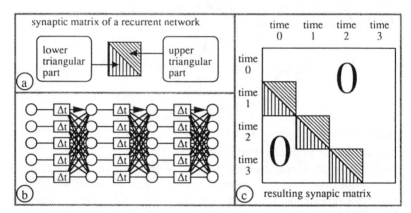

Figure 9.11 "Unfolding" a synchronous recurrent network into a feedforward network.

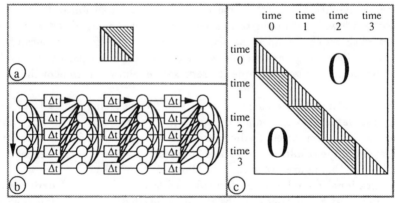

Figure 9.12 Converting an asynchronous recurrent neural network into a feedforward network.

9.3.4 Back-Propagation Learning

TOTAL GRADIENT ALGORITHM

The error back-propagation algorithm [RHW86] is a gradient method, the computations of which have been cleverly organized to reduce their complexity in time and memory space. It is shown below that this complexity is $\mathcal{O}(n_W)$ for the presentation of a training pattern, where n_W is the number of synaptic coefficients of the network. Moreover, this learning method is local, i.e. the modification of a weight w_{ij} depends on data available in postsynaptic neuron i and presynaptic neuron j. This property is useful for designing an efficient parallel implementation.

This algorithm is described below for every feedforward architecture.

It is assumed that a pattern k is composed of a couple of vectors $\mathbf{I}(k)$ and $\mathbf{d}(k)$. A boolean vector ω is the mask of outputs: for each neuron of the network, there is a component of $\mathbf{I}(k)$, $\mathbf{d}(k)$ and ω. If neuron i is not an input neuron, $I_i(k) = 0$; if it is not an output neuron, the value of $d_i(k)$ is not defined and $\omega_i = 0$. If neuron i is an output neuron $\omega_i = 1$. The goal of training is reducing the discrepancy between vector $\mathbf{d}(k)$ supplied by a "teacher" and $\sigma(k)$ computed by the network. This discrepancy, for pattern k, may be expressed as a quadratic cost $J(k)$:

$$J(k) = \sum_{i=1}^{n} \omega_i (d_i(k) - \sigma_i(k))^2 \tag{9.9}$$

The quadratic cost has to be minimized for every pattern k that comes to minimize the global quadratic cost: $J = \sum J(k)$:

$$J = \sum_{k=1}^{s} \sum_{i=1}^{n} \omega_i (d_i(k) - \sigma_i(k))^2 \tag{9.10}$$

where s is the number of patterns of the training set.

At every iteration of the gradient algorithm, the most simple way is to update coefficients w_{ij} by adding Δw_{ij} specified by the next expression:

$$\Delta w_{ij} = -\eta \frac{\partial J}{\partial w_{ij}} \qquad \eta > 0$$

Gradient step η must be chosen large enough to reduce the number of iterations at best, but not so large that the algorithm converges.

The neurons of the network are indexed according to the order described above, i.e.: if the state of neuron i depends on the state of neuron j, then $j < i$.

Each neuron can own an external input; it can be an external output as well.

$$\Delta w_{ij} = \eta \sum_{k=1}^{s} \delta_i(k)\, \sigma_j(k) \tag{9.11}$$

where

$$\delta_i(k) = f'(V_i(k)) \left\{ 2\omega_i (d_i(k) - \sigma_i(k)) + \sum_{l=i+1}^{n} w_{li}\, \delta_l(k) \right\} \tag{9.12}$$

$f'\left(\mathbf{V}_i(k)\right)$ is the derivative of the transition function. It is assumed that the summation shown on the right of expression (9.12) does not exist if $i = n$.

Clearly, if neuron i is an output neuron then $\delta_i(k)$ is expressed by the term $(d_i(k) - \sigma_i(k))$ that represents the error generated by the desired output $d_i(k)$. Moreover, $\delta_i(k)$ depends on values of $\delta_l(k)$, where l is the index of a postsynaptic neuron. This information is backward propagated from upper layers (outputs) to lower layers (inputs). It only depends on the synaptic weights and errors of output neurons. It is as if the algorithm was assigning an error for every neuron of the network, even hidden neurons. These considerations justify the name of this learning rule: the *back-propagation of the errors* algorithm.

Remember that, in the case of a general feedforward network, vector $\sigma(k)$ is given by expressions (9.3) and (9.4).

Expression (9.11) can be written in matrix form:

$$\Delta\mathbf{W} = \eta\mathbf{C} \times \left(\sum_{k=1}^{s} \delta(k).\sigma^{\mathrm{T}}(k)\right) \qquad (9.13)$$

where $\mathbf{C}$ is the adjacency matrix and operator "$\times$" represents the matrix extension of the multiplication.

The matrix form of expression (9.12) needs similar notations to those used for expressions (9.3) and (9.4):

$\delta^{\lambda+1..L}$: error sub-vector for layers $\lambda + 1$ to L
$f'()$: vector extension of the derivative of the transition function
$\mathbf{d}^{\lambda}(k)$: error sub-vector for layer λ
$\mathbf{W}_-^{\lambda\,\mathrm{T}}$: transpose of $\mathbf{W}_-^{\lambda}$
ω^{λ} : mask vector of outputs of layer λ

Values of σ can be computed simultaneously for all the neurons of a given layer; it is possible to deal similarly with values of δ. That allows the expression of the back-propagation algorithm in matrix form:

While the error of output neurons is too great do:
    For every pattern k do:
        Computation of state for every layer from $\lambda = 0$ until L:
        $\mathbf{V}^{\lambda}(k) := \mathbf{W}_+^{\lambda}.\sigma^{0..\lambda-1}(k) + \mathbf{I}^{\lambda}(k)$
        $\sigma^{\lambda}(k) := f\left(\mathbf{V}^{\lambda}(k)\right)$
        Computation of the error for every layer from $\lambda = L$ until layer 1:
        $\delta^{\lambda}(k) := f'\left(\mathbf{V}^{\lambda}(k)\right) \times \left\{2\omega^{\lambda} \times \left(\mathbf{d}^{\lambda}(k) - \sigma^{\lambda}(k)\right) + \mathbf{W}_-^{\lambda\,\mathrm{T}}.\delta^{\lambda+1..L}(k)\right\}$
    End for
    Updating weights after presenting all training patterns:
    $\Delta\mathbf{W} := \eta\mathbf{C} \times \sum_{k=1}^{s} \delta(k).\sigma^{\mathrm{T}}(k)$
    $\mathbf{W} := \mathbf{W} + \Delta\mathbf{W}$
End while

The above algorithm computes an exact value of the gradient: it is called the *"total gradient"* algorithm. By definition, a *training epoch* consists in presenting all the patterns of the training set once. In the case of the total gradient, there is only one update of weights for a training epoch. Two conditions have to be present in order for the algorithm to be used:

- Network is feedforward.

- Transition function is differentiable.

STOCHASTIC GRADIENT ALGORITHM (LMS ALGORITHM).

The total gradient algorithm may be very slow: whether the training set is large or small, the gradient is only known after a training epoch, which implies an updating of weights per epoch.

It could appear more interesting to estimate the gradient computed from subsets of the training set. In this way, there would be more updates of synaptic coefficients per epoch and the gradient algorithm would be speeded up accordingly.

At most, it can be shown that $-\delta_i(k).\sigma_j(k)$ is an unbiased estimation (in statistical terms) of the global gradient $\frac{\partial J}{\partial w_{ij}}$ [WS85]. Then, for each presented pattern, synaptic coefficients are updated as:

$$\Delta \mathbf{W}(k) = \eta \mathbf{C} \times \delta_i(k).\sigma_j(k) \tag{9.14}$$

where η is the positive number allowing the fastest convergence of the algorithm.

This algorithm is known as the *stochastic gradient algorithm*. A demonstration of its convergence is presented in [WS85] for two-layer linear neural networks. In practice, the stochastic gradient algorithm often converges faster than the total gradient algorithm for non-linear feedforward neural networks.

BLOCK GRADIENT ALGORITHM: BLMS (BLOCK LEAST MEAN SQUARE)

However, the stochastic gradient algorithm may converge more slowly than expected because the estimation of the gradient is very inaccurate. A better estimation of the cost function for all patterns is given by considering a block of b patterns in place of only one pattern [MC88].

The training set is divided into blocks of b patterns. An updating of the synaptic matrix occurs after the presentation of each block ξ according to the following expression:

$$\Delta \mathbf{W}(\xi) = \frac{\eta}{b} \left\{ \sum_{k=b\times\xi}^{b\times(\xi+1)-1} \mathbf{C} \times \left(\delta^{1..L}(k).\sigma^{0..L-1\ \mathrm{T}}(k) \right) \right\} \tag{9.15}$$

where $0 < \xi < \lceil s/b \rceil$; $\lceil s/b \rceil$ is the ceiling function of s/b.

The synaptic matrix is updated $\lceil s/b \rceil$ times during a training cycle.

TRAINING RECURRENT NEURAL NETWORKS WITH THE BACK-PROPAGATION ALGORITHM.

The back-propagation algorithm is suited only to feedforward networks. Training a recurrent neural network with back-propagation implies unfolding the network into a feedforward network according to its dynamics as described above (Figures 9.11 and 9.12) [RHW86, RF87] by replicating it as many times as needed. The number of network copies is determined by the length of the state sequences to learn. It must be noticed that, for a given sequence, the learning involves the storage of both state and error vectors at any moment of the sequence in order to compute matrix $\Delta\mathbf{W}$ at the end of the sequence. Obviously, the amount of memory is always bounded. That means that the length of sequence to learn must be bounded as well. This is an important limitation of the back-propagation algorithm when it is applied to a recurrent network. The Real Time Recurrent Learning Algorithm [WZ89] overcomes this limitation. However, the time complexity of an iteration is $\mathcal{O}(n^4)$ while the spatial complexity is $\mathcal{O}(n^3)$, which is considerable in comparison with back-propagation learning; n is the number of neurons in the network.

9.3.5   Other Supervised Learning Algorithms

ADALINE AND PERCEPTRON

The Adaline learning algorithm clearly is a particular case of the back-propagation algorithm for a two-layer linear network (an input layer, an output layer).

There is a formal identity between the Perceptron algorithm, presented above, and the back-propagation algorithm applied to the training of the decision cells by replacing variables in the matrix form of the back-propagation algorithm given in section 9.3.4 as follows:

- ϕ in place of σ^1

- d in place of $\mathbf{d}^1$

- X in place of $\sigma^0(k)$

- 1 in place of η

- H in place of $f(\mathbf{V}(k))$

- 1 in place of $f'(\mathbf{V}(k))$

Then, associative cells are on layer 0, and decision cells are on layer 1. The Perceptron algorithm is presented in section 9.3.1. However, in spite of this formal identity, the back-propagation algorithm cannot be derived from the minimization of the cost yielded by expression (9.9).

Consequently, parallel implementations of the Adaline and Perceptron algorithms will be similar to the parallelization of the back-propagation algorithm.

TRAINING HOPFIELD NETWORKS

A Hopfield network is trained for working as an associative memory [KH90]. Learning consists of presenting the *prototype vectors* to be memorized to the network. Learning must force the prototypes to be attractor steady states of the network.

There are several suitable methods to train a Hopfield network. Originally, Hopfield used the Hebb rule [HOP82]. However, this rule did not assure the correct storage of prototypes when they were not mutually orthogonal. A notable improvement was presented by Personnaz *et al.* [PGD85] which allowed a reliable storage of all prototypes with good attractivity while their number was less than the number of neurons in the network.

However, this method, known as the *pseudo-inverse rule*, or *projection rule*, needed complicated non-local computations. Thus, it was unsuitable for modeling biological reality and for implementations on massively parallel computers.

Diederich and Opper [DO87] showed that the Widrow–Hoff algorithm was suitable for the learning of a Hopfield network and that it was giving the same synaptic matrix as the pseudo-inverse rule when the initial synaptic coefficients were zero for a given set of prototypes.

The Widrow–Hoff algorithm is presented above for training a feedforward network. To apply it to a Hopfield network, the latter must be transformed into a feedforward network by replication in time as described above (Figure 9.11). Only one time unit has to be considered because only fixed points are learned. Thus, the unfolded feedforward network has two layers. Let p be a prototype: p is presented to the input of the network at time 0 on layer 0, and the output σ^1 of the network is available at time 1 on layer 1. The desired output of the network is p because p is a fixed point.

Consequently, training a Hopfield network can be considered as a particular case of the back-propagation algorithm in recurrent networks.

9.4 UNSUPERVISED LEARNING ALGORITHMS FOR NEURAL NETWORKS: KOHONEN MAPS

9.4.1 Architecture of Kohonen Maps

The network model known under the name of *Kohonen self-organizing feature maps* is inspired from both competitive learning concepts and biology, more specifically from the modeling of mammal perception systems, such as sight and hearing. Since the last century, biologists have observed that the brain presents an organization into areas corresponding to various specific functions. As far as hearing is concerned, certain areas seem to be more sensitive to certain phonemes than others; moreover cells sensitive to similar phonemes are located in neighboring areas. This idea has been taken up by Kohonen for the implementation of his "neural phonetic typewriter" [KOH88]. The definition of self-organizing feature maps and their use as an associative memory date from 1984 [KOH84].

The network architecture is that of an artificial neural map, often a two-dimensional one, each unit of which is connected to all the input units (Figure 9.13). Inputs can take real values. To each unit j of the map is associated a weight vector $\mathbf{W}_j = (w_{j1}, ..., w_{jNi})$; each connection is weighted by w_{ji} and links the input cell i to the

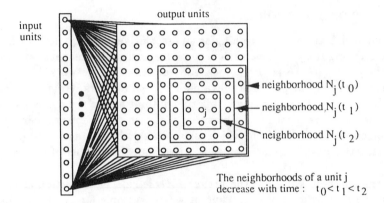

Figure 9.13   Scheme of a 2-D Kohonen map.

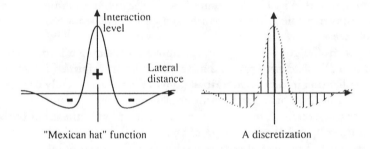

Figure 9.14   "Mexican hat" function.

output cell j. This matrix of weight constitutes the set of *external connections*. Within the map coexist lateral connections between output cells, which will be referred to as *internal connections*.

9.4.2   The Propagation Activation Rule

The propagation activation rule of the Kohonen model is inspired from biology: inside the brain, every neuron of a sensory area interacts with neighboring cells with a strength that depends on the distance from the considered cell. This dependence can be represented by the *"Mexican hat"* function, the discretization of which enables one to fix the values of weights ω_{jk} of the internal connections. Both functions are shown in Figure 9.14 in the case of a one-dimensional map.

Propagation rule of the activations on a Kohonen map:

$$(\forall j \in \{1, ..., No\}) \qquad s_j(t) = f\left(\sum_{i=1}^{Ni} w_{ji}(t)x_i(t) + \sum_{k \in K_j} \omega_{jk}s_k(t-1)\right)$$

where Ni and No are the number of input and output units respectively,
$\quad s_j(t)$ is the output, at time t, of cell j of the map (output unit),

f is a sigmoid function,

$\mathbf{X}_t = (x_i(t))_{1 \leq i \leq Ni}$ is the vector presented at time t to the input units,

$\mathbf{W}_t = (w_{ji}(t))_{1 \leq j \leq No, 1 \leq i \leq Ni}$ is the external weight matrix at time t,

$\Omega = (\omega_{jk})_{1 \leq j,k \leq No}$ is the matrix of internal weights (lateral connections),

K_j is the influence area of unit j (Mexican hat)

For a given pattern presented to the inputs, the map reaches a steady state where the cells which are in a localized area of the map are activated and constitute an "activity bubble".

The principle of self-organizing maps is based on the above property. The output unit j^*, whose vector $\mathbf{W}_{j^*}$ of the presynaptic weights is nearest to vector $\mathbf{X}$, is elected to be the center of the activity bubble. Kohonen has proved that, under given hypotheses, the elected unit is the one that has a maximal activation for the input vector [KOH84]. The width of the bubble is defined by a *topological neighborhood*, the characteristics of which are parameters of the map.

9.4.3   Training a Kohonen Self-Organizing Feature Map

Learning consists of forcing the map to give similar output patterns to similar input patterns. No desired output is supplied: it is an *unsupervised learning*. During the learning process, numerous input patterns are presented to the map. For each pattern presented at a time t, an input unit is elected and its external weight vector and those of all units in its neighborhood are modified in order that they are closer to the pattern. The width of the neighborhood decreases with time. The learning algorithm of a Kohonen map is presented next:

Self-organization rule (learning) of the Kohonen maps:

At time $t = 0$, initializing matrix $\mathbf{W}$ to small random values.

For each pattern randomly drawn with a uniform probability in the training set S, do:

  $t := t + 1$;

  Presenting pattern $\mathbf{X}(t) = (x_i(t))$ to the input units;

  Electing output unit j^*, the weight vector of which $\mathbf{W}_{j^*}(t-1)$ is the closest of $\mathbf{X}(t)$:

$$\delta_{j^*}(t) = \min\{\delta_j(t)/1 \leq j \leq No\} = \min_j \left\{ \sum_{i=1}^{Ni} (x_i(t) - w_{ji}(t-1))^2 \right\}$$

  Updating the weights of unit j^* and its neighbors:

  $\forall j \in N_{j^*}(t), \forall i \in \{1..Ni\}, w_{ji}(t-1) + \alpha(t)(x_i(t) - w_{ji}(t-1))$

  $\forall j \notin N_{j^*}(t), \forall i \notin \{1..Ni\}, w_{ji}(t) = w_{ji}(t-1)$

End for;

The coefficient $\alpha(t)$ is generally chosen as a decreasing function of time in the interval $[0, 1]$ such that:

$$\alpha(t) = 1 - e^{-\frac{1}{t}}$$

	a	a	c	k	k	**k**	k	l	l
b	**b**	c	**c**	c	f	k	l	**l**	l
d	b	e	c	f	**f**	f	f	l	t
d	e	e	e	f	f	g	g	t	t
h	h	e	s	s	g	g	g	t	**t**
h	**h**	h	s	s	s	g		q	t
i	h	m	m	s	s	o	q	**q**	q
i	m	**m**	m	n	o	**o**	o	q	r
j	m	m	**n**	n	o	p	r	**r**	
j	j	m	n	n	p	p	**p**	p	r

A bold character indicates the unit that has the highest activity for the given example.

Topological organization is evident.

Figure 9.15   After the learning phase, a Kohonen map can be labeled.

A satisfactory stopping criterion would be that all the minimal distances δ_{j*} for all the patterns X in S are less than the smallest distance between two patterns of the training set S. In practice, this criterion is too complex to be evaluated after each pattern presentation. Generally, the maximum of all the distances δ_{j*} is once compared to a fixed threshold after each presentation of the whole training set.

After the learning phase is complete, the map is *labeled*, by locating the cells which react, beyond a given threshold, to each of the patterns. Then the map can be used in the *generalization* phase, by presenting it with new patterns in order to associate them to the labels of the most activated units. For instance, a student in our laboratory, Berthomé, trained a two-dimensional Kohonen map on a set of 20 characters and labeled it as shown in Figure 9.15.

9.5   PETRI NETS FOR MODELING PARALLELIZATION OF SUPERVISED LEARNING ALGORITHMS

We have previously seen that most of the standard supervised learning algorithms, such as the Perceptron rule, are formally identical to the back-propagation algorithm. That is why we are going to study the parallelization of the back-propagation algorithm in its more general version: the BLMS algorithm.

A Petri net [PET81, BRR] has been used to model the behavior of the back-propagation learning rule.

9.5.1   Petri Nets

Next is a short description of Petri nets in the field of computer science. A Petri net is a labeled graph which possesses two kinds of nodes called: *places* and *transitions* (Figure 9.16). Successors of a place are always transitions. Successors of a transition are always places. Predecessor places of a transition are its *input places*; successor places are its *output places*. A place can be marked by one or several *tokens*. All tokens constitute the *marking* of the network. A transition is *enabled* if each of its

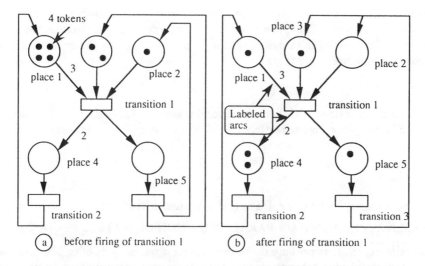

(a) before firing of transition 1   (b) after firing of transition 1

Figure 9.16 A Petri-net before and after firing of transition 1. The layout of part *b* is an abbreviation that allows one to clearly trace dense Petri-nets.

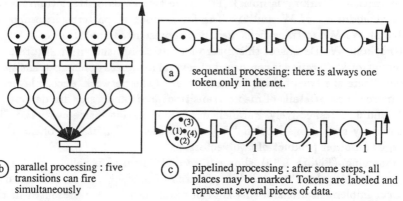

(a) sequential processing: there is always one token only in the net.

(b) parallel processing : five transitions can fire simultaneously

(c) pipelined processing : after some steps, all places may be marked. Tokens are labeled and represent several pieces of data.

Figure 9.17 Examples of modeling: parallel processing, sequential processing, pipelined processing.

input place has more tokens than the label associated with the corresponding arc. If an enabled transition is *fired*, tokens are removed from their input places and added in their output places according to the weights on the arcs.

With such a diagram, one may model the behavior of a parallel program in the following way. A transition is associated with a computation that may involve a change of state of the machine. A place is associated with the state of a variable or a set of variables of the parallel program. The marking represents the actual state of the machine. Figures 9.17 (a), (b) and (c) respectively show the modelings of a sequential program, a parallel program and a pipelined program. The capacities "1" under the places of Figure 9.17 (c) specify that they accept one token at maximum, otherwise the predecessor transition(s) cannot fire.

Now some Petri net extensions useful for our purpose are described.

Interpretation extension: As regards the neural networks, most variables are indexed, like synaptic coefficients. Then, there is a special interpretation for tokens: tokens may be labeled by the index of the variable that is going to be used by the next transition(s) of the considered place.

Representation extensions: If there are several tokens labeled with consecutive indices from a to b in one place, one token labeled $(a..b)$ will be represented instead of the full list.

9.5.2   Selecting Ways for Parallel Implementations

PARALLELIZATION BASED ON PARALLELIZATION OF MATRIX PRODUCTS

The vectorial expressions presented above show an obvious form of exploitable parallelism: the simultaneous computation of both state and error vectors on each layer, modeled by matrix–vector products. This is not the only possible form, and others can be revealed by an adequate modeling.

There are several ways of modeling the BLMS algorithm. Figure 9.18 shows a possible first method. Marking is initial. There are two kinds of transitions: transitions Σ represent additions of $\mathbf{W}$ and $\Delta\mathbf{W}(k)$ for a block of patterns in order to get a new value of $\mathbf{W}$. Macro-transitions *iteration* represent computation of $\Delta\mathbf{W}(k)$ from $\{\mathbf{I}(k), \mathbf{d}(k)\}$ and $\mathbf{W}$. Details of this macro-transition are shown in Figure 9.19 for a four-layer network. *Iteration* is composed of several instances of macro-transitions *state* and *error*. There are two of these for each layer of the network, except layer 0 which is much more simple. Details of macro-transitions *state* and *error* are depicted in Figures 9.20 and 9.21 respectively. Parallelism of computation inside every layer is taken into account by transitions labeled "." that represent computation of matrix–vector products, or an outer product of two vectors.

This modeling (Figure 9.18) shows a second form of parallelism of the back-propagation BLMS algorithm: all the patterns of a block can be processed in parallel. Direct implementations of this kind of parallelization are presented in the next chapter.

Other methods of parallelizing the algorithm may be derived from the Petri net depicted in Figure 9.18, by modifying the graph of the Petri net, its initial marking or its interpretation. Details of two other variants of parallelization are presented next.

THE FIRST VARIANT

All the pattern vectors of a block ξ can be grouped in such a way that they form a b column matrix. Now, all labels $\mathbf{d}$ and $\mathbf{I}$ are interpreted as matrix variables and the Petri net is modified as depicted in Figure 9.22. Transitions labeled "." used in macro-transitions *iteration*, *state* and *error* (Figures 9.19, 9.20 and 9.21) are interpreted as matrix–matrix products. In this chapter, "matrix back-propagation" refers to this type of parallelization.

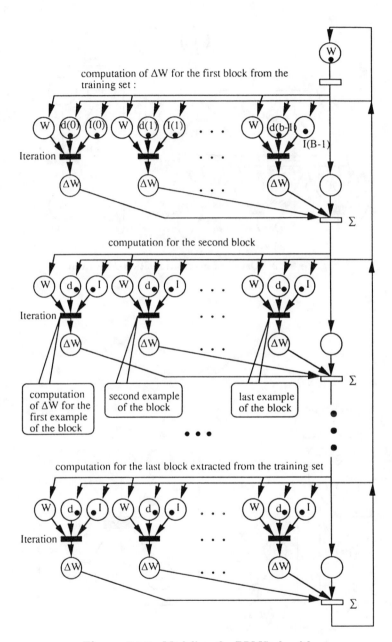

computation of ΔW for the first block from the training set :

computation for the second block

computation
of ΔW for the
first example
of the block

second example
of the block

last example
of the block

computation for the last block extracted from the training set

Figure 9.18 Modeling the BLMS algorithm.

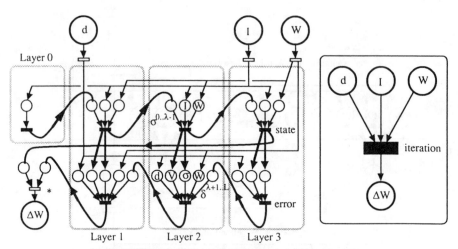

Figure 9.19 Detail of macro-transition *"iteration"*.

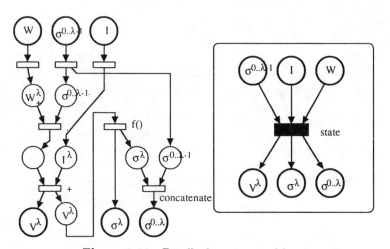

Figure 9.20 Detail of macro-transition *"state"*.

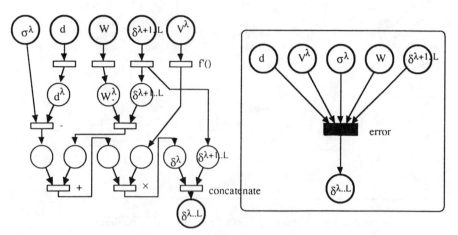

Figure 9.21   Detail of macro-transition *"error"*.

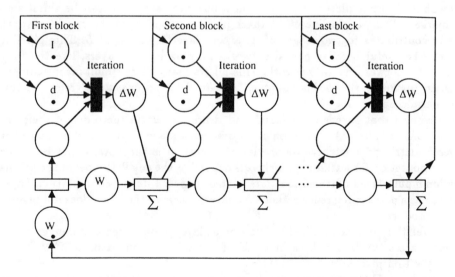

Figure 9.22   A first variant of parallelization modeling.

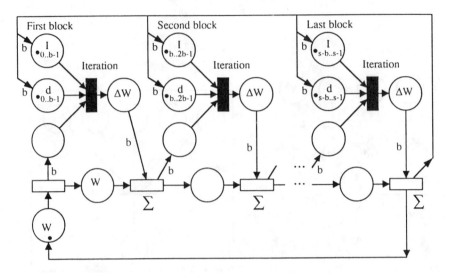

Figure 9.23   A second variant of parallelization modeling.

A SECOND VARIANT OF MODELING

A second variant is based on the presentation of the patterns of a block in succession. When looking at the structure of macro-transition *iteration* (Figure 9.19), it appears that all input places of macro-transitions *state* and *error* can be simultaneously marked. Thus, a pipeline effect takes place and a layer of the neural network generally contributes to two stages of it, except layer 0 and layer L. This pipeline effect may be useful because neural networks may own many layers, like the fully connected feedforward neural network. This allows many more simultaneous computations. In further parts of this chapter, "*pipelined back-propagation*" refers to this type of parallelization.

It is assumed that tokens on places I and d are labeled in the order of their use by transitions *iteration*. A transition is considered a stage of the pipeline only if it involves a matrix product because the latter operation is the slowest. Let α be the step of computation for a training block; α is defined as the smallest label of the tokens present on input place I of transition *state* related to layer 1 during computation. Layer 1 is chosen as a point of reference rather than layer 0 because the latter does not involve a matrix product.

Now, a relation may be established between α, layer λ and index k of a given token on input place $\sigma^{0..\lambda-1}$ as well as index k' of the token on input place $\delta^{\lambda+1..L}$, i.e. $k = \alpha - \lambda + 1$ on place $\sigma^{0..\lambda-1}$.

Thus, on layer L, the token on place $\sigma^{0..\lambda-1}$ is $\alpha - L + 1$. There is little value into considering the transition *error* of layer L as a stage of the pipeline because it does not involve a matrix product. Thus, label k' of token on place $\delta^{\lambda+1..L}$ of layer $L-1$ is equal to label k on place $\sigma^{0..\lambda-1}$ for layer $L-1$.

Consequently $k' = \alpha + \lambda - 2L + 1$ on place $\delta^{\lambda+1..L}$ for layer λ.

MODELING PARALLELIZATION OF RECURRENT NEURAL NETWORKS

Obviously, the parallelization of recurrent neural networks is similar to the parallelization of feedforward neural networks. However, if the training set is composed of one long sequence of states, all the parallel implementations described above could not take advantage of the parallel processing of several patterns. If that happens, parallelization will be based only on the parallelization of matrix products, which might be inefficient if the neural network included many layers. That may appear as a paradox for pipelined back-propagation, but in fact the succession of states of a sequence is considered as only one long state vector used by the unfolded recurrent network, not as several vectors presented in succession, and the pipeline will not be properly initialized.

9.6 ALGEBRAIC PARTITIONING OF SUPERVISED LEARNING ALGORITHMS

9.6.1 Introduction

Error back-propagation learning makes use of three types of matrix products:

$$\mathbf{V} = \mathbf{W}.\sigma, \quad \mathbf{E} = \mathbf{W}^\mathrm{T}.\delta, \quad \mathbf{D} = \delta.\sigma^\mathrm{T}$$

If there is only one neuron per layer (like the fully connected feedforward network), the synaptic submatrix related to a given layer degenerates into a row vector. If pipelined computation or the stochastic gradient algorithm were implemented, σ or δ would be column vectors, otherwise they would be matrices of b columns.

Methods of parallelization are numerous and only a few of them can be described here. In this chapter, the parallelizations are essentially based on parallelization of matrix products. In effect, these operations are the more time-consuming and are common to most neural network paradigms and training algorithms. Another choice has been fixed : all the matrix products involved in training or retrieving phases are performed by the same processors in order to use machine architectures that do not depend on the neural architecture. Consequently, matrix products are performed successively. The matrices are not explicitly transposed in order to minimize the communication times. Therefore, these products are implemented by specific algorithms which guarantee an optimal sequence of computations.

It has been shown that matrix products are efficient on the nearest neighbor architectures such as the hypercube, the two-dimensional torus or the ring [FOH87]. As we have used a network of transputers [INM87] that have only four links of communication per processor, we have studied the parallelization only on a "square" two-dimensional torus and a ring (Figure 9.24) because these implementations do not need a time-consuming routing software.

Matrix products are not sufficient to implement the back-propagation algorithm. It also requires the computation of extensions of scalar operations such as multiplication, the sigmoid function, etc. For a parallel computer, such operators can be local to each processor. Then, only matrix products need to communicate data in order to implement the back-propagation algorithm and have to be more thoroughly studied.

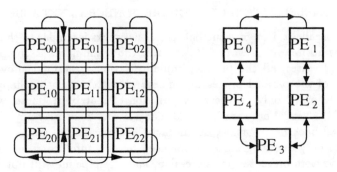

Figure 9.24 A torus of 3×3 processors and a ring of five processors.

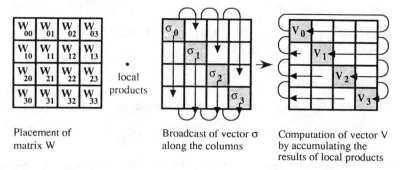

Placement of matrix W

Broadcast of vector σ along the columns

Computation of vector V by accumulating the results of local products

Figure 9.25 Matrix vector product $\mathbf{V} = \mathbf{W}.\sigma$ on a torus: wavefront algorithm.

9.6.2 Parallel Matrix Products

Two families of parallel matrix product algorithms are described in this section: the wavefront algorithms and the Fox-like algorithms [FOH87]. They will be used for parallelizing the back-propagation algorithm. Each family has specific properties which will be exploited in order to get maximal performance for parallel implementation in accordance with the characteristics of neural applications.

WAVEFRONT ALGORITHMS

Wavefront algorithms are suitable for matrix–vector products [KH89]. For computing on a torus of processors the product $\mathbf{V} = \mathbf{W}.\sigma$, the matrix $\mathbf{W}$ is partitioned into $Q \times Q$ blocks of similar size $\mathbf{W}_{ij}$ which are placed on processor PE_{ij} located at row i and column j of the torus, for all i and j in interval $[0, Q)$. Vector σ is divided into subvectors σ_i which are placed on diagonal processors PE_{ii}. To perform a matrix product, the wavefront algorithm requires a broadcast of the vector σ along the columns of the torus. The results of the local products within each processing element PE_{ij} of $\mathbf{W}$ with σ are accumulated along the rows on the processors PE_{ii} in order to get vector $\mathbf{V}$ on the diagonal of the torus (Figure 9.25).

A similar algorithm is used to compute the product $\mathbf{E} = \mathbf{W}^{\mathbf{T}}.\delta$. Placement of matrix $\mathbf{W}$ is identical to the one described above. Vector δ is placed like vector σ. In this case, the computation is performed as follows: vector δ is broadcast along the lines of the torus. Then local products $\mathbf{W}_{ij}^{\mathbf{T}}.\delta_i$ are simultaneously performed by each processor

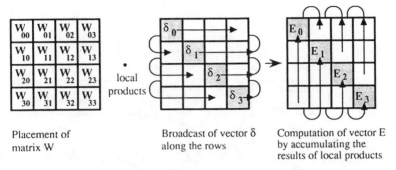

| Placement of matrix W | Broadcast of vector δ along the rows | Computation of vector E by accumulating the results of local products |

Figure 9.26   Matrix vector product $\mathbf{E} = \mathbf{W}^T.\delta$ on a torus: wavefront algorithm.

PE_{ij}. Lastly, local results are accumulated along columns on the diagonal processors in order to get vector **E** (Figure 9.26).

The outer product of vectors δ and σ requires the broadcast of σ along the columns and the broadcast of δ along the rows from the torus diagonal. Then, simultaneous local outer products of broadcast subvectors give matrix **D** which will be placed on the torus in the same way as matrix **W**.

FOX-LIKE ALGORITHMS

When learning needs matrix–matrix products, it may be more advantageous to use the Fox algorithm on a torus. All matrices M are divided into $Q \times Q$ blocks $\mathbf{W}_{ij}$, each of them being stored in the memory of processor PE_{ij}. This placement on a "square" torus (Figure 9.24) enables the best communication performances [FOH87].

Computation of the product $\mathbf{V} := \mathbf{W}.\sigma$:

The matrix product requires Q steps of computation. At step k, blocks $\mathbf{W}_{i,k+i}$ are broadcast along the rows such that $\mathbf{X}_{ij} = \mathbf{W}_{i,k+i}$, then local products $\mathbf{W}_{i,k+i}.\sigma_{ij}$ are performed by every processor PE_{ij}, and at the end of step k, matrix σ is shifted along the columns. Figures 9.27 and 9.28 illustrate the execution of the Fox algorithm.

Similar algorithms are used to compute $\mathbf{W}^T.\delta$ and $\delta.\sigma^T$ without performing explicit transposition.

The product $\mathbf{E} = \mathbf{W}^T.\delta$ needs Q steps of computation on a $Q \times Q$ torus:

At step k, $(k = 0$ to $Q - 1)$, for all processors $PE_{i,j}$:

- Submatrices $\mathbf{W}_{i,i-k}$ placed on diagonal of processors $PE_{i,i-k}$ are broadcast along rows : $\mathbf{X}_{ij} := \mathbf{W}_{i,i-k}$

- Local products $\mathbf{E}_{ij} := \mathbf{X}_{ij}^T.\delta_{ij} + \mathbf{E}_{ij}$ are performed

- Submatrices $\mathbf{E}_{i,j}$ are shifted along columns : $\mathbf{E}_{ij} = \mathbf{E}_{i-1,j}$

The results of all arithmetic expressions are modulo Q. The first step of this algorithm is shown in Figure 9.29.

The computation of $\mathbf{D} = \delta.\sigma^T$ is performed in a similar way:

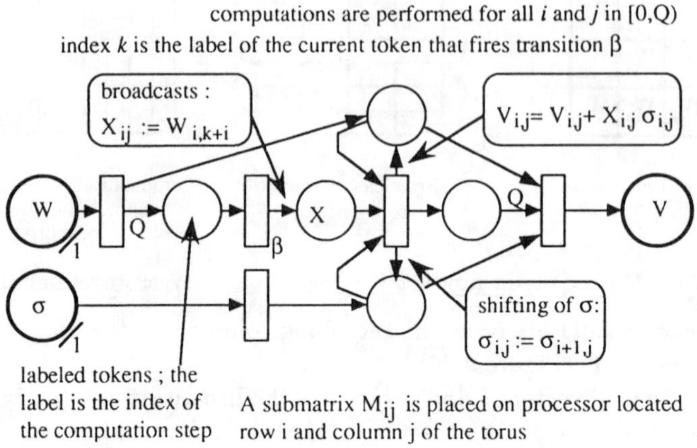

A. PETROWSKI, H. PAUGAM-MOISY

computations are performed for all i and j in $[0,Q)$

index k is the label of the current token that fires transition β

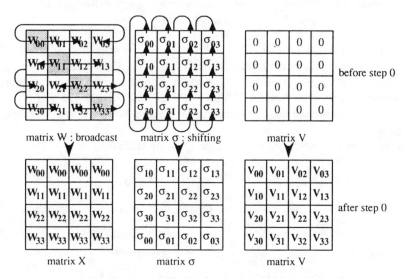

broadcasts :

$X_{ij} := W_{i,k+i}$

$V_{ij} = V_{ij} + X_{ij}\,\sigma_{ij}$

shifting of σ:

$\sigma_{ij} := \sigma_{i+1,j}$

labeled tokens ; the label is the index of the computation step

A submatrix M_{ij} is placed on processor located row i and column j of the torus

Figure 9.27 Fox algorithm modeled by a Petri net : matrix–matrix product $\mathbf{V} = \mathbf{W}.\sigma$ on a torus.

matrix W : broadcast

matrix σ : shifting

matrix V

before step 0

matrix X

matrix σ

matrix V

after step 0

Figure 9.28 State of matrices used for the product $\mathbf{V} = \mathbf{W}.\sigma$ before and after the first step of the Fox algorithm on a 4×4 torus.

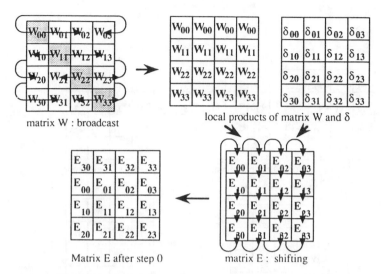

Figure 9.29 State of matrices used for the product $\mathbf{E} = \mathbf{W}^T.\delta$ before and after the first step of the matrix product algorithm on a 4 × 4 torus.

At step k, $(k = 0$ to $Q - 1)$, for all processors $PE_{i,j}$

- Local products $\mathbf{X}_{ij} = \delta_{ij}.\sigma_{ij}^{\mathrm{T}}$ are performed

- Submatrices $\mathbf{X}_{ij}$ are accumulated along rows into processors $PE_{i,i+k}$ in order to get $\mathbf{D}_{i,i+k} : \mathbf{D}_{i,i+k} = \sum_{j=0}^{Q-1} \mathbf{X}_{ij}$

- Submatrices σ_{ij} are shifted along columns : $\sigma_{ij} = \sigma_{i+1,j}$

The first step of this algorithm is shown in Figure 9.30.

9.6.3 Processor Network, Architecture and Placement

Matrices $\mathbf{W}$ and $\Delta\mathbf{W}$ are lower triangular and a simple placement on a torus such as the one described in the previous section for parallel matrix product is not adequate because the computation load would not be balanced [DZC90]. To overcome this problem, these matrices are placed on the network as follows. Let $\mathbf{M}$ be a lower triangular matrix divided into $Q \times Q$ blocks $\mathbf{M}_{ij}$ stored in the memory of the processing element PE_{ij}. In order to distribute the computation load evenly among all processors, rows and columns of the synaptic matrix have to be permuted before their placement on the processor network. The coefficients located at row i and column j must be transferred to row i', column j' given by :

$$i' = (i \backslash Q) \times (n/Q) + (i/Q) \quad \text{and} \quad j' = (j \backslash Q) \times (n/Q) + (j/Q)$$

where Q is the number of processors per row or column and n is the number of neurons of the network (Figure 9.31); "\" is the "modulo" operator.

The placement of the state vector and error vector depends on the parallelization

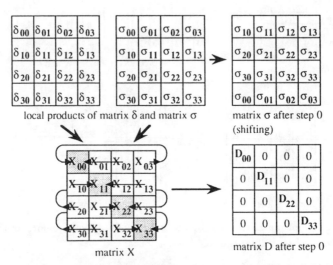

local products of matrix δ and matrix σ

matrix σ after step 0
(shifting)

matrix X

matrix D after step 0

Figure 9.30 State of matrices used for the product $\mathbf{D} = \delta.\sigma^{\mathrm{T}}$ before and after the first step of the matrix product algorithm on a 4 × 4 torus.

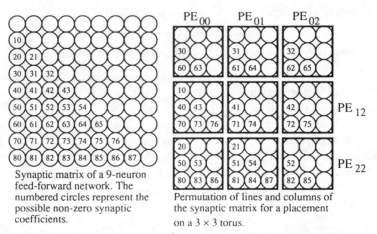

Synaptic matrix of a 9-neuron feed-forward network. The numbered circles represent the possible non-zero synaptic coefficients.

Permutation of lines and columns of the synaptic matrix for a placement on a 3 × 3 torus.

Figure 9.31 An example of placement of $\mathbf{W}$ or $\Delta\mathbf{W}$ on a torus of 3 × 3 processors.

method. For example, if the Fox algorithm is used to implement matrix products, the set of state vectors and error vectors corresponding to a block of the training set will be considered as matrices of b columns and n rows, where b is the size of a block of patterns and n is the number of neurons in the network. Rows of these matrices are permuted as explained above; however, it is useless to permute columns. If b is too small, the block of patterns will not be evenly distributed among processors of the torus and the number of its columns should be decreased. For instance, $b = 1$ for the stochastic gradient method; in this case, the number of columns of the torus should be decreased to 1 and it has to be replaced by a ring as shown in Figure 9.32.

For the wavefront algorithm, the patterns are placed on the diagonal of the torus, the processors of which are indexed as PE_{ii} for all i in $[0, Q)$. This placement is adequate whatever the size of a pattern block is.

9.6.4 Parallelizing the Back-Propagation Algorithm

BACK-PROPAGATION BASED ON A PARALLEL FOX MATRIX PRODUCT ALGORITHM

The parallel implementation of the back-propagation based on the Fox algorithm is straightforward because the parallel matrix products presented above can be linked without performing additional communication(s). Thus, the parallel algorithm is deduced from the one described in section 9.3.4, the parallelism being wholly expressed in matrix operations:

While the error of output neurons is too great do:
  For every pattern block ξ do:
    Computation of state for every layer from $\lambda = 0$ until L
    $\mathbf{V}^\lambda(\xi) := \mathbf{W}_+^\lambda . \sigma^{0..\lambda-1}(\xi) + \mathbf{I}^\lambda(\xi)$
    $\sigma^\lambda(\xi) := f\left(\mathbf{V}^\lambda(\xi)\right)$
    Computation of the error for every layer from $\lambda = L$ until layer 1:
    $\delta^\lambda(\xi) := f'\left(\mathbf{V}^\lambda(\xi)\right) \times \left\{2\omega^\lambda \times \left(\mathbf{d}^\lambda(\xi) - \sigma^\lambda(\xi)\right) + \mathbf{W}_-^\lambda{}^{\mathrm{T}}.\delta^{\lambda+1..L}(\xi)\right\}$
    Updating weights after presenting a block:
    $\Delta\mathbf{W} := \eta\mathbf{C} \times \delta(\xi).\sigma^{\mathrm{T}}(\xi)$
    $\mathbf{W} := \mathbf{W} + \Delta\mathbf{W}$
  End for
End while

If a block owns too few patterns in comparison with the number of processors per row or per column, the computation load will not be properly balanced and the computation will be quite inefficient. In this case, the computation on a torus is inadequate and one of two other implementations should be considered:

- a Fox algorithm implemented on a ring

- a wavefront algorithm running on a torus

To adapt the Fox algorithms to a ring, it is enough to consider that all the processors of a given row of the torus are replaced by only one processor. Then, broadcasts along

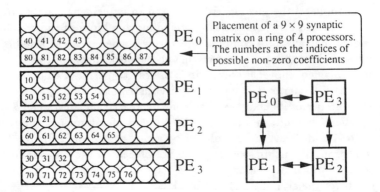

Figure 9.32 An example of placement of $\mathbf{W}$ or $\Delta\mathbf{W}$ on a ring of 4 processors.

rows of matrix blocks are replaced by reading and writing data in the local memory of the processing element. On the other hand, shifts along columns of vector σ and $\mathbf{E}$ are unchanged.

Implementing a neural network on a ring seems to be a more general method. However, communications on a ring are far more time consuming [PPD89], and an implementation on a torus should be used when possible.

If the number of neurons on a layer is too small in comparison with the number of processors per row or per column, the computation load in a torus of processors will not be properly balanced too. Moreover, a ring does not improve the computation load with the placement described above. In order to overcome this problem, a pipelined implementation would be considered.

A PARALLEL WAVEFRONT BASED PIPELINED BACK-PROPAGATION

The back-propagation algorithm allows one to simplify the wavefront matrix products presented above. Thus, to perform the product $\mathbf{V}^\lambda(k) := \mathbf{W}_+^\lambda . \sigma^{0..\lambda-1}(k)$, the subvector $\sigma^{\lambda-1}(k)$ has to be broadcast along the columns of the torus instead of $\sigma^{0..\lambda-1}(k)$, because the subvector $\sigma^{0..\lambda-2}(k)$ was already broadcast during the previous steps for computing the potential subvector $\mathbf{V}^{0..\lambda-1}(k)$. For a similar reason, a broadcast of subvector $\delta^{\lambda+1}(k)$ along rows is required to perform the product $\mathbf{E}^\lambda(k) := \mathbf{W}_-^{\lambda\ \mathrm{T}} . \delta^{\lambda+1..L}(k)$. The last product, $\mathbf{D}(k) := \delta(k) . \sigma^\mathrm{T}(k)$, does not need broadcasts of vectors δ along rows and σ along columns because these vectors were already broadcast at the moment of computation of $\mathbf{V}$ and $\mathbf{E}$.

Simple wavefront matrix product algorithms are efficient for implementing a parallel back-propagation only if the number of neurons per layer is large enough in comparison with the number of processors per row or per column of the torus. For example, consider a fully connected feedforward neural network: As the number of neurons per layer is one, the computation of $\mathbf{V}^\lambda$ needs a broadcast of $\sigma^{\lambda-1}$; the local matrix products involve only one column of processors; and finally, the accumulation of local matrix product results involves only one row of processors. Consequently, $2Q$ processors are concerned with this computation while there are Q^2 processors in the torus. The efficiency would be very low!

The pipelined implementation described is section 9.5.2.3 is applied to the wavefront matrix product algorithms in order to improve its efficiency. Let α be the current step of computation. At the end of step α, layer λ receives the state related to pattern $\alpha + 1 - \lambda$. For various patterns, the computations related to every layer of the network are simultaneous. The computations are not performed when the index of the pattern on a layer is negative or greater than s.

$\sigma^0(\alpha) = f(\mathbf{I}^0(\alpha))$
//for $\lambda = 1$ to L do $--$ state evaluation; "//" means "parallel"
        $\mathbf{V}^\lambda(\alpha + 1 - \lambda) := \mathbf{W}^\lambda_+ . \sigma^{0..\lambda-1}(\alpha + 1 - \lambda)$
end //for
//for $\lambda = 1$ to L do
        $\sigma^\lambda(\alpha + 1 - \lambda) := f(\mathbf{V}^\lambda(\alpha + 1 - \lambda) + \mathbf{I}^\lambda(\alpha + 1 - \lambda))$
end //for

At the end of step α, the sub-vector δ^λ on layer λ is related to the pattern $\alpha + 1 - 2L + \lambda$.

$\delta^L(\alpha - L) := f'(\mathbf{V}^L(\alpha - L)) \times \omega^L \times \left(\mathbf{d}^L(\alpha - L) - \sigma^L(\alpha - L)\right)$
//for $\lambda = L - 1$ to 1 do $--$ back-propagation
        $\mathbf{B}^\lambda(\alpha + 1 - 2L + \lambda) := \mathbf{W}^\lambda_-{}^{\mathrm{T}} . \delta^{\lambda+1..L}(\alpha + 1 - 2L + \lambda)$
end //for
//for $\lambda = L$ to 2 do
        $\delta(\alpha + 1 - 2L + \lambda) := f'(\mathbf{V}^\lambda(\alpha + 1 - 2L + \lambda)) \times (\mathbf{B}^\lambda(\alpha + 1 - 2L + \lambda) +$
        $\omega^\lambda \times (\delta^\lambda(\alpha + 1 - 2L + \lambda) - \sigma^\lambda(\alpha + 1 - 2L + \lambda)))$
end //for

If $L > 1$, at the end of step α, both sub-vector $\delta^{1..L}(\alpha + 2 - 2L)$ and state $\sigma(\alpha + 2 - 2L)$ are computed. Therefore, matrix $\Delta \mathbf{W}$ can be updated:

$$\Delta \mathbf{W} := \Delta \mathbf{W} + \eta \mathbf{C} \times \left(\delta(\alpha + 2 - 2L) . \sigma^{\mathrm{T}}(\alpha + 2 - 2L)\right)$$

If $L = 1$, at the end of step α, sub-vector $\delta^1(\alpha)$ is computed, and the updating of $\Delta \mathbf{W}$ is performed for pattern α at step α.

The whole training set is presented during a learning cycle: α takes its values between 1 and $s - 2 + 2L$ if $L > 1$; if $L = 1$, α must take its values between 1 and s.

The efficiency of a pipeline is high if it operates on vectors whose length is much larger than the number of its stages, otherwise the pipeline cannot be properly initialized. In the case of the pipelined back-propagation, a processor can implement approximately L/Q stages of the layer pipeline. Consequently, it is as if the actual number of stages was $2Q$. The pipelined back-propagation will be efficient if the size of the pattern blocks is sufficiently larger than Q [PDG91].

EXPERIMENTAL RESULTS

Results of performance obtained from the implementation based on the matrix product Fox algorithms are slightly superior to those of pipelined wavefront algorithms provided that the computation load is balanced. This condition implies that the number of patterns in a block and the number of neurons per layer are larger than the number of processors per row or column of the torus. An implementation on a ring requires fewer conditions to balance the computation load; however, the level of performance will be far lower because communication times are much higher. These results are discussed in [PPD89].

In fact, pipelined back-propagation can be used efficiently, for more neural architectures or algorithms than back-propagation based on Fox algorithm matrix products. That is why experimental performance measurements for *pipelined back-propagation* are presented below. Theoretical assessments are developed in [PDG91].

In order to obtain the parallel execution time t_{par}, the experiments were performed on a two-dimensional torus of 16 T800 transputers programmed in the OCCAM language.

A *transputer* [INM87] is a 32-bit microprocessor with four 20 Mbit/s serial bidirectional communication links. The transputer can access 4 gigabytes of memory through a 32-bit private bus. Part of this space is on-chip memory (T800: 4 Kbytes, access time: 50 ns). The computation speed reaches 10 MIPS for a clock rate of 20 MHz. In addition, the T800 provides an internal floating point unit running at 1.5 MFlops for 64-bit real numbers. The transputer was designed for efficiently implementing the high level OCCAM language [INM88]. OCCAM allows the implementation of sequential processes that communicate by sending and receiving messages on logical channels, some of which correspond to physical links. A transputer can run several processes by time-slicing. The code generated by OCCAM is compact and efficient, making direct algorithm implementation in machine language unnecessary.

From a single transputer configuration, we obtained the measurement of the sequential execution time t_{ser}. The speedup is defined as the ratio t_{ser}/t_{par}.

For these experiments, auto-associative learning is performed on a set of random binary vectors. The synaptic coefficients were randomly initialized. The measurements have been performed for a fully connected network and a three-layer network in order to easily compare the performances obtained for very dissimilar network architectures. The number of neurons of the three-layer network is the same for every layer.

Measurements of time for both kinds of architecture have been performed for networks of 12 to 192 neurons with steps of 12 neurons. The blocks contain 64 patterns. The speedups reached by the parallel program for the different architectures are shown in Figure 9.33. One can see that the speedups are almost the same for both the fully connected networks and the three-layer networks for a given number of neurons.

The number of synaptic weights updated per second, N_Δ, is estimated for this parallel transputer-based implementation of the back-propagation as follows:

$N_\Delta = (n_W \times s)/t_{cycle}$, where t_{cycle} is the duration of a learning cycle, and n_W is the number of non-zero synaptic coefficients. The time measurements are given for 16 processors:

Fully connected, 192 neurons : $t_{cycle} = 2.57$ s, $N_\Delta = 457000$ connections/second

3 layers, 192 neurons: $t_{cycle} = 1.34$ s, $N_\Delta = 587000$ connections/second

Provided that the distribution of the synaptic matrix is balanced, theoretical assessments developed in [PDG91] show that speedup asymptotically reaches the number of processors when the number of neurons n increases for a pipelined back-propagation. On the other hand, the speedup does not go beyond the square root of the number of processors of a "square" torus when a non-pipelined back-propagation is implemented

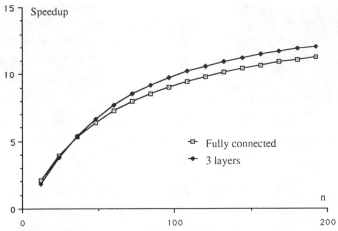

Figure 9.33 Speedup for a network of 16 processors.

to train a fully connected feedforward neural network. Performance of the pipelined back-propagation is far less sensitive to the architecture of the neural network.

9.6.5   Parallelizing the Hopfield Network

The back-propagation algorithm is a good algorithm for training a Hopfield network: it is much more reliable than the Hebb rule. The training phase often uses the stochastic gradient algorithm, where the synaptic matrix is updated after the presentation of each pattern of the training set. However, other gradient methods could be used. During the retrieval phase, when a pattern is presented, the network has to reach a steady state before another pattern is presented. Thus, the patterns have to be presented sequentially, one by one, to a given network, although it is possible to take advantage of a pipeline effect as described in [BH88].

The parallelization described below is standard and is suitable for both the training phase and the retrieval phase [KH89, WEI89]. This algorithm may be deduced from the Fox parallel matrix products. The synaptic matrix of a Hopfield network is square and its placement by interleaving as described in section 9.6.3 is useless.

Patterns are presented sequentially during the training phase as well as the retrieval phase. Consequently, matrix–vector products have to be computed. In this case, only the ring implementation can be suited to the Fox algorithms because, otherwise, data would not be evenly distributed on a torus. Products $V = W.\sigma$ and $D = \delta.\sigma^T$ have to be computed, but not $E = W^T.\delta$ because it is useless to compute subvector δ^0 which is related to layer 0.

The presentation of a pattern during training involves the following operations:

Let P be the number of processors, let $I^0(k)$ be pattern k of the training set, let $d^1(k)$ be the desired output for pattern k. In the case of a Hopfield network, $I^0(k) = d^1(k)$, and $\sigma^0 = I^0(k)$.

- Computing product $V^1 := W.\sigma^0$ (P steps of computation, one shift of σ^0 per step)

	processor 1
	processor 2
	processor 3
	processor 4

(a) Straightforward block mapping.   (b) Mapping improving the load balancing.

Figure 9.34   Mapping of a 2-D Kohonen map on a ring or a linear net of processors.

- Computing the error $\delta^1 := \mathbf{d}^1 - \mathbf{V}^1$: local operations

- Computing product $\mathbf{D}^1 := \delta^1.\sigma^0{}^\mathrm{T}$ (P steps of computation, one shift of σ^0 per step)

- Updating matrix $\mathbf{W}$: $\mathbf{W} := \mathbf{W} + \eta \times \mathbf{D}$: local operations

In the retrieval phase, the parallel algorithm for a synchronous iteration is:

- Computing product $\mathbf{V}^1 := \mathbf{W}.\sigma^0$ (P steps of computation, one shift of σ^0 per step)

- Thresholding: $\sigma^0 := \mathrm{sign}(\mathbf{V}^1)$: local operations

These parallel algorithms are very simple and have been used for VLSI implementations of Hopfield networks [WEI89]. In effect, if a processor is used for each neuron, a shift of σ^0 consists of communicating one boolean value from one processor to another. A processor accesses all the presynaptic weight values of its associated neuron in such a way that the memory can be a shift register.

Parallelization of a Hopfield network on a torus or a mesh of processors is possible: communication times would be less than on a ring. However, the machine is efficient in the retrieval phase only if a pipeline is implemented, otherwise few processors would work at any time. More details are in [BH88].

9.7   PARALLELIZING KOHONEN MAPS ALGORITHMS

9.7.1   A Straightforward Parallel Algorithm

Since the weight matrix of Kohonen maps is not a sparse one, parallelizing the learning phase for Kohonen maps seems to be easier than parallelizing back-propagation learning for multilayer networks. Since each cell of the map receives a weight vector, which comes from the input cells, distributing the neural units of the map on the processors is equivalent to distributing the weight matrix.

A straightforward parallel algorithm consists of equally distributing consecutive rows of the weight matrix on the different processors of the parallel computer. This is equivalent to mapping successive bands of units to every processor (Figure 9.34(a)).

The sequential learning algorithm of topological maps was presented in a previous section. The parallel algorithm is nearly the same. The only differences are as follows:

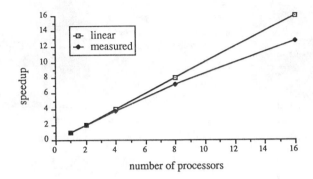

Figure 9.35   Speedup in implementing a Kohonen map on a hypercube of transputers.

- each pattern is diffused to all the processors

- election of the unit j^* which realizes the minimum distance to the input is thus decomposed:

    1. on every processor P_k, election of unit j_k^* with locally minimum distance

    2. global election of unit j^* with minimum distance to the input

    3. diffusion of j^* to all the processors

All other steps of the algorithm remain unchanged. They are performed in parallel by all the processors. Speedups of 7.1 for 8 processors and 12.8 for 16 processors were obtained by J.M.Auger [DA89] on a hypercube of transputers (Figure 9.35).

9.7.2   Improvements of Load Balancing

The straightforward parallel algorithm does not take into account the fact that the weight update should only occur in a neighborhood of the elected unit j^*. Hence the load balancing can be improved by better mapping the units to the processors.

Several authors have proposed various answers to this mapping problem. Since it is the most widely used, the case of a 2-D Kohonen map is next discussed.

The simplest improvement consists of interleaving successive lines of the map [US89, WHW91]. If the network is composed of p processors, the units in lines 1, $p+1$, $2p+1$, etc., are mapped on the first processor, the units in lines 2, $p+2$, $2p+2$, etc., are mapped on the second processor, and so on (Figure 9.34(b)). This mapping is well-suited to an implementation on a linear net or on a ring of processors. Every processor is kept busy while the neighborhood diameter is greater than or equal to p.

To implement a 2-D Kohonen map on a 2-D mesh of processors, the mapping array has to be generalized. The second direction of the mesh can be taken into account in the same way as for a 1-D processor topology (Figure 9.36(a)). Assuming that the mesh consists of $p \times p$ processors, numbered in sequence (line after line), a unit with coordinates given by (x, y) on the map is implemented on the processor numbered $x \bmod p + (y \bmod p) \times p$ [WHW91, DM92].

When the 2-D map is not wrapped like a torus, units at the border of the map have less probability of being modified than inner units. In the case of the previous

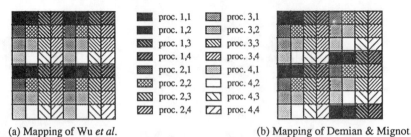

proc. 1,1	proc. 3,1
proc. 1,2	proc. 3,2
proc. 1,3	proc. 3,3
proc. 1,4	proc. 3,4
proc. 2,1	proc. 4,1
proc. 2,2	proc. 4,2
proc. 2,3	proc. 4,3
proc. 2,4	proc. 4,4

(a) Mapping of Wu *et al.*　　　　　　　　(b) Mapping of Demian & Mignot

Figure 9.36   Improvements in mapping units of a 2-D Kohonen map to a processor network (e.g. a mesh).

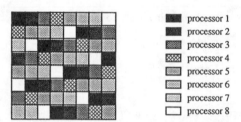

processor 1
processor 2
processor 3
processor 4
processor 5
processor 6
processor 7
processor 8

Figure 9.37   Mapping of an 8 × 8 Kohonen map on a network of 8 processors.

mapping, these units all lie on the processors which are on the border of the mesh. This remark leads to a new improvement (Figure 9.36(b)). A unit, the coordinates of which are (x, y) on the map, is now implemented on the processor numbered $(p \times y + x) \bmod p^2$ [DM92]. The units which lie on the lower and upper borders of the map are equally distributed over the processors. Note that this mapping does not depend on the topology of the processor network. Since the numbering of the processors realizes a sequence, this mapping can be applied to a ring or to a linear net as well.

The method for mapping neural units to a processor network should be generalized, as described before, and by using a modulo of the number of available processors. For instance, an $(8 \times k) \times (8 \times k)$ Kohonen map can be mapped to a three-dimensional hypercube as shown in Figure 9.37.

9.7.3   Improvements of the Communication Times

In order to reduce the communication times, patterns can be diffused and pipelined by blocks to the processors. The number of exchanges can also be minimized by arranging the minimal distances in blocks. These two modifications lead to a new learning algorithm. Each processor determines several local winners by processing a certain number of patterns (called a block) between two successive communications. Then, all the processors determine the global winners associated with the patterns of a block.

The alteration of the learning algorithm came from the fact that all the winners in a block are evaluated with the same map, and hence with the same weight matrix. Experiments were performed on an iPSC/860 computer, in training a 32 × 32 map to learn the unit square [DM92]. These experiments proved that 100 patterns per block provide very good speedup, and that perturbation is quite negligible for a number of iterations equal to at least 60,000.

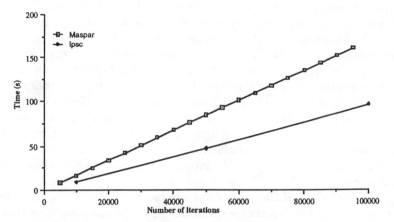

Figure 9.38 Computation time on the iPSC and on the MasPar.

9.7.4 Comparing MIMD and SIMD Implementations

The training of a Kohonen map on the unit square was implemented both on an iPSC/860 computer and on a MasPar computer [DM92]. Another comparison was performed between a transputer systolic ring and a Connection Machine CM-2. The application was a modeling of the synaptic organization in the hand-region of the somatosensory cortex [ORS90].

These experiments allow a comparison between MIMD and SIMD processing systems. Since the number of processors is far greater on a SIMD computer than on a MIMD one, SIMD implementations usually map one neural unit per processor. However, all the above improvements to mapping units can be applied if necessary.

For training a map on the unit square, the iPSC implementation proves to be more efficient than the MasPar implementation (Figure 9.38).

Time measurements on the transputer ring and on the CM-2 show that, in the low-communication case of the classical topological map algorithm, a transputer system should require 510 nodes in order that its level of perfomance becomes equivalent to the joint performance of 16K CM-2-processors and 512 Weitek-FPUs [ORS90]. Hence, in practical experiments, the transputer network is much less efficient than the Connection Machine. Nevertheless, in the high-communication case of an extended algorithm, which explicitly includes the computation of lateral interactions on the map, the relative performance of the transputer system improves significantly [ORS90].

9.8 CONCLUSION

Parallelizing the BLMS variant of the back-propagation algorithms allows one to implement a generic method for parallelizing other supervised learning algorithms. The parallelization of the underlying matrix products achieves good performance on a loosely coupled machine. Parallelization may be efficient even for small neural networks. Furthermore, the greater the size of the neural network, the better the speedup and the efficiency of the parallel algorithm.

Several parallelization variants may be used. The simplest deals only with parallel matrix product algorithms on a ring. However, the cost of data communication in a ring is high and an implementation on a torus should be selected when possible. Two families of parallel algorithms have been presented: the wavefront matrix products and the Fox parallel matrix products. The latter is efficient on a square torus if the number of neurons per layer is larger than the square root of the number of processors Q. Let b be the number of patterns presented between two updates. During the training phase, b has to be larger than Q as well. If this condition is not verified, then wavefront algorithms should be used. If the number of neurons per layer is too small and if b is large enough, a pipelined back-propagation algorithm has to be implemented. Although pipelined back-propagation is slightly less efficient than parallelization based on Fox algorithms, the performance of the pipelined algorithm is almost independent of the neural architecture.

Parallel implementations of Kohonen maps are easier to implement than those of multilayer neural networks. Greater speedups can be easily obtained. The choice between MIMD and SIMD parallel computers is not straightforward. It strongly depends on the type of the processors, on the details of the implementation (mapping of units, pipelining patterns,...), and on the size of the Kohonen map.

Some improvements in the communication times imply alterations of the learning algorithm. In the case of computation by blocks, as long as the blocks stay sufficiently small, actual speedups can be observed without significant decay of performance. More elaborate modifications of the learning algorithms should be defined, in order to turn the parallelization to the best account. The case of a two-layer learning vector quantizer has been addressed by Kotropoulos et al. [KAP92]. The new algorithm is based on splitting the set of patterns in blocks, and duplicating the first layer LVQ's. This method takes place between algebraic partitioning and network duplicating. This latter family of parallelizations will be developed in the next chapter.

ACKNOWLEDGEMENT

The authors wish to acknowledge Prof. M. Becker of the "Institut National des Télécommunications" for a critical reading and Prof. C. Girault of the "Université Pierre et Marie Curie" for his generous help.

REFERENCES

[BAR89] Barlow H.B. Unsupervised Learning. *Neural Computation*, (1):295–311, 1989.

[BH88] Blayo F., Hurat P. Aplysie : un Réseau Systolique à Réinjection pour la Reconnaissance selon l'Algorithme de Hopfield (in French). *Annales du Groupe Carnac*, EPFL, 1988.

[BRR] Brauer W., Reisig W., Rosenberg G. (eds) *Petri Nets: Central Models and their Properties*. Lectures Notes in Computer Science, Goos G. and Hartmanis J. (eds) Springer Verlag, 1987.

[DA89] Dorizzi B., Auger J.M. Implémentation de l'Algorithme des Cartes Topologiques de Kohonen sur Transputers (in French). *La Lettre du Transputer*, (3):17–29, 1989.

[DEP89] Deprit E. Implementing Recurrent Back-Propagation on the Connection Machine. *Neural Networks*, (2):295–314, 1989.

[DM92]   Demian V., Mignot J.C. Implementation of the Self-Organizing Feature Map on Parallel Computers. *Proc. of CONPAR-92 / VAPP-V*, Springer-Verlag, Sept. 1992.

[DO87]   Diederich S., Opper M. Learning of Correlated Patterns in Spin-Glass Networks by Local Learning Rules. *Physical Review Letters*, (58):949–952, 1987.

[DZC90] Di Zitti E., Chirico M., Paganini M., Bisio G.M. Partitioning Large Neural Computations on 2–D Meshes of Transputers. In *Proc. of Esprit PCA Workshop*, Ispra, Dec. 1990.

[FOH87] Fox G., Otto S., Hey A. Matrix Algorithm on a Hypercube: Matrix Multiplication. *Parallel Computing*, (4), 1987.

[GH89]   Ghosh J., Hwang K. Mapping Neural Networks onto Message-Passing Multicomputers. *Journal of Parallel and Distributed Computing*, (6):291–330, 1989.

[HOE90] Hoekstra J. System Architecture of a Modular Neural Network Using 400 Simple Processors. *Microprocessing and Microprogramming*, North Holland, (30):257–262, 1990.

[HOP82] Hopfield J.J. Neural Networks and Physical Systems with Emergent Collective Computational Abilities. *Proceedings of the National Academy of Sciences*, (79):2554–2558, 1982.

[INM87] INMOS Ltd. *IMS T800 Transputer Data Sheet*, 1987.

[INM88] INMOS Ltd. *OCCAM 2 Reference Manual*. Prentice Hall International Series in Computer Science, C.A.R. Hoare, Series Editor, 1988.

[KAP92] Kotropoulos C., Augé E., Pitas I. Two-Layer Learning Vector Quantizer for Color Image Quantization. *Proc. of EUSIPCO'92*, Brussels, 1992.

[KH89]   Kung S.Y., Hwang J.N. A Unified Systolic Architecture for Artificial Neural Networks. *Journal of Parallel and Distributed Computing*, (6):358–387, 1989.

[KH90]   Kamp Y., Hasler M. *Recursive Neural Networks for Associative Memory*. John Wiley and Sons, 1990.

[KOH84] Kohonen T. *Self-organization and Associative Memory*. Springer Verlag, 1984.

[KOH88] Kohonen T. The 'Neural' Phonetic Typewriter. *IEEE Computer*, 11–22, 1988.

[MC88]   Mulgrew B., Cowan C.F. *Adaptive Filters and Equalizers*. Kluwer Academic Publishers, 1988.

[MCP43] McCulloch W.S., Pitts W. A Logical Calculus of the Ideas Immanent in Nervous Activity. *Bulletin of Mathematical Biophysics* (5):115–133, 1943.

[MP69]   Minsky M., Papert S. *Perceptrons*. MIT Press, Cambridge, MA, 1969.

[NF89]   Núñez F.J., Fortes J.A.B. Performance of Connectionist Learning Algorithms on 2–D SIMD Processor Arrays. *Neural Information Processing Systems 2*, Denver, 810–817, 1989.

[ORS90] Obermayer K., Ritter H., Schulten K. Large-Scale Simulations of Self-Organizing Neural Networks on Parallel Computers: Application to Biological Modeling. *Parallel Computing*, (14):381–404, 1990.

[PDG91] Petrowski A., Dreyfus G., Girault C. Performance Analysis of a Pipelined Back-Propagation Parallel Algorithm. Report 91.59, Laboratoire MASI, Université Pierre et Marie Curie, Nov. 1991.

[PET81] Peterson J.L. *Petri Net Theory and the Modeling of Systems.* Prentice Hall, 1981

[PGD85] Personnaz L., Guyon I., Dreyfus G. Information Storage and Retrieval in Spin Glass Like Neural Networks. *J. Phys. Lett.*, (46):359–365, 1985.

[PIN87] Pineda F.J. Generalization of Back-Propagation to Recurrent Neural Networks. *Physical Review Letters*, (59):2229–2232, 1987.

[PPD89] Petrowski A., Personnaz L., Dreyfus G., Girault C. Parallel Implementations of Neural Network Simulations. In Andre F. and Verjus J.P. (eds), *Hypercube and Distributed Computers*, North Holland, 205–218, 1989.

[RF87]   Robinson A.J., Fallside F. Static and Dynamic Error Propagation Networks with Application to Speech Coding. *IEEE Conference on Neural Information Processing Systems - Natural and Synthetic*, 1987.

[RHW86] Rumelhart D.E., Hinton G.E., Williams R.J. *Learning Internal Representation by Error Propagation*, volume 1 of *Parallel Distributed Processing*. MIT Press, 318–362, 1986.

[ROS58] Rosenblatt F. The Perceptron: a Probabilistic Model for Information Storage and Organization in the Brain. *Psychological Review*, (65):386–408, 1958.

[RW89]   Robert F., Wang S. Implementation of Neural networks on a Hypercube F.P.S. T20. In Cosnard M., Barton M.H. and Vanneschi M. (eds), *Parallel Processing*, North Holland, 189–200, 1989.

[US89]   Ultsch A., Siemon H.P. Exploratory Data Analysis: Using Kohonen Networks on Transputers. Report 329, Dept of Computer Science, University of Dortmund (Germany), Dec. 1989.

[WEI89] Weinfeld M. A Fully Digital CMOS Integrated Hopfield Network Including the Learning Algorithm. *International Workshop on VLSI for Artificial Intelligence*, Delgado-Frias J.G. and Moore W. (eds), Kluwer Academic, 1989.

[WH60]   Widrow B., Hoff M.E. Adaptive Switching Circuits. 1960 IRE WESCON, Convention record, New York: IRE, 96–104, 1960.

[WHW91] Wu C.H., Hodges R., Wang C.J. Parallelizing the Self-Organizing Feature Map on Multiprocessor Systems. *Parallel Computing*, (17):821–832, 1991.

[WL90]   Widrow B., Lehr M.A. 30 Years of Adaptive Neural Networks: Perceptron, Madaline, and Back–propagation. *Proceedings of the IEEE*, (78):1415–1442, 1990.

[WS85]   Widrow B., Stearns S.D. *Adaptive Signal Processing.* Prentice Hall, 1985.

[WZ89]   Williams R.J., Zipser D. Experimental Analysis of the Real-Time Recurrent Learning Algorithm. *Connection Science*, (1):87–111, 1989.

[WZ90]   Witbrock M., Zaghia M. An Implementation of Back-Propagation Learning on GF11, a Large SIMD Parallel Computer. *Parallel Computing*, (14):329–346, 1990.

[YNM90] Yoon H., Nang J.H., Maeng S.R. Parallel Simulation of Multilayered Neural Networks on Distributed–Memory Multiprocessors. *Microprocessing and Microprogramming*, North Holland, (29):185–195, 1990.

10

Parallel Neural Computing Based on Network Duplicating

HELENE PAUGAM-MOISY

10.1 INTRODUCTION

Whereas the previous two chapters presented parallel neural computing based on partitioning networks, we now adopt a radically different perspective. In order to exploit the parallelism which is inherent in the presentation of multiple data to a connectionist model, a neural network is now duplicated on several processors, instead of distributing it. It will be seen that this method is in fact a general principle for parallelizing connectionist models, in the recognition as well as in the learning phase.

Another way of computing parallel samples of neural networks consists in distributing several copies of the same connectionist model, with different network architectures or learning parameters. In this case, they all receive the whole training set for performing their learning phase. Thus their performances can be stored or compared in order to find the best neural networks for a given application. The method can be applied to any connectionist model, and to any set of parameters.

This indirect method of parallelizing neural networks does not improve the learning speed of a fixed network. However, a developer of applications will see it as a method for improving the learning phase. It is now acknowledged that the greatest difficulty, when dealing with real-world problems, is to determine nearly optimal conditions for applying a connectionist model to the problem. The major drawbacks are, first, that theoretical results are inefficient in concrete cases, and second, that developing a large number of learning phases is time-consuming.

Parallel Algorithms for Digital Image Processing, Computer Vision and Neural Networks, ed. I. Pitas
© 1993 John Wiley & Sons Ltd

Therefore the development of real-world applications can be improved both by accelerating each learning phase and by avoiding useless computations by parallel automatic selection of the best parameters.

The layout of this chapter is as follows. Sections 2 and 3 develop methods, implementations and experiments, for parallelizing the recognition and the learning phases of the most widely used model, i.e. *multilayer neural networks* with *back-propagation* learning. Section 4 deals with the parallel method for selecting best parameters, and presents applications to *multilayer neural networks* and *Kohonen topological maps*.

10.2   PARALLELIZING THE RECOGNITION PHASE

10.2.1   Partitioning the Pattern Set

The recognition phase of new patterns is generally much faster than the learning phase. For instance, for multilayer neural networks, a single feedforward pass is sufficient for each pattern, while the learning phase requires a lot of feedforward and feedback passes, and weight updates, for each example. One may imagine that parallelizing the recognition phase would further slow down this phase by wasting time in communications costs. That is probably true if parallelization is attempted by distributing cells or computations on processors.

If, on the other hand, the network is replicated in multiple copies and the patterns are distributed to each of them, this method can give high dividends for low-level applications with large data flows, such as robotics and signal processing. In fact, parallelizing the recognition phase by partitioning the data set is a widely applicable method. It can be applied to any connectionist model, without loss of speedup. This is a general way for optimizing the computation time in the development phase.

10.2.2   Parallelizing the Multilayer Networks Recognition Phase

A parallelization of *multilayer neural networks* by partitioning the set of patterns, has been experimented on a large dataset. The method has been implemented in a parallel C language [LS89], on a parallel MIMD computer, a T.node [Nic88] of 32 T800 transputers. A ring topology is mapped on the T.node, including the frontal node (Figure 10.1). The front-end sends the patterns by packets through one link toward each processor and receives the results through the other link.

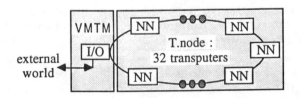

Figure 10.1   A ring of neural networks.

Let k be the size of the packets sent by the front-end to each processor, and p be the number of processors on the ring. For a multilayer network, each processor computes

k results by a feedforward pass through the neural network. The load is balanced as shown on Figure 10.2. For each packet of k computations, a processor π must

1. receive k patterns,

2. pass $k(p - \pi)$ patterns, from its predecessor to its successor,

3. send its k results,

4. pass $k(\pi - 1)$ results, from its predecessor to its successor.

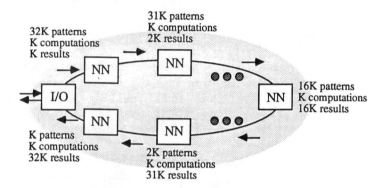

Figure 10.2   Load balancing around the ring.

The speedup obtained in that way is very good, as a function both of k and of p. The sum of the message-passing and of the computation times are shown on Figure 10.3, as a function of the packet size, on different rings of 1, 2, 4, 8, 16 and 32 processors. The multilayer neural network in this experiment had 300 connections. A set of 1920 patterns can be processed in about 0.3 seconds using 32 processors.

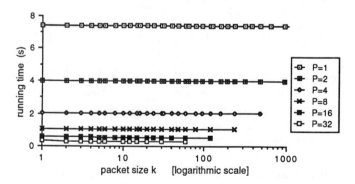

Figure 10.3   Running time as a function of the packet size and the number of processors.

Speedups grow slightly with the size of the packets. Both the smallest and the largest are compared with the ideal curve (Figure 10.4). Some numerical values for speedups are 1.99 with 2 processors, 7.12 with 8 processors, and 24.5 with 32 processors.

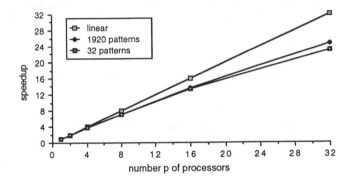

Figure 10.4 Speedup as a function of the number of processors and the packet size.

There exist different ways for arranging the communication and computation phases in time. The C language [LS89], which has been used for these experiments, is OCCAM based. Hence message-passing instructions are blocking instructions. Nevertheless in that language one can write parallel processes on the same processor. This is an indirect way to achieve non-blocking communications between transputers.

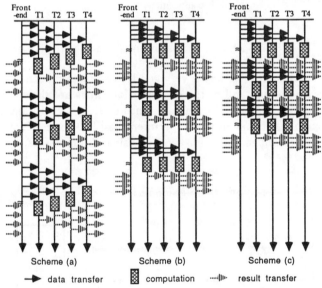

N.B. Because of the ring topology, right arrows (output of the transputer T4) are the same as left arrows (input of the front-end).

Figure 10.5 Communication on a uni-directional ring of 4 processors.

Without parallel processes, a time simulation on 4 processors and the front-end can be seen on scheme (a) in Figure 10.5. Note that, even in the steady state, each processor is often inactive. A first improvement consists in running a receive process and a send process in parallel on every internal transputer. Scheme (b) shows how communication time can be thus reduced. Scheme (c) represents a second improvement obtained by also implementing parallel send and receive processes on the front-end.

Several remarks are in order :

- in the framework of a real application, data messages and result messages often have different sizes, which could reduce the harmony of scheme (c);

- the computation times are nearly proportional to the number of weights in the network, and currently they are far longer than the communication times;

- on the front-end, apparent inactive periods of time (denoted by $\approx$ marks on the schemes) may become very helpful and busy for reading data on external peripheral devices (disks, tapes, analog sensors, photodetectors), or for storing or exploiting results (disks, tapes, robot arms, etc.). Hence their length should not be necessarily reduced.

Different schemes could be built up, on different topologies, in order to make computations and communications overlap. However, scheme (c) is optimal on a unidirectional ring of processors, since each processor receives its own data just before computing them, and sends its own results just after having calculated them. Neural computations are performed synchronously on all processors. Since the neural network and the number of patterns to compute on each processor are the same, the computation time is exactly the same for each node on the ring.

Following Desprez and Tourancheau [DT90], the time for sending or receiving a message of length ℓ bytes between two transputers can be accurately modeled by :

$$\beta + \ell\tau \qquad\qquad \text{where} \quad \beta = 3.9 \ \mu s \quad \text{and} \quad \tau = 1.1 \ \mu s \qquad\qquad (10.1)$$

The time for sending or receiving such a message between the front-end and a transputer can be modeled by :

$$\beta' + \ell\tau' \qquad\qquad \text{where} \quad \beta' = 15.4 \ \mu s \quad \text{and} \quad \tau' = 1.8 \ \mu s \qquad\qquad (10.2)$$

As before (Figure 10.2), k is the number of patterns which are computed by each processor, at each step, and p is the number of processors on the ring. The variables λ and r represent respectively the lengths, in bytes, of a pattern data and a result. The number of weighted links of the neural network is denoted by w. For this parallelized recognition phase, the total time is obtained by adding the communication time to the calculation time. The following model is proposed :

$$T_{total} = T_{comm} + T_{calc}$$

with

$$T_{comm} = \frac{1}{k} \left(2\beta' + k(\lambda + r)\tau' + \left(1 - \frac{1}{p}\right) (2\beta + k(\lambda + r)\tau) \right) \qquad (10.3)$$

and

$$T_{calc} = \frac{1}{p}(\gamma + \delta w) \qquad\qquad (10.4)$$

T_{total} represents the average total time of estimation per pattern. The values for γ and

δ have been evaluated from multilayer neural networks of size $w \in \{300, 1200, 2400\}$.

$$\gamma = 150 \, \mu s \qquad \text{and} \qquad \delta = 13 \, \mu s$$

These values are quite stable when p varies from 1 to 32. The model is very accurate for many different values of p and k. From this model and the results shown previously (Figures 10.3 and 10.4), the following facts can be deduced :

- the influence of the packet size on the execution time is negligible,

- the communication time is small compared to the computation time.

10.2.3   Conclusion

Implementation, experimental results and modeling have been presented, for improving the execution time of the recognition phase in multilayer neural networks. The parallel algorithm is obvious, and achieves quasi linear speedups, even in the case of a straightforward implementation on a non-optimized topology. This work aims to show the efficiency of partitioning the pattern set, at least in the case of the recognition phase, which is rarely mentioned in the literature.

A similar behavior can be forecast for the recognition phase in most of the classical connectionist models. Difficulties arise only when parallelizing the learning phases. While distributing the patterns does not affect the recognition computations, distributing the examples to be learned often involves alterations of the learning algorithms. This question is addressed in the next section.

10.3   PARALLELIZING BACK-PROPAGATION LEARNING

10.3.1   Parallel Training of Multilayer Neural Networks

As pointed out by A.Singer [Sin90a], there are at least three degrees of parallelism in training *multilayer neural networks*. First, there is the parallel processing performed by the numerous nodes at each layer. Second, there is the parallel processing of the many training examples. A third parallel aspect stems from the fact that the forward and backward passes of different training patterns can be pipelined. Various implementations of these aspects have been experimented, and some of them are presented in previous chapters of this book, but several difficulties remain. Distributing the nodes on all the processors requires a critical study of the network connectivity and an adapted grain of parallelism [GH89]. It is not easy to achieve an optimal load-balancing for a given neural network on a given topology for parallel processors [Dod89, Wan89]. When parallelizing the matrix–vector products, a critical point is that the degree of parallelism is limited by the architecture of the neural network, because of sparse weight matrices. Distributing the examples among different copies of a neural network, each of them computed by a single processor, was recently presented as a much more effective parallel algorithm [Sin90b]. The purpose of this section is to show that, unfortunately, the speedups which are actually obtained when considering the whole *back-propagation* learning phase are not as good as those performed on a single *epoch*, i.e. one presentation of each example of the whole training set.

The following section focuses on the parallel processing of many examples. One copy of the same multilayer neural network is fully implemented on each processor of a parallel computer. The training set is divided into packets. Each processing element receives a different packet of examples and processes it independently. The only communication required by this implementation occurs when the weights are updated.

When processing the examples in a packet, each processor collects the weight corrections to be applied to the weight matrix, but cannot apply them immediately, because the various copies of the neural network must stay globally the same. While the computations can be independent, weight updating requires synchronization. After all the processors have completed processing their own packets, corrections are exchanged and they are all added up everywhere. A new stage can now start, with other packets of examples.

The crucial issue is as follows. The larger the packets, the higher the speedup afforded by the parallel algorithm. Conversely, the smaller the packets, the more frequent the weight updates, and the faster the convergence of the learning phase, afforded by back-propagation. The problem is to find the appropriate packet size so as to achieve an optimal overall speedup for a parallel implementation.

10.3.2   On the Convergence of Back-Propagation

10.3.2.1   VARIATIONS OF THE BACK-PROPAGATION ALGORITHM

Since weight-updating is a linear operation in the back-propagation algorithm, this parallelization is a correct algorithm. Nevertheless it is not an exact one. For most of the examples, corrections are computed with an obsolete weight matrix, and the evaluation of the cost function slightly differs from the real one. These approximations are not unbearable, but it is important to be aware of them.

Some precisions need to be made about *back-propagation*. As a matter of fact, there exist a lot of variants of back-propagation. Even when considering the most basic algorithms, without additional refinements such as gain factors [KM91] or second order terms [BL89, Fah89], two important variants should be distinguished, the total gradient descent and the stochastic gradient algorithm. These two variants have been well studied by L.Bottou in his PhD thesis [Bot91].

The *total gradient descent* consists in minimizing a global cost function C which is computed from the whole training set. The weight update occurs only after a complete presentation of all the examples according to

$$W_t = W_{t-1} - \varepsilon_t \mathrm{grad}_W C(W_{t-1}) \tag{10.5}$$

where W_t is the weight matrix at time t, and ε_t is the learning rate at time t. Total gradient back-propagation has been proved to converge [Hec90], but no theoretical bound is known on the number of presentations of the training set that this convergence requires.

The *stochastic gradient descent* differs on the weight update, which occurs after every presentation of an example according to

$$W_{t'} = W_{t'-1} - \varepsilon_{t'} \mathrm{grad}_W J(x_{t'}, W_{t'-1}) \tag{10.6}$$

where $x_{t'}$ is the example x presented at time t', and $J(x, W)$ is the local cost, i.e. an approximation of the global cost on a single example x. For instance, with a quadratic error function

$$J(x, W) = J((e, d), W) = \| d - f(e, W) \|_2^2$$

where e is the input vector of example x, d is its desired output vector, W the current weight matrix, and f the function realized by the neural network. It is important to notice that the time scales are not the same in the two formulas.

Stochastic gradient descent is not a pure gradient descent method. The reduction of the local cost $J(x, W)$ at each step does not actually imply the reduction of the global cost C. Though the convergence of stochastic gradient algorithms has been proved in the Adaptive Filter literature, the convergence of back-propagation has not yet been proved. Some proofs have been derived for stochastic back-propagation, under restrictive assumptions, and for continuous time [Bot91], but no exact results are known yet about the speed of convergence. Nevertheless, empirical studies show that often the same level of learning can be obtained 10 to 100 times faster with a well implemented stochastic back-propagation than with a total gradient algorithm. This behavior seems to be justified by the amount of redundancy contained among the various examples of a training set.

When implementing the parallel processing of training examples, weight updates occur after the presentation of every block of $b = kp$ examples, where k is the number of examples computed by each of the p processors between two successive synchronizations, i.e.

$$W_{t''} = W_{t''-1} - \varepsilon_{t''} \sum_{i=1}^{b} \mathrm{grad}_W J(x_{i,t''}, W_{t''-1}) \tag{10.7}$$

This hybrid implementation of back-propagation will be further called a *block-gradient algorithm*. This is an intermediate case between stochastic and total gradient back-propagation. It is equivalent to the stochastic gradient method only when $b = 1$. This case implies $k = 1$ and $p = 1$, which is not very parallel! The alternative possibility consists in dividing the training set S, of size s, in p packets of $k = \frac{s}{p}$ examples, where p is the number of available processors. Then the weight updates occur only once after the presentation of the whole training set, and the network computes a total gradient back-propagation. All intermediate values of b imply $\frac{s}{b}$ weight updates per epoch.

10.3.2.2 AN EXPERIMENTAL LAW FOR THE LEARNING RATE AS A FUNCTION OF BLOCK SIZE

The behavior of a sequential back-propagation algorithm was observed for various sizes of blocks between two successive weight updates. Both the cost function and the success ratio on the training set are computed after each epoch (i.e. a single presentation of all the examples). The examples were always presented in the same order.

The application consists in classifying the patterns into three classes. The neural network is a one-hidden layer network, with 27 input cells and 3 output cells. The input layer is fully connected to the hidden layer, which is fully connected to the output layer. To each cell is associated the quotient of a constant value ε, called the *learning rate value*, by the number of input weights.

For stochastic back-propagation, and for the particular size of the training set, the number of hidden units and the learning rate value are chosen equal to 55 cells and $\varepsilon_0 = 0.15$ respectively. A first experiment was performed with a learning rate value $\varepsilon = \varepsilon_0$ constant in time and independent of the block size b. The results are presented below (Figure 10.6). As expected, the larger the size of the blocks, the more chaotic the behavior of learning. For total gradient back-propagation $(b = s)$, no convergence seems to be possible under these conditions.

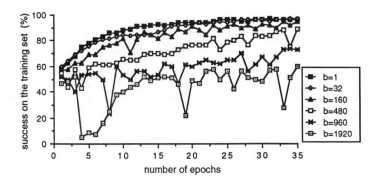

Figure 10.6 Learning behavior with constant learning rate $(b = kp)$.

This behavior is well known to be typical of back-propagation divergence for too large learning rates. In a rough approximation, when training a neural network with total gradient back-propagation, a learning rate equal to ε_0 divided by the size of the training set is currently recommended. The purpose of a second experiment was to refine this law, and to adapt it to intermediate block sizes. Then separate trials were performed, for different sizes of blocks, so that a critical learning rate value can be found, at the limit of the chaotic behavior of learning. A logarithmic regression of the results is shown in Figure 10.7.

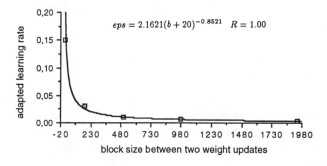

Figure 10.7 Empirical determination of a dependence law.

Finally, further experiments were performed, under the same conditions as the first ones, except for the learning rate value which follows this new law of block size dependence. The results are significantly better Figure 10.8. The learning curves are no longer chaotic; they are just slower when b increases, since ε decreases.

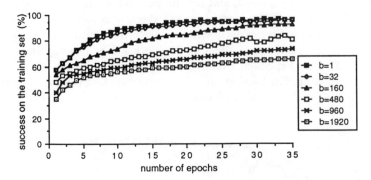

Figure 10.8 Learning behavior, with adaptive learning rate ($b = kp$).

Based on a fine study of the behavior of back-propagation on a classification problem, the following experimental law has been established :

$$\varepsilon = 2(b + 20)^{-0.85}$$

This law was confirmed by E.Fleury and C.Parent[1] on a character recognition application. They observed that the learning curves became smoother, but slower, when
applying an adaptive learning rate value as follows :

$$\varepsilon = 0.075 \, b^{-0.66}$$

More generally, an exponential dependence law between the learning rate ε and the
size b of the blocks may behave like

$$\varepsilon = k_1 b^{-\alpha} \qquad \text{with} \qquad 0 \le \alpha \le 1 \qquad (10.8)$$

where k_1 is a positive constant, and α is slightly smaller than 1. Though numerical values are application-sensitive, these dependencies seem to be widely applicable
to real-world problems. Nevertheless they will have to be confirmed and refined by
theoretical analyses.

10.3.2.3 AN EXPERIMENTAL LAW FOR THE SPEED OF CONVERGENCE AS A FUNCTION OF BLOCK SIZE

Since in the general case no theoretical convergence is ensured for back-propagation,
the word *convergence* must be understood in terms of some pre-determined stop-
criterion. In most cases, the learning phase ends when a given threshold has been
reached either by the success ratio on the training set (upper bound), or by the cost
function (lower bound).

The previous curves (Figure 10.8) show that, with an adaptive learning rate value,
the larger the blocks, the slower the growth of the success ratio. To make this observation precise, learning phases were run up to two successive stop-criteria (80%
and 90%) of success on the training set. New experiments were performed on various

---

[1] E.Fleury and C.Parent are "Master" students at L'Ecole Normale Supérieure de Lyon (France)

training sets, with various neural networks. In the case of the largest training set, the number of epochs is stored and visualized on Figures 10.9 and 10.10.

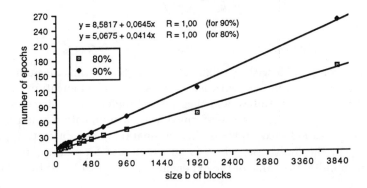

Figure 10.9   Convergence speed vs block size : a linear experimental law.

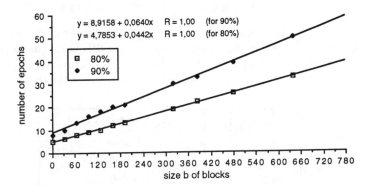

Figure 10.10   Convergence speed vs block size : magnification near the origin.

In every case, the following experimental law has been verified :

> When applying the block-gradient algorithm with an adaptive learning rate, the number of epochs required for a given convergence level is a linear function of the block size.

10.3.2.4   A CONSEQUENCE OF PREVIOUS EXPERIMENTAL LAWS FOR THE SPEED OF CONVERGENCE AS A FUNCTION OF THE LEARNING RATE

In the previous paragraphs we established two experimental laws in terms of the block size b. The first law asserts that an adaptive learning rate ε for parallel training may be given by equation (10.8). The second law asserts that the number of epochs N necessary to reach a given level of convergence varies linearly with block size, i.e. $N = k_2 b$. These laws imply further conclusions in agreement with established results. In fact, since

$$\varepsilon = k_1 \left(\frac{N}{k_2} \right)^{-\alpha}$$

and

$$\frac{N}{k_2} = \left(\frac{\varepsilon}{k_1}\right)^{-\frac{1}{\alpha}}$$

it follows that

$$N = k_3 \varepsilon^{-\frac{1}{\alpha}} \qquad \text{with} \qquad 0 \le \alpha \le 1 \qquad (10.9)$$

This result is comparable with the claim of A.Sato [Sat91] that the number of epochs is proportional to the ratio $\frac{1-\omega}{\varepsilon}$ with learning rate ε and momentum ω. This result was inspired by empirical studies, and then proved under rather strong assumptions. Since all of our experiments were performed with a momentum equal to zero, the experimental law established above is thus comparable, and, in fact, appears to be more general. In the limit case, which is an exact case for a linear neural network without hidden units, the value of the exponent α is equal to 1 and the two laws then coincide.

10.3.3 Speedup of a Parallel Algorithm

10.3.3.1 AN IMPLEMENTATION ON A NET OF TRANSPUTERS

Back-propagation learning, with parallel processing of training examples, was implemented on a T.node [Nic88] of 32 transputers, in a parallel C language [LS89]. Here the ring includes internal transputers of the T.node only (Figure 10.11), while for the parallelization of the recognition phase, the ring also includes the front-end.

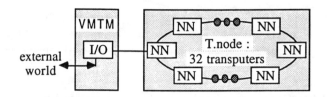

Figure 10.11   A ring of transputers on the T.node architecture.

The neural network to train is duplicated on each of the p processors of the ring (Figure 10.12). Two types of communications must be considered :

a scattering strategy : for sending examples from the frontal node towards each processor. Every block of $b = kp$ examples is pipelined in p packets of k examples each. In a simpler frame, without the calculation phases, this algorithm was proved to be optimal for scattering on an oriented ring of processors [FMR90].

a gossiping strategy : for exchanging the weight corrections ΔW_π computed by each processor on the ring.

Since locally

$$(\forall \pi \in \{1, p\}) \quad \Delta W_\pi = \sum_{i=1}^{k} \Delta W\left(x_i(\pi)\right)$$

then globally

$$\Delta W = \sum_{\pi=1}^{p} \Delta W_{\pi}$$

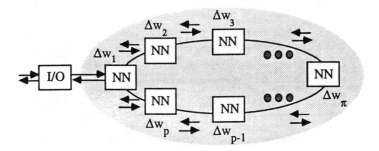

Figure 10.12 Parallel processing of examples, on a ring of p processors.

Between these two communication phases, each processor π keeps a packet of k examples and computes the feed-forward and the feed-back passes of back-propagation for each of them. For communicating the weight corrections, each processor adds the content of the current ΔW to its W matrix and then sends it to its successor. It also receives the corresponding ΔW from its predecessor in the ring (Figure 10.12). After $p-1$ steps, every processor has achieved its weight updating.

Figures 10.13 and 10.14 show the computational times, and Figure 10.15 the speedups, for a single epoch, according to the block size, the number of processors, and the number of examples which are computed by each processor at each step.

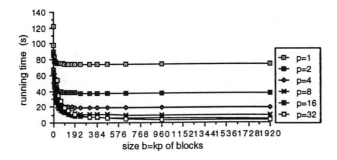

Figure 10.13 Computation times for one epoch, as a function of block size b and number p of processors.

Before the block size becomes sufficiently large for stabilization, many crossings can be observed on the curves. This can be explained by the pipelining of the examples, which actually wastes time when the blocks are small. This implementation has been selected to allow efficient training on possibly large data sets, which would be too large to be stored in every processor's local memory. As usual with algorithms, saving memory implies wasting time. Here the drawback disappears as b grows.

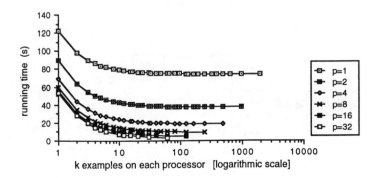

Figure 10.14 Computation times for a single epoch, according to the number k of examples computed by each processor, and to the number p of processors.

It is interesting to notice that total computation time by epoch is reduced from 122 seconds on a single processor (stochastic back-propagation), to 3 seconds on 32 processors (total gradient back-propagation). The main reason for this large difference is that the communication time for examples pipelining from the front-end to the ring of processors becomes prominent when the ring is reduced to a few processors. The right halves of the curves (large block size) are more significant for measuring speedups. When the blocks are sufficiently large, some very good speedup values are obtained, such as 3.96 for 4 processors, 7.76 for 8 processors, and 23.0 for 32 processors.

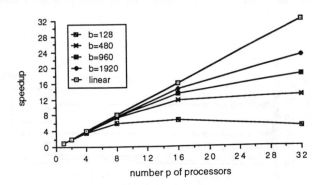

Figure 10.15 Speedups in terms of the number p of processors and the block size b.

10.3.3.2 MODELING

The implementation described above can be modeled by adding communication time and computation time. The startup time β and the 1-byte communication time τ were previously given in equations (10.1) and (10.2). For the communication time, we obtain the following formula, for a single presentation of a training set S :

$$T_1 = \frac{s}{b}[p(\beta' + k\ell\tau') + (p-1)(\gamma + \beta + w\tau)]$$

where

s is the size of the training set S

b is the size of blocks

p is the number of processors

k is the number of examples learned by each processor at each step

ℓ is the length of each example message

γ is the startup time for two parallel processes on a transputer

w is the size of the weight updates.

The first term inside the square brackets accounts for pipelining the examples, the second term accounts for diffusing the weight updates. Only significant, non-zero weights are actually transmitted, as a vector data structure. Since $b = kp$, dividing T_1 by s yields the average communication time T_{comm} per example,

$$T_{comm} = \ell\tau' + \frac{1}{k}(\beta' + \gamma + \beta + w\tau) - \frac{1}{kp}(\gamma + \beta + w\tau) \qquad (10.10)$$

The computation time can be modeled by the following formula :

$$T_2 = \frac{s}{b}[Aw + k(B + Cw) + pDw]$$

with the same notations as above, and where A, B, C and D are constant factors. The first term corresponds to initializing the weight corrections to zero, the second term to the time for back-propagation algorithm on k examples, and the last one to weight updating. Since $b = kp$, one obtains the average computation time per example T_{calc} by dividing T_2 by s,

$$T_{calc} = \frac{1}{k}Dw + \frac{1}{p}(B + Cw) + \frac{1}{kp}Aw \qquad (10.11)$$

Many experiments have been performed for $w \in \{300, 1650, 2400\}$ (respectively 10, 55, 80 hidden cells). They show that this model is rather accurate, and confirm that the communication time is smaller than the computation time.

The total time can thus be rewritten as a function of w :

$$T_{total} = T_{comm} + T_{calc} = X + wY$$

From the three experimented values of w, both X and Y have been evaluated for several values of k with constant $p = 32$ (Table 10.1), and for several values of p with constant $k = 20$ (Table 10.2).

k	1	6	12	20	30	60
$X(\mu s)$	150	60	45	44	44	43
$Y(\mu s)$	16.6	3.37	2.05	1.52	1.25	0.99

Table 10.1   Evaluations of X and Y, for various k, with $p = 32$.

p	1	2	4	8	16	32
$X(\mu s)$	310	170	104	74	59	44
$Y(\mu s)$	24.0	12.4	6.59	3.69	2.24	1.52

Table 10.2   Evaluations of X and Y, for various p, with $k = 20$.

From these values of X and Y, evaluations of the constant factors can be set as follows :

$$A \approx 2\ \mu s \qquad B \approx 500\ \mu s \qquad C \approx 23\ \mu s \qquad D \approx 15\ \mu s \qquad \gamma \approx 200\ \mu s$$

The computations of C and D values are fairly accurate. The other values must be taken as rough evaluations.

10.3.4   Speedup Versus Convergence

10.3.4.1   A CONDITION FOR SPEEDUP

Assuming that the number of epochs which are necessary to reach a given threshold of convergence (success percentage, or value of cost function) follows the experimental law established above, a condition for actual speedup can now be deduced.

We are looking for an expression for the learning rate $\varepsilon = \varepsilon(k, p)$ as a function of the number of examples k computed by each processor at every step, and of the number of processors p.

The total learning time is equal to the product of the number of epochs and the time required for a single epoch. With the notations above,

$$T = NT_{1epoch} = Ns(T_{comm} + T_{calc})$$

Hence

$$T = (\lambda\varepsilon^{-\frac{1}{\alpha}})(T_{comm} + T_{calc})$$

$$T = (\lambda\varepsilon(k, p)^{-\frac{1}{\alpha}})\theta(k, p)$$

where λ is a new parameter, derived from s and the previous constant k_3, and $\theta(k, p)$ is equal to $T_{comm} + T_{calc}$.

In order to study the variations of T, its partial derivatives according to k and to p are calculated :

$$\frac{\partial T}{\partial p} = -\frac{\lambda}{\alpha}\frac{\partial\varepsilon}{\partial p}\varepsilon^{-\frac{1}{\alpha}-1}\theta + \lambda\varepsilon^{-\frac{1}{\alpha}}\frac{\partial\theta}{\partial p}$$

and

$$\frac{\partial T}{\partial k} = -\frac{\lambda}{\alpha}\frac{\partial \varepsilon}{\partial k}\varepsilon^{-\frac{1}{\alpha}-1}\theta + \lambda\varepsilon^{-\frac{1}{\alpha}}\frac{\partial \theta}{\partial k}$$

It follows that $\frac{\partial T}{\partial p}$ and $\frac{\partial T}{\partial k}$ are identically zero when $\varepsilon(k,p) = \theta(k,p)^{\alpha}$, which gives

$$\varepsilon = \left[\ell\tau' + \frac{1}{k}(\beta' + \gamma + \beta + w\tau + Dw) + \frac{1}{p}(B + Cw) + \frac{1}{kp}(Aw - (\gamma + \beta + w\tau))\right]^{\alpha}$$

This expression differs from our law for ε as a function of $b = kp$ by the presence of a term in $\frac{1}{k}$ and a term in $\frac{1}{p}$. This means that one may hope for T not to be constant with respect to k and p (i.e. partial derivatives identically zero).

A condition for the existence of actual speedup is obtained by assuming that λ, ε and θ are positive (which is true under realistic conditions of experiments), and ensuring that $\frac{\partial T}{\partial p} < 0$ and $\frac{\partial T}{\partial k} < 0$.

$$\frac{\partial T}{\partial p} < 0 \qquad \text{implies that} \qquad \frac{\frac{\partial \varepsilon}{\partial p}}{\varepsilon} > \alpha\frac{\frac{\partial \theta}{\partial p}}{\theta}$$

$$\frac{\partial T}{\partial k} < 0 \qquad \text{implies that} \qquad \frac{\frac{\partial \varepsilon}{\partial k}}{\varepsilon} > \alpha\frac{\frac{\partial \theta}{\partial k}}{\theta}$$

The actual measurements of constant values in time modeling are not precise enough to check whether these conditions are satisfied, but the next section shows that actual optimal conditions can be observed experimentally.

10.3.4.2 EXISTENCE OF OPTIMAL CONDITIONS : EXPERIMENTAL RESULTS

Optimal value of k, for a fixed number p of processors

Starting from the numbers of epochs computed experimentally and from the times measured, the histograms shown in Figure 10.16 are obtained, for a fixed number of processors $p = 32$. They show how, given a limited number of processors, the optimal size of blocks, and hence the number k of examples to be computed on each processor at each step, should be chosen.

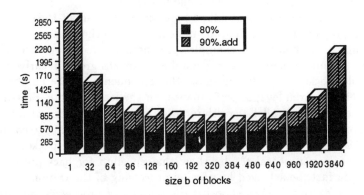

Figure 10.16 Optimal conditions exist for effective speedup.

For the experiment described herein, the optimal speedups are obtained for block size b in the range $[192, 384]$. Since $p = 32$, the best values for the size k of example packets are in the range $[6, 12]$. This packet size provides convergence to 80% and to 90% of learning success about four times faster than a small packet size $k = 1$, and at least three times as fast as a large packet size $k = 120$.

Optimal value of p, for a fixed example packet size k

Several evaluations have been computed from the previous measurements (Figure 10.17). They show that the number $p = 16$ of processors provides optimal speedup for small sizes k of example packets, and $p = 8$ becomes better in a higher range of k.

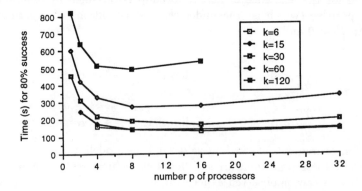

Figure 10.17   Optimal number p of processors, as a function of k, the packet size.

10.3.5   Conclusion

In order to design an efficient parallel implementation of back-propagation by distributing the training set, it is important to be aware of the alterations which the parallel algorithm implies for the gradient descent method. Even if actual speedup can be obtained, the performances, for complete learning, are far weaker than what the number of Mips [Sin90b] would lead one to expect.

In this section, three experimental laws were established about the speed of convergence of back-propagation. The first one indicates how to choose an adaptive learning rate according to the number of examples presented between two successive weight updates. The second law shows that the number of epochs grows linearly with the size of the example blocks. The last one shows the dependence on the number of epochs required to reach a given level of performance, on the learning rate. Starting from an implementation of the parallel algorithm on an MIMD computer, certain conditions on the value of the learning rate were proved necessary and sufficient to ensure optimal choices for the number of processors and the size of the example packets.

In conclusion, experimental results show that speedup for back-propagation convergence can, in fact, be achieved by parallel processing of the training set. However, caution must be exercised when choosing the number of processors, and hence when partitioning the training set.

10.4   PARALLEL SELECTION OF BEST PARAMETERS

The topic of this section is how to improve neural networks by searching and selecting the best conditions for learning with regard to a given application.

Nowadays a wide public has an interest in applications of neural networks to a variety of areas (pattern recognition, signal processing, expert systems, robotics, etc.). The world market was estimated to be \$ 7M in 1987 and \$ 138M in 1991, and an amount of \$ 584M is forecast in the perspective of 1994 [FG91].

However, the developer of applications still faces a lot of difficulties. The behavior of a connectionist model, according to the network architecture and the learning parameters, depends strongly on the application. Hence obtaining the best performances for a neural network implementation remains a difficult optimization problem.

We propose an optimization tool, called a *spy of parallel neural networks*. Its various aspects will be developed in sections 10.4.2 to 10.4.4. We digress briefly to make some precisions.

10.4.1   About the Optimization Problem

Some theoretical results have been established in the last few years, such as a lower bound for connectivity in local-learning neural networks [Abu88], some theorems on the power of multilayer perceptrons [Bau88, BH89], results proving that one hidden layer would suffice ([Cyb88, Fun89] based on Kolmogorov's work [Kol57]), and other mathematical proofs that multilayer feedforward networks are universal approximators [HSW90]. But these results often remain too theoretical to be used efficiently by the developers of applications. Most of the time, the only methods actually used are based on heuristics.

Empirical studies have been conducted with interesting results, for instance on learning capabilities of back-propagation networks [Fah88, Rae90], but they have often been tested on toy problems because of the long computation time that the learning phase requires. On the other hand, other studies reveal a chaotic behavior of neural networks [VVM90] so that most of the time developers ignore them, sometimes simply not knowing how to exploit them.

The problem of optimizing a neural network for a given application can be best viewed as a constraint satisfaction search [Ack87]. A distinction can be drawn between satisfying strong constraints :

> for a given function $f : \mathcal{D} \to \mathbf{R}$, find a point $x \in \mathcal{D}$ such that $f(x) \geq \gamma$, where γ is a fixed criterion (for instance $\gamma = \max_{x \in \mathcal{D}} f(x)$)

and satisfying weak constraints :

> for a given function $f : \mathcal{D} \to \mathbf{R}$, find a point $x \in \mathcal{D}$ which is as good as possible, with respect to some conditions

For instance, if these conditions are reduced to a stopping criterion, the distinction between strong and weak constraints becomes similar to Simon's distinction between *optimizing* and *satisfying* [Sim82]. From another viewpoint, this distinction can be viewed as the distinction between finding *the best point* and finding *a good point* [Ack87].

In the case of optimizing neural networks, the problem is that of a weak constraint satisfaction search. The set of parameters to be tuned defines the set $\mathcal{D}$. The function f is the performance of the neural networks on the application. We next develop an optimizing method for solving this problem.

10.4.2   The Spy of Parallel Neural Networks

A master process runs the *spy* process, and is linked to a farm of slave processes, each of which implements a complete neural network with its learning algorithm (Figure 10.18).

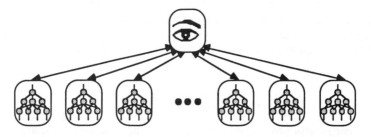

Figure 10.18   The master process and its farm of slave processes.

The spy process

- broadcasts the parameters which differ from a neural network copy to another,

- diffuses the examples to be learned or the patterns to be recognized,

- recalls the performances from each neural network.

When used as an exploration tool, the spy only stores the performances into files which can be exploited later on by drawing softwares. When used as an automatic selector, the spy program includes an algorithm for optimizing and selecting new sets of parameters. These topics will be detailed in further sections.

Many samples of a connectionist model need to be compared and the learning phase accelerated, so distributed parallelism is well suited to this task. The spy works with a large number of neural networks, all of the same type, learning from the same set of examples, tested on the same set of patterns, but differing from one another in some of their parameters. The neural networks work independently and require a local memory of large size to store and update their weights, so it seems natural to use a MIMD parallel computer, with message-passing communications. A straightforward implementation consists of a linear net of neural networks.

The spy is the only process which needs network wide communication. It has to broadcast the data to each neural network and to collect their results. The time of calculation of each network is very large with regard to the small number of results to send (for instance, a percentage of success after each epoch of learning). Moreover, the computation times of the various networks are different because of the different parameters, so the messages do not reach the spy at the same times. Therefore no bottle-neck is to be feared in message-passing.

The system was implemented on a T.node of 32 transputers [Nic88], with the aid of the TéNOR package [Bon90, ADT91] for the layout and communications. Transputers T800 were efficient calculators (see Table 10.3). They have been overtaken recently by fast workstations or by i860 processors, but the future transputer T9000 may make a comeback.

Machine and language	Learning time (s)	Testing time (s)	Total time (s)
PC - Pascal	95.00	54.00	153.00
Sun 3.60 - Pascal	12.52	7.98	20.76
Sun 3.60 - C	12.40	7.48	20.07
T800 transputer - C	5.25	3.18	10.74
Sparc-station-2 - C	3.43	2.15	5.65
i860 processor - C	0.68	0.48	5.61

Table 10.3   Running times for back-propagation.

Each transputer presents four communication links. The T.node accepts any configuration, on the condition that the order of its graph remains lower than four. Hence a star topology all around the spy is out of the question. A straightforward implementation consists of a linear net of transputers, each computing one copy of the neural network to be evaluated, and communicating with its neighbors (Figure 10.19).

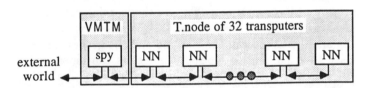

Figure 10.19   A linear net of neural networks.

The front-end is the only node of the T.node which deals with I-O devices, so it has been chosen to implement the *spy* process. All the other nodes, named NN (Figure 10.19), compute a complete neural algorithm, called the *neural net* process, which may be a back-propagation learning, or any other. All the NN nodes receive the same set of patterns but differ from one another in some of their parameters.

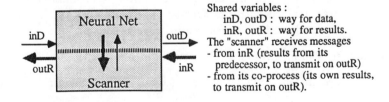

Figure 10.20   Two processes in parallel on the same transputer.

During the phase of evaluation, on each of the NN nodes, a *scanner* process runs in parallel with the *neural net* process, to take in charge the message-passing towards the spy, without stopping the calculations (Figure 10.20). The *scanner* sends each result as soon as it arrives from its own node or from the previous nodes on the linear net. At the end of the string, the node named last-NN is the only one which does not receive information from any other, hence its *scanner* process is slightly simplified.

To summarize, three types of processes are involved :

- the *spy* process broadcasts the parameters, different from one neural network to another, diffuses the examples to be learned or the patterns to be recognized and recalls the performances from each net, after each computation;

- the *neural net* process completes an entire neural network;

- the *scanner* process takes care of the communications, in parallel with calculations, both looking at the previous node and looking at its co-process on the same node.

10.4.3   An Exploration Tool: the Plain Spy

The *plain spy* is a collector of results and it allows one to draw landscapes of learning capabilities in some space of parameters, for a given connectionist model. Consider an example: assuming that an application has been chosen, the multilayer perceptron, with back-propagation learning, is selected. For this connectionist model, the two parameters which are the most difficult to adjust are the number of hidden units, which sets the architecture of the neural network, and the learning rate, which exercises an influence on its speed of convergence. So, let the plain spy explore a lot of values for both of these parameters and recall the learning and the generalization performances after an arbitrary fixed number of epochs. The results can be shown in a 3-D map: percentage of success, as a function of the number of hidden units and of the learning rate. If the number of epochs is considered as another variable parameter, then the result is a 4-D map, but it becomes rather difficult to represent graphically.

Parallelism is essential for constructing experimental diagrams of dependency between two or more parameters, because of the very long time of computation required by most of the learning algorithms. Applying the spy device, we obtain in one week results that would require seven or eight months, with sequential programming!

10.4.3.1   APPLICATIONS TO MULTILAYER NETWORKS

Experiments focus on the learning and generalization performances for feedforward *multilayer networks*, trained with the *back-propagation* algorithm [LeC85, RHW86]. Percentages of success have been measured in terms of two parameters :

1. the number of hidden units, in a unique hidden layer;

2. a constant coefficient, called Kalpha, such that the learning rate is defined by :

$$\text{learning rate} = \frac{\text{Kalpha}}{\text{fan-in}}$$

where fan-in is the number of input links to a unit.

Stochastic back-propagation is performed, with weight updating after each presentation of an example. A number of 35 epochs was fixed for these experiments. To compare the potential performances of a network, perfect convergence is not necessary. It may be sufficient to get the tendencies from a certain number of epochs. The following figures show how convergence profiles can be inferred from only 10 presentations of a data set (Figures 10.21 and 10.22). For instance, when the learning rate is too low (e.g. Kalpha = 0.05), the convergence is slow; when it is too high (e.g. Kalpha = 0.6) the learning becomes chaotic and no longer converges.

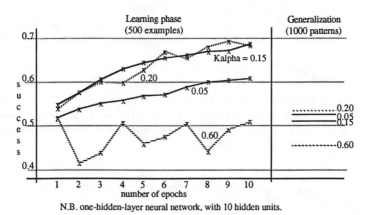

Figure 10.21 Convergence profiles after a small number of epochs: different values of Kalpha, with 10 hidden units.

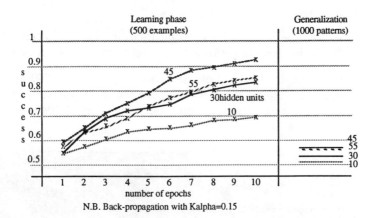

Figure 10.22 Convergence profiles after a small number of epochs: different numbers of hidden units, with Kalpha = 0.15.

It may be explained by considering energy landscapes, when expressing the error-function in terms of the weight space. If the learning rate is low, the steps of the gradient descent are small. Hence the progression towards the local valley is slow. If this coefficient is too high, the steps are so large that the state of the connections hurries here and there and jumps over from one valley to an other without reaching any minimum.

Using these parameters, two applications are experimented for back-propagation learning :

- a database of 5478 *configurations of a Tic-Tac-Toe board*, to be classified according to their nature (winner, loser or drawn game); these data are binary valued, the multilayer net having 27 input units and 3 output units;

- a database of 208 *sonar signals* used for experiments by Gorman and Sejnowski [GS88]; these real valued data belong to either the class of mines targets or that of rocks targets, the multilayer net having 60 input units and 2 output units.

10.4.3.2 EXPERIMENTAL DIAGRAMS

A great amount of numerical results are collected by the plain spy. To bring out the variations of the performances, a graphic representation is adopted. Each result is associated with a square: the darker the square, the better the performance. All the diagrams respect the following shade scale :

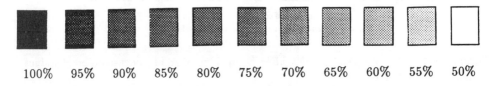

100%   95%   90%   85%   80%   75%   70%   65%   60%   55%   50%

Three diagrams are shown in the following pages. They represent fine-grain landscapes of various experiments, as detailed below.

1. For the Tic-Tac-Toe boards classification (learning stopped after 35 epochs), Figure 10.23 shows learning performances from a training set of 500 examples.

2. For the sonar signals classification (learning stopped after 200 epochs), Figure 10.24 shows learning performances from a set of 104 examples [GS88], and Figure 10.25 shows generalization performances on a set of 104 other patterns.

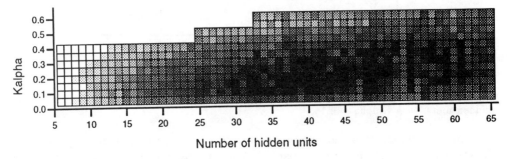

Figure 10.23   Learning performances from a set of 500 Tic-Tac-Toe examples.

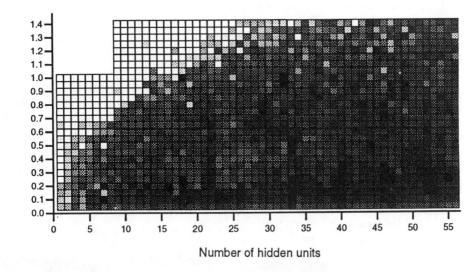

Figure 10.24 Learning performances from a set of 104 sonar examples.

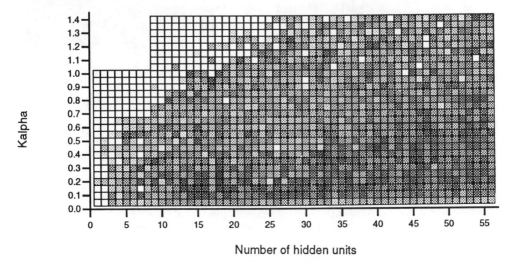

Figure 10.25 Generalization performances on a set of 104 sonar patterns.

When considering and comparing all these diagrams, a number of remarks have to be made. First, the diagrams share some common features that can be summarized in these terms :

1. fine-grain landscapes are rather chaotic ones, but a region of best performances can be discerned,

2. the shape - but not the size - of these good regions are roughly the same: ovoid, slightly tilted on the horizontal,

3. various isolated vertical strips of good results may be observed, for some peculiar number of hidden units, nearly independent of the value of Kalpha,

4. the behavior becomes more and more chaotic as Kalpha and the number of hidden units grow.

Of course the generalization performances give paler diagrams than the learning ones, but shape and location of good regions are similar. In order to display the good regions of parameters, an arithmetical mean was computed on horizontal bars of five consecutive numbers of hidden units. The coarse-grain diagrams obtained are shown in Figure 10.26. Each of them clearly bears out the region of good performances, the location of which depends on the size of the learning set. These observations enforce the following conjecture :

As the number of examples increases, the number of hidden units increases and the learning rate decreases.

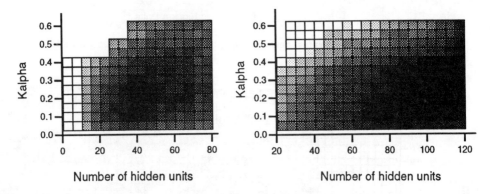

Figure 10.26 Coarse-grain landscapes, for Tic-Tac-Toe experiments. Left: training set of 500 patterns. Right: training set of 2739 patterns.

In each good region, the interest of the developer is to choose (a) the smallest number of hidden units since the number of weights, and hence the learning time, increase linearly with it; and (b) the lowest learning rate for which the learning success is more continuous and stable, hence the results are more reliable.

10.4.3.3   EXTENSION TO DIFFERENT PARAMETERS

Even when considering back-propagation learning in multilayer neural networks, the set of parameters to be explored can be different from those previously discussed.

For instance, during the development of an industrial application, it becomes evident that two-hidden-layer neural networks are more efficient than one-hidden-layer networks. Hence the spy is involved in the search for the best numbers of hidden units on the first layer and on the second layer respectively.

The behavior maps of both learning and generalization phases show the same features: performance is bad under a hyperbolic line which points out the necessity of a minimum number of about 300 weights. A graphic visualization of the learning performance is presented on a grey-level map (Figure 10.27).

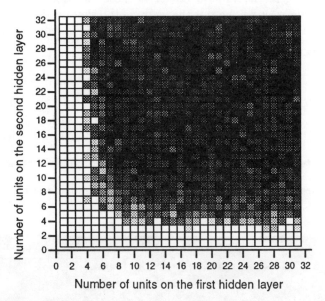

Figure 10.27 Grey-level map of learning performances, according to the number of hidden units in each of two hidden layers.

10.4.3.4 APPLICATION TO KOHONEN MAPS

The unsupervised learning algorithm of *Kohonen topological maps* was described in chapter 9. At each time t, the selected weight vector $w_{j*}(t)$ and its neighbors $w_j(t)$ in $V_{j*}(t)$ have to be updated according to the formula

$$w_j(t+1) = w_j(t) + \alpha(t)\left(x(t) - w_j(t)\right)$$

In order to take the adaptation gain $\alpha(t)$ and the neighborhood $V_{j*}(t)$ into account, a scalar kernel function may be introduced, as recommended by Kohonen himself [Koh90]. Let the lateral distance between neural units be denoted by v_{j*j}. The function

$$h_{j \cdot j}(t) = h_0(t)v_{j \cdot j}(t) = h_0(t)\exp\left(-\frac{\parallel r_j - r_{j \cdot} \parallel^2}{\sigma^2(t)}\right)$$

allows one to rewrite the weight update as

$$w_j(t+1) = w_j(t) + h_{j \cdot j}(t)\left(x(t) - w_j(t)\right) \quad (\forall j \in \{1..N_s\})$$

V.Demian [Dem91] used the spy to study two parameters which are relevant to the behavior of Kohonen maps learning, in the frame of a character recognition application. He makes the kernel function $h_{j*j}(t)$ more accurate by defining

$$v_{j \cdot j}(t) = \exp\left(-\frac{\parallel r_j - r_{j \cdot} \parallel^2}{S^2}t\right)$$

with $S = \frac{T-bord}{konst}$ where the value of *konst* is chosen so that the influence of the selected unit on its nearest neighbor is the learning threshold which determines where the learning algorithm halts. The neighborhood of unit $j*$ is reduced to $\{j*\}$ exactly when the learning time reaches the value $T - bord$:

$$h_0(t) = \frac{1}{1 + t\frac{1-H}{HT-bord}}$$

the gain coefficient H being equal to the gain $h_0(t)$ when t reaches the value $T - bord$. These two parameters appear to be the most determinant ones of the learning phase :

- $T - bord$ determines the rate at which the neighborhoods contract,

- H determines the rate at which the adaptation gain decreases.

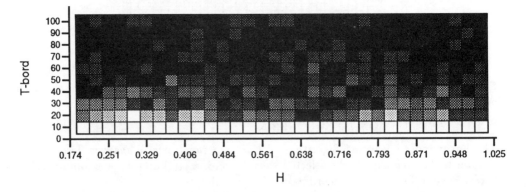

Figure 10.28 Performances of Kohonen map, according to the rate of neighborhood contracting, and the rate of gain decreasing.

The number of well identified patterns has been measured and the learning success ratio is represented by grey-level squares. Figure 10.28 shows performances of a 225-unit map, after learning on a training set of 20 characters.

10.4.4   An Optimization Tool : the Clever Spy

The spy becomes a *clever spy* when it analyses the results after receiving them and when it takes some decisions, depending on these results, with the objective of zeroing in on the parameters providing best performances.

More precisely, the connectionist model is supposed to have been determined by the developer, and then, among the mass of all the neural networks that are potential solutions for a given application, the clever spy selects one or a few nets which provide good learning and generalization performances. The problem is not only to select the good weights for the connections (for which learning algorithms have been created), but to select a good architecture (i.e. the number and the places of the connections themselves) and a good set of parameters for the network. The difficulty comes from the fact that an architecture and some parameters must be frozen before applying the learning algorithm, while the performances can be evaluated only after a long time of computation for the learning phase. Therefore parallel computation is essential for this task: the clever spy observes many different neural networks learning in competition and it adjusts the parameters so as to yield better and better performances.

The difference between the plain spy and the clever spy appears to be significant for the user, as shown in Table 10.4. This difference may become fundamental when designing a new neural network simulator. Most of those in existence nowadays [GLMB89, Nes88, Neu89, Mim91] urge the user to give the parameters of the model and, most of the time, this stage of the work puts him in trouble.

	"plain" spy	"clever" spy
who gives the patterns ?	the user	the user
who gives the parameters ?	the user	*the spy*
who collects the results ?	*the spy*	*the spy*

Table 10.4   A fundamental difference between the plain spy and the clever spy.

10.4.4.1   ALGORITHMS AND STRATEGIES

For a given connectionist model and a given application, with sets of patterns proposed by the user, the spy implements the following algorithm :

```
Choose an initial set of parameters;
Repeat
    send their own parameters to each of the neural networks;
    receive the performances from each of the networks;
    sort the networks by decreasing performances;
    choose a new set of parameters, from the best ones;
until the parameters are stabilized.
```

Each pass through the repeat-loop will be referred to as a *test*.

The first set of parameters may be chosen according to the size of the learning sets and with the help of theoretical results, if they already exist for the connectionist model in consideration. For instance, with back-propagation learning, the number of hidden units must be increased when the size of the learning set becomes larger. In the Hopfield model, the size of the net may be chosen according to the number of patterns to discriminate, according to the law that at most 0.15 x units number of patterns may be learned. For Kohonen maps, the dimension and the size of the map have to be adapted to the space and to the size of the training set. In any case the initial ranges of the various parameters should be set as wide as possible, and the notion of *performance* should be defined by the user.

For lack of other information, a rather general rule, called *strategy number 1*, may be applied. At each test, the spy computes the performances of all the neural networks involved in the learning phase. Then it selects the N networks which give the best performances, and it linearly interpolates new parameters from the best ones.

Another problem is how to stop the loop of tests. Most of the time the system stabilizes on small ranges of parameters, and the criterion to stop calculations may be a threshold in the size of variations of the different sets of parameters. But sometimes it falls into a cycle, which is another criterion for halting the loop, though often the results are poor: too wide ranges for one of the parameters, number of hidden units for instance. One solution is to restart from another set of initial parameters.

In the case of the back-propagation learning, *strategy number 2* has been developed to avoid this lack of convergence. The spy selects the M networks which give the best performances, sends new learning phases for the P networks with neighboring numbers of units, and it computes *in-average-performances* as illustrated on Figure 10.29. The end of the test is the same as for strategy number 1.

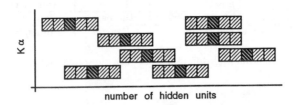

Figure 10.29   Neural networks for computing *in-average-performances* ($M = 8$ and $P = 4$).

The advantages of this second strategy are decisive. The results are more reliable and the spy avoids staying bound in a locally good region. But some drawbacks develop. The time of computation is increased by two learnings at each test and there is a larger risk of redundancy (several learnings with the same parameters can occur). Moreover strategy number 2 is adapted to back-propagation and to the number of hidden units, but it is probably not much more general.

10.4.4.2   APPLICATIONS TO BACK-PROPAGATION LEARNING

The clever spy algorithm and its various strategies have been tested both on the *Tic-Tac-Toe boards* learning and on the *sonar targets* classification. For a better understanding of the behavior of the clever spy, two diagrams develop the successive tests of the selecting algorithm for Tic-Tac-Toe experiments (Figure 10.30).

Grey rectangles represent the ranges of values for the two parameters. Small squares point out the five best networks after each test. The difference between the two strategies is shown on two experiments, starting from the same initial sets of parameters, with the same training and testing sets.

The interest of the developer is to choose the smallest number of hidden units and the lowest learning rate, so for each parameter the tables mention the final ranges proposed by the clever spy. The outcomes are comparable for the two databases: after a maximum number of six tests, either the sets of parameters have been sufficiently reduced, or a cycle has been detected. It may be noticed that no cycle has been detected when applying strategy number 2.

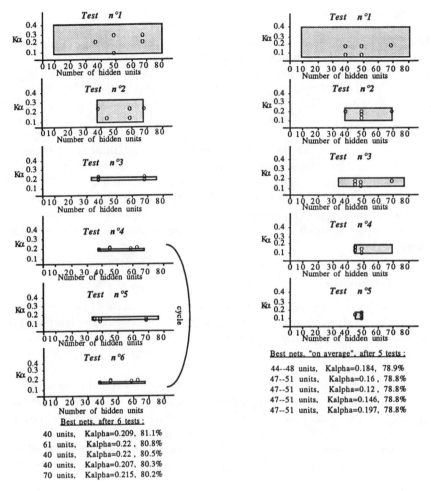

Best nets, "on average", after 5 tests :

44--48 units,   Kalpha=0.184, 78.9%
47--51 units,   Kalpha=0.16 , 78.8%
47--51 units,   Kalpha=0.12 , 78.8%
47--51 units,   Kalpha=0.146, 78.8%
47--51 units,   Kalpha=0.197, 78.8%

Best nets, after 6 tests :

40 units,   Kalpha=0.209, 81.1%
61 units,   Kalpha=0.22 , 80.8%
40 units,   Kalpha=0.22 , 80.5%
40 units,   Kalpha=0.207, 80.3%
70 units,   Kalpha=0.215, 80.2%

Figure 10.30 Behavior of the clever spy for the Tic-Tac-Toe classification: differences between two strategies.

10.4.4.3   APPLICATION TO QUICKPROP ALGORITHM

The *quickprop* algorithm has been developed by S.Fahlman [Fah88], in order to accelerate the learning phase for multilayer neural networks. The method is based on back-propagation learning, and on the use of local approximations of error by parabolas in weight space. This algorithm introduces a new μ parameter which controls the growth of the weights. The influence of this parameter μ on the quickprop behavior was studied by A.Fouilloux[2] , with the help of the spy, on the Tic-Tac-Toe classification. Experiments proved that the best values for parameter μ are in the interval $[1.25, 4.0]$. These results confirm and enlarge Fahlman's statements which recommend choosing $\mu = 1.75$.

---

[2] A.Fouilloux is a first-year student at L'Ecole Normale Supérieure de Lyon (France)

10.4.4.4 EXTENSIONS

The algorithm of optimization presently used by the spy process is an original one. It has the advantage of being simple to implement. It has already shown its efficiency on many occasions, for industrial applications [PMH92], as well as for perception modeling [APR92]. It presents several analogies both with *hillclimbing* methods and with *genetic algorithms* [Gol89]. The idea of working with several collections of neural networks, the performances of which become better and better after each *test*, appears to be similar to the genetic improvement of a population from generation to generation. The main differences are that the spy process does not yet implement crossover nor mutation. Some authors have proposed optimization methods for neural networks which are based on genetic algorithms, sometimes implemented on parallel computers [HSG89, MTH89, MK89, Kit90, Gru92, GU92, DM92]. The difficulty is then to find a well suited encoding for the significant features of the neural networks. A good direction for further research is probably the mixing of the spy principles and genetic algorithms.

10.4.5 Conclusion

The *plain spy* allows empirical studies on a large scale because of parallel computing. The time scale is reduced but it is clear that the complexity of the learning problem remains unchanged. Meanwhile, in a parallel direction with a theoretical approach, the results will help to investigate some of the still mysterious laws which govern the behavior of neural networks.

The *clever spy* gives promising results and needs to be expanded as a tool for designing real-world applications. This evaluation tool should be driven by a description language, as natural as possible, where the user will no longer guess the good parameters: this tedious task will be undertaken by the spy-system.

It is important to notice that the spy device can be applied to any set of parameters and to any connectionist model. It could be easily integrated into connectionist simulator software.

10.5 FINAL REMARKS

In this chapter, several ways of exploiting replication of neural networks on several processors were developed. In the first section, the neural networks are assumed to be copies of the same fixed neural network, without any modification of its weights, and to perform a recognition phase on pipelined pattern packets. This implementation provides the developer with very good speedups and allows real-time exploitation. However, it requires, prior to the recognition phase, a neural network which performs the application as well as possible. Hence the learning phase should have been previously improved. This is the problem addressed in the two other sections.

In the second section, the neural networks are assumed to be identical copies of the same neural network, the weights of which are to be adapted by learning, from pipelined example packets. In the case of back-propagation, the communication defers the application of weight updates and alters the learning algorithm. Hence the speedup obtained during the whole learning phase is not very good. Nevertheless, speedup is actually achievable by adapting the learning rate value, and by implementing this parallel learning phase with optimal example block size, in terms of the number of available processors.

In the third section, the neural networks are assumed to be different samples of the same connectionist model, and to perform their learning phase concurrently, each of them on the whole training set, so that the best parameters and architecture of the network are found. This parallel optimization tool is very efficient. It helps the developer in finding an effective implementation of his application, without wasting time in accelerating and automatizing this quest phase.

While the spy of parallel neural networks and the parallelization of the recognition phase by distributing patterns can be easily extended to any connectionist model, the parallelization of the learning phase is a much more difficult problem. Several solutions are proposed in this chapter and in the previous ones, principally for back-propagation learning and Kohonen maps training, arguably the most widely used algorithms to date [FG91]. The proposed methods are broadly discussed, but the review is far from being exhaustive. For further reading, one may recommend several articles dealing with transputer implementations of various models, such as [Abb88] for McCulloch and Pitts networks, [TFM90] for neocognitrons and [Tie90] for complex neural networks. Other authors have written general purpose articles [BS89, MW89], and application specific papers [CF88, LV89].

REFERENCES

[Abb88] Abbruzzese F. A transputer implementation of a McCulloch-Pitts network. In *Parallel processing and applications*, Chiricozzi E. & D'Amico D. editors, North-Holland, 1988.

[Abu88] Abu-Mostafa Y.S. Lower bound for connectivity in local-learning neural networks. *Journal of Complexity*, 4:246–255, 1988.

[Ack87] Ackley D.H. *A connectionist machine for genetic hillclimbing*. Kluwer Academic Publishers, 1987.

[ADT91] Adamo J.M., Dupont C.,Trejo L. C_NET, a C^{++} based language for parallel programming. Report 91-17, Laboratoire de l'Informatique du Parallélisme, Ecole Normale Supérieure de Lyon, France, 1991.

[APR92] Amghar S., Paugam-Moisy H., Royet J.P. Learning methods for odor recognition modeling. *Proc. of IPMU'92*, Palma de Mallorca, July 1992.

[Bau88] Baum E.B. On the capabilities of multilayer perceptrons. *Journal of Complexity*, 4:193–215, 1988.

[BH89] Baum E.B., Haussler D. What size net gives valid generalization? *Neural Computation*, 1(1):151–160, 1989.

[BL89] Becker S., Le Cun Y. Improving the convergence of back-propagation learning with second order methods. In *Proc. of the 1988 Connectionist Models Summer School*, Morgan Kaufmann, 29–37, 1989.

[Bon90] Bonello C. TéNOR : un configurateur symbolique pour l'architecture T.node, manuel de référence. Technical Report 90-01, Laboratoire de l'Informatique du Parallélisme, Ecole Normale Supérieure de Lyon, France, 1990.

[Bot91] Bottou L. *Une approche théorique de l'apprentisage connexionniste; applications à la reconnaissance de la parole.* PhD dissertation, Univ. Paris-Sud/Orsay, LRI, France, February 1991.

[BS89] Board J.A., Shue-Jen Lu J. Performance of parallel neural network simulations. In *Proc. of North American Transputer Users Group*, Salt Lake City, 1989.

[CF88] Chong M.W., Fallside F. Implementation of neural networks for speech recognition on a transputer array. Report CUED/F-INFENG/TR.8, Engineering Dept, Cambridge University, UK, 1988.

[Cyb88] Cybenko G. Approximation by superpositions of a sigmoidal function. *Math. Control, Signal Syst.*, 2:303–324, 1988.

[Dem91] Demian V. Etude des paramètres, pour les cartes auto-organisatrices de Kohonen, sur ordinateur parallèle Master dissertation, Ecole Normale Supérieure de Lyon, France, June 1991.

[DM92] Dasgupta D., McGregor D. Designing application-specific neural networks using the structured genetic algorithm. In *Proc. of COGANN-92*, 87–96, 1992.

[Dod89] Dodd N. Graph matching by stochastic optimization applied to the implementation of multi-layer perceptrons on transputer networks. *Parallel Computing*, 10:135–142, 1989.

[DT90] Desprez F., Tourancheau B. Modélisation des performances de communication sur le Tnode avec le Logical system transputer toolset. *La Lettre du Transputer et des Calculateurs Distribués*, (7):65–72, 1990.

[Fah88] Fahlman S.E. An empirical study of learning speed in back-propagation networks. Report CMU-CS-88-162, School of Computer Science, Carnegie Mellon University, Pennsylvania, 1988.

[Fah89] Fahlman S.E. Faster learning variations on back-propagation: an empirical study. In *Proc. of the 1988 Connectionist Models Summer School*, Morgan Kaufmann, 38–50, 1989.

[FG91] Fogelman F., Gallinari P. Neural networks: from theory to industrial applications. In *Tutorial Proc. of Neuro-Nimes'91*, EC2, France, 2–10, 1991.

[FMR90] Fraigniaud P., Miguet S., Robert Y. Scattering on a ring of processors. *Parallel Computing*, 13:377–383, 1990.

[Fun89] Funahashi K. On the approximate realization of continuous mappings by neural networks. *Neural Networks*, 2(3):183–192, 1989.

[GH89] Ghosh J., Hwang K. Mapping neural networks onto message-passing multicomputers. *Journal of Parallel and Distributed Computing*, 6(2):291–330, 1989.

[GLMB89] Goddard N., Lynne K., Mintz T., Bukys L. Rochester Connectionist Simulator. Technical Report 233, revised, Computer Science Dept, University of Rochester, NY, 1989.

[Gol89] Goldberg D.E. *Genetic algorithms in search, optimization and machine learning.* Addison-Wesley, 1989.

[Gru92] Gruau F. Genetic synthesis of boolean neural networks with a cell rewriting developmental process. In *Proc. of COGANN-92*, 55–74, 1992.

[GS88] Gorman R.P., Sejnowski T.J. Analysis of hidden units in a layered network trained to classify sonar targets. *Neural Networks*, 1:75–89, 1988.

[GU92] Guo Z., Uhrig R. Using genetic algorithms to select inputs for neural networks. In *Proc. of COGANN-92*, 223–234, 1992.

[Hec90] Hecht-Nielsen R. *Neurocomputing*. Addison-Wesley, 1990.

[HSG89] Harp S., Samad T.,Guha A. Toward the genetic synthesis of neural networks. In *3rd International Conference on Genetic Algorithms*, 360–369, 1989.

[HSW90] Hornik K., Stinchcombe M., White H. Universal approximation of an unknown mapping and its derivatives using multilayer feedforward networks. *Neural Networks*, 3(5):551–560, 1990.

[Kit90] Kitano H. Designing neural network using genetic algorithm with graph generation system. *Complex Systems*, 4:461–476, 1990.

[KM91] Kruschke J.K., Movellan J.R. Benefits of gain: speeded learning and minimal hidden layers in back-propagation networks. *IEEE Trans. SMC*, 21(1), 1991.

[Koh90] Kohonen T. The self-organizing map. *Proceedings of the IEEE*, 78(9):1464–1479, 1990.

[Kol57] Kolmogorov A.N. On the representation of continuous functions of many variables by superposition of continuous functions of one variable and addition. *Doklady Akademii Nauk, SSSR*, 144:679–681, 1957.

[LeC85] Le Cun Y. Une procédure d'apprentissage pour réseau à seuil asymétrique. In *Proc. of Cognitiva 85*, Paris, France, 599–604, 1985.

[LS89] *Logical Systems Transputer Toolset*. version 88.4, Copyright 1989 by Logical Systems, 1989.

[LV89] Leman M., Van Renterghem P. Transputer implementation of the Kohonen feature map for a music recognition task. In *Proc. of the Second International Transputer Conference*, Antwerp, Belgium, 1989.

[Mim91] *Mimenice* Mimétics S.A., Chatenay-Malabry, France, 1991.

[MK89] Muhlenbein H., Kinderman J. The dynamics of evolution and learning - toward genetic neural networks. In Pfeifer R., Schreter Z., Fogelman F.,Steels L., editors, *Connectionism in perspective*, North-Holland, 1989.

[MTH89] Miller G., Todd P., Hedge S. Designing neural networks using genetic algorithms. In *3rd International Conference on Genetic Algorithms*, 379–384, 1989.

[MW89] Muhlenbein H., Wolf K. Neural networks simulations on parallel computers. In *Proc. of Parallel Computing 89*, Evans et al., editors, 365–374, Elsevier, North-Holland, 1989.

[Nes88] *The Nestor Development System*. Nestor'Inc., 1988.

[Neu89] *Neuralworks Connection*. A Quarterly Publication of NeuralWare'Inc., Klimasauskas C.C., editor, 1(1), 1989.

[Nic88] Nicole D.A. Reconfigurable transputer processor architecture. ESPRIT Project 1085. In *Proc. of CONPAR 1988*, 81–89, 1988.

[PMH92] Paugam-Moisy H., Mignot J.C., Hartmann F. Recherche d'une méthodologie pour la prédiction par réseaux neuronaux. ESPRIT COMETT Seminar, Autrans, France, April 1992.

[Rae90] Raeth P. Using 3-D surfaces maps to illustrate neural network performance. In *Proc. of INNC-90 Paris*, 733–737, 1990.

[RHW86] Rumelhart D.E., Hinton G.E., Williams R.J. Learning internal representations by error propagation. In *Parallel Distributed Processing*, volume 1, 318–362, The MIT Press, 1986.

[Sat91] Sato A. An analytical study of the momentum term in a back-propagation algorithm. In *Proc. of ICANN-91*, Kohonen T. et al., editors, *Artificial Neural Networks*, volume 1, 617–622, Elsevier, North-Holland, 1991.

[Sim82] Simon H.A. *The sciences of the artificial*. The MIT Press, 1982.

[Sin90a] Singer A. Implementations of artificial neural networks on the Connection Machine. *Parallel Computing*, 14:305–316, 1990.

[Sin90b] Singer A. Exploiting the inherent parallelism of artificial neural networks to achieve 1300 million interconnects per second. In *Proc. of INNC-90 Paris*, 656–660, 1990.

[TFM90] Takayuki I., Fukushima K., Miyake S. Realization of a neural network model neocognitron on a hypercube parallel computer. *International Journal of High Speed Computing*, 2(1):1–16, 1990.

[Tie90] Tietz C. et al. Object-oriented simulation of complex neural architectures on parallel computers. In *Proc. of Cognitiva 90*, Madrid, Spain, 1990.

[VVM90] Van Der Maas H.L., Verschure P.F., Molenaar P.C. A note on chaotic behavior in simple neural network. *Neural Networks*, 3(1):119–122, 1990.

[Wan89] Wang S. Reducing the communication cost in simulating layered neural networks on a hypercube machine. In *Proc. of Parallel Computing 89*, Evans et al., editors, 375–380, Elsevier, North-Holland, 1989.

11

PARALLEL EIKONA: A Parallel Digital Image Processing Package

THOMAS KILINDRIS, IOANNIS PITAS

11.1 INTRODUCTION

PARALLEL EIKONA is a software package for parallel digital image processing. It has been developed at the Department of Electrical Engineering, University of Thessaloniki, during the ESPRIT Parallel Computing Action (1990-1992) [Pit91]. It combines high performance parallel implementation and a user friendly interface. PARALLEL EIKONA is written entirely in C. It currently runs on transputer machines under the HELIOS operating system and its user interface is supported by MICROSOFT WINDOWS. The whole application was initially developed on a Telmat T.Node machine consisting of 24 T800 transputers under the HELIOS 1.1A operating system. It was ported subsequently on MS-Windows based HELIOS 1.2 to make use of the windows facilities. Special attention has been paid to the portability of the package. Therefore, it can be easily ported on parallel Digital Signal Processing environments (e.g. Texas Instruments TMS320C40) and can be easily hooked under X-Windows.

The selection of HELIOS C, instead of another transputer-oriented language, was made because of the generic perspective adopted by the HELIOS operating system. Although HELIOS was originally developed for transputer networks, it can support various processors by providing a machine specific kernel. Another reason is the communication facilities. The programmer does not have to be concerned about communication topics, such as channels or protocols, as in OCCAM 2, because they are managed

---

Parallel Algorithms for Digital Image Processing, Computer Vision and Neural Networks, ed. I. Pitas
© 1993 John Wiley & Sons Ltd

by HELIOS in four levels [Per91]. The four levels provided range from a high level, machine independent, POSIX communication interface using the `write()`, `read()` functions to machine specific, transputer link access operations. The C language is suitable due to the internal structure of the application, the data objects needed and the shared data between concurrent processes. The support of MS-Windows by HELIOS is another important issue for digital image processing applications, particularly for PC transputer boards. The use of a processor pool supported by HELIOS allows multi-user applications and does not have the limits of single user application provided by development systems. UNIX compatibility also facilitates software development.

Several problems have been confronted during application development. Some of them are related to the transputer architecture (e.g., the absence of a memory management unit) and others were related to the operating system itself. The documentation of the message routing and of the entire environment inheritance was rather poor. Tools that would monitor the queued messages waiting at every link would help in developing programs using the POSIX level of communication, which are very hard to debug once they deadlock.

11.2   FROM TASKS TO PARALLEL PROGRAMS

The *Communicating Sequential Processes* (CSP) model has been adopted, which is very tightly coupled with the transputer architecture. According to this model, the program is decomposed in self-contained processes which have to be synchronized for coherent execution. Once they are synchronized, they can exchange data. This model is adopted by OCCAM and is used in HELIOS as well. Every process in HELIOS comprises a *Task*. Tasks may be composed of a number of very small subprocesses called *Threads*. There is a difference between Tasks and Threads: Tasks are usually executed on separate processors, whereas Threads run on the same processor on a time shared basis. Threads communicate to each other via *Streams* implementing the CSP concept on the Task level. Tasks can also communicate to each other via Streams, building the largest program construct, the *Task Force*. According to the CSP model a sequential program has to be partitioned into small independent parts. These parts can be either Threads or Tasks. The program that uses well defined threads has a more flexible structure and is called *fine grained*. If decomposition in Tasks is employed, a *coarse grained* structure is obtained. The optimum selection depends on the nature of the problem as well as on the available hardware implementation, although a majority of problems tend to be realized in a more or less coarse grained approach.

One of the essential jobs of an operating system is process scheduling as well as execution in the environment of resources provided. In the HELIOS distributed operating system this job is not trivial, due to the presence of a number of processors and the existence of complex program structures (Task Forces). A special language, the *Component Distribution Language* (CDL), serves to describe the Task Force, defining the Streams connecting the Tasks and several Task or machine related features. The presence of the CDL language is essential but not sufficient, since there are cases where networks are very hard to describe in CDL formalism. The object code created from the CDL compiler has all the necessary information to feed the *Task Force Manager*, a server responsible for Task creation, Stream allocation, and Environment inheritance.

Thread creation is a job that has to be carried out by every Task separately, as well as the synchronization and message exchange. A master Task and several worker Tasks exist in our application, depending on the configuration selected. In the rest of this chapter we shall refer to a worker Task as a worker process and to a master Task as a master process.

When the application starts, the worker processes enter a loop waiting for incoming requests. When a request is received via a Control Vector, a dispatcher unit decodes the operation requested, hands the Control Vector to the appropriate operation interface for execution and responds back to the master process. The worker processes spawning, including communication setup (Stream creation, Environment inheritance), are all left to the CDL shell - Task Force Manager cooperation [Per90]. The CDL script is written so as to support a generic $N \times N$ torus of processors [Cyp89, Pit91] and a private connection to the master process. As mentioned above, a Task Force includes also its inter-Task communication facilities. Actually, these facilities are streams. A stream is realized on a transputer link. Several streams may share a transputer link. Thus, the total number of stream connections may be greater than the total links available. Furthermore, the total number of processes can be greater than the number of processors, because several processes can reside on the same processor.

Some information about stream allocation made by the CDL is included in the master process module in order to realize the above mentioned scheme. Thus, the user has just to recompile the CDL script, whenever a network of a different size is used, by passing the number of processor elements N. An executable program is produced that spawns the appropriate worker tasks. A description of the software architecture follows.

11.3   SOFTWARE ARCHITECTURE

The model of data partitioning or data parallelism (also called *processor farming*) was adopted because it fulfills critical design goals:

- Balanced distribution of the workload across the processor network

- Automatic distribution of the application over any processor network

- Reasonable level of programming effort.

It is assumed that the network topology is a mesh of size $N \times N$. Although any other topology can be supported as well, mesh topology is close to the two-dimensional image geometry and preserves image neighborhood information, which is very important for low- and intermediate-level digital image processing that is the target of this software package. A modular software architecture has been chosen. Modularity facilitates portability on different hardware systems by changing the appropriate module. The surface complexity of the application is shown in Figure 11.1. The internal structure of the master task is illustrated in this figure. An instance of a worker process is shown in Figure 11.2. It can be clearly seen that the only module involved in the control of the processor network is the Cntv module. Other system specific modules are MSwmenus and MSevents, which are needed to implement the graphical user interface and to capture several MS-Windows related events respectively.

11.3.1   Data Representations

The internal representation of the images in PARALLEL EIKONA is the following. Two image formats are currently supported: 8 bit gray level (black and white, BW) images, and 24 bit true color images. The images are stored in a user specified pre-allocated image buffer pool. The buffer pool can be viewed as an array of **unsigned char** image buffers.

```
typedef image unsigned char * unsigned char *;
```

The declaration of the image buffer follows:

```
typedef struct ImagePoolElements{
BYTE Mode;      /* It indicates if the buffer is a monochrome
or a color one. */
BYTE State;     /* It indicates if the buffer is free or not. */
char *FileName; /* The name of the file where the image resides. */
SHORT X;        /* The X and Y size of the buffer. */
SHORT Y;
image MyImage;  /* Pointer to an unsigned char array. */
struct ImagePoolElements *Next; /* A pointer to link pool
elements in a list when dynamic allocation is invoked. */
```

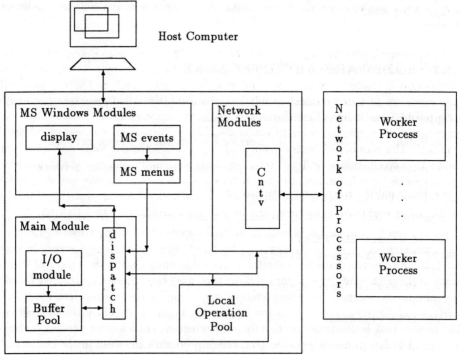

Figure 11.1   The surface complexity of PARALLEL EIKONA.

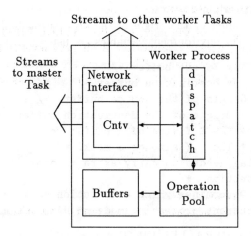

Streams to other worker Tasks

Figure 11.2 A worker process. Streams connect worker processes as well as the master to workers.

```
} ImagePoolElements;

ImagePoolElements *ImagePool; /* The root of the image buffer pool. */
image *Img_Buffer;
```

Each image buffer has a pointer **MyImage** to a two dimensional array of type **image** where the image data are stored. It also contains a link in order to form buffer lists. No distinction is made between color and gray level image buffers. Color image buffers are made up of three consecutive BW buffers, each of them representing the Red, Green and Blue image channel respectively. This representation allows monochrome processing on a specific color image channel, e.g., histogram calculation of the Red channel. The number of buffers allocated is predefined by the user on the command line and is fixed. Image buffers cannot be destroyed. They can be used to store either monochrome or color images on user request. Another object is the user selected *Area Of Interest* (AOI). It contains information on the area of interest specified by the user either from keyboard or by using the mouse. Its definition is the following:

```
typedef struct SLCTAREA{
SHORT X0; /*The upper left corner of the area of interest. */
SHORT Y0;
SHORT XX; /*The lower right corner of the area of interest. */
SHORT YY;
} SLCTAREA ProcArea;
```

Digital image processing routines usually have source and destination image buffers. The user refers to image buffers by a descriptor which is currently an integer number, limited by the selected maximal buffer number. Image processing takes place either on an entire source image buffer or on an AOI, according to the contents of an environment variable. Environment variables are used to specify frequently used values, such as the processing mode of a buffer or the origin of the destination buffer, where the result image will be placed. The environment variables are listed below:

```
int SRCBUF;        /* Source buffer */
int DSTBUF;        /* Destination buffer */
int XORG,YORG; /* Origin of the source buffer. */
int XDORG,YDORG; /* Origin of the destination buffer. */
int X_SIZ,Y_SIZ; /* The X,Y size of a buffer. */
int WX,WY;        /* The X,Y size of a mask. */
int INVERSE; /* Flag needed to carry extra information, or inverse
invocation of a function. */
int ACTV_MASK; /* Determines which Convolution mask is active. */
int MODE; /* The current processing mode of PARALLEL EIKONA. */
```

As mentioned above, PARALLEL EIKONA is capable of processing monochrome as well as color operations, by toggling the Environment variable MODE. Whenever a buffer is affected, its **State** and **Mode** are modified. A special function provides information to the user about the settings of the current buffers.

11.3.2   Module Description

Modular design was chosen to ensure flexibility and porting capabilities to several machines. Some of the modules are machine specific, e.g., the **display** module has the mission to visualize the contents of the buffer on display devices. The **MSevents** module captures events sent by MS Windows. Such events are the pointing device (mouse) coordinates, keyboard input, or window resize requests. As can be seen in Figure 11.1, **MSevents** drives the menu module. The whole user interface is defined in this module. Although MS Windows support the creation of menu driven applications, this is not the case with the graphics library for HELIOS. Thus, a lot of trivial facilities had to be written again from scratch such as the folded menu table, input boxes, etc.

The **main** module is the place where the image buffers as well as all Environment variables are defined. It includes a module to handle several I/O functions, such as loading a raw image or a user predefined convolution mask. This module contains also a **dispatcher unit**, which is used to interconnect several modules together. It handles messages from the **MSmenus** module, e.g. "display buffer", and sends the appropriate message to the related module. In the above mentioned example, the **display** module will be called to display the buffer pointed to by the **SRCBUF** descriptor. The dispatcher unit also drives the **Cntv** module and the **Local Operation Pool** in which several operation routines reside and are executed only on the master. The **Cntv** module contains all the network related functions including data as well as Control Vector transmission and reception functions.

A worker process has a slightly simpler structure. The **Cntv** module is present and is responsible for listening on the streams connecting it to the master for incoming requests as well as for delivering the entire communication traffic from/to the master and the neighbor worker tasks. Once a message arrives, a dispatcher unit chooses the appropriate "shell", which will be explained later in detail, in which the image processing operation will be executed. All the available image processing operations reside in the `Operation Pool`. The communication management will be discussed in detail in the following subsection.

11.3.3 Communication Management

All network-related activities pass through the `Cntv` module. This module is responsible for the data exchange between the master process and the worker processes across the processor network. Special functions that split an image buffer into smaller blocks and distribute them to the worker processes are part of that module. These functions automatically generate the boundary border area needed for neighborhood operations (convolution, median, etc.) on the image blocks. The image distribution subroutine has the following form:

```
void sendimage(WORD *CntVec,a,N,M,LN,LM,N1,M1,N2,M2)
image a;
int N,M,LN,LM,N1,M1,N2,M2;
```

An explanation of the symbols involved follows. The first argument `CntVec` is the Control Vector for task interaction that will be discussed later on. The second argument is a pointer to the **image** array of the selected buffer. The remaining arguments are the buffer dimensions, the processing window size and the coordinates of the area of interest of the specified buffer. Usually, images are split into square blocks. Another approach is to split them into slices. The second approach is simpler to implement but needs slightly more boundary data to be transmitted. A special control vector must be sent to each worker process to request a service from the processor network. Because of the large number of parameters that must be passed to each worker and the relatively large overhead introduced (1.4 ms) [Pow90, Per91] for every transmission (even for a single byte) when using the POSIX or the System level of communication, we have decided to use a control vector containing any related information to the process to be passed to the worker tasks. The control vector is currently an array of 32 words (128 bytes) as can be seen in Figure 11.3.

Length of Vector	Command id	. . .	Run State	. . .	Proc. Time	. . .

Figure 11.3 The Control Vector.

Its length is constant, although the related functions for the control vector transmission and reception can handle a variable length. The first field of the control vector contains the total length of the vector in bytes. The length field is examined; it is checked if it differs from a default value (indicating that a Control Vector of different length will be used for the current interaction), and the rest of the Control Vector is received. Some of its fields are listed below:

```
#define _LENGTH         0
#define _COMMAND        1
...
#define _RUN_STATE      10
#define _PRC_TIME       12
#define _INMASK         13
...
```

The variable length of the control vector has many possible usages. One of them is to encapsulate into the vector small pieces of data related to the process that will follow, thus avoiding additional transmission. An example of such a use is the convolution operation with a specific user defined mask. The mask often contains only a small amount of data (e.g., 9 numbers for a 3×3 mask) that does not exceed 256 bytes. In this case the encapsulation of the mask into the Control Vector is shown to the worker via the _INMASK field. An additional pointer field points to the start of the mask in the vector, thus allowing the worker to recover the mask data. The workers reply with an identical control vector indicating any possible errors that occurred during the operation performed. The specific function that is used by the master to send the Control Vector is the following:

...

```
send_CNTV(StrId,CntVec); /* Send the control vector to the worker
    using stream StrId. */
```

...

On the worker side, the corresponding worker has to wait until it receives the data required:

...

```
getCNTV(CntVec); /* The worker is waiting by default at StrId 0
    for master requests. */
```
...

When a specified operation must start, the master process transmits the Control Vector to all worker processes. After operation end, the opposite is performed: the worker processes transmit their control vectors and the master process is the receiver. The operation is finished when the master process rearranges the data received and saves them on the specified destination buffer. Each image processing operation belongs to a specific class. Neighborhood operations form one of these classes. Every operation of a class is executed via a standard "shell" which is specific to this class. WinPrc() is the "shell" for neighborhood operations. Every "shell" handles the allocation of the resources needed and performs performance measurement as well. The structure of WinPrc() is as follows:

```
void WinPrc(WORD *CntVec, void (*function)());
{
...

Carrier *fast_mem;

/* Allocate memory resources  receive buffer and
   result buffer, a,b. */

...

/* Receive the data vector and measure the
   reception time taken. */
...

/* Ask for fast memory resource. */
/* Measure the time taken for processing. */

if ((fast_mem)=AllocFast(OP_SIZE,&MyTask->MemPool))==(Carrier*)NULL)
/* EXECUTE Operation using the external RAM */
(*function)(a,b,Np,Mp,LN,LM);
else{
/* EXECUTE Operation using the fast RAM */
Accelerate(fast_mem,function,6*sizeof(WORD),a,b,Np,Mp,LN,LM);
speed_desc='f'; /* Indicate that operation was
    executed on the fast memory. */

}

/* Encapsulate the runstate of the operation and the
timing values in the CntVec. */

...

/* Return the resources allocated back to the system. */

FreeMem(fast_mem);
...
}
```

The application makes use of the fast memory resource provided by the on-chip RAM of the transputer. An acceleration of 33% can be achieved by using the special memory management handling functions provided by HELIOS. If no space on the fast memory is available, the execution of the operation takes place at the normal (external) RAM.

11.4   EXAMPLES

Many low- and intermediate-level image processing operations have been included in the package. The following classes of operations are included in its demo version:

- Window Processing Functions: Mean, Median, Min, Max, Convolution.

- Edge detectors: Sobel, Laplace.

- Global operations: Histogram calculation, output for further processing.

- Primitives: Addition, Subtraction, ANDing, ORing, EXORing and Inverting.

- Auxiliary operations: Clipping, Display, AOI selection, performance statistics, several I/O functions.

New operations can be easily integrated by adding appropriate modules in the Operation pool.

Operation	T_t (s)	T_{Com} (s)	T_{Proc} (s)
Sobel	3.50	0.750	2.580
Mean 5 × 5	6.64	0.760	5.710
Median 7 × 7	83.70	0.760	82.740
Conv 7 × 7	19.00	0.760	18.070
Sobel	1.60	0.180	0.657
Mean 5 × 5	2.39	0.182	1.440
Median 7 × 7	21.76	0.182	20.690
Conv 7 × 7	5.52	0.182	4.510
Sobel	1.24	0.028	0.166
Mean 5 × 5	1.49	0.032	0.363
Median 7 × 7	6.44	0.031	5.180
Conv 7 × 7	2.29	0.035	1.077

Table 11.1   Performance measurement for parallel digital image processing operations. Each table section corresponds to a 1, 4, 16 transputer network respectively.

The main goal in parallel processing is to achieve a possibly linear speedup versus the number of processors used. The package can display processing statistics such as data transfer time, elapsed processing time, etc. Table 11.1 depicts such information. The three parts of Table 11.1 correspond to 1, 4 and 16 worker processors respectively. T_t denotes the total time elapsed for the specific operation where T_{Com} is the time spent on data transfer and T_{Proc} is the average processing time. All times were measured in seconds. T_{Com} actually represents the time taken to transfer the data from the master process to the worker process only. Time spent for synchronization, routing, etc., is not taken into account in T_{Com}. Thus $T_t > T_{Proc} + T_{Com}$. These times were obtained by loading one worker task per processor. The image size was 256×256 bytes. The size of the processing window used is indicated in the table as well. The transputers used were T800s at 20 MHz with a link speed of 10 Mbits/s. An almost linear speedup was achieved for operations that require a large amount of computational power, e.g. data sorting or floating point arithmetic. The median filtering is such a case. An overview of the speedup of some operations is presented in Table 11.2. A graphical representation of the speedup achieved can be seen in Figure 11.4. The speedups of median filtering and Sobel edge detector are depicted because they represent the best and the worse speedup in the neighborhood operation class respectively.

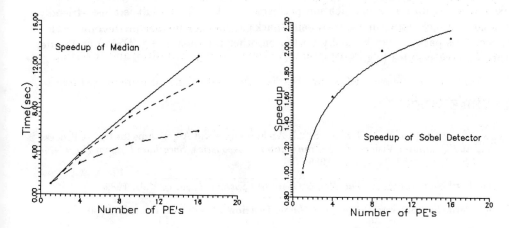

Figure 11.4 Speedup of median filtering and Sobel edge detector.

	Speedup			
Operation	Number of PE's			
	1	4	9	16
Sobel	1.0	1.61	1.98	2.08
Mean 3 × 3	1.0	1.59	1.94	2.01
Mean 5 × 5	1.0	2.39	3.40	3.83
Mean 7 × 7	1.0	2.89	4.81	5.67
Median 3 × 3	1.0	2.92	4.78	5.96
Median 5 × 5	1.0	3.61	7.19	10.53
Median 7 × 7	1.0	3.80	7.70	12.84
Max 3 × 3	1.0	1.83	2.35	2.50
Max 5 × 5	1.0	2.65	4.02	4.77
Max 7 × 7	1.0	3.13	5.31	6.86
Conv 5 × 5	1.0	2.85	4.50	5.47
Conv 7 × 7	1.0	3.27	5.77	7.89

Table 11.2 Speedup of operations versus the processor number.

Sobel speedup is poor because its code was written so as to obtain optimal execution (low computational load). Therefore communication overhead is large compared to the processing time. Median filtering uses shell sorting which is slow (on purpose). Thus, its computational load and, subsequently, the speedup is high.

11.5 CONCLUSION

A research prototype software system for parallel digital image processing has been presented in this chapter. It runs under the HELIOS operating system on transputer machines. Its user interface is based on Microsoft Windows. HELIOS has been chosen for its generic parallel perspective. Although it is a good tool conceptually, its use created difficulties due its documentation and instability. Special measures have been taken to speed up its communication performance. The final result is a user-friendly, modular parallel digital image processing package having very good numerical performance. This package can be easily ported on other processors (e.g. DSPs) and under other window systems (e.g. X-Windows).

REFERENCES

[Cyp89] R. Cypher and J. L. C. Sanz. SIMD Architectures and Algorithms for Image Processing and Computer Vision, *IEEE Transaction on Acoustics, Speech and Signal Processing*, ASSP-37(12):2158–2174, Dec. 1989.

[Per89] Perihelion Software. *The Helios Operating System*, Prentice Hall, 1989.

[Per90] Perihelion Software. *The CDL Guide*, Distributed Software Limited, 1990.

[Per91] Perihelion Software. *The Helios Parallel Operating System*, page 236, Prentice-Hall, 1991.

[Pit91] I. Pitas. ESPRIT Parallel Computing Actions: an Overview, in T.S. Durrani, W.A. Saudham, I.J. Soraghan, S.M. Forbes, *Application of Transputers 3*, pages 26–31, IOS Press, 1991.

[Pow90] J. Powell and N. Garnett. Helios Performance Measurement. Tech. Report No. 22, Perihelion Software, February 1990.

12

Parallel Architectures and Algorithms for Real Time Computer Vision

ERNEST HIRSCH

12.1 INTRODUCTION

One of the goals set for the integration of parallel architectures (e.g. transputer networks) in real-time vision systems for medium to high level processing is to contribute to the development of heterogeneous parallel processing structures for real time image processing and vision based applications. Furthermore, such structures should also be usable either as a development system for vision applications, or as hardware platforms for actual applications, integrated in the corresponding application environments.

In order to achieve application dependent "real time" performance, it is necessary, with the technology available today, to use heavily parallelism for image processing and some higher level treatments. Specifically, the hardware has to be matched to the type of processing to be run on it. This leads to the design and implementation of heterogeneous pipelined structures, due to the various processing levels usually implied by an application. Then, the synchronized use of such systems calls for a carefully designed programming environment, facilitating the implementation of the desired application on the system. Two distinct approaches have been used for the design of image processing systems. The first is based on a modular functional point of view, whereas the second one aims to implement a reconfigurable, flexible and fully programmable structure. Both approaches lead to the realization of systems able to carry out most of the low level image processings in video real time. Development of methods and design of new architectures call thus for careful studies and possibly experimentation. This should be facilitated by the set-up of development centers grouping hardware and software resources. A possible configuration of such an integrated development system for computer vision applications will be indicated, together with some representative applications.

Parallel Algorithms for Digital Image Processing, Computer Vision and Neural Networks, ed. I. Pitas
© 1993 John Wiley & Sons Ltd

12.2 USE OF PARALLEL ARCHITECTURES FOR COMPUTER VISION APPLICATIONS

Most of the current industrial applications of machine vision, relying on image processing systems with high computation power, are concerned with inspection, quality control, assembly, control of manufacturing processes, autonomous vehicle guidance and robotics. Optical sensing of the application environment, evaluation of the images of the scene and physical reaction after interpretation of the image contents are among the most effective and efficient means for the analysis of the environment and for acting in an appropriate way. Machine vision is thus a way to automate in a flexible and intelligent manner the chain of actions for the applications previously described in which almost the same happens more or less quickly. Vision, in fact, provides a huge amount of information about our environment without any direct physical contact. That is why a lot of efforts have been made to give technical systems the capability to "see", more precisely to sense, the world or at least a part of it. This leads to *artificial vision* (see [Hor86]) that combines theories and/or results from various scientific fields such as information processing theory, decision theory, biology and psychology, with also a strong dependence on computer technology and its evolution. The goal of computer or machine vision is then to extract high-level information about the environment from the low-level information contained in one or a sequence of images of that environment. Because of the amount of information contained in an image, machine vision calls for high computing power. Provided the required hardware is available, this leads to the development of vision systems that aim to solve these problems automatically, with a computation speed compatible to that needed by the application to be solved. This naturally leads to the use of parallel computer architectures, and more precisely to heterogeneous pipelined structures. A lot of computer vision systems have been designed, built and used in recent years for the extraction of the required information from images of the application environment [Mil85, TTC85, San88]. In these systems, the fact that illumination and part and/or actuator can be controlled is usually taken into account, as well as other aspects like cost, accuracy, speed and flexibility.

However, the different systems, proposed for the industrial applications quoted above, can often not provide the performance and processing speed needed at reasonable cost. This is also the case for more sophisticated applications such as, for example, the automated vision based on-line inspection of manufactured parts in order to detect and locate different defects on the part under control to optimize the production rate. The solution of this kind of problem requires again detection, comparison and/or classification, identification, estimation and description. Specific requirements for the vision systems running such vision tasks have thus firstly to be defined and secondly to be satisfied. With the technology available today, in order to run the application in "real time", it is necessary to use heavy parallelism for the image processing and some higher level treatments required by the application. More specifically, one has also to match hardware to the envisioned processing. This leads to the design and implementation of heterogeneous pipelined structures, in which each component is optimized with respect to the type of processing it has to perform. Furthermore, the elements of the pipeline often imply an internal parallelism (for example, systolic processors, arrays of processors such as transputer networks). Last but not least, the synchronized use of such systems calls for a carefully designed programming environment, partly relieving the user of the burden of programming such systems.

The following section introduces the definitions and concepts involved in the design and implementation of such vision systems. Section 12.4 describes two image processing systems already realized, using two different approaches. The first system, designed and built at the IITB-Fhg Institute, Karlsruhe, FRG, uses a modular functional approach; whereas the second one, developed by ENSPS/LSIT in the framework of an ESPRIT Project, aims to implement a reconfigurable, flexible and fully programmable structure. Both systems are able to carry out most of the low level image processing in video real time. In the last section, representative applications using the two systems are presented. The contribution is concluded by a brief discussion, giving tentative rules for the design of such heterogeneous, real time oriented vision systems considering the applications.

12.3 DEFINITIONS AND GENERAL CONCEPTS

In vision applications, two different processing steps can usually be defined. The first step deals with the so-called image processing, which transforms an input image into a modified output image in order to, for example, enhance the image quality (e.g. noise reduction and distortion correction), correct the image acquisition conditions or prepare a subsequent feature extraction. Then some segmentation of the enhanced image is done in order to delimit different regions in the image. Regions can be defined, for example, as zones of uniform brightness or can be delimited by detecting the contours of these regions. The extracted features represent (or model) some characteristic properties of the information content of the scene (perimeter, connectivity, moments, etc.). Thus, after having extracted the features required by the application and having computed a description of the image content, the second step exploits this description in order to compute statements about the meaning of the image content. These statements are then further used for firstly defining and secondly carrying out the actions on the environment implied by the application. Thus, this interpretation of the image is used to achieve a well defined goal (e.g. recognizing objects, taking decisions, vehicle guidance, inspection, acting on the real-world, etc.). This two step process (the truncated grey rectangles in the figure) is illustrated in Figure 12.1. The processing performed by the machine vision system can be referred to as image processing applied to visual perception. A machine vision system, taking into account the above defined processing steps, can then be seen as a technical system having to analyze images in order to produce a description of what is represented in the image (see Figure 12.1).

The imaging device (generally a CCD camera) produces as input for the machine vision system a pixel image. The purpose of the vision system is to transform the low-level information content of the input image into a number (as small as convenient) of high-level information pieces, in order to deliver a description of the real-world scene. This description can be further used to take a decision, which, in turn, leads to one or more actions to be carried out on the real-world through a feedback-loop. Instead of the feedback free processing model of Figure 12.1, a more complex processing scheme, including a feedback loop called the interpretation loop, has to be imagined. Figure 12.2 shows the model first proposed by Kanade [Kan78, Kan80] and modified by Nagel [Nag78, Nag85, Nag87]. It should be noted that this model allows iterative image description interpretation and eventual control of the data acquisition parameters. Furthermore, the model implies different types of knowledge for the interpretation process in both the image (low level) and scene (high level) domains. More and more industrial vision applications rely on such a processing scheme, as the examples in section 12.5 will illustrate.

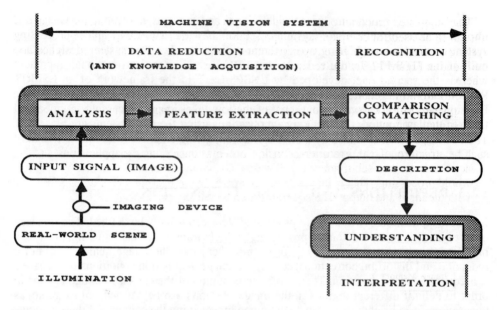

Figure 12.1 A typical scheme for visual perception indicating the processing steps for a typical computer vision application.

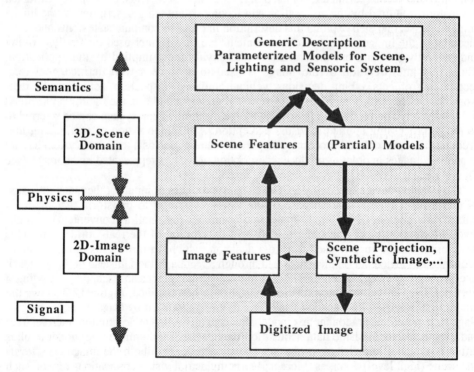

Figure 12.2 Computer vision as an iterative interpretation process (after [Nag78, Nag85]).

The suggested processing model can be applied to the design of an image processing system to be used for complex vision applications. Figure 12.3 exemplifies how a system relying on this knowledge based approach treats the image data. The interpretation loop can be found in Figure 12.3 if one recognizes that :

- Going from the generic description down to the scene projection (or synthetic image) implies *a priori* knowledge in both the image and scene domains and the results of the executed computing loops. This is summarized in Figure 12.3 through the two knowledge blocks.
- The structure of the processing track from raw data up to interpretation results and actions is further subdivided in sub-processes having in charge specific parts of the whole processing. This is indicated in Figure 12.3 with truncated rectangles associated with the input and output data structures used by the sub-processes.

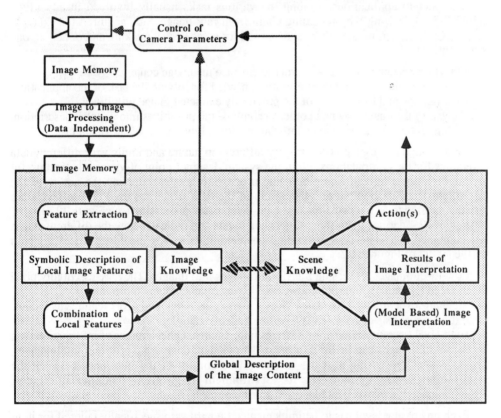

Figure 12.3   Image processing hardware model for vision based applications (after [Nag88]).

The proposed model for the hardware is a direct result from the fact that actual image processing and industrial vision systems are mainly based on a modular approach for the implementation of the path from raw data up to interpretation data of the processing model of Figure 12.2, the other processing path being mainly implemented using software approaches. In the following, we will thus focus on the first, direct processing path.

The treatment of image data, excluding the determination of action control, starts, following the model of Figure 12.3, with some data independent pre-processing, preparing the determination of the required image primitives (e.g. elements of a contour), carried out in a second step. Then several steps of combination of extracted primitives take place, leading to a description hierarchy in the image domain:

- the image description is a combination of image objects (e.g. the image content),
- an image object is a combination of image structures (e.g. an object in the image),
- an image structure is an assembly of image elements (e.g. the four contour segments of a square in the image),
- an image element is the already mentioned image primitive (e.g. an edge segment of a contour).

It follows from the above that image processing implies very different processing tasks with respect to applications. Among the various tasks usually involved in any given application, following the processing chain from raw image data, acquired for example using a CCD sensor, up to high level data used for some decision taking and/or action, one can mention :

- correction of acquired images in order to enhance the image content,
- extraction of the specific image primitives needed for solving the task of the application,
- identification and localization of the previously extracted image primitives,
- analysis of the imaged scene in order to combine the primitives into a global description,
- exploitation of the image data combinations for solving the specific vision task.

These image processing tasks are very different in nature and imply very different data structures for the computations. From the system designer point of view, it is then useful to sub-divide a complete vision task into processing levels, reflecting the nature of the operations to be carried out and the nature of the data structures used. These levels are usually referted to as low, medium and high-level image processing (see Figure 12.4).

Figure 12.4 defines these three processing levels and indicates how the different stages are combined in a sequential processing scheme, implementing the direct processing path of the model of Figure 12.2:

- Low-level image processing transforms images into images. They are essentially pixel oriented operations: threshold, lowpass filtering, mathematical morphology.
- Medium-level image processing needs images as input and gives features as output. Extraction of lists of contours is a widely known example.
- High-level operations transform features into features. Other sources of information than the initial images can be used (*a priori* knowledge, databases, artificial intelligence). High-level processing also has in charge the control of the interfaces between the machine vision system and its environment (e.g. man—machine interfaces, communication network interfaces, actuator interfaces).

Each processing level has to be implemented on hardware specifically tailored for it, in order to perform efficiently its tasks.Taking this matching into account, leads then directly to the design of heterogeneous pipelined image processing structures for complex vision applications. It has also to be noticed that the information density is increasing from the low-level to the high-level stage, together with the complexity of the operations performed. The amount of data to be computed is decreasing from the low-level to the high-level stage, and less and less computing power is needed, but more and more flexibility is required.

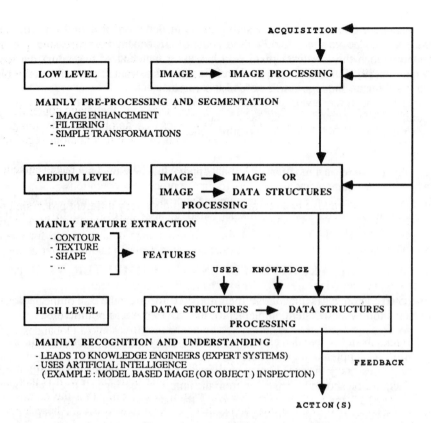

Figure 12.4 Processing levels and operation chaining for a typical vision based application.

Following Figure 12.4, the basic structure of an image processing system can also be defined around three parts, each having different requirements to the processing architecture :

- The acquisition, pre-processing and restitution of images.
- The processing in the image domain or the so-called iconic processing step. In this case, the needed algorithms and data structures are nearly directly related to the pixel organization in the image.
- The model based exploitation of image primitives and content or the so-called symbolic processing step. In this case, the data structures implied are almost exclusively a function of the type of computation to be carried out.

As already mentioned, many recent publications show how to implement a vision system based on the described approach (for a discussion, see, for example, [San89, Duf90]). Three basic structures, for so-called general purpose systems, are today clearly emerging :
- arrays of mesh-connected processors with more or less computation power,
- pipelines and cascaded structures, chaining different hardware modules with more or less flexibility,
- bus-oriented processing structures with powerful, more or less specialized micro-processors.

For special purpose processing, systolic arrays or dedicated LSI or VLSI integrated circuits can also be very efficiently used [Fou86]. However, bootlenecks are usually encountered when the low-level pixel data has to be matched with the high-level data structures [Duf89], [Duf90]. It seems therefore not possible to design a system able to perform well for all the algorithms needed in computer vision. However, heterogeneous structures for the three levels of processing, with an integrated control strategy and incorporating different modes of parallelism, appear to be today the best compromise. With respect to the use of such systems, two approaches, exemplified in the next sections, are possible :

- The first is based on a modular functional approach, where the user has just to choose the appropriate chaining and parameters for image processing operations.
- The second is based on a fully programmable approach, where the user can develop his own software for all the system components and organize his own data flows and image processing sequences.

12.4 PARALLEL ARCHITECTURES FOR COMPUTER VISION

Sophisticated vision tasks like those mentioned in the Introduction imply numerous requirements for a vision system, implemented into the systems to be described :

- Bottlenecks should be avoided either by extending or by specially organizing the system. Addition of supplementary modules for parallelization and the support of general purpose processors with special hardware processors help to remove these bottlenecks.
- Image acquisition should be separated from the image processing and interpretation steps (see Figures 12.2 and 12.3) in order to process the data at maximum speed.
- The organization of the data should not be fixed in order to give the system the greatest flexibility.
- With respect to signal acquisition, storage and display, different sensors must be available, differing in format but also in physical nature, in order to be able to process multidimensional images and multisensorial signals.
- The processing of images, isolated, endless or in sequence, should be possible. Furthermore, the system hardware must be able to adapt to particular classes of tasks, varying in complexity, in order to allow a cost effective match of the system to the application to be solved. Bus-oriented multiprocessor architectures whose modules are the processing elements can efficiently be used. These modules can be classified into three categories (for details see [PHN+88, DD190]) :

    1. video I/O modules for acquisition, storage and display,
    2. pixel oriented image processing modules working synchronously with the pixel rate and offering the possibility of parallel and pipelined processing, for data compression in the iconic stage (image processing and feature extraction),
    3. non pixel oriented data processing modules working asynchronously with the pixel rate, for statement generation in the symbolic stage.

- The system should offer the possibility of being used as a development system (e.g. for testing the image processing or evaluating the processing steps needed for solving a vision task), or as part of a workstation (e.g. for the solution of real problems in the industrial environment). A hierarchical layered approach can be retained for the software organization, which does not require the user to be a low level programming expert. Furthermore, an exhaustive package of image processing and evaluation programs should be provided. The development of problem oriented software should be possible using a high level language and ergonomic man—machine interfaces helping the user in his application software developments.

The architecture of the parallel vision machines developed (see Figures 12.5 and 12.10) implements the requirements stated in the preceding section and is matched with the three processing levels described in Figure 12.4. The image to be interpreted is sent to the low-level processing unit. The result is then fed to the medium-level processing unit which produces features for the high-level processing unit.

A feedback-loop has to be foreseen from the high-level stage to the medium and low-level stages (use of high-level knowledge to guide the processing of the lower stages). The general architecture looks like a system of pipelined processing elements, each of the processing units being able to make use of its own internal parallelism, adapted to the type of computation to be performed (leading to the concept of multi-parallelism).

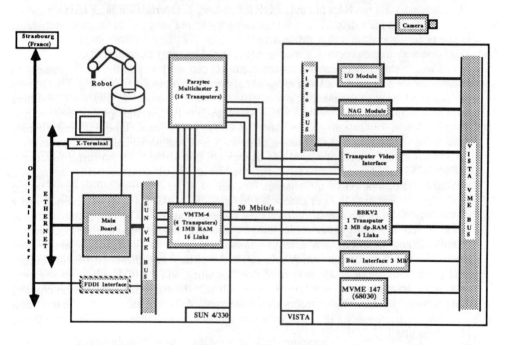

Figure 12.5   The machine vision system developed at IITB-Fhg.

12.4.1 The Low-Level Processing Units

The low-level processing is performed either with a VISTA system (Visual Interpretation System for Technical Applications) developed at the Fraunhofer Institut-IITB in Karlsruhe, Germany [PHN+88] — illustrating the modular functional design approach — or with dedicated hardware build around a mesh of 1 bit processors at ENSPS in Strasbourg, France

[PGC+88, PHE+88] — exemplifying the reconfigurable, flexible and programmable design approach.

The VISTA Approach

VISTA is a bus-oriented multiprocessor architecture whose modules are the processing elements. The functional block-diagram of this system, satisfying the requirements described, is given in Figure 12.6.

A control unit is in charge of the coordination of the whole system and the communication with peripherals. Connections between system components are established by the processor bus (VME bus), and by a pixel and data bus (Video bus) relieving the processor bus. With respect to vision system architectures, VISTA has a functionally dedicated architecture (use of heterogeneous modules) using a bus-oriented structure for interconnecting the processing elements. Special modules are used for the iconic stage as well as for the symbolic stage:

- Video I/O unit.
  The corresponding modules are interfaces for camera, line sensors or laser scanner and an interface for a video display. An image memory acting as a buffer memory separates image acquisition from image processing.
- Pixel oriented image processing modules (low-level image processing).
  In this iconic stage, different processing elements can work in parallel on the same data stream, and/or several processing elements can work in a pipeline chaining. This allows on-line processing of the images. Among the available modules are filtering (IIR-filters with self-adjusting thresholds, FIR-filters to detect contour pixels and staged morphological operations for binary images), component labeling and feature processing (extraction and evaluation of geometrical and statistical features) modules. As an example of processing modules developed, one of the most powerful functions, called VISTA-NAG and designed for the detection of contour pixels using the standardized derivation of a Gaussian function, will be described. Low-level image processing is performed in our case with this module. NAG has been designed in order to accelerate the first steps of methods for contour detection.The board transforms at video speed incoming gray-scale images into double-channeled gradient images (amplitude and direction), and, after non-maxima suppression, into contour images, the lines of which are at most two pixels thick. Amplitude and direction of the contour pixels are then handed as images of contour lines, via the video bus, to the next processing stages (i.e. other modules), where firstly the contour pixels can be chained and secondly the evolving contours chains interpreted. The board can also be used as a standard programmable FIR-filter with two independent channels, the data rate being able to go up to 15 MHz.
- Non pixel oriented image processing modules.
  In this symbolic stage, the computation speed can be matched with the task to be solved. At low speed, the control computer can be used, whereas at medium to high speed, more microprocessors (e.g. a network of Transputers) and/or special processing modules (e.g. a list generator module) can be used. Again buffer memories are used in order to avoid the transfer limitation of the VME processor bus.

When planning a vision system, it is necessary to provide "universal" tools in order to relieve partly the user of the burden of programming such complex systems.

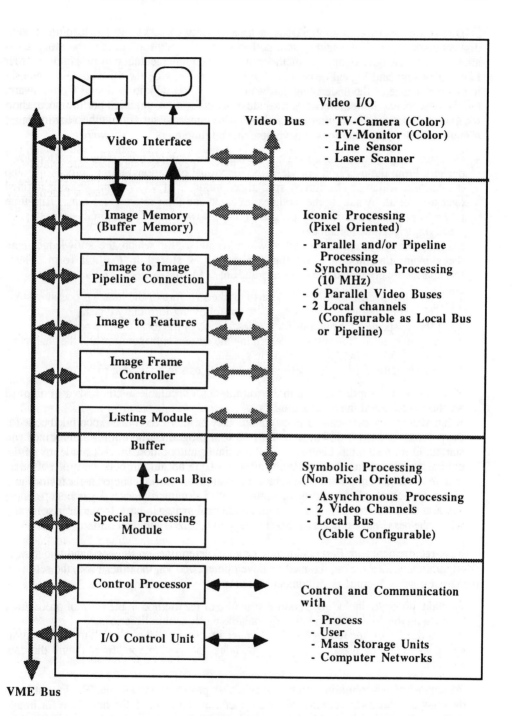

Figure 12.6   Modular functional architecture of the VISTA system (source: Fhg-IITB).

Due to the envisioned applications, a great variety of tasks results, leading to very distinct operating facilities and system performance. Furthermore, in the laboratory, tools are needed for the development of methods and for the implementation of programs in order to test their time and logical behaviors. The tools must provide facilities enabling the user to take advantage of the underlying hardware without special knowledge of the hardware. On the other hand, the requirements for industrial applications are high performance, short reaction time and minimum user interaction. These requirements led to the following basic principles of programming for the development and running of user software :

- Complex image processing operations are parsed into simple processing steps (top down design). From the user point of view, the functional operational unit or processing step is a routine, which can be run by specialized modules of VISTA and which is defined once and for all by stating the modules involved and their interconnections. "Run-time parameters", included in user programs, can, however, affect a processing step by modifying procedure parameters.
- Image processing steps are described within formularies in which the knowledge about the system, the modules and the application is stored in explicit form. These formularies are organized hierarchically and are of four types :

  1. Function specific formularies describing the structure of the image processing step. These formularies include pointers to the following formulary types.
  2. Module specific formularies for the description of the local module parameters.
  3. System specific formularies describing the system configuration and the character- istics of all the modules used in the system.
  4. User specific formularies defining the data objects to be used at run-time.

  Based on the descriptions stored in the formularies, executable instructions are compiled for the modules and the control unit.
- Image processing steps can be run autonomously or interactively. The compiled code for the processing steps is downloaded into the user program, where it is parametrized and started. Once a step has been started, it continues autonomously, independently of the calling user program and synchronized with it via an autonomous control software. Within the target environment, several processing steps can be chained and executed as a string. During development, the operating mode is interactive and only one step can be run at a time. At the end of each step, the control switches back to the user software, where the next image processing step can be parametrized and then started.

Task requirements are first explored in order to determine, on the one hand, the system configuration needed during the method development and, on the other hand, the set-up of the target system. Method development results in :

- A main program including a control structure of the method in the form of procedures running on the control computer and available partly within libraries.
- A description of the required steps of image processing containing all the information about the intended use of the system modules, the system specific data and the data objects.

At the end of programming, an executable user program is available. The lowest layer is the computer hardware controlled by an operating system and the hardware for image processing controlled by a special piece of software implemented as an independent process. Communication between the control software and the user software occurs through a common data file containing, at call time, user commands and parameters and, at the end of the execution of a processing step, results and status. The highest layer, within a run-time environment in autonomous execution mode, contains the user program. This layer also includes modules for the communication with the user of the system. During method development, an additional shell around the set of user programs constitutes an interactive user interface. The described software development process is sustained through a set of tools among which are a formulary editor, a code generator which compiles formularies, a loader, a sequencer which addresses and controls the hardware modules, menu-driven dialog modules, a development programming environment and a diagnosis and test tool.

In conclusion, tools for parametrizing the use of the modules and a set of basic functions are provided to support the programming of the system. Furthermore, automatic translation of explicit knowledge on system configuration, features of the modules and application requirements into machine code for the modules and the control system is available.

The Flexible Reconfigurable and Programmable Approach

The second system, realized at the University of Strasbourg, France., and partially developed in ESPRIT I Project P26 "Advanced Algorithms and Architectures for Speech and Image Processing" [PGC+88, PHE+88], is based on the reconfigurable, programmable approach and is basically a video real time computer based on a multi-parallel architecture. Design studies focused on SIMD networks of 1 bit processors for lower level, data independent computations, and on MIMD machines for medium level processing, involving complex data dependent calculations. Subsequently, a flexible and reconfigurable architecture, based on both commercially and specifically designed processors, has been developed, combining several modes of parallelism and able to experiment with different approaches (for details, see [PGC+88, PHE+88, Hir91b, HPMG91]). The oversimplified block-diagram of the image processing system is given in Figure 12.7.

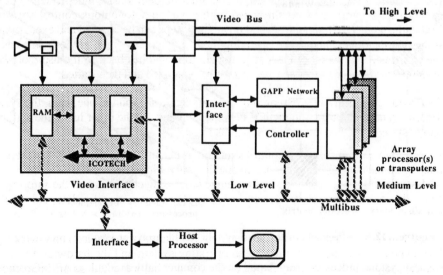

Figure 12.7 Heterogeneous image processing system for real time applications.

A continuous stream of pictures is acquired through the video interface, and fed into the low level image processing stage (GAPP machine). The resulting data are then sent to the medium stage (transputer or array processor based machine), in order to extract the features, possibly in real time, needed for the understanding stage. A host computer is connected to all the above blocks, in order to configure the system according to various operating modes, and to allocate software modules, implementing required algorithms, throughout the system. A general I/O device (i.e. the ICOTECH iconic workstation) is used for image acquisition and restitution in video real time, and for managing the data streams between all the image processing blocks. Some position independent image manipulations can also be carried out by the workstation.

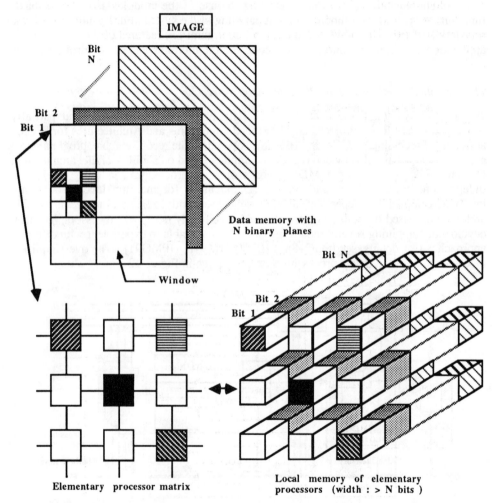

Figure   12.8   Principle of the quasi-systolic GAPP array for low level processing.

A quasi-systolic processor array, based on the commercially available GAPP (Geometric Arithmetic Parallel Processor) from NCR, which is based on chips containing 6*12

Processing Elements (PEs), has been used for the low level stage. Due to its SIMD structure, this processor is intented to support low-level processing, such as pixel or position independent neighborhood operations. The principle of this type of low level processing is given in figure 12.8.

Due to the large computation power needed at this level, a basic hypothesis for the implementation is the association of one elementary processor of the array with one image pixel, leading to heavy or high (fine grain) parallelism for the low level processing hardware. But, even with the technology of today, it is not feasible to build a processor array of the size of a standard image. The image has thus to be split into sub-images called windows. Therefore, this requires the development of a specific interface between the input/output image data flows and the processing array, in order to feed the processors, in real time, with a sequential flow of image windows of approximately the size of the processor network. The GAPP machine structure is shown in Figure 12.9.

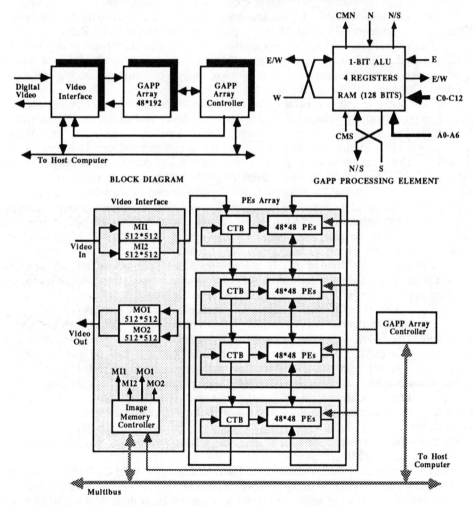

Figure 12.9 Architecture of the GAPP machine.

Basically, it is composed of three main parts. The first one, the video I/O interface, is a board particularly designed for this architecture which performs real time data formating, image windowing and data exchange synchronization. The PEs array is organized in sections of 48*48 elements, and also includes the data formating device (CTB), needed for the bit-serial handling and processing of the data. Finally, the controller, built around a conventional programmable micro-sequencer, runs the system being connected to the host computer.

12.4.2 The Medium-Level Processing Unit

For the medium level processing stage, two different solutions have been studied and then implemented, in order to compare different specific kinds of parallelism.

The first solution, coupled with the low-level system of the University of Strasbourg, is based on a commercially available array processor, the MERCURY ZIP3216, and is arranged into a set of one to four array processors, which can be configured to implement a MISD pipeline, SPMD or MPMD structures. In order to achieve this flexibility a special interface, which controls the data multiplexing and/or partitioning among the array processors, has been specifically developed.

A second possible solution is based on a fixed mesh network of transputers and is a general purpose processor which has been specifically developed within the P26 project. It has a MIMD structure, particularly adapted to data dependent computations, like the treatments needed in medium and/or high level image processing. The core of the transputer based solution is an array of 16 transputer-based processing elements having been developed by Thomson-LER, France. Each processing element comprises a processing unit, built around a transputer, and a video memory unit, which is an element of the global distributed memory of the system. The processing units are interconnected in a static 4*4 mesh network, used for data and message exchange during processing. The video memory units are interconnected in a macro-pipeline way to handle acquisition and restitution of images. The associated video I/O interface broadcasts the video data to the array. Input images are divided into 16 sub-images of 128*128 pixels, and to each sub-image a processing element is dedicated. A master processor, made of an Inmos transputer board plugged into the host computer, is used to support software development.

The various architectures can successfully process isolated pictures (in order, for example, to validate algorithms) or continuous flows of images. Various benchmarks have been implemented to assess the performance of each parallel machine. A set of performance parameters, to be used for evaluation of processing time needed in various applications, has been derived. As foreseen, the GAPP machine performs better than the MIMD machines on benchmarks with intensive data independent computations. For 512*512 images, real time processing is achieved on all benchmarks with a network of 48*192 PEs. For example, a 7*7 convolution on the image takes 10.3 ms of computation time and 3.6 ms for network loading, both operations being done in overlap. On the other hand, benchmarks needing complex data dependent computations, as for example edge following, perform better on the MIMD system.

For the integration of the specialized I/O interfaces, the low level GAPP processor and the medium level transputer or array processor machines, and for the cooperation between these two levels, a software structure similar to what has been described for VISTA has been implemented.

The P26 transputer-based module is, however, too specifically oriented toward image (or signal) processing, and, for that reason, not particularly adapted for medium and high level processing, such as those used in the vision applications described in section 12.5. A similar approach is, thus, quite difficult to use for the realization of hardware platforms for complex vision based applications. In these situations, it is more advisable to use transputer-based systems of more general purpose (e.g. T-Node from Telmat, Multi-cluster from Parsytec, etc.). Systems based on this second approach allow much more flexibility with respect to the very diverse kinds of processing involved in the applications to be described later. This solution has thus to be retained for our system implementations.

A network of 16 T800 transputers (Multicluster 2 from Parsytec or T-Node from Telmat) has been chosen as a medium-level processing unit. The transputer technology has, however, been retained because of its flexibility in efficiently accommodating the computation needs, as the complexity of processing increases from the low-level to the medium-level [Pai89]. At this level, OCCAM has been used as the programming language for transputers, because it provides the advantages of a high-level language and permits easy exploitation of concurrency. The OCCAM compiler is also very well optimized as regards executable code size and execution time. As the inputs of the medium-level stage are images, an interface between the low-level stages video-bus (VISTA and GAPP machine) and transputer links of the network has been developed to optimize data transfer rates between the low and medium processing stages [Gen90b]. The integration of the transputer based systems is shown in Figures 12.5 and 12.10.

The integration of the specialized I/O interfaces, the low level processor modules, the medium level transputer networks and the cooperation between the two levels is achieved through partitioning of the processing algorithms over the two stages, taking into account the characteristics of each processor and the kind of algorithms that each processor can optimally execute. Consequently, the feasibility of an efficient combination of the SIMD and MIMD approaches for low and medium level image processing has been confirmed. The processing capabilities in actual applications have also been verified (see section 12.5). This should lead to a tentative definition of the domains of use of each type of parallelism, leading to rough rules for finding an optimal architecture for a given application and/or a given time performance requirement.

12.4.3 The High-Level Processing Unit

The high-level processing units are SUN 4/3xx workstations. Each of these workstations is receiving features from the medium-level processing unit in order to interpret the initial real-world scene content. Programs running on these workstations are written in C or C++, an object oriented programming language, which allows a flexible and easy manipulation of the feature data coming from the medium-level stages and usually packed into specific objects. The SUN workstation initializes, configures and loads either of the two vision systems and the transputer networks with appropriate algorithms and is used as an interface between the machine vision system and its environment (Ethernet, robot control, etc.). Communication (and feedback-loop) with the low/medium level stages is done using either specially developed transputer based interfaces, or a transputer board (BBKV2 from Parsytec) with dual-ported RAM between the transputer memory bus and the VME or Multibus-bus of the low level stages, or a bus interface between the workstation bus and the low-level system buses. Communications with the transputer network are performed with the help of another transputer based board (VMTM from Parsytec).

A software structure, connected to the software pieces described in the preceding sections, is in charge of the high-level unit. It can be seen as the overall system management software, including the man—machine interface. This man—machine interface is running on the SUN workstations and is developed under X-windows and OSF/MOTIF, which allow the development of menu-driven applications.

12.4.4 Discussion and Concluding Remarks

A model of machine vision architecture has been implemented using different functional levels, leading to a general purpose parallel computer for machine vision. The machines are based on pipelined low, medium and high-level processing units, each having its own well-suited parallelism.

As a result of experimentation carried out with the vision systems described, the assessment of SIMD and MIMD parallel architectures for low/medium level processing tasks and the development of knowledge based methodologies for the high level applications, should allow improved performance and competitiveness in the development of a wide range of image understanding applications, all based on two common, very flexible parts :

- A kernel of image processing routines for software. The results of using the techniques of artificial intelligence for image understanding show that this approach is well suited to realize a general software kernel for vision systems. Such a kernel would allow the designer to go from one application to the other only by changing the knowledge specific to the application (model of the scene under examination and of its content), instead of changing the whole software.
- A heterogeneous parallel machine for hardware. The demonstrated feasibility of programmable hardware for image processing enables faster implementation of a wide range of industrial applications. With only one programmable parallel machine, it will be possible to solve a number of disparate computer vision applications related to various domains.

The performed comparison and evaluation of the proposed architectures for image recognition, now enables the choice of the optimal combination of algorithms and architectures for a given application area; however, further work is necessary in this field, as research must be continued with the aim in particular of building a better SIMD machine and of improving the coupling with the MIMD machines. In addition, it is necessary to develop an extensive software support, as software implementation of algorithms will definitely be the major cost factor in developing new applications. Furthermore, the future realization of vision systems, able to be integrated in industrial applications, will be influenced in particular by :

- The development of more and more integrated electronic devices and of modules incorporating them, leading to some *de facto* standardization of the communication buses,
- the continued development of image processing and (mainly) interpretation methods, in particular the use of binocular or trinocular vision and the modeling of the image content,
- the integration of vision systems as sub-systems in complex applications, possibly in

the feedback path of the control loop (see Figures 12.3 and 12.4) of these systems in order, in particular, to control the sensors and/or the lighting conditions (active sensing) for an automated, dynamically optimized, data acquisition.

Up to now, the design of vision systems has been dominated by the image processing and interpretation methods themselves. In the future, however, it will be necessary to optimize not isolated vision systems but complete systems, where vision is only a component, as, for example, in the field of Computer Integrated Manufacturing (CIM). The resulting increased requirements for the number and performance of the sensors used will further lead to new evaluation criteria, which must be taken into account in the design of vision systems. The systems should also be integrated in local array networks (Ethernet or the newer FDDI) in order to exchange data with other sub-systems. Integration within an overall manufacturing environment should also be foreseen, for example by using MAP (Manufacturing Automation Protocol). These concepts have led to the solution proposed in Figures 12.16 and 12.17 for the inspection application (see section 12.5). Development of methods and design of new architectures call thus for careful studies and possibly experimentation. This should be facilitated by the set-up of development centers grouping hardware and software resources. Possible configurations of such integrated development workstations for computer vision applications are indicated in simplified block-diagram form in Figures 12.5 and 12.10.

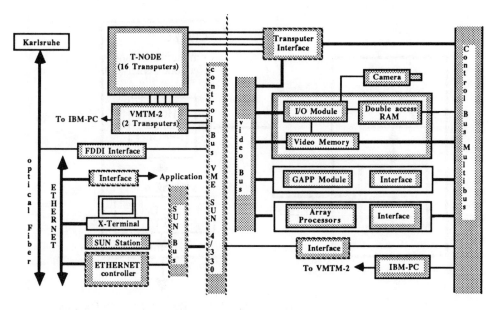

Figure 12.10   Vision and image processing development system configuration at ENSPS.

12.4.5 Interconnection of the Two Systems

In order to setup a very complete and powerful distributed (transputer network based) development tool, the two transputer networks of the systems shown in Figures 12.5 and

12.10 will be interconnected using an optical fiber [HPMN90, HPMN91]. The two systems, the first located in Strasbourg (see Figure 12.10), and the second in Karlsruhe (see Figure 12.5), will be interconnected through an already existing optical fiber between the two institutes involved in the application. The protocol chosen for data exchange is the newly available FDDI standard. The performances of this standard are such that the overall performance of the distributed transputer network should not be lowered. The connection also punctually allows the access by one institute to the whole shared resources, when high computing power is required. The distributed system can then be seen as a very complete development system for vision applications, joining the resources of the two institutes and enabling the use by each institute of the two different low-level processing units.

The structure to be implemented at the University of Strasbourg (ULP) for this interconnection is shown in over-simplified form in Figure 12.11. This figure illustrates also how the vision system of Figure 12.10 is connected to the optical link joining the two partner institutes. A similar structure is used by the German partner, in order to connect its vision system (see Figure 12.5) to the optical link. For both partners, the complete hardware, including the border-crossing optical fiber, is already installed. First tests on a local FDDI loop have been carried out and are very promising. For the final border-crossing connection, the authorization and sponsoring of the two concerned postal agencies (France-Télécom and Deutsche Telekom) is expected in the very near future for first experimentations.

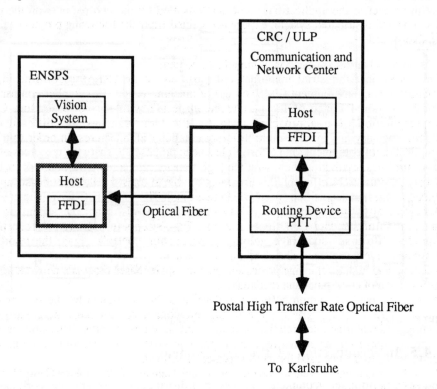

Figure 12.11 Connection of the vision system of Figure 12.10 to the optical link.

The applications implemented on these systems aim to develop a large set of image processing procedures of medium and high level. Furthermore the transputer based systems have been connected to low level processing stages, able to carry out the operations on either single images or continuous image sequences in video real time. It must also be recalled that image processing performance for vision applications can only be assessed when taking into account the actual data flows. The transputer systems should thus not limit the overall performance of the systems, by insufficient computation power. The low level video real time processing capabilities should not be lowered due to too small medium/high level systems. A limited array size could, in this sense, constitute a bottleneck which should be avoided. For that reason, the best compromise, with respect to transputer network size and cost, is an array of 32 processors.

With respect to research activities, splitting the resources will allow integration of the global experience of the two institutes, as it cannot be envisaged at the present time to group at a common place researchers of the two laboratories, even though exchanges of workers are taking place. Splitting of resources will also hasten development time, each institute having its own facilities.

However, it is *very* important to note that the resources will be able to be *joined whenever required* (for teaching purposes as well as research activities), through use of the available fiber optic link between the two institutes, transfering data at very high speed, in such a way that these transfers do not constitute a bottleneck for the overall application performance.

With respect to the applications to be implemented by the two partners on the pilot interconnected distributed system, experience gained from the following projects will be intensively used :

- Vision based on-line inspection of manufactured parts.
  In this project industrial manufactured parts are to be controlled on-line in the manufacturing environment (FMS) by use of machine vision. This implies comparison of the acquired image of the part to be inspected with the corresponding CAD representation. The approaches used by the two branches are different but complementary and involve quite different computer architectures. In order to avoid duplication of equipment (and effort), it has been proposed to share the resources of the two institutes, by linking them with the high transfer rate communication link (optical fiber). In order to be efficient, this link must be able to transfer data (in our case, digital video images) at acquisition speed (video real time). The structure to be implemented is schematically shown on Figure 12.12. This project also puts the accent on the integration of standard CAD tools and on CIM concepts (especially the concept of "product life time" and 100% automated production control). Again the resources implied are very expensive and should thus be shared.
- Medium and high level image processing on a transputer based processor network for the comparison of conceptual and real images.
  In this project, a common software toolbox is to be developed by the two project partners. As a result, with the use of the interconnected structures, automated and application real time interpretation of image content will be possible. This could lead to a great impact on the industrial use of machine vision. The structure to be used is comparable to the one used for the first project described.
- Set-up of a German—French Demonstration and Transfer of Technology Center for the for the Applications of Vision.
  As a major output, it is already scheduled to merge the scientific and the technological

(hardware and software) competences of the two partners in a common center of competence, conceived as a joint, border crossing, structure with the goal to propose also services and consultancies to industry.

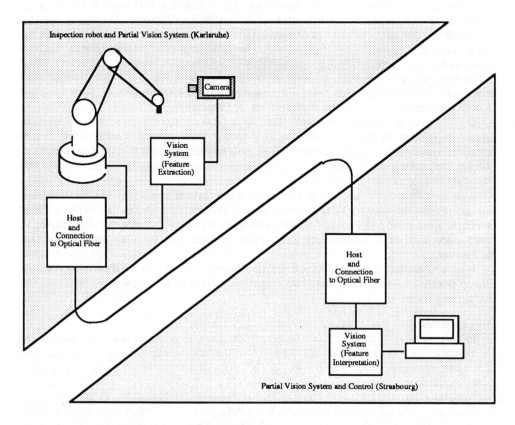

Figure 12.12 Example of a future possible link of resources installed in Strasbourg and Karls-ruhe for a typical treatment of a vision-based industrial application.

12.5 APPLICATIONS

The machine vision systems described are able to deal with quite a lot of applications. A brief description of three of these follows.

12.5.1 Real-World Scene Interpretation [Mül91]

A typical goal in machine vision is to understand an image of a real-world scene in order to perform some actions on the scene. Two applications were developed to recognize 3D objects using evaluation of CCD images and pick up the objects with a robot arm [Gen90a, Mül91]. The vision system used for these applications is the one illustrated in

Figure 12.5. The transputer network is loaded from the SUN workstation using the VMTM plugged-in transputer board. The BBKV2 transputer board runs a program which initializes and configures the VISTA modules used.

Three images of the same object (trinocular vision), taken from three different positions, are gained by using either three fixed or one movable CCD camera. For the latter solution, the camera is placed on the arm of the robot. All four cameras are connected to the VISTA video interface. Via the video bus, the images are transmitted to the first module in the processing chain, the NAG module, which performs the extraction of edges out of the grey value images in order to deliver "edge images", encoding in our case maxima of amplitude and direction of the image gradient. The result of this step is stored in different matrices, the components of which represent either the maxima of amplitude or the direction of the gradient in grey value image. The results from the low-level image processing system are next sent to the medium-level processing stage (transputer network) through a specially designed interface (TBK), which establishes a connection between the VISTA video bus and the transputer network links. The data transfer via this interface is realized by subdividing the data flow in a sufficient number of data packages, the size of which is small enough to use the normal data transfer rate of (several) transputer links for sending the packages without lowering the overall transfer/video speed. Due to the fact that for 3D object recognition three different images have to be evaluated, the data packages (having a size of half an image) are sent to the next stage (the medium level evaluation stage), using a set of six transputer links. The set of operations just described is performed in about 250 ms for the complete set of three images. A faster version of this program, having only to transmit one image and using eight transputer links, needs only about 50 ms to send the whole data. This faster version is to be used, in future work, for active vision tasks, currently in the development stage. Figure 12.13 shows the structure of the interconnected transputer set used for the application just described.

Each of the three "edge images", corresponding to one initial image of the 3D scene, is processed by a pool of two transputers (the processed image being divided into two sub-images). The corresponding transputers, each evaluating half an image, perform in the next step an approximation by line segments of the contours which have straight line shapes in the "edge images". The results of this step are six lists of line segments and are forwarded to the next processing level, where the line segments belonging to the same initial picture are merged into one complete line segment list. These lists are then used to calculate the projected corner points of the objects depicted in the images of the scene. This processing step is done using three transputers, each evaluating the line segment list corresponding to one image.

As output of this processing stage, a list of line segments and corner points, describing the objects in the scene, is delivered. These data are handled as cues to a procedure, having to build up the scene description. In order to get the 3D scene description, the information from the images taken from different viewpoints must be combined, using stereo vision techniques. Therefore, the 3D coordinates of the corners of the objects in the scene are recovered from the previously calculated 2D corner point coordinates, using calibration data (one particular data set for each camera and for each camera position). The calibration data have to be obtained in an off-line step, to be described later. To calculate these scene point coordinates, a single transputer, located hierarchically at the next processing level, is used.

This leads to the use of 10 or 14 transputers (out of the 16 available) for a parallel processing of the three initial images, with a total processing time for the steps just described of the order of 600 ms for the complete set of three images. The total processing

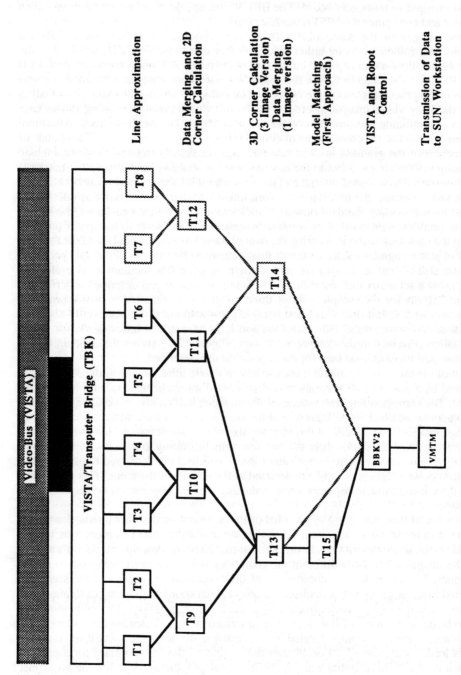

Figure 12.13 The structure of the interconnected transputers in the case of the slower three image version (solid lines) and the faster one image version (solid and dashed lines). The interconnection between T11 and T13 is only established in the first, the three image version.

time obviously depends on the complexity of the 3D scene, i.e. the number of objects and their complexity. The processing time values for the various steps are given in table 12.1 and correspond to a scene of medium complexity, containing of the order of 5 polyhedral objects.

It should be noted that calibration of camera(s) has to be done only once, since the cameras are mounted in a fixed manner or moved to defined locations, with defined orientation, by the robot. The calibration method used is from [FT86, Tsa86, Tsa87, Len88, LT88, TL89] and is fully automated, starting from the acquisition of a calibration pattern image and ending with the output of the calibration parameters of the cameras and their positions. This process is also running on a set of four transputers and takes about 2 s. The 3D accuracy achieved is one part in 4000.

Results from the medium-level processing stage are then transmitted either to the SUN workstation through the VMTM transputer board or to a further transputer, in order to undertake the object recognition and the 3D scene interpretation. Two approaches are implemented for the recognition task. The first one uses a model of the object, which represents a description with full details to be recognized in the images. The second approach is more sophisticated and makes use only of abstract knowledge about the objects expected in the images to be evaluated. This approach is restricted to nearly polyhedral scenes and is based on the method developed by Sugihara for the interpretation of line drawings [Sug86].

The extracted input line drawing of the depicted objects, coming from the previous processing stages, is then tested to see whether it can be considered as a correct polyhedral sketch of nearly polyhedral objects. If the corresponding constraints are fulfilled, it will then be possible to reconstruct the scene, using the line description and the 3D vertex information provided by the trinocular vision system. Therefore the system is able to recognize and localize objects in the scene without any complete *a priori* knowledge, with the unique restriction that the objects have to be nearly polyhedral. As a result of this processing level, the 3D location and the spatial orientation of the objects in the scene are known. Finally, a robot arm can be moved in order to pick up the objects, after computation of appropriate control information.

The complete processing time for the fully parallelized version of the first, model-based, recognition, starting with the acquisition of the three initial real-world images and ending, after recognition and localization of the objects, with the computation of the robot arm actions is of the order of 2 s. For the other approach, the processing time values are given in table 12.1.

Work is now in progress in order to parallelize most of the high-level processing algorithms running on the SUN workstation, in order to implement them onto the transputer network. The complete processing time is then expected to be well below one second. Also, in order to enhance the scene description, the use of circular and elliptic segments as features is currently under investigation.

12.5.2 Comparison of CCD and CAD Data for Inspection Tasks. Vision Based Inspection of Manufactured Parts

An example of a ;more sophisticated application to be run on the hardware described is given in [PHN+88] (identifying and locating surface defects in wood) or by the on-line inspection in the manufacturing environment of parts being manufactured using computer vision [HL90, Hir91a].

Processing Times

Hardware	Data	Speed
Trinocular Vision	3 Images	40 ms
Vision System	Edge Detection and Data Transmission (3 Image Version)	250 ms
Vision System	Edge Detection and Data Transmission (1 Image Version)	50 ms
Transputer Network	Line Approximation	250 ms
Transputer Network	Data Merging and 2D Corner Calculation	150 ms
Transputer Network	3D Corner Calculation (3 Image Version)	200 ms
Transputer Network	Data Merging (1 Image Version)	5 ms
Transputer Network	Model Matching (First Approach)	400 ms
Transputer Network	VISTA and Robot Control	10 ms
Transputer Network	Data Transmission to SUN workstation	1 s
SUN workstation	Model Matching (First Approach)	2 s
SUN workstation	Object Reconstruction (Second Approach)	40 s

Table 12.1 Table of processing times of the developed hardware configuration and approaches. The processing times of the transputer network and SUN workstation are mean values, because of the dependency of the evaluation extent from size of data.

This section presents an automated system, based on a parallel computer architecture, as a solution to the 100% control of manufactured parts in a Flexible Manufacturing System (FMS) environment. This prototype is aimed to be able to replace mechanical sensors with the same accuracy (of the order of 10 to 100 μm) within the overall volume of the part to be inspected. The system will work on-line in an FMS , in order to increase productivity and reduce manufacturing costs, using modern techniques of vision systems. The technique used is based on comparison between real pictures acquired through a vision system and the corresponding synthetic picture based on CAD product data. Specifically, in order to inspect the geometrical properties, the image of the current field of view is compared with the information generated by a simulation system. The image acquisition is done by use of direct light, structured light and Moiré techniques. The whole of manufacturing industry is thus concerned by this new non-contact, CAD connected inspection system.

Introduction

Inspection of manufactured parts on-line during the manufacturing process is an essential part of the future integration of FMS in production, in order to increase productivity and reduce costs. Classical inspection methods compare a reference part with the set of parts to be evaluated. The method implemented in this work is based on the comparison of a conceptual reference image with actual images taken from the manufactured parts. The reference image is obtained through a Planning and Simulation system, which stores in its database all the information necessary for the simulation of the part to be inspected.

Inspection takes place through comparison of CCD images and corresponding conceptual representations gained using the CAD model of the piece. Comparison takes place at feature level as well as at image level. All kinds of inspections, ranging from conformity checking up to metrology, can be achieved through use of a user friendly planning system. Due to the limited resolution of the imaging sensors used today for digital image processing, the sensor is moved in order to scan larger workpieces in their entire extent.

CAD-based knowledge is also required and used for efficient performance of such hybrid mechanical and electronic inspection tasks. To inspect the geometrical properties, the image of the current field of view is compared with the information stored in the database of the associated CAD system, with or without use of structured light. Comparison takes place after segmentation and registration of the actual image with a synthetic projection of the CAD module. Furthermore, the 3D data coming from the CAD system is used to generate a 2D representation corresponding to the angle of view of the sensor. The output of the inspection stage is used for retrofitting by the manipulator in case of a possible remanufacturing.

System Architecture

Figure 12.14 shows the principal steps of the treatment and the functional blocks of the inspection system. In order to be able to compare the reference image with the real image, it is necessary to :

- plan and simulate the real inspection session, in order to generate a synthetic image,

- segment the real image acquired through the camera,
- extract the features (e.g. contours) of the part under analysis, or the skeleton of the structured light on the surface of the part,
- compare the synthetic and transformed real images.

Also, in order to realize dimensional measurements, the comparison involves differences between contours for different object projections and differences between the deformation of structured light on the object's surface and the corresponding deformations, due to the structured light, simulated on the conceptual reference object.

The advanced inspection system described consists of knowledge processing and engineering at the top level, but the first layers will consist of simulation, pre-processing, feature extraction (e.g. filtering, identification, segmentation) followed by recognition (registration, inspection) and decision taking. Concerning the steps to achieve, going from real data acquisition up to the comparison of the real features and the conceptual features, three processing levels can be defined and implemented onto the systems to be used for implementation and described in the previous section (see Figure 12.15). Figure 12.15 indicates also the various types of processing implied and the associated data structures.

Again, the inspection task is the chaining of different processing tasks. The three processing levels defined in section 12.3 and implemented in the systems described in section 12.4 can be easily recognized on Figure 12.15, together with the type of hardware used for each processing level. It is noteworthy to see that the same model can be used for a wide range of applications (pick and place, autonomous vehicle guidance, robotics, for example) just by changing the *a priori* knowledge (e.g. the CAD database).

The first step is to analyze the input CCD signal so as to remove noise, enhance the images and end up with suitably segmented images. Suitable combinations (after registration) of these pictures are then chosen as global features to be used in the subsequent stages of processing. In the next step, some form of matching or comparison is greatly simplified and undertaken accurately through use of specially designed light sources (structured light). Furthermore, the scanning of the manufactured part is under the control of an inspection sequence module using CAD data.

The comparison may take the form of a simple distance measure (for example, as is suitable for difference determination between the original and real parts). Alternatively, more complex processing such as feature descriptor based methods (modified Fourier descriptors, for example) may be used to compare the images obtained from the CCD sensor and those synthesized from the CAD database.

Furthermore, in general the images are not compared in the representation of grey-scale pictures, but rather using an abstraction extracted from them. Also, the synthetic images are gained from the analytic perspective geometric description of the outlines and surfaces of the workpiece adapted to the position of the camera. In general, the output from the "comparison" stage is a single decision (good or bad) or a more complex response ("differences" and how to reprocess the part).

A further stage of processing can then take place using, for example, a retrofitting technique to the CAD/CAM system or the associated host computer. The most complex component is the "understanding" part which is some kind of knowledge system (possibly an expert system for remanufacturing) which uses the knowledge about the parts (and the manufacturing process) and the knowledge extracted by the lower level stages. There may be, of course, an interaction and feedback (assisted in a first step by an operator) between the inspection system and the manufacturing system as shown in Figure 12.15.

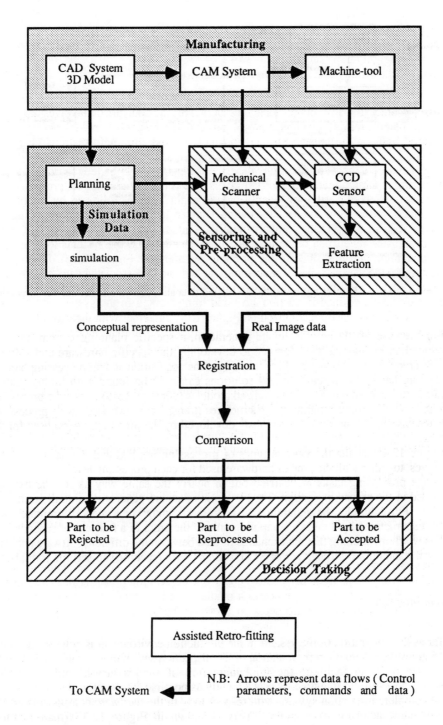

Figure 12.14 Functional block diagramm of the inspection system.

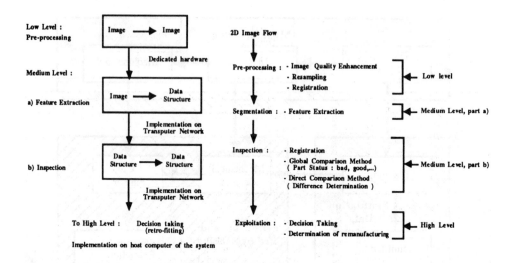

Figure 12.15   Processing levels and associated data and hardware structures for inspection.

For the case of 2D graphic image generation, a specific planning system has been developed, effort having been devoted to developing the specific hardware and software modules required by this approach. However, for the acquisition and preprocessing part, the processing has to be in realtime and solutions can only be found with highly parallel architectures realized either with specialized modules (wired processors, systolic processors) or with general purpose programmable structures (transputer networks or array processors), as is the case for the hardware (previously developed by the project partners) used for this system.

Figure 12.15 recalls the various types of processing implied and the associated data structures, together with the type of hardware used for each processing level.

Image processing tasks are carried out in nearly the same way as for the example described in the preceding section. The simulation data are generated using the transputer network. For example, the generation of a synthetic image of a scene illuminated with projected structured light takes a computing time of the order of a few tens of seconds.

It is worth mentioning that the exchange of data between the different software packages has been standardized through use of STEP and/or DMIS (specific sub-set) file formats.

System Integration

As far as the integration of the system in the production environment is concerned, Figure 12.16 gives the schematic representation of the inspection set-up in a manufacturing cell.

But, in order to facilitate the implementation of such a vision application, it is definitely necessary to integrate, as transparently as possible for the user, the vision system in the complete inspection system, with respect to both the hardware components and the overall manufacturing environment. This is shown in Figure 12.17 (manufacturing environment).

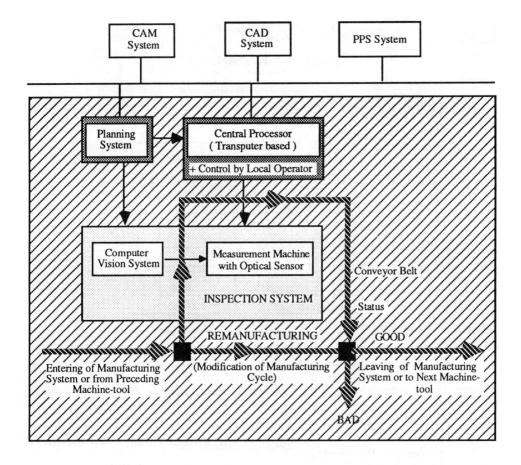

Figure 12.16   Inspection system integration in PMS/FMC environment.

Conclusion

As a conclusion to this section, a non-contact inspection system, based on real time computer vision, has been extensively described. Inspection is carried out through comparison of conceptual images and actual object pictures. The system is oriented toward metrology, measurements having to be carried out with an accuracy of 10 to 100 µm. This necessitates a careful calibration of the inspection system as well as the definition of references. The method is based on the fact that several images of an object, after combination, lead to a satisfactory object representation. The inspection is on-line and controls 100% of the parts.

This is aimed to decrease inspection time and increase production rate. The hardware and software components have been described and some specific application domains have been defined. The project, however, does not aim to develop a restricted system, as the whole of manufacturing industry is concerned by this non-contact, CAD connected and FMS integrated inspection system.

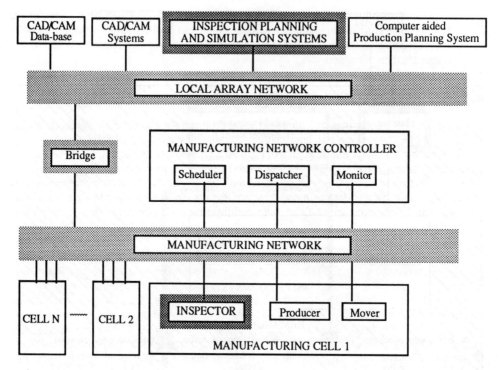

Figure 12.17 Integration of the inspection system (inspector) in the manufacturing environment.

12.5.3 Comparison of CCD Images with Synthetic Images. Application to Image Processing

Parallel to image processing, the field of image synthesis has developed so that one can now dispose of "perfect" images, sometimes difficult to distinguish from real images. The most realistic images are obtained using techniques based on the physical description of the interaction between light and matter (e.g. so-called ray tracing techniques [GN71]). These images are used in the fields of art, architecture, the automobile industry and medicine, for instance. But, with respect to image processing, the generation of a very realistic image, in he sense that it can be compared with reality, requires a lot of computing power. This again calls for the use of parallel computer architectures.

A key problem in machine vision is to provide a description of a part of the world (the scene to be depicted) which is robust, as a correct interpretation of the surrounding environment is often very critical. A solution to improve robustness is to use *a priori* knowledge about that environment. This information can be used at different levels during image processing. For example, one can use *a priori* knowledge at the low-level image processing stage by comparing a synthetic image and a real image of the scene to be understood. This is the topic of the work to be described below and assumes that both images (the artificial and the real one) are comparable. In other words, results of treatments applied to synthetic images can be compared with results obtained using the real image.

The parallel machine vision system described in section 12.4 has been used for our experiments. In the following, the ray tracing algorithm and its parallel implementation will be presented. Experimental results concerning the comparison between synthetic and real images are then discussed.

The Ray Tracing Algorithm

This section will briefly describe the ray tracing program used to produce synthetic images and its implementation on a transputer network realized by Bertrand [Ber91].

Ray tracing methods use results from physics (reflection, refraction, etc.) in order to compute synthetic images [Gla89]. The basic principle is to compute the intersection of each ray starting from the observation point with the objects in the scene. The light source distribution and the physical properties of the objects (tranparency, color, etc.) are taken into account to compute the color of the resulting pixel. The intensity at a given point is given by :

$$I_{point} = I_{surrounding} + I_{diffused} + I_{reflection} + I_{refraction}$$

The objects can be described using surfaces or volumes (Constructive Solid Geometry). Most of the computing time needed by ray tracing is devoted to computing the intersection between objects and rays. This task can easily be split into several sub-tasks, each having to compute the intersection of a sub-set of the rays and the objects. Multi-processor computers are very well suited for such applications [CWBV86, Pri89] and in particular transputer based computers [GM91]. The ray tracing program implemented is Rayshade, written by C. Kolb, D.C. Hoffman and D. Dobkin from Princeton University, 1988. This is a very complete and powerful software allowing the use of textures, of different kinds of light sources, of atmospheric effects and of anti-aliasing techniques, for example. The scene to be displayed is described by :

- the screen resolution (in pixels),
- the eye position in space,
- the point at which the eye is looking,
- the "up" direction,
- the field of view,
- the light source description (type, position, intensity),
- the surface description (color, reflectivity, transparency, texture),
- the object descriptions using surface definitions and volume primitives,
- the object positions in the scene.

Rayshade was implemented on the transputer network (Multicluster-2 from Parsytec). The initial software, written in C, was translated into OCCAM in order to improve speed and parallelized on a pipelined structure of 16 transputers using a farming programming model. The scene description is still interpreted by the SUN workstation and then fed into the transputer network, which computes the ray—object intersections and sends the computed image pixels back to the SUN workstation. The use of 16 T800 (20 MHz) transputers (24 Mflops) gives a fourfold increase in speed on an IBM RISC 6000-320 (9 Mflops) machine, for example. The performance also increases nearly linearly with the number of transputers used (tested for 1 up to 16 transputers). This permits synthetic images such as those generated in these experiments to be computed in about 40 seconds. This computing time is small enough to consider the use of "on-line generated" synthetic images in some computer vision applications. With the next transputer generation (e.g. T9000), it should be possible to compute synthetic images within a couple of seconds. One can then think of generating images as often as needed during the execution of a vision application, leading to improved robustness and flexibility for machine vision applications.

Use of Synthetic Images for Image Processing

Using synthetic images in image processing is not a new idea [BJ85] and already some applications have been realized. One can mention for instance 2D or 3D object recognition [CM91, KSSZ90], where synthetic images of the object to be recognized are used to improve the matching process, and image sequence analysis [LR91], where synthetic image sequences are generated to test the modeling of movement. It is stressed in such applications that the synthetic images to be used should be "realistic enough", in order to get results which are comparable with those obtained with real images.

However, this is still not a really mature field of research and experiments need to be done in order to determine what synthetic images can really contribute. The important question here is wether synthetic images can be compared, at the pixel level (intensity and location), with corresponding real images. A positive answer would lead to important implications, as image synthesis could then be used as a powerful and comfortable tool to efficiently model and study the photometric aspects of image processing. One could then also easily study and test some image processing methods (edge detection, for instance) on synthetic images, in order to allow some control of important image formation parameters (lighting conditions, for example). Their influence on the results of performed processing could also be better assessed. It should, however, be noted that this kind of approach can only be used if the computing time for producing synthetic images is reasonable (that is, of the order of a few minutes). An efficient implementation of a ray tracer, such as was described in the previous section, is then important.

The experimental setup used to take an image allows to fix the image formation conditions. The following parameters are experimentally known :

- the light position and lighting direction,
- the camera parameters (position, orientation, focal length, etc.) determined by camera calibration,
- the object parameters : dimensions, position on the calibration plate and surface characteristics (color, reflectivity). This information can be obtained from a CAD system.

The eye position, viewpoint and field of view needed by the ray tracer are obtained from the camera parameters. All these data are fed into the Rayshade program which produces the synthetic image of the object. This image will then be directly compared with the real image of the object (if the camera lens radial distortion cannot be neglected, one should also apply such a radial distortion to the synthetic image). A way to compare the two images at the pixel level is to compare the two corresponding edge images (obtained, for example, using the Canny edge detector) :

- The same edge is present in the two images if the gradient amplitude is comparable in the synthetic and real images (that is to say the grey level values are comparable up to a scale factor),

- this edge is located at the same position in the two images if the pixel positions are the same in the synthetic and real image.

If the two images really match, one can then for instance use the synthetic image to isolate real edges corresponding to the object(s) to be localized or recognized, classify real edges as object edges, reflection edges or shadow edges, or detect highlights as described in the next section.

Results

The experimental results were obtained using the previously introduced experimental set-up. The synthetic images were computed within a few tens of seconds (26 s to 48 s, depending on the complexity of the scene), using a 16 transputer network. Edge detection is then performed on these images. From these results, one can tentatively conclude that, under the chosen experimental conditions, synthetic images can be generated, which are comparable to real images at the pixel level (intensity and location). Indeed, the same edges (object, reflection, shadow edges) are present in the real and synthetic images and they are located at the same position ($\pm$ one pixel). This has a very important consequence, since it is now possible to efficiently model real images. Below, a non-exhaustive list of possible applications is given :

- The influence of imaging parameters (camera parameters, lighting conditions) can be more easily studied, together with image processing methods, since it is possible to control these parameters in the synthetic image formation process. A synthetic image with very specific photometric features can thus be generated and the behavior of a given image processing method can be studied with respect to these photometric conditions (the behavior of gradient based edge detectors at corners, for example, is very well reproduced with synthetic images).
- With given camera parameters, lighting conditions and object model, it should be possible to use synthetic images of this object in order to match and recognize it among other objects in the scene to be processed.
- The application to classification of edges can be envisaged.
- The avoidance of lighting effects such as highlights on objects can be achieved. This means that it is possible to simulate images with various camera and light source positions and to retain the position corresponding to the best photometric conditions (no highlights, good contrast) for a further edge detection process, for instance. The camera and light source positions selected can then be taken into account within the experimental set-up to produce a real image of the object, which a known optimal photometric aspect for the process to follow on. This can be useful for some industrial inspection tasks using computer vision and could lead to the definition of optimal camera/light source positioning strategies in order to optimally extract image features. This kind of approach could also be of some interest for deriving self-adaptive image feature detectors.

Conclusion

Using a general purpose parallel computer, based on pipelined low, medium and high-level processing units, and in particular on a transputer network, a ray tracing algorithm was efficiently implemented. With this it was possible to perform some productive experiments into the use of synthetic images in image processing. It has been shown that "perfect" synthetic images, whose formation process is completely controlled, can be compared (at pixel level) to real images. Ray tracing can thus generate images which model reality very closely. This allows the use of such artificial images to test and understand the behavior of some image processing methods (edge detection, for instance) under varying and controlled image formation conditions. Photometric optimal strategies, in connection with image processing, could be studied and tested, for instance. Synthetic images can also be used to isolate specific objects in an image, classify image edges or detect and prevent lighting effects such as highlights.

The use of artificial images in computer vision is still a young field of research but seems to be very promising. Up to now it has been difficult to work with realistic synthetic images since their generation was very time consuming. One can, however, expect a "typical" synthetic image in some tens of seconds, and, with the announced T9000 transputer, it should be possible to compute such artificial images in a couple of seconds. One can then think of generating synthetic images as often as needed during a computer vision application. This should contribute to improving robustness and flexibility in machine vision systems.

ACKNOWLEDGEMENTS

The author wishes to thank his colleagues at the LSIT and IITB-Fhg Institutes, especially Dr C. Müller, Dr P. Paillou, Dr U. Lübbert, Dr D.Paul and C. Draman, for having provided part of the material for writing this contribution and for their kind permission to use some of the illustrations.

REFERENCES

[Ber91]   D. Bertrand. Parallèlisation d'un algorithme de lancer de rayon sur un réseau de trans-
             puters. Master Thesis, Université de Strasbourg I, Louis Pasteur, July 1991.

[BJ85]   P. J. Besl and R. C. Jain. Three Dimensional Object Recognition. *Computing Sur-
             veys*, 17: 75-145, 1985.

[CM91]   C.-H. Chen and P. G. Mulgaonker. CAD-Based Feature-Utility Measures for Auto-
             matic Vision Programming. In *Proc. of IEEE Workshop on Directions in
             Automated CAD Based Vision*, pages 106-114, Maui, Hawaii, 1991.

[CWBV86]   J. G. Cleary, B. M. Wywill, G. M. Birtwistle and R. Vatti. Multiprocessor Ray Tra-
             cing. *Computer Graphics Forum*, 5 : 3-12, 1986.

[DD190]   Deliverable D1 of ESPRIT Project P2091. External Specifications of the Overall
             VIMP System. March 1990.

[Duf89]   M. J. B. Duff. In J. C Simon, editor, *From Pixels to Features*, pages 403-413, Else-
             vier Science Publishers B.V. (North-Holland), Amsterdam, 1989.

[Duf90]   M. J. B. Duff. I n P roc. 1 0th *International Conference on Pattern Recognition
             ICPR-90*, pages 24-33, Atlantic City, NJ, June 1990.

[Fou86]   T.J. Fountain. In *Proc. 8th International Conference on Pattern Recognition ICPR-
             86*, pages 24-33, Paris, 1986.

[FT86]   O. D. Faugeras and G. Toscani. The Calibration Problem for Stereo. In *Proc. IEEE
             Conf. Computer Vision and Pattern Recognition*, pages 15-20, Miami, FL, 22-26
             June, 1986.

[Gen90a]   V. Gengenbach. Master Thesis, Institut für Algorithmen und Kognitive Systeme, Fakultät für Informatik, Universität Karlsruhe (TH), January 1990.

[Gen90b]   V. Gengenbach. Internal Report, Fraunhofer-Institut für Informations- und Datenverarbeitung, IITB, Karlsruhe, 1990.

[Gla89]   A. S. Glassner. *An Introduction to Ray Tracing*. Academic Press, New York, 1989.

[GM91]   D. Gassiloud and B. Mignot. Image Synthesis on the T_Node. In *Computing with Parallel Architectures*, pages 123-136, Kluwer Academic Publishers, Amsterdam, 1991.

[GN71]   R. A. Golstein and R. Nagel. 3D Visual Simulation. *Simulation*, 6 : 25-31, 1971.

[Hir91a]   E. Hirsch. Vision Based On-line Inspection of Manufactured Parts. In *Computing with Parallel Architectures*, pages 173-196, Kluwer Academic Publishers, Amsterdam, 1991.

[Hir91b]   E. Hirsch. Heterogeneous Parallel Processing Structures for Real Time Image Processing : Reconfigurable and Flexible Structures Versus Modular Functional Structures. In J.C. Simon, editor, *From Pixels to Features : Parallelism in Image Processing*, pages 327-346, Elsevier Science Publishers B.V. (North-Holland), Amsterdam,1991.

[HL90]   E. Hirsch and U. Lübbert. In L. Faria and W. Van Puymbroeck, editors, *Computer Integrated Manufacturing*, pages 76-90, Springer-Verlag, Berlin, Heidelberg, New York, 1990.

[Hor86]   B. K. P. Horn. *Robot Vision*. The MIT Press, Cambridge, MA, 1986.

[HPMG91]   E. Hirsch, P. Paillou, C. Müller and V. Gengenbach. A Versatile Parallel Computer Architectures For Machine Vision. In P.H. Welch, editor, *Multiprocessing with Transputers*, pages 828-844, IOS Press, Amsterdam, 1991.

[HPMN90]   E. Hirsch, P. Paillou, C. Müller and H.-H. Nagel. In *Proc. First ESPRIT Parallel Computing Action Workshop*, pages 77-80, Southampton, UK, 1990.

[HPMN91]   E. Hirsch, P. Paillou, C. Müller and H.-H. Nagel. In *Proc. Second ESPRIT Parallel Computing Action Workshop*, pages 365-371, Ispra, Italy, March 1991.

[Kan78]   T. Kanade. In *Proc. Int. Joint Conf. Pattern Recognition*, pages 95-105, Kyoto, Japan, 7-10 November, 1978.

[Kan80]   T. Kanade. *Computer Graphics and Image Processing* , 13 : 279-297, 1980.

[KSSZ90]   A. Korn, G. Saur, W. Schwerdtmann and G. Zimmermann. Signalverarbeitung in einem autonomen Sensorsystem : Wissensgestützte Auswertung von Bildern natürlicher Szenen zur Erkennung dreidimensionaler Objekte. Technical Report T/RF33/I0042/I1237, Fraunhofer Institut für Informations- und Datenverarbeitung IITB, Karlsruhe, Germany, December 1990.

[Len88]   R. Lenz. Zur Genauigkeit der Videometrie mit CCD-Sensoren. In H. Bunke, O. Kübler and P. Stucki, editors, *Proc. 10. DAGM-Symposium*, pages 179-189, Zürich, September 1988, number 180 in Informatik-Fachberichte, Springer-Verlag, Berlin, Heidelberg, New York, 1988.

[LR91]   W. Leister and K. Rohr. Voruntersuchungen von Bildsynthesemethoden zur Analyse von Bildfolgen. Technical Report, University of Karlsruhe, Germany, 1991.

[LT88]   R. K. Lenz and R. Y. Tsai. *IEEE Transactions on Pattern Analysis and Machine Intelligence* , 10 (5) : 713-720, 1988.

[Mil85]   R.K. Miller. *Machine Vision for Robotics and Automated Inspection*, volume 1, 2 and 3 of Technical Insights, Fort Lee, NJ, third edition, 1985.

[Mül91]   C. Müller. *Verwendung von Bildauswertungsmethoden zur Erkennung und Lagebestimmung von generischen polyedrischen Objekten im Raum*. PhD Dissertation, Institut für Algorithmen und Kognitive Systeme, Fakultät für Informatik der Universität Karlsruhe (TH),1991.

[Nag78]   H.-H. Nagel. In J. P. Foith, editor, *Angewandte Szenenanalyse*, number 20 of Informatik-Fachberichte, pages 3-21, Springer-Verlag, Berlin, Heidelberg, New York, 1978.

[Nag85]   H.-H. Nagel. In W. Brauer and B. Radig, editors, number 118 of Informatik-Fachbe-richte, pages 170-199, Springer-Verlag, Berlin, Heidelberg, New York, Tokyo, 1985.

[Nag87]   H.-H. Nagel. In J. P. Haton, editor, *Fundamentals in Computer Understanding : Speech and Vision*, pages 113-139, Cambridge University Press, Cambridge, 1987.

[Nag88]   H.-H. Nagel. In *Proc. 1st International Exhibition and Conference on Applied Vision Systems ,Vision '88*, pages 15-23, Stuttgart, FRG, 1988.

[Pai89]   P. Paillou. Master Thesis, Ecole Nationale Supérieure de Physique, Université Louis Pasteur, Strasbourg, June 1989.

[PGC+88] G. Perucca, S. Giorcelli, T. De Couasnon, E. Hirsch and H. Mangold. In CEC-DGXIII, *Putting Technology to Use*, pages 543-561, North-Holland, Amsterdam, 1988.

[PHE+88] F. Pierre, Y. Hervé, R. Eugène, C. Draman and S. Wendling. *In Proc. 2th PIXIM Conference*, Paris, 1988.

[PHN+88] D. Paul, W. Hättich, W. Nill, S. Tatari and G. Winkler. *IEEE Transactions on Pattern Analysis and Machine Intelligence*, 10 (3) : 399-407, 1988.

[Pri89]   T. Priol. *Lancé de rayons sur des architectures parallèles : Etude et mise en oeuvre.* PhD Dissertation, Université de Rennes I, June 1989.

[San88]   J. L. C. Sanz. Introduction to the Special Issues on Industrial Machine Vision and Computer Vision Technology. *IEEE Transactions on Pattern Analysis and Machine Intelligence*, 10 (1) and 10 (3), 1988.

[San89]   J. L. C. Sanz. *Machine Vision and Applications*, 2 : 167-173, 1989.

[Sug86]   K. Sugihara. *Machine Interpretation of Line Drawings*. The MIT Press, Cambridge, MA, 1986.

[TL89]   R. Y. Tsai and R. K. Lenz. A new technique for fully autonomous and efficient 3-D robotics hand/eye calibration. *IEEE Transactions on Robotics and Automation*, 5 (3) : 345-358, 1989.

[Tsa86]   R. Y. Tsai. An efficient and accurate camera calibration technique for 3-D machine vision. In *Proc. IEEE Conf. Computer Vision and Pattern Recognition*, pages 364-374, Miami/FL, 22-26 June, 1986.

[Tsa87]   R. Y. Tsai. *IEEE Transactions on Robotics and Automation*, 3 : 323-344, 1987.

[TTC85]   Tech. Tran. Consultants, Inc. *Machine Vision Systems: A Summary and Forecast.* Tech. Tran. Corp., Lake Geneva, Switzerland, second edition, 1985.

Index